WRITING SPECULATIVE FICTION

Science Fiction, Fantasy, and Horror

STUDENT EDITION

Lelia Rose Foreman

Copyright 2017 by Bear Publications, LLC

All rights reserved. No part of this publication may be reproduced, distributed or transmitted in any form or by any means, including photocopying, recording, or other electronic or mechanical methods, without the prior written permission of the publisher, except in the case of brief quotations embodied in critical reviews and certain other noncommercial uses permitted by copyright law. For permission requests, write to the publisher, addressed "Attention: Permissions Coordinator," at the address below.

Lelia Rose Foreman

Bear Publications

1229 Sun Valley Drive

Wichita Falls, TX 76302

www.bearpublications.com

Note: All interior artwork and three images on the front cover were taken from speculative fiction magazines or book covers from the early to mid-1900s. All cover artwork included has entered the public domain and may be reproduced without permission from this publisher.

Ordering information:

WRITING SPECULATIVE FICTION: Science Fiction, Fantasy, and Horror   1st Edition

ISBN 978-1-64008-440-7

TABLE OF CONTENTS

- INTRODUCTION ... 5
- CHAPTER ONE: GENRE ... 7
- CHAPTER TWO: CULTURAL WORLD-BUILDING ... 23
- CHAPTER THREE: MORE CULTURAL WORLD-BUILDING ... 39
- CHAPTER FOUR: PHYSICAL WORLD-BUILDING ... 57
- CHAPTER FIVE: PLOT ... 71
- CHAPTER SIX: MORE PLOT ... 88
- CHAPTER SEVEN: CHARACTER ... 106
- CHAPTER EIGHT: HEROES, VILLAINS, SIDEKICKS, AND BYSTANDERS ... 130
- CHAPTER NINE: CHARACTER ARC ... 144
- CHAPTER TEN: DESCRIPTION ... 161
- CHAPTER ELEVEN: CONFLICT AND TENSION ... 175
- CHAPTER TWELVE: EDITING, REVISING ... 192
- CHAPTER THIRTEEN: YOUR FIRST CHAPTER ... 206
- CHAPTER FOURTEEN: VOICE ... 222
- CHAPTER FIFTEEN: WORDS AND WORLDVIEWS ... 238
- CHAPTER SIXTEEN: SCIENCE FICTION ... 263
- CHAPTER SEVENTEEN: FANTASY ... 280
- CHAPTER EIGHTEEN: HORROR ... 295
- EXTRA CREDIT ACTIVITIES ... 316
- GLOSSARY ... 317
- LISTS OF RECOMMENDED WORKS ... 320
- HELPFUL WEBSITES ACTIVE AT TIME OF PUBLICATION ... 326
- INDEX ... 327
- AUTHOR & CONTRIBUTORS ... 333

VOCABULARY QUIZZES (answers in Teacher's edition) 335

INTRODUCTION

Out of all the trillions of things to pick up in this world, you picked up this book. I'm glad you did.

When I was a teenager, I tried so hard to become a writer. I read every book on writing I could find.

They did not help.

Either my brain wasn't developed enough to understand what the books said, or the books did not address what I needed to know. I read thousands of speculative fiction stories, but I could not SEE how the writers did their magic. I flailed through my teens, my twenties, and my thirties trying to learn how to write.

Today, there are so many good books and websites that can tell you how to write, that I finally figured out how to write a story that was good enough to be published. In this book, I have brought together some of the best books and websites for learning how to write and condensed some of their advice. If I had known what is in this book, I would have been published decades before I was.

This is an eighteen-week writing course. During the course, I will introduce you to famous writers and to writers you might otherwise never learn about. My dream is that you will SEE how the magic is done.

I had planned to not use any excerpts from my work because that seemed egotistical and maybe not ethical. But, I reached a chapter where I needed to SHOW a concept and not merely tell you about that concept. The showing would provide spoilers. I know some of the writers in this book. I did not want any of them coming after me with an ax because I put in spoilers. Me, I didn't care if one of my stories was "spoiled" by giving away the ending. So I went ahead and showed the concept which also allows you to judge whether or not I learned how to write skillfully.

(Please note that all the excerpts, save three public domain ones, are copyrighted and used with permission. If you want to use the excerpts, you will need to contact the writer or publisher for permission.)

I will give you some of the writing techniques and tropes that will help you write stories in whatever genre you pick with the goal that your writing can be understood by people who enjoy reading in that genre.

Some people write for the same reason that other people journal or dance. They use these methods as a way to express themselves or to imaginatively explore some of the mysteries of the universe. Some people want their writing to bring glory to God. Others want to bring glory to themselves and hope to become famous. Yet other people want to make enough money to pay their bills.

Here's a hard truth: if you do not learn the techniques of writing compelling stories, you will not achieve any of those goals. Here is another hard truth: to grow as a writer, you will need to be willing to write badly for a long time. Certainly longer than eighteen weeks. (But hopefully less than decades.)

No Olympic ice skater popped out of her mother's womb wearing skates and leotards, and ready to pirouette. She had to learn to crawl and then to walk. She needed to be willing to fall down a lot. And then she needed to pay attention to a teacher.

No famous quarterback came out of kindergarten able to lob a long pass. He needed to practice running and throwing. He needed to listen to a coach yell at him and then follow his instructions.

This book will be a coach telling you one way to dribble a ball. During this course, you will write a short story of your own.

I will not teach you grammar, spelling, homonyms or homophones. If you do not know how baited differs from bated, or passed from past, please find a book, a website, or a friendly teacher to explain these things to you. I will also not teach you how to write romance or mysteries or treatises on nuclear physics.

I will, however, try to teach you some techniques that apply to nearly all writing as well as some specialized techniques that apply to speculative fiction. I will try to teach you how to write in a manner that other people will consider skillful. I will try to teach you good writing techniques, though I admit that what is considered good will vary from historical age to age, and from one person to another.

Some of you might be thinking, "Why should I bother? I'm going to write the way I want to write. After all, many badly-written books are best sellers."

Here's why you should bother. Every trade has its jargon and its tools. If you want to be a professional anything, you will need to learn the names of the tools and their uses. A reader may not be able to say, "This writer is using gerunds and participles wrongly," or "These motivation reaction units are jumbled." But the reader will be able to say, "This is confusing." If you confuse the reader too many times, he or she will find something else to read unless they are being forced to read the piece by the instructor. As a writer, you need to learn how to write sentences that won't confuse your target audience.

It is a truth that many bad books as declared by English teachers will be picked up by readers who say the book is good. There are also many great books written with soaring language, deep truths, and rich in symbolism and metaphor that some readers will call bad.

How does that happen?

Now think about the following questions: What do people read when nobody is forcing them to? Why do people read when nobody is forcing them to?

Answers: People read what they like. What they like depends on what emotion they want to feel when they read. People read fiction of any sort to experience feelings. Some readers want to experience awe, some excitement, some wish-fulfillment, and some comfort. A few readers will want to be challenged and yet others to be reassured.

And SOME readers want to read speculative fiction. If that's what you want to write, let's talk about how you can do so in a skillful way.

CHAPTER ONE:

GENRE

Day 1 defining

So what is speculative fiction? Speculative fiction is 1. Fiction (surprise!) 2. A literature that speculates or asks "What if?" questions about a great many things 3. A zoo of genres, subgenres, subsubgenres, and mingled creatures that defy easy categorization. I am dividing speculative fiction into three broad categories: science fiction, fantasy, and horror. Science fiction and fantasy are genre designations which focus on setting, a setting that for them is always speculative. "Horror" is a genre designation based on the effect it has on the reader. The effect exists whether horror is speculative or not. Some horror in fact is not speculative fiction, but we will confine our discussion of horror to that which is speculative.

Each of the three genres can be further divided. Just as bears can be divided into grizzly, black, sun, panda, and teddy bears, so can each genre be divided into subgenres. What all the genres and subgenres have in common is that at least one element of the work involves something that does not exist. The something may exist in some future, or the something might never exist or be unknowable.

Orson Scott Card in his excellent book, *How to Write Science Fiction & Fantasy*, said:

> … If the story is set in a universe that follows the same rules as ours, it's science fiction. If it's set in a universe that doesn't follow our rules, it's fantasy.
>
> Or in other words, science fiction is about what *could* be but isn't, fantasy is about what *couldn't* be.

Science fiction will generally have lots of science-type words in it or have concepts that come from the physical or sociological sciences. Logic based on and rooted in these sciences is expected. Problem solving is prized.

Fantasy will often have magic and magical creatures and will have its own internal logic based on the world-building within the novel.

Horror may or may not have magic, but will often have words with spiritual, psychological, and perhaps ecological connotations. One of its common themes is facing the unknown, especially if that unknown is uncontrollable, terrifying, and somehow hidden or occultic.

In case you're wondering, here's why we care how to categorize a story: Librarians want to know where to put the book, as do bookstores. Catalogs need some way to sort the books. Teachers making assignments want to know what they're telling their students to read. And READERS want to know. People who liked one steampunk talking-teddy bear book will often go to bookstores and libraries to find more steampunk talking-teddybear books. If that's what you write, you want your book to sit on the science fiction and fantasy shelves. Unless your teddybear kills everyone in horrible ways, and then you want the thing in the horror section.

Here are some science-fiction subgenres:

AFROFUTURISM: Stories imbued with African sensibilities set in the future. An example is *Binti* by Nnedi Okorafor.

ALTERNATE HISTORY: Stories in which one or more historical events differ from reality, such as Philip K Dick's *The Man in the High Castle* where Germany won WWII. STEAMPUNK falls under this as a subsubgenre.

ALTERNATE REALITY: also known as ALTERNATE UNIVERSE: Stories in which different laws of physics apply or Earth is different from the Earth we know. PARALLEL UNIVERSE: Stories with a self-contained separate world, universe, or reality coexisting with the real world.

APOCALYPTIC: Stories about the end of the world or civilization. An example is *The Blue Afternoon that Lasted Forever* by Daniel H. Wilson.

POST-APOCALYPTIC: Stories about the surviving remnant from an apocalypse. Examples include: *A Time to Die* by Nadine Brandes, *Black Tiger* by Sara Baysinger, and *Thunder* by Bonnie S. Calhoun

CYBERPUNK: Stories that are usually dystopic futures where daily life is impacted by rapid technological change, a ubiquitous datasphere of computerized information, and invasive modification of the human body. Examples include: *A Star Curiously Singing* by Kerry Nietz, *Flashpoint* by Frank Creed, and *Cinder* by Marissa Meyer. Most cyberpunk stories can also be called cyberthrillers, such as *Eternity Falls* by Kirk Outerbridge

DIESELPUNK: Stories similar to its more well-known cousin steampunk that combines the aesthetics of the diesel-based technology of the time between the two world wars through to the 1950s with retro-futuristic technology and postmodern sensibilities. *The Leviathan Trilogy* by Scott Westerfield is an example, as is *Storming* by K. M. Weiland.

DYSTOPIA: Stories where an oppressive government uses technology to oppress people. Examples include *Hunger Games* by Suzanne Collins, *Divergent* by Veronica Roth, and *Captives (The Safe Lands)* by Jill Williamson

UTOPIA: Stories where a benign government solves all the problems of the world. I think few are worth reading unless you are studying worldviews. You might try *Dinotopia* by James Gurney.

HARD SCIENCE FICTION: Stories where the science is accurate as far as is known by the current level of science. There are bonus points for having a science fact, such as the melting point of molybdenum, be a plot point in the novel. Examples include nearly all books by Hal Clement, Isaac Asimov, and Poul Anderson. A more recent example is *Thunderwell* by Doug Beason.

SOFT SCIENCE FICTION: Stories in which physical laws are sometimes paid attention to and sometimes not, and the setting of a space station or new planet is only a backdrop to a traditional romance, murder mystery, or revenge story. A story might also be labeled soft when the science that is speculated about is one that is harder to measure, such as sociology and psychology. When the story gets too soft, it can be scooted over to fantasy. Any of the subgenres of science fiction have soft versions. Most of the subgenres of science fiction have hard versions.

HUMOROUS SCIENCE FICTION: Stories where the tropes of science fiction are used, sometimes inappropriately for the purposes of humor. Examples include *There Goes The Galaxy* by Jenn Thorson and *The Hitchhiker's Guide to the Galaxy* by Douglas Adams

MILITARY SCIENCE FICTION: Stories where the focus is on war, strategy, and the experiences of soldiers. Examples include *Knox's Irregulars* by J Wesley Bush and *The Chaplain's War* by Brad R Torgersen

SPACE OPERA: Substitute a space ship for a horse and a ray gun for a six-shooter. Adventure in space where a single hero can make a difference. When there is some deference to physical laws, this can go under science fiction. When the writer doesn't even pretend to follow a single physical law of the universe, the book will be slotted under fantasy. Examples include *Edge of Oblivion* by Joshua A. Johnston, *Truce at Bakura* by Kathy Tyers, *The Worker Prince* by Bryan Thomas Schmidt, and *A New Threat* by Aaron DeMott.

STEAMPUNK: This is nearly more of a fashion, an aesthetic choice. These are alternate reality stories with gears, goggles, and steam reigning as a motive power. Usually the characters will dress and speak in a Victorian style. Often there is magic which makes steampunk straddle a fence between science fiction and fantasy. Examples include *Curio* by Evangeline Denmark, *Lady of Devices* by Shelley Adina, *Nyssa Glass and the House of Mirrors* by H. L. Burke, *The Clockwork Golem* by LeAnna Shields, and *Steampunk Fairy Tales* by several authors, including Angela Castillo.

SUPERHERO: This goes under science fiction despite all the fantasy elements because the genesis of the superhero nearly always has a bafflegab or technobabble explanation. A human gains one or more superpowers and excitement ensues. Examples include *Failstate* by John W. Otte and *Hero* by Jim Miles. My favorite superheroes are Spiderman and Nightcrawler.

TIME TRAVEL: Time travel stories can involve moving forward or backward on the arrow of time. They can also involve characters moving from a given timeline to an alternate timeline. If there is machinery involved, it is considered science fiction. If magic is the mechanism, the subgenre will slide over to fantasy. Examples are *Saving Lucas Biggs* by Marisa De los Santos and David Teague, and *The Map of the Sky* by Felix J. Palma.

VIRTUAL REALITY: Stories where most of the action takes place inside a computer simulation. Examples include the Disney movie *TRON* and the book *The Hidden Level* by A. J. Bakke.

WEIRD: Stories that contain tropes of science fiction but the story is so odd because of the style in which it is written, or the concepts defy human comprehension such that it defies classification. Some people think Cordwainer Smith's stories belong here.

MASHUP: Any of the genres and subgenres and subsubgenres can be combined in a mashup. Isaac Asimov combined science fiction with mystery in *The Caves of Steel*. Terri Main combined cozy mystery with science fiction in the *Dark Side of the Moon* Mysteries. Steampunk romance is common. Paranormal is most commonly combined with romance, though horror is also common. A movie that represents a mashup is *Cowboys versus Aliens*.

Here are some fantasy subgenres:

ALLEGORY: A story or novel in which abstract ideas and principles are described in terms of characters, figures and events with the purpose of teaching an idea and a principle or explaining an idea or a principle. The main characters are likely to be symbols. Examples include *Pilgrim's Progress* by John Bunyan and *Flatland* by Edwin Abbott.

ANIMAL: What separates this from Fable, is that the story could fit under one or another of the other subgenres except the actors are animals. *Owls of Ga'Hoole, Watership Down, Warrior Cats, Redwall, Plague Dogs,* and *Wings of Fire* might be examples of this.

FABLE: Very short stories that utilize talking objects (usually animals) to make a comment on the human condition or make a political point. Examples include Aesop and his tales, and the prophecy of Jotham in Judges 9 speaking to Abimelech. There are also some novel-length fables such as *Animal Farm* by George Orwell and *The Book of the Dun Cow* by Walter Wangerin Jr.

FAIRYTALE: Stories about magical or imaginary beings and lands that were told at one time by adults to adults and slowly slid into being classified as children's literature, and now are regaining adult status, especially as reimagined with elements and worldview changes.

HIGH or EPIC FANTASY: Fantasy that is obviously set on an alternate earth or magical land. It will usually involve royalty and mythical people such as elves and fairies, and whatever happens in the story will change the entire land. The theme is often summed up as "A boy (or girl) goes on a journey." It will generally follow the basic tropes of the Hero's Journey. In most cases, the prince or princess is in a battle to earn or keep the throne or land to which he is entitled. One classic example is *Lord of the Rings* by J.R.R. Tolkien.

HUMOROUS FANTASY: A story where the tropes of fantasy are used for a humorous effect. Examples are the *Dragonspell (The Fairy Godmother Dilemma Book 0)* by Danyelle Leafty, *Of Mice and Momphibraks* by Lia London, *Even a Stone* by Jane Lebak, *Live and Let Fly* by Karina Fabian, and *A Twist of Fae* by Rebekah Shafer.

LOW FANTASY: There is so much disagreement about this that I will only state what some of those who consider themselves experts in fantasy say: If the fantasy is set in the supposed real world, then it is low fantasy. An example is *Mary Poppins* by Dr. P. L. Travers and nearly all urban fantasy.

MAGIC REALISM: Stories with a style associated especially with Latin American writers that incorporates fantastic or mythical elements into otherwise realistic fiction —called also magical realism. They tend to be literary. Many are subversive. *The Lost Mission* and *The Cure* by Athol Dickson, and *Memory's Door* by James L. Rubart represent North American magical realism

MYTHPUNK: Stories that use traditional myths and fairytales and reconstruct them using postmodern literary techniques. They are meant to be subversive. One example is *Odd and the Frost Giants* by Neil Gaiman

MYTHOPOEIA: Stories that use religious mythology, traditional myths, folklores and history and then recast them into a re-imagined realm created by the author. They tend to uphold traditional values. An example is *Lord of the Rings* by Tolkien.

PARABLE: Parables are a type of allegory and can be as short as a sentence or several paragraphs long. They are told to make one point. The parable of the prodigal son may be the most famous one. Longer literary parables include *The Little Prince* by Antoine de St. Exupery, *The Trial* by Franz Kafka, and *The Alchemist* by Paul Coelho.

PARANORMAL: Stories set in the everyday world with lots of fantasy elements added. Often synonymous with urban fantasy. Paranormal is the most likely to include romance. An example is *The Mermaid's Sister* by Carrie Anne Noble.

PORTAL FANTASY: Stories that involve people of this world entering a magic world through a portal. Examples include *The Lion, The Witch, and The Wardrobe* by C. S. Lewis, *Finding Angel* by Kat Heckenbach. And *The Tethered World* by Heather L. L. FitzGerald.

SUPERNATURAL: Opinions of how supernatural and paranormal differ are both confusing and contradictory. Many say that supernatural is more likely to be about spiritual things such as angels, demons, and ghosts, while paranormal is more like to be about creatures such as vampires, shape-shifters, and dragons. One writer says a story with a ghost in it is supernatural. If the main character falls in love with the ghost, it is a paranormal. Another writer says that in supernatural stories, the general population knows about the fantasy elements of the story, but in paranormal stories the population either does not know of or is skeptical of the fantasy elements. You may argue about this among yourselves.

SWORD AND SORCERY: Stories in which the main weapon is a sword and there are lots of spells cast. It is closely akin the high fantasy in that the hero usually exists in a world filled with hierarchy, and intrigue. However, the hero of a sword and sorcery story is primarily a warrior on a quest and not a prince or princess attempting to keep the throne. One example is *Conan the Barbarian* by Robert E. Howard.

TALL TALES: Folk lore about heroes that exaggerates one or more of their traits. Examples include Paul Bunyan, Slue-foot Sue, and Pecos Bill.

URBAN FANTASY: Stories that deal with magical or paranormal elements in a real world, contemporary (or urban) setting. Synonymous with Paranormal. The movie *Twilight* and the book *Girls Can't be Knights* by Lee French exemplify this.

WEIRD: Stories that are so odd or so oddly told, such as slipstream, that they are difficult to classify end up here. One example is *The Phantom Tollbooth* by Norton Juster. Stories by Cordwainer Smith are sometimes slotted here.

Here are some horror subgenres:

HUMOROUS HORROR: Stories that use the tropes of horror to elicit laughter. The most important aspects of these stories, as in all jokes, is the buildup to the laugh. Humorous horror works best when the reader can commiserate with the protagonist's fears at a safe distance. This subgenre may or may not be speculative depending on whether or not there are speculative elements. One example is *The Ghost of Briardale* by Grace Mullins.

GHOST STORIES: Ghosts in these stories are usually haunted by an unfulfilled desire, regret, or mission. Often there is a need for justice towards a particular person, family, or region. Whether they are aware that they are dead or not, they are either powerless and lost or, alternately, quite powerful. The ghost can either be the protagonist or the antagonist. They are often bound to a certain place. Good ghost stories elicit feeling of terror and loss. Ghost stories are as old as the *Bible* (the story of Samuel) and the *Odyssey*. They are the most common way in which popular culture discusses the afterlife and death. This subgenre is always speculative.

GORE/SPLATTER/SPLATTERPUNK: The focus of these stories are on crimes, bloodletting, and violation. Usually the violation is based on a casting-off of societal and moral rules. In gore, the protagonist is at the mercy of one or more antagonists whose only joy and power is the ability to destroy another. Think serial killer, clown killers, and emotionally-damaged bullies. Unless this subgenre is mixed with other speculative subgenres, this is not speculative fiction.

GOTHIC: Stories with a style of writing that is characterized by elements of fear, horror, death, and gloom, with very high emotion. These emotions can include fear and suspense and can include romance. The term Gothic actually originated as a term belittling the architecture and art of the

1700s and 1800s, which was dark, decaying, and dismal. This is where genre of horror began. Examples include the tales of Edgar Allan Poe, *Wuthering Heights* by Emily Bronte, and *Jane Eyre* by Charlotte Bronte. Not all Gothic is speculative.

MONSTER STORIES: Stories that involve a monster and sometimes a Big Boss Battle with said monster. Examples include *Beowulf*, many Greek myths, and the movie *The Thing*. The monsters can be creatures—either an ancient evil awakening or a modern monster created through mankind's tampering with nature and biology. The monster can also be a human who has changed somehow, perhaps through self-experimentation, insanity, or some disturbance in the natural state of things. This is always speculative.

PSYCHOLOGICAL HORROR: While most horror focuses on our communal fears—of disease, stranger, death, abandoned houses, dead bodies etc,—psychological horror often focuses on the fears of one particular character or group. Sometimes the reader may understand the main character in the beginning, but after a while, the reader and protagonist must part ways because the protagonist has proven to be unreliable, unlikable, or psychologically abnormal. Sometimes the stories can be understood on two levels. Classical stories that fall into this category include *The Turn of a Screw* by Henry James, *Tell-tale Heart* by Edgar Allen Poe, and Lord Dunsany's *Ghosts*. Modern examples with a likable and reliable protagonist include *Intensity* by Dean Koontz. Again, this may or may not be speculative depending on whether or not there are speculative elements in the story.

Activities:

A. *Read*:
After the stranded biologist cut Mr. Reese down from her rope trap on an alien planet.

Her fingers plucked at the hem of her tunic. "Why'd SARC send you now?"

Nervous. She doesn't like that I showed up.

He spread his hands. "Who can understand the bureaucratic mind?"

Now that he was on his feet, confidence grew. The training locked in place. Observe. Assess. Prepare.

Her jaw flexed. "Find anything while you were snooping around?"

He managed a disarming smile. No use lying. She was not stupid. "Doesn't hurt to know who you're working for."

Good thing she had no idea who *he* actually worked for.

"Nothing piqued your curiosity?"

"Nope." He shrugged. That had to be the biggest lie so far. "But what's with the trap?" He sought the name of the planet's most dangerous predator. "Tereph?"

"They're for marauders."

"They? More than one trap?"

"Yes. There's another behind the shed."

Interesting that she would volunteer the information. "You expect pirates? Empusa III is so far off shipping routes that few know it exists."

She tilted her head. "Still pays to be cautious. We've all heard stories of murdered scientists."

Murder...intriguing choice of words. Hadn't she murdered her last assistant?

He indicated base camp in a sweeping gesture. "From what I've seen, you don't have much anyone would want."

"Let's hope *they* believe that." She motioned toward the cabin. "Thirsty?"

"Yes. It was quite a trek from the landing site."

"I didn't hear the drop-off ship."

"Newer technology. Much quieter."

She appeared to buy the lie. Good. His arrival two days prior had given him time to stash extra supplies and do some scouting. Though he hadn't located Geoffrey's body, Sean prided himself on his determination. He *would* find it.

"I have some juice you might like." She turned.

He followed. Her dark brown braid, bobbing against the knife's handle, drew his attention. Swaying with every step, the weapon reminded him why he was there.

Not for one second could he forget his secret orders to assassinate her.

Anna Zogg   *The Paradise Protocol*

1) Which genre is this? How do you know?
2) What creates tension in this excerpt?
3) List three subgenres of science fiction and their characteristics.

B. *Read*:

The fever returned to Northern Marst in the spring of my eighteenth year and rocked the capital city of Kaeson to its foundations.

After several years with only the odd case or two, new cases cropped up every day, keeping me and my fifteen-year-old apprentice, Princess Renelan, frantically busy. Most of our patients responded to a regimen of rest, gruel, and fluids, but for the serious cases, I needed to use my gift of healing.

El had called me to be a healer at age twelve, but these days I hesitated to use the gift. People gave me doubtful, sidelong looks as if to say, Lady Elilan couldn't even heal her own husband. Less charitable people whispered, "I heard Elilan caused Lord Jayson's death."

Kathrese McKee   *Healer's Curse*

1) Which genre is this? How do you know?
2) Can you tell which subgenre this is?
3) List three subgenres of fantasy and their characteristics.

C. *Read*:

> Unreal!—Even while I breathed there came to my nostrils the breath of the vapor of heated iron! A suffocating odor pervaded the prison! A deeper glow settled each moment in the eyes that glared at my agonies! A richer tint of crimson diffused itself over the pictured horrors of blood. I panted! I gasped for breath! There could be no doubt of the design of my tormentors—oh! most unrelenting! Oh! most demoniac of men! I shrank from the glowing metal to the centre of the cell.

Edgar Allan Poe *The Pit and the Pendulum*

1) Which genre is this? How do you know?
2) Can you tell which subgenre this is?
3) List three subgenres of horror and their characteristics.

Day 2 fanfic

To fanfic or not to fanfic. Fanfic is short for fan fiction, works that are set in a universe already created by someone else. If you write a story using, say, Star Trek or Nintendo characters, you are writing fanfic.

Writing fanfic can be a lot of fun. If you write fanfic for your own amusement or to share with other fanfic writers, there is no harm done. BUT (Danger, Will Robinson! Danger!) if you try to make money by selling your stories set in a famous franchise, lawyers will drop on you like a ton of octopuses faster than gravity would call for. Just don't. You can't afford the grief you would bring upon yourself.

Some people use fanfic as practice and a springboard for their own writing. Some people think fanfic is cheating. Why? Because most of the work has been done for you. The characters are premade. You don't need to put any thought into the attributes and motivations of the people in your story. The world (universe) has already been built. You don't need to do the hard work of world building such as figuring out the society and its rules, laws, and customs. You don't need to describe the clothing or the appearance of the spaceship corridors. Writing fanfic can let you develop lazy habits.

The short story you will write for this course cannot be fanfic. Cannot. You will need to invent your own story with your own universe and your own characters. The length should be between 3,000 and 10,000 words. I picked those lengths because I want your short story to be long enough to include all or most of the elements of writing I will discuss, and yet short enough to finish before your time is up. Also, many of us find out we need to redo the beginning once we reach the end of our story. I do.

Activities:

A. *Read*:

> "Good morning," the small, quavering voice comes from the medical bed. "Is that you, Paul?"
>
> Today I am Paul. I activate my chassis extender, giving myself 3.5 centimeters additional height so as to approximate Paul's size. I change my eye color to R60, G200, B180, the average shade of Paul's eyes in interior lighting. I adjust my skin tone as well. When I had first emulated Paul, I had regretted that I could not quickly emulate his beard; but Mildred never seems to notice its absence. The Paul in her memory has no beard.
>
> The house is quiet now that the morning staff have left. Mildred's room is clean but dark this morning with the drapes concealing the big picture window. Paul wouldn't notice the darkness (he never does when he visits in person), but my empathy net knows that Mildred's garden outside will cheer her up. I set a reminder to open the drapes after I greet her.

                          Martin L. Shoemaker   *Today I Am Paul*

1) Which genre is this? How do you know?
2) Can you tell which subgenre this is?
3) List three subgenres of science fiction and their characteristics

B. *Read*:

> "You think this is bad? You should see what he did to a whole village back that way." The tugolith handler pointed back across the road and into the trees. As Pelmen turned to look, he could easily see the path the beast had made for himself through the underbrush. Fallen trees and broken shrubs marked it clearly.
>
> "What had the village done to cause your beast to go on such a rampage?"
>
> The man shrugged. "It got in his way. It's hard to teach a tug to go around something he could just as easily go through." Pelmen raised his eyebrow in response. "By the way," the man went on, "if you will, call him by his name—Evanlitha. He's sensitive, and if he hears someone call him a beast he gets offended."
>
> Pelmen nodded thankfully and filed that bit of information for future reference. There was no creature he knew of that was larger or more powerful than a tugolith, save the dragon himself. It didn't seem healthy to offend something that big.

           Robert Don Hughes   *Pursuit of a Lost Tugolith*   *A Tale of Pelmen Before the Dragon Was Divided.*

1) Which genre is this? How do you know?
2) Can you tell which subgenre this is?
3) List three subgenres of fantasy and their characteristics

C. *Read*:

Silvery cascades leafed the bronze woods, burnishing bark and bough with sterling highlights.

An unusual mineral content in the rain might have lent it this slight phosphorescence.

Or . . . having come in from the west, through the soiled air above Los Angeles and surrounding cities, perhaps the storm had washed from the atmosphere a witch's brew of pollutants that in combination gave rise to this pale, eerie radiance.

Sensing that neither explanation would prove correct, seeking a third, Molly was startled by movement on the porch. She shifted focus from the trees to the sheltered shadows immediately beyond the glass.

Low sinuous shapes moved under the window. They were so silent, fluid, and mysterious that for a moment they seemed to be imagined: formless expressions of primal fears.

Then one, three, five of them lifted their heads and turned their yellow eyes to the window, regarding her inquisitively. They were as real as Molly herself, though sharper of tooth.

Dean Koontz *The Taking*

1) Which genre is this? How do you know?
2) Can you tell which subgenre this is?
3) List three subgenres of horror and their characteristics

Day 3 things to do, things to don't

Earlier I mentioned a steampunk talking teddybear novel. I don't know that such a thing has been written, though I wouldn't be surprised. At the time of publication of this textbook, over a million new books are published in the English-speaking world every *year*. A good chunk of those are speculative fiction. It is impossible to know everything that is written in the field of speculative fiction. It is *almost* impossible to write a story with elements that no one else has ever written about before. Perhaps you'll be the one to do the almost impossible and come up with an idea that thousands of other writers copy because it's such a wonderful idea.

Later, we will discuss voice, which is what will make your telling of stories unique even if you and thirty other people try to write the exact same story.

During this course, we are not asking you to come up with something brilliant no one has ever thought of before. You'll burn out your brain trying. That does *not* mean you should not try to be creative and use ideas that you personally have never seen before. What I do mean is that if you find out your new idea isn't so new after all, don't worry about it.

While I'm on the subject, soon I'll be asking you to write practice paragraphs. I don't expect you to write brilliant paragraphs. I do expect you to write wretched paragraphs. If you're a new writer and you don't write awful paragraphs, you're doing it wrong. Either you are editing while you write a decent paragraph, or you are plagiarizing. Don't edit while you write your practice paragraphs. I want you to splat words on a page. Editing comes later. First, put words on that page. We can work with words that are marking up the pretty paper. We can't work with words that aren't in physical form yet.

Plagiarize means to use someone else's exact words while pretending they are yours. You can certainly use other people's ideas. You can use other people's words as long as you attribute them and obtain permission. There is only one idea in this entire textbook I did not take directly from someone else's speech or book. I did not attribute *all* the words in this textbook because I wrote about ideas that are spoken and written in hundreds of writer's conferences and books about writing. Most of the things I tell you are common knowledge among professional writers. I may have accidentally repeated phrases or sentences first written by someone else because there are only so many ways you can organize the sentence, "Write clearly," or "Don't ever plagiarize."

Still. Don't ever plagiarize. Don't ever plagiarize. Don't ever plagiarize. You will be found out. Maybe not today. Maybe not this year. But eventually someone will find out, and then you will watch your career go up in flames. You will regret that lazy shortcut you took. If you never want to hide the newsfeed from your children or grandchildren, don't ever plagiarize.

Let me repeat: that does not mean you cannot take other people's ideas and twist them into another shape. Your voice is what will make your story of (Cinderella, First Contact, Demonic Serial Killer) different from the others.

Activities:

A. *Read*:

"The future," the mathematician intoned, "is both unknown and unknowable," which seemed an interesting contention at the time, somewhere near the end of the meal, when all were pleasantly sated and ready for one of their usual debates. "There are, after all, a huge number of variables involved in any outcome."

The group, a military engineer, two mathematicians, a physicist, and a philosopher had met at this *beir stuben* every month to share a pleasant meal, frothy beer, and conversation. Their political member had demurred, begging other pressing issues, as usual.

"An interesting conceit," the engineer replied. "But flawed. Any future event must have a cause and, since there are only a few relevant factors involved, we can certainly predict what will happen." He sat back with a self-satisfied look.

"Of course, that only applies on the macro scale," the philosopher said. "Our physicist here can probably think of a dozen reasons that wouldn't apply on the quantum level."

The physicist threw back his head and chuckled. "He also forgot that chaos theory says that seemingly unrelated factors can cascade into any given event. The number of past events need not be large at all."

Bud Sparhawk   *Causes and Effects*   *Daily Science Fiction*

1) Which genre is this? How do you know?
2) Can you tell which subgenre this is?
3) List three subgenres of science fiction and their characteristics. (Different from the ones you listed before.)

B. *Read:*

TRUE! --nervous --very, very dreadfully nervous I had been and am; but why will you say that I am mad? The disease had sharpened my senses --not destroyed --not dulled them. Above all was the sense of hearing acute. I heard all things in the heaven and in the earth. I heard many things in hell. How, then, am I mad? Hearken! and observe how healthily --how calmly I can tell you the whole story.

It is impossible to say how first the idea entered my brain; but once conceived, it haunted me day and night. Object there was none. Passion there was none. I loved the old man. He had never wronged me. He had never given me insult. For his gold I had no desire. I think it was his eye! yes, it was this! He had the eye of a vulture --a pale blue eye, with a film over it. Whenever it fell upon me, my blood ran cold; and so by degrees --very gradually --I made up my mind to take the life of the old man, and thus rid myself of the eye forever.

Now this is the point. You fancy me mad. Madmen know nothing. But you should have seen me. You should have seen how wisely I proceeded --with what caution --with what foresight --with what dissimulation I went to work! I was never kinder to the old man than during the whole week before I killed him. And every night, about midnight, I turned the latch of his door and opened it --oh so gently! And then, when I had made an opening sufficient for my head, I put in a dark lantern, all closed, closed, that no light shone out, and then I thrust in my head. Oh, you would have laughed to see how cunningly I thrust it in! I moved it slowly --very, very slowly, so that I might not disturb the old man's sleep. It took me an hour to place my whole head within the opening so far that I could see him as he lay upon his bed. Ha! would a madman have been so wise as this? And then, when my head was well in the room, I undid the lantern cautiously-oh, so cautiously --cautiously (for the hinges creaked) --I undid it just so much that a single thin ray fell upon the vulture eye. And this I did for seven long nights --every night just at midnight --but I found the eye always closed; and so it was impossible to do the work; for it was not the old man who vexed me, but his Evil Eye. And every morning, when the day broke, I went boldly into the chamber, and spoke courageously to him, calling him by name in a hearty tone, and inquiring how he had passed the night. So you see he would have been a very profound old man, indeed, to suspect that every night, just at twelve, I looked in upon him while he slept.

Edgar Allan Poe   *The Tell Tale Heart*

1) Which genre is this? How do you know?
2) Can you tell which subgenre this is?
3) List three subgenres of horror and their characteristics

C. *Read*:
In previous pages we have learned that Riette's parents are dead and she must take care of her little brother who has autism and the ability to feel magic. Al'Zjhon soldiers have been stealing people who are different.

"Fly Dragon Airways! Because who don't want to fly on a dragon?"

"Does he breathe fire?" Riette heard Emmet ask even as she ran. After a few more darting steps, she reclaimed her mother's note. The Al'Zjhon drew ever closer, and neither the plane nor the airship appeared ready to take off. It made her sick to realize she'd wasted two silvers on a flight she might never take. As ever, she found herself needing to be responsible for both her and Emmet and coming up short.

The tall man was now kneeling before Emmet and handing him a marshmallow on a stick. Riette sucked in a deep breath and pumped her legs. Before she could shout in warning, her little brother stood before the aging but nonetheless formidable beast. Only then did Riette see the dragon's entire face, and it left her speechless. Most of what had once been one side of its face was now gone, in its place weathered copper—deep orange in color but marbled with streaks of green. Within a masterfully forged enclosure, intricate in its detailed re-creation of the creature's wasted face, rested a piercing eye that stared back.

After a deep breath, the dragon regarded Emmet and the marshmallow, rearing up over him. Riette screamed as the dragon struck, snatching the marshmallow from the stick in a single swift motion, leaving the stick and its bearer intact. Emmet never moved an inch.

"You horrible man!" Riette shouted as she got closer. He regarded her with no more expression than a stone. Not taking the time to tell him what she thought, she dragged Emmet away. The tall man watched them go, and Emmet turned to meet his eyes. He pointed back and said, "Magic."

At this the tall man's face finally showed some reaction, which alarmed Riette even more. Dragging Emmet away, she scanned the remaining ships, looking for any ready to take off, yet all appeared to be somewhere in the process of refueling. The first plane she'd thought she would board was now taking on passengers, one of which was almost certainly Al'Zhjon. Two more continued their search. She'd run out of time.

Others had begun to notice the Zhjon as well. It resulted in a wave of startled exclamations followed by utter silence. All the fighting troops were at the front, and even those on their way were not yet ready for a fight.

"Fly Dragon Airways because we're leaving *right now*."

Brian Rathbone *Dragon Airways*

1) Later we will introduce you to the story writing concept of the ticking clock, which is the device that increases tension within a story. What is it that adds to the tension of this excerpt?

2) What does this excerpt show about the world this story is set in?

3) What is the main character trait that we see in Riette? Do you think that later she will toss her brother off a cliff? Why or why not?

Day 4 choosing

Mashups: Most of us enjoy them even though they can make classification difficult. The science fiction/romance. The paranormal/adventure journey. The horror noir. The fairytale/alternate history. The Jane Austin/zombie. The steampunk/supernatural

If you want to write a mashup, go for it. But I would like you to consider a couple things. First, your book needs to go on *some* shelf and be listed under *some* category. If you come up with a supernatural alternate history romance cyberpunk allegory superhero book, what is the poor cataloger supposed to do? The usual advice is to pick one thing and make that the dominant tone of the book, while the other elements play lesser roles.

If you pick science fiction as the dominant tone for the book, you will have more adherence to science facts and more logic in the plot than if you pick allegory. If you pick romance, you will have more smoldering looks, green eyes, and spinning heads than if you pick horror. Hmm, or maybe not, but those tropes will mean something different in a book that is predominantly horror.

Whatever your book starts out as, don't change it later unless you are willing to go back to the beginning and rewrite it with the tropes of the new genre you picked.

Activities:

1) Choose the genre and possibly subgenre of the short story you will write. You can change your mind later, but today choose. If choosing is too hard today, roll dice to make a choice.

2) What have you chosen?

3) Answer these questions: (1) What do you like about the genre you chose? (2) Is there anything about the other genres you didn't choose that you don't like? (3) What about the genre you did choose do you not like? (4) Will you need to do research to make your story believable? For example, if your fairy queen is a manatee, maybe you should look up what manatees are like. If so, start today. Don't wait until week eighteen. Seriously, don't.

4) If you have ever watched a movie mashup, how did the genres mix and match with each other?

Day 5 suspending disbelief

Wikipedia says: The term *suspension of disbelief* or *willing suspension of disbelief* has been defined as a willingness to suspend one's critical faculties and believe the unbelievable; sacrifice of realism and logic for the sake of enjoyment.

People want to enjoy your story. One of the ways they can enjoy your story is for them to suspend their disbelief. People who don't believe in ghosts or magic wands or alien gasbag people on Jupiter are willing to believe such things during the time they are reading your story so they can immerse themselves in the adventure and feel what the hero is feeling. Those who like a certain genre will readily believe in the story being presented to them. But if the writer makes wands that work too easily or a ghost who seems like nothing more than a Saturday morning cartoon, the reader will not feel that he is in good hands.

You must make it easy for people to trust your story, your skill, and your characters. You make it easy by ensuring that all the real things in your story are true. True to the common earthly reality, true to human nature, and true to the nature of the ghost or alien you have created. You don't place Seattle in the middle of China. You don't have water freezing at a hundred degrees Celsius, and mercury at 70 degrees Fahrenheit. You don't have a sixteenth-century man time travel into the twentieth century and immediately fit into the culture. You don't have ghosts that say, "Boo!" (Unless you're deliberately trying to achieve humorous silliness.)

You need a coherent storyworld. For example, you don't have your characters speaking formal Elizabethan English for most of the book, and then have one of the main characters shout, "Bummer, dude!"

Another way to immerse your target audience reader is to appeal to what they already believe. For example, one reader won't believe a story that doesn't include evolution. Another reader will toss a book that mentions evolution aside.

Aside from a coherent storyworld, you need coherent people. The girl who solves problems by kicking people in the face is not going to pick up knitting to solve the Big Boss Battle unless you show us how she changes her mind. People who have phobias about spiders are not suddenly going to keep them as pets. Without very good reasons, people who speak one way will not suddenly speak another way. Your characters must act within the characteristics you have given them. If your plot requires your character to act in a way they would *not* to make a certain plot point happen, then you need to change your character or you need to change your plot. Or you could write an awful story. Your choice.

Activities:

1) Write at least one practice paragraph of your story set somewhere near the beginning of the story. This paragraph is unlikely to be inserted into the story you will turn in, so don't fuss overmuch about it. Save this and all the other paragraphs in a file. You will come back to them.

2) List the things in your paragraph that indicate which genre you have chosen.

3) Do not begin writing your story for this course yet. You will be writing practice paragraphs for a while. Answer this question: What will you need to do to create suspension of disbelief in the reader of your particular story?

CHAPTER TWO:

CULTURAL WORLD-BUILDING

World-building occurs in all stories and all genres, but speculative fiction requires bushels of the stuff. Your story needs to happen someplace, even if all the action is in the middle of a white room. A story that takes place in our "common" reality might only need to show the hero's class, her family history, and her hometown in its setting. Historical fiction might need to add a bit more world-building for readers to understand the story. But the history, geography, weather, technology, cultures, and social mores of a speculative world are unknown to the reader of a science fiction or fantasy story until the writer tells the reader what they are. These facts and matter-of-facts of the speculative fiction should not be presented to the reader in the form of an infodump (a dumping of information on the reader.) Infodumps interfere with the forward movement of the plot, and are easily forgotten because all that information often is not needed in the scene the reader is currently involved in.

Many writing instructors say the reader wants to be carried away to another world. In speculative fiction that is especially true.

World-building is so much fun. More fun even than building landscapes for model trains or putting together plastic building bricks. But there can be traps within world-building. You might spend so long on delving into the intricacies of your world that you never get around to actually writing a story set within it. Or you could make the world and rules so complex that no reader can follow the plot. Or, quoting from Janeen Ippolito's book:

World-Building From the Inside Out began because of a mistake.

My mistake.

I'd been world-building for over ten years. I'd studied cultures and anthropology at a college known (and infamous) for its thorough humanities program. I'd taught classes on world-building and coached people through the process individually.

And yet, when it came to incorporating world-building into my own speculative novels, I failed.

Over and over again.

My worlds were well-designed. My races looked cool and had neat clothing and weaponry. And the names! Oh yes, I loved making up all those crazy names.

But I had missed one key factor that I should have remembered from my very first literature class: a story is about plot and characters, working towards a goal, and having disasters thrown at them. It's about excitement. Adventure. Emotional depth. Pacing.

I had beautifully-formed races with no heart. No soul. No motivation.

No reason to go along with my plot other than because I said so.

For some reason, that made for some pretty shallow cultures!

To use a favorite expression from my college days, I was missing the **cultural worldview**.

Worldview, the essential collection of beliefs that frame how an individual and a society perceives, interacts with, and makes decisions about the world.

Once I stopped banging my head on my desk, I did what any self-respecting, hyper-planning teacher would do. I began writing a curriculum for myself. I researched all sorts of different ideas on world-building and tried out character builder profiles with pages and pages of questions.

I sifted my way through cultures and societies, trying to fuse together a comprehensive way of building a culture from the worldview and moving out.

The result is *World-Building From the Inside Out*.

The next two chapters will be taking a lot of the discussion from Janeen Ippolito's book, but will not go as deeply as her book does. Also, I am dealing with topics in a different order. For instance, this textbook does not deal specifically with worldview until chapter fifteen while Ippolito's book tackles the issue first thing.

Day 1 knowing your world

You should *not* reveal all the characteristics of the world in your story, but *you* want to know all the rules so your characters will behave believably. For example, it might be logical in present-day America for a woman to go into a senator's office to present a petition to legalize current illegal drugs. Unless she wants to go to jail, it would be illogical for that woman to enter a senator's office and inject herself with an illegal recreational drug. But in an alternate USA, it might be legal for a senator to pass out recreational, addictive drugs to voters.

Whatever the personal traits of a character are, she acts within a society that will influence the manifestation of those traits. Rebellion looks like one thing in one world, and entirely different in another world. Obedience in one world might involve murdering a neighbor, and in another world blessing and aiding a neighbor.

Randy Ingermanson says in his book, *Writing Fiction For Dummies*, that you should know one hundred times more things about your world than you place in your story. I think that might be too high a ratio. I think you could get away with ninety-nine times.

Also, you might not need to know *everything* before you begin, even though that is useful. Sometimes, the peculiarities of a world emerge as a writer writes and discovers the ramifications of the social, scientific, and technological world he or she is creating.

Activities:

A. *Read*:

Orlo fidgeted with the pieces of metal he had collected during his travels. He squinted to place a tiny pin between two gears and then reached into the pocket of his trousers to see what else he could attach. The warmth in the crowded room made his hairless head sweat under his clean, but well-used, tweed cap. Orlo stretched his long legs out in front of him and wiggled his toes to keep them from falling asleep in his work boots. He was tall for thirteen, nearly as tall as most of the men assigned as deliverers. Tiny holes in the ground puffed a warm gentle mist of glowing steam around his feet. He slid his foot over the opening and then let it go. A burst of light shot up in front of him—eventually to blend into the hovering mist that illuminated the congested cavern.

Orlo had purposely chosen to sit on the back row so no one would sit beside him, but the Slub was busier than usual and seating was limited. He had never been told, nor had he thought to ask, why the deliverers of long ago had nicknamed the Hall of Deliverers the Slub. Since *Slub* was easier to say, Orlo had allowed it to easily settle into his vocabulary.

"Whatcha doin', mate?" the tiny boy sitting beside Orlo asked.

"Don't know. Just messin' around , I guess," Orlo mumbled, wishing the boy would leave him alone.

He honestly did not know what he was doing with the metallic pieces in his hand. His caretaker in the Hall of Orphan Care said that he was born a fidgeter. The elders of garden must have been aware of his fidgeting as well. On the day of assigning the gardener had said, "Busy people must be kept busy. We have the perfect assignment for you, Deliverer." From that point on, Orlo spent nearly every day of the week in the Slub.

"Where did you get it?" the boy, at least three years his junior, persisted. The pale child pushed the goggles that were slipping down on his forehead back upon his greasy, matted hair. There'd been a time when Orlo thought he would never grow into his own goggles.

The boy looked around as if to see if anyone was listening. With a huge grin, he asked, "Did an inventor give it to ya?"

Orlo was shocked. "Of course not!"

"What's it do?"

Orlo squinted. "Nothing. It doesn't do anything, okay?"

"Course it does, mate? Look! Those pieces are movin' up and down." Orlo stared at what he had done. "You have the gifting," the boy said in an awed whisper.

"Listen, kid. I'm a deliverer, that's all. Deliverers don't have giftings. We make the deliveries and that's it. Got it?

"I got it, mate," the boy said as he slumped over.

It was against the law to be unkind to others. Orlo did not think he had crossed the line into unkindness, but he remembered what it was like to be little and to have his feelings hurt by the older deliverers. He placed the gadget in his black satchel, clasped his hands together, and looked at the sad child. "So, do you have a guardian?"

Lauren H. Brandenburg   *Orlo: The Created*

1) What have you learned about this world from the first few pages of *Orlo: The Created*?
2) Which genre do you think this is, and why?
3) List at least three characteristics not shown that you think would exist in this world.

B. *Read:*

There was a saying in the land as old as the dust that stood ten inches deep in the back of his cavern, as old as the diamonds that he loved to toss from mouth to mouth. "Two heads are better than one," Vicia-Heinox would hear a passerby say, and he would nod with both of his in sage agreement, then eat the traveler whole. Vicia-Heinox was a two-headed dragon, the only one there had ever been—the only one which *has* ever been.

To say that Vicia-Heinox was the most powerful living creature anyone would remember is to understate the case. A one-headed dragon is a national emergency. A two-headed dragon, sitting astride the only truly usable pass on the north-south trade route, is a world problem. Vicia-Heinox was an environmental feature. He not only altered cultures, he was a factor in producing them. Three ancient nations feuded and skirmished around him, for he sat on the only frontier the three realms held in common. He had been actively involved in the history of each, and all held him in awe.

One could say that the dragon helped preserve the peace, for he refused to let armies march through his pass. On the other hand, one could say his presence constantly argued for war, for he strangled economic interchange between the giant powers. The only merchants he allowed to pass were very rich merchants. They had to be very rich, in order to pay his incredibly high toll in goods and slaves and still make a profit. They were also very wise merchants, who knew how to show honor and respect to the dragon who insured their financial well-being. No wisecracking merchant ever made his way through Dragonsgate. A misplaced remark about two heads, dropped thoughtlessly amid the bargaining with the beast, had been the bane of many a family fortune. Over a period of centuries this process of unnatural selection resulted in a very small company of sour, mean-tempered, closemouthed merchants controlling all of the interempire traffic.

This provided the primary cause of friction between the nations. Everyone knew that it was the merchants who controlled their economy. And because the merchants kept to themselves, each family holding a number of private estates scattered through each one of the kingdoms, the people of every land viewed the merchant families as foreigners. Because they hated merchants, the public hated foreigners. Because they hated foreigners, they warred on their neighbors.

But Vicia-Heinox straddled Dragonsgate and armies couldn't march. The three lands waged no hot, quick wars on sunny days, moving in colorful array across great remembered battlefields. Instead, the three realms wrestled in one slow, dark war, a night war, fought in black and white. Skirmishes and raids replaced marches and charges. Generals were made by intrigue, not excellence. Cruelty was valued over bravery. The great-hearted leaders of memory had long since been replaced by thieves. It was not a good world in which to live.

Except for Vicia-Heinox, who felt it couldn't be better. There were rulers of lands, but he ruled the rulers. The merchants controlled the countryside, but he controlled the merchants. And he ate well.

...

And naturally, he was also in constant need of food. Now some dragons preferred to eat cattle. ... But Vicia-Heinox was a perverse sort of dragon, the kind that gave all dragons a bad name. Vicia-Heinox took pleasure in talking to his dinner before he ate it. How the hideous beast came by this disgusting proclivity for dinner conversation cannot be dealt with here. It must simply be said that this was an old habit, one not easy for the dragon to break, even had he been so inclined. And this had resulted in a rebirth of the long-dead institution of slavery.

Robert Don Hughes   *The Prophet of Lamath*

1) What do we know about this world from the excerpt of the first few pages?

2) What do you think the genre of this story is?

3) What might this story be about? If you were writing this, what would happen next?

C. Read:

Jonah took off, clambering higher till he could reach with his left hand for one of the independent dangle vines that sometimes laced the gaps between pinyons. With his right hand he flicked with his belt knife, severing the dangler a meter or so below his knees. Sheathing the blade and taking a deep breath, he launched off, swinging across an open space in the forest . . . and finally alighting along a second giant bole. It shook from his impact and Jonah worried. *If this one was weakened, and I'm the reason that it falls, I could be in for real punishment. Not just grandma-tending duty!*

A "rascal's" reputation might have been harmless, when Jonah was younger. But now, the mothers were pondering what amount Tairee Dome might have to pay, in dowry, for some other bubble colony to take him. A boy known to be unruly might not get any offers, at any marriage price . . . and a man without a wife-sponsor led a marginal existence.

But honestly, this last time wasn't my fault! How am I supposed to make an improved pump without filling something with high-pressure water? All right, the kitchen rice cooker was a poor choice. But it has a gauge and everything . . . or, it used to.

After quivering far too long, the great vine held. With a brief sense of relief, he scrambled around to the other side. There was no convenient dangler, this time, but another pinyon towered fairly close. Jonah flexed his legs, prepared and launched himself across the gap, hurtling with open arms, alighting with shock and painful clumsiness. He didn't wait though, scurrying to the other side—where there *was* another dangle vine, well positioned for a wide-spanning swing.

This time he couldn't help himself while hurtling across open space, giving vent to a yell of exhilaration.

Two swings and four leaps later, he was right next to the bubble's edge, reaching out to stroke the nearest patch of ancient, vitrified stone, in a place where no one would see him break taboo. Pushing at the transparent barrier, Jonah felt deep ocean pressure shoving back. The texture felt rough-ribbed, uneven. Silver flakes rubbed off, dusting his hand.

"Of course, bubbles were younger then," the old woman had said. "More flexible."

Jonah had to wrap a length of dangle vine around his left wrist and clutch the pinyon with his toes, in order to lean far out and bring his face right up against the bubble—it sucked heat into bottomless cold—using his right hand and arm to cup around his face and peer into the blackness outside. Adapting vision gradually revealed the stony walls of Cleopatra Canyon, the narrow-deep canyon where humanity had come to take shelter so very long ago. Fleeing the Coss invaders. Before many life spans of grandmothers.

Several strings of globelike habitats lay parallel along the canyon bottom, like pearls on a necklace, each of them surrounded by a froth of smaller bubbles . . . though fewer of the little one than there were in olden times, and none anymore in the most useful sizes. It was said that, way back at the time of the Founding, there used to be faint illumination overhead, filtering downward from the surface and demarking night from day: light that came from the mythological god-thing that old books called the *sun*, so fierce that it could penetrate both dense, poisonous clouds and the ever-growing ocean.

But that was way back in a long-ago past, when the sea had not yet burgeoned so, filling canyons, becoming a dark and mighty deep. Now the only gifts that fell from above were clots of detritus that men gathered to feed algae ponds. Debris that got stranger every year.

These days the canyon walls could only be seen by light from the bubbles themselves, by their pinyon glow within. Jonah turned slowly left to right, counting and naming those farm enclaves he could see. *Amtor . . . Leininger . . . Chown . . . Kuttner . . . Okumo . . .* each one a clan with traditions styles all their own. Each one possibly the place where Tairee tribe might sell him in a marriage pact. A mere boy and good riddance. Good at numbers and letters. A bit skilled with his hands, but notoriously absentminded, prone to staring at nothing, and occasionally putting action to rascally thought.

He kept tallying: Brakutt . . . Lewis . . . Atari . . . Napeer . . . Aldrin . . . what?

Jonah blinked. What was happening to Aldrin? And the bubble just beyond it. Both Aldrin and Bezo were still quivering. He could make out few details at this range through the milky, pitted membrane. But one of the two was rippling and convulsing, the glimmer of its pinyon forest shaking back and forth as the giant boles swayed . . . then collapsed!

The other distant habitat seemed to be *inflating*. Or so Jonah thought at first. Rubbing his eyes and pressing even closer, as Bezo habitat grew bigger . . .

. . . or else it was rising! Jonah could not believe what he saw. Torn loose, somehow, from the ocean floor, the entire bubble was moving. Upward. And as Bezo ascended, its flattened bottom now reshaped itself as farms and homes and lagoons tumbled together into the base of the accelerating globe. With its pinyons still mostly in place, Bezo Colony continued glowing as it climbed upward.

Aghast, and yet compelled to look, Jonah watched until the glimmer that had been Bezo finally vanished in blackness, accelerating toward the poison surface of Venus.

Then, without warning or mercy, habitat Aldrin imploded.

David Brin   *The Tumbledowns of Cleopatra Abyss...The Year's Top Ten Tales of Science Fiction 8*   http://www.davidbrin.com/

1) David Brin never explains what a pinyon is. It's a type of pine tree with edible nuts. He never says, but we can assume the trees have been genetically altered, or gengineered, for bioluminescence. One of the joys of reading science fiction is figuring out the world as you read along. As a mystery reader likes to guess who committed the murder, so science fiction fans like to gather clues to what this fictional world is like and what of today's technologies were extrapolated into wondrous uses and improvements. So, tell us about this world.

2) How do you think food is produced in this world?

3) Why might the people of this world have the attitude toward boys that they have?

Day 2 fictional religion

If your world contains humans, it is quite likely that a subset of them will worship one God or other. Oftentimes, religions are affected by culture. Different clans might have completely different religions or might worship the same god in different ways.

In addition to festivals and holidays, many writers invent one or more religions for their storyworld. With so many existing religions on present-day Earth, why would anyone feel the need to invent a religion? There are several reasons.

Adding a religion with interesting trappings and practices can enrich a storyworld and make it feel deeper. The writer might want the texture religion adds to life, but not want adherents of different religions or none to stop reading the book because a particular religion offends a swath of the intended audience.

An invented religion can provide motivation to a character that do not exist for an intended reader and thereby explain the character's otherwise puzzling actions.

Another reason might be that the writer wants to investigate some facet of the God they do worship, but to do so in disguise so the reader doesn't automatically throw up a defense, saying "But my God is not like that." Instead the reader will absorb the story, and maybe think new ways about their God.

Also, the disguise of an invented religion might present a doctrine that an adherent has grown bored with over a long time of adherence and cause an excitement over a fresh presentation of that doctrine. Think how many people cried over the death of Aslan (in the *Chronicles of Narnia*) who can no longer produce tears over the six-hundredth reading of the crucifixion of Jesus.

And yet another reason for an invented religion might be that the writer wants to show how stupid the religion they are disguising, or for that matter, any religion, is.

Or a writer might want to demonstrate how evil a particular present religion is without gaining a ban, shunning, or trouble from relatives.

Another writer might wish there existed a religion like the one invented because she is dissatisfied with current offerings.

Hollywood is fond of using invented religions to cause danger for the hero, as well as humor.

Using competing invented religions to provide conflict can let the writer create a story that is not a commentary on present-day Earth conflicts.

I'm sure you can think of a few more reasons.

Activities:

A: *Read*

> I turned a corner in the road and hit the edge of the crowd. The Servant's crier was on my left, the Vanguard on my right. The edict of tolerance had forbidden fighting among the orders, but that didn't keep their adherents from going at it by proxy.

> "The purpose of man is to serve others, placing them above himself," the Servant's crier proclaimed, his brown robe ruffling in the breeze. "If every man looks to use his gift in his own interest, we will descend into selfish barbarity." His clear tenor carried above the crowd. Many in the loose assembly that filled the large square framed by the cathedrals nodded their heads in agreement.

> "I must take issue with my brother," a brazen-throated woman in white declaimed. "While service is a noble goal, there will always be evil in this world. Unless we are bold in confronting the enemy's malice, servanthood will only provide

fuel for its excesses." Tall, her auburn hair floated in the breeze, wreathing her head in a flaming halo atop her spotless white robe. "The gifts of Aer are given so that we might eradicate evil from the world."

I dismounted and led Dest through the crowd on foot, grinding my teeth at the delay. Yet it would be quicker than having to apologize to some merchant if my horse stepped on his toes. The criers for the Absold and Merum loomed ahead. I looked around at the throng. I'd been through Crier's Square any number of times. Most of the faces never changed, but even in their newfound strangeness, I noted the presence of new adherents.

The Abshold crier—they were almost always attractive blue-clad women—had the largest portion of the crowd. Many of the men gazed at her with something other than religious fervor. I moved to my left to get by.

"While I can sympathize with the desire to serve and to fight evil, as my brother and sister so eloquently express, I must disagree. Our principle purpose here is not dependent on what we do, but on what we are. We are all fallen. Only be extending forgiveness freely to each other, in imitation of Air's forgiveness for us, can we free ourselves from those internal chains that make us less than we are. Then you will see your gift shine forth."

The Merum priest, dressed in red, waited for her to finish. The crowd in front of his stand, a simple stack of granite slabs at odds with the massive cathedral behind it, was smaller than the other three, and most of them waited passively, their faces neither pained nor expectant. "The strictures are these," the priest intoned, reciting the daily office. "You must not delve the deep places of the earth, you must not covet another's gift, and above all you must honor Aer, Iosa, and Gaoithe in all." He stopped. The Merum never debated. They quoted the office in pieces between the proclamations of the other three. Most people, even those who didn't adhere to their division, had heard it so many times, they could recite it themselves.

Patrick W. Carr   *The Shock of Night*

1) Why might the writer have invented this divided religion?

2) How do you think this religion might be important in this story?

3) List the descriptions of each priest.

B. *Read*:
During a college debate about whether or not "great men" or circumstances propel history:

In 2028 on the world of Terra, in what was then called Uzbekistan, a new religion arose. It was one of those volatile times when economic and moral chaos reigned. The people of the region were looking for answers and the Prophet supplied them. Preaching in the name of the Mogdukh, or "Power-Spirit," he synthesized a religion from the varied strands of Central Asia, revamped Marxism, Islam and a generous dash of pseudoscientific mysticism.

The faith spread with frightening rapidity. In eight years Nirsultanev took control of Central Asia, Siberia, Iraq, northern Iran, the Caucuses and even portions of Russia west of the Urals. His followers came to call themselves Khlisti, or "Whips," in reference to the self-flagellation that figured prominently in their rituals.

The Prophet taught that his followers would usher in the next stage of human evolution through asceticism, collective living, and the unifying conquest of humankind in worship of the Mogdukh. Over time man would transcend the corruption of the physical and become pure spirit, as the Mogdukh was. Individual humans were nothing more than experiments created by the Mogdukh in this process of Becoming.

Through terror, the Prophet crushed dissent and seized the industrial and governmental positions previously held by corrupt oligarchs. The rigid, centralized economy he instituted failed to bring prosperity, as such economies always do, but it did elevate the poor to a common level of misery.

Even more ambitious than the economic "reforms" were the radical revisions he made upon the area's culture. He turned a demoralized region into a militaristic power bent upon converting its neighbors at the point of the sword. Over time, the Khlisti regime became a humanitarian and security crisis even the Europe Union could not ignore. This led to war with the Atlantic powers and the Khlisti Empire was broken apart.

Were it not for an "accident" of history, Nitsultanev's sect would have become a historical footnote. As his Empire was being subjugated, a joint project of Caltech and Tsinghua University made the theoretical breakthrough in physics that opened the door to faster-than-light travel. Within a quarter-century colony ships were rocketing off for distant stars and disaffected Khlisti were among the first to leave.

J. Wesley Bush   *Knox's Irregulars*

1) What type of story would use this kind of religion?

2) A science fiction writer of some renown invented a religion called Scientology and then made a lot of money from it. Why else might someone invent a religion?

3) What kind of holidays might a Khlisti religion have? What sort of sayings would the parents teach the children?

C. *Read:*
Pelman is talking to his friend's son who has been assigned to guard him, and to a princess he rescued from a dragon and is still trying to rescue from all the people hunting for her:

"But if the three lands were once united, why would they choose to divide?" Bronwynn wondered.

"P-p-perhaps they d-didn't choose," Rosha muttered. "P-perhaps it was chosen for them."

"It was both chosen for them and they chose, Rosha. Few changes that great occur from a single cause. Many factors worked on our fathers of old to destroy the one land. All are described in that book Bronwynn holds."

"Please, Pelmen, tell us! It's so much easier to hear you explain it than try to read it all."

Pelmen nodded, then reached out to take the book from her and seated himself on the stone shelf. Bronwynn scooted the stool away to give him room. Then she leaned against the wall beside Rosha. The small cell seemed more so with all three of them crammed inside, but to Pelmen it seemed the safest place to pursue their study.

He placed the lamp to one side, closed his eyes, and began. "It's hard to condense factors without making generalizations, but the breaking of the one land resulted from our fathers' inability to integrate all they discovered in the one land's last age. There were so many people then—many more than live today—and so much happened so fast. Various groups of men began to cluster around ideas they held in common. There were those who saw the powers of the air as inanimate forces that could be controlled by physical means. They built devices to harness these powers as spirits of the wind and hold them in tension. Others viewed these powers as spirits of the wind and fire, that could only be controlled by magic. These were the ancient powershapers, who scoffed at using tools to bend the powers. Still others clustered around various leaders, men who taught that the powers aided only those who worshipped them. None of these groups could live with the others.

"Too much took place to sketch here—that's why I want you to read the book, my Lady—but it seems that man is foolish enough to believe that if he can hurt another man sufficiently, that other man will come to agree with him."

Robert Don Hughs   The Prophet of Lamath

1) The worshippers of the two-headed dragon Vicia-Heinox are divided into churches that say the dragon is one, and the churches that say the dragon is two. What kind of practices do you think worshippers of a dragon engage in?

2) What have you learned about this world from this excerpt?

3) What do you think about Pelmen's last sentence?

Day 3 technology

Technology can include anything from a sharpened stick to 3-D printers and space ships. Your storyworld will have some level of technology. What level of technology the story has will deeply influence what the characters will be able to do. And, conversely, technology is only invented and used where it is needed. A sea-faring society (traders, raiders, whalers, or fishermen) might be better at sea technology (navigating by the stars, managing the sea winds, ship-building) than a land-locked society where war (horses, swords, etc) and agriculture (planting, hybridization, animal husbandry, etc) are considered more important.

For example, a woman cannot kill a man with a machine gun if the only weapons available are arrows and knives. A man cannot travel a thousand miles in a day on horseback. Unless it's a magic horse. So . . . can we include magic under the label of technology? We think so, if technology and magic are both seen as tools that allow a person to manipulate nature or do work beyond what a person's hand and body alone are able to do. So even if you have a magic world, you need to know what the limits and possibilities of your invented magic are.

Yes, even superheroes must follow some rules. Their powers must be established at the beginning of the story and those are the powers they must use. If they can have any power that they can use at any time, what kind of story can you have with them? It would be like, "Look! There's a problem." Bam! Solved. The end. Well, that was exciting, wasn't it? No.

In one of the poorer nations of Africa, I have seen students walking out of homes that were made by slathering mud on a framework of sticks and bamboo. While talking on cell phones. The students, not the homes. Technology can be unevenly distributed, and certainly is here on Earth. One of the things you can ask yourself as you build your storyworld is, "How is the technology distributed? Why do some people have (a technology) and other people do not?" The easy and wrong answer is that mean people keep all the good stuff for themselves. That answer ignores how wealth and innovation are produced. You might want to think how the nations of your world generate or dissipate wealth. You might look at resource-rich Congo and resource-poor Singapore and ask, "Which nation has the greater percentage of wealthy people? Why?" Why do some nations have thousands upon thousands of inventors and innovators, and some do not?

What technology or object has high enough status that everybody in your world wants one?

Activities:

A. *Read:*

Los Angeles—2081

Too close.

Horns and screeching tires yelled at him from behind as Rick Macey counter-steered, sliding the silver Lexus sideways before nearly sideswiping a cab. He tuned his neural net to the local traffic satellite, its overhead image minimizing in the corner of his vision as he careened through another intersection in the turbocharged sedan.

Pouring rain turned the city streets into tar-black mirrors. Traffic signals and holographic billboards reflected in a disorientating array of flashing neon and laser light. He forced his eyes to see through it as he neutrally shifted gears, plowing through a hazily reflected red light—rain pounding his car top in a snare drum roll.

Artificial adrenalin heightened his senses. He warned slower vehicles with a constant blaring of the horn, weaving restlessly behind them like an Indy car driver waiting for the pace car to pull away. Finally he spotted open roadway ahead on the traffic-sat. He punched the gas, wiper jets barely maintaining visibility as the methanol engine roared and his speed increased.

100…120…130

No way was he letting the killer get away.

Not this time.

Not when he had the location pinned.

Macey locked his comm onto the police band, scanned the channels for confirmation of the kill. His neural net queued up a series of transmissions and he let them play, his AI ciphering through and discarding the impertinent bits according to his search algorithm. A cacophony of voices relayed their various pieces of information.

<confirmed homicide…>

<twenty year old Hispanic female…>

<single head wound…>

<20mm shell extracted from wall forty mete…>

<shot origin estimated at two miles plus…>

Two miles. That sealed it. It was the Streetwalker Sniper for sure.

Kirk Outerbridge   *Eternity Falls (Rick Macey Book 1)*

1) The writer wasted no time letting the reader know exactly what the setting was. This is a cyberthriller, and many cyberthrillers use the same technique to start every chapter. Is this something that would fit with the type of story you want to write? Why or why not?

2) What is the technological level here? What can Macey do that he wouldn't be able to if he were a peasant in medieval Norway?

3) Does this technology seem like a logical extrapolation of present-day technology to you? Why or why not?

B. *Read:*

I must admit to being impressed. As traps go, this is a pretty good one. They've got me in a warehouse and have rigged the lighting from hard light to soft light which is diffusing the shadows, and when your superpower is controlling shadows, that's a bit of a problem. Not that the shadows are gone, but being diffused I can't really use them because I can barely see them. Also the warehouse has a high ceiling which allows a flyer to maneuver. Now my three opponents have spread out in front of me so I am trapped between them and the wall behind me. I guess I should be scared, and I am, but fortunately I'm also a little cranky.

I did mention that I haven't had my coffee yet, right?

Okay, this is not the end of the world. So I'm outnumbered, and currently outpowered. So what? In spite of all of that, I am the first-born daughter of Lightning Lass and Quazar, the greatest supercouple ever! Even more important, I am a child of God, and no one can stand against HIM! Provided saving me from The Squad is in His plan.

God, please let that be in your plan.

In any case, it's time to get this show on the road. So, I put my defensive strategy into play and try to look bored.

Now, I know that sounds dumb, and it may very well be, but the worst thing I can do right now is let these bullies think I'm scared of them. I am, of course, but that is beside the point. Of course, my acting may all be for naught, because they say Wildcat Woman can smell fear. In a way I hope that's true, because I must stink to high heaven.

I hope it burns her sensitive little nose.

Sorry, like I said, I'm cranky right now. I don't like coming up with battle plans on the fly at any time, but especially when I miss my coffee.

C. L. Ragsdale   *Chasing Lady Midnight*

1) What's the limitation for a flying superhero?

2) Being able to control shadows sounds cool, but how do you think that helps against a Wildcat Woman?

3) There's not much yet directly said about this storyworld, but there is a great deal implied. There is lighting that can be rigged, and can be hard or soft. That implies the kind of technology that can produce light bulbs, controllable electricity, and enough infrastructure to support laying wires to control that electricity. What else is implied in this excerpt?

C. *Read:*

> Mist removed two large coins from the blue money box on the counter and walked outside her shop. Closing the door, she reached for the ideograph placard which read, "Closed, but unlocked. Take what you need and leave your payment in the coin box." The signboard in place, she stuffed the "D" volume of her interplanetary Webster's Dictionary into her quilted backpack, strapped it on her back and walked into the dusty bustle of the open-air market.
>
> The market still basked in the heat although First Dusk had already come and Second Dusk had begun rolling across the sky. Using her marriage scarf to shield her face from the dusty streets, Mist headed towards the fruit stands where the Federation-approved traders sold exotic foods gathered from across the galaxy.
>
> In the distance, near an Ormat tree, four Federation off-worlders with ear-caps on their heads talked among themselves. One man carried something long and metallic on his shoulders. Another had a metallic box with a glass tube on one side. The only woman among them was looking through a metallic tube at the reddening sky. For several seconds, Mist studied the movement of their lips but could decipher nothing.
>
> The purple warning lights of the market flashed: three slow blinks, then two long ones. Mist felt a cold chill run down her back. A dread unsettled her mind and she glanced nervously at the Town Square stage. Two women with children strapped in chest-packs raced past her.

Carole McDonnell   *Lingua Franca*

1) If you were paying attention, these few paragraphs told you a lot about this world. List the things you learned about this world while following the main character around.

2) What was your first clue that everybody (until the Federation showed up) on this planet was deaf?

3) What other accommodations for deafness might this society have?

Day 4 circle of life

Unless the characters in your story are fixed in number, immortal, and existed before time began, they will need to be born. We won't discuss the physicality of birth yet, but rather how society forms around birth.

In your society, what will be the rituals around birth? Will the father make an announcement, and if so, how? Who gives whom presents after birth? Will the father or mother care what gender the child is? Will there be mourning for one and rejoicing for another? What will birth order mean for the baby?

Will the baby remain unnamed for a certain amount of days or months until the family believes the baby will survive the high infant mortality rate of the society? Will the child be given a nasty name so the demons won't be attracted to it? Will it be important what the mother sees first after giving birth? Is the process of birth private, public, or something in between? Is it family or specialized healers who attend the birth? Who will name the baby? The parents? The grandparents? The leader/king/shaman of the group? Will all but one baby from a multiple birth be killed? If the father does not accept the child, is the child left outside to be eaten by scavenger animals? What ritual might accompany acceptance? All the mentioned possibilities happen or happened somewhere on Earth. Perhaps you could come up with new rituals for your fae or alien or human living among aliens.

Will mothers wear clothing and hair arrangements different from those who have not given birth? Will they have better or different food? Are babies or mothers given special tattoos? Is the baby shaved at birth, or the hair allowed to grow for at least one year before cutting? Who feeds the baby, and how? How is the baby dressed, and who dresses it?

Are birthdays celebrated? In one society of Earth, the only important birthdays are the first and the sixtieth. Do the people of your society believe the date of one's birth determines its destiny? Are portents looked for during the birth? Will the baby be allowed a fairly carefree childhood, or will it be expected to work as a small, weak adult as soon as it can be whipped into working?

So, there's birth, and then there's death. Perhaps even the immortal beings can be killed. In your storyworld, what happens when someone dies? Does everybody in the house in which the person died move out and burn down the house? Is a wife or daughter required to chop off a finger? Is there loud lamentation with hired mourners to cry with great clamor? Are family members expected to grieve privately? Are family members expected to throw themselves on the body or casket? Are huge monuments built for the body to be buried under or in? Or are burials done quickly with unmarked graves?

How are the bodies treated? Are they eaten? Are they mummified? Are body parts taken as talismans? Are some of the mourners required to cut off a finger to make sure somebody is crying for the dead? Are live people or possessions buried with the body? And where is the body buried? At one time, a few of the First Nation tribes placed their dead in ceremonial canoes and hoisted the canoes into trees. In another part of the world, bodies are reverently placed on special hilltops for the vultures to eat. Perhaps the body is burned on a bier or in a boat floating on a river. What is done with the ashes?

What happens to the belongings of the newly deceased? Which family members claim the belongings? Or perhaps a king seizes them? Can his side of the family drive out the wife, keeping the children and possessions, but leaving her to starve? (Yes, there are places on Earth where this occurs.) What happens to the debts of the dead person? What happens to the remaining family?

Are there ritual foods or clothing or colors associated with funerals? What are people expected to say during a funeral?

Knowing the answers to these and more questions can enrich your storyworld and keep it from reading just like middle-class American life. So here's a few more questions to keep your mind buzzing:

What types of clothing will your characters wear, and why?

How did your characters arrive at the location of your story?

What is the racial background of your characters and their appearance?

Are sports important? What kind? Competitive or cooperative, or a mixture like basketball is? How lethal are the games allowed to be?

Activity:

1) Now write at least three practice paragraphs set in the world of your story. They won't need to go into your story, so don't fuss. Practice writing that shows how your world

works. Each paragraph should answer one of the above questions. Save them in the folder for your story.

Day 5 art and music

Art and Music are important to most of us. One can envision a society without either, but we would rather not. Advertising of every sort could be done with only words of a plain font, but if your characters are anything like most humans, they won't like it much. Visual art, which includes advertisements, architecture, painting, drawing, photography, literature, calligraphy, dance, mime, acting, seasonal decorating, décor, furniture making, clothing and hair styling, jewelry, packaging, product design, etc. can tell much about your world in a few words. If all the art your characters see in a city are focused on battle and bloodshed, what does that tell the reader about that society?

Will your society expect everyone to create art of some kind, or will the creation be limited to professionals? How will your characters be trained in arts? Will people paint patterns on the outside of their houses? On the inside? Will some expensive colors be limited to royalty or elite? Will people expect their food to be artistically displayed?

Must all the art conform to government propaganda? Is the art uplifting, or degrading? Is most of the art religious in nature? Are certain subjects or objects banned from being used in art?

Music can tell much about a culture as well. Are harvests, children growing, and historical events subjects of lyrics, or are all the songs about sex? Are there hymns? Are there national anthems? Are there specific birth, funeral, promotion, demotion, coronation, coming of age, etc. songs? Are the hymns atonal chants, or melodic? Do the people of your storyworld sing songs in groups? Are only certain people allowed to sing? Are there times music is paid for? Are the different genders allowed to sing together? Might music be a component of magic, mesmerism, or command?

What sort of instruments are used? Music that uses only percussion instruments is radically different from that which uses only wind instruments. Humans can clap, click, and use vocal cords to make music. If your storyworld has aliens, how might they make music? (I'm thinking here of stridulating crickets.) Is the music scale based on the octave, pentatonic, microtonal, maqamic or something else altogether? Does the music require a regular beat?

How is the music of your world physically perceived? Dogs can hear sounds of too high a frequency for humans to hear. Elephants hear lower frequencies than humans can hear. Some insects can perceive radio waves. Katydid ears are on their front legs. Grasshopper ears are on their abdomens. What would music that dipped in and out of human hearing sound like to humans? (You could ask someone who is growing deaf and losing perception of different frequencies.)

Music can be used as a sensory detail involving hearing to enrich your storyworld. (Note: If you write more than a few lines of lyrics, most readers will skip over it. Sad fact.) Still, a little is wonderful.

Activity:

1) Write at least three more practice paragraphs set in your story world. What do those paragraphs reveal about your world? Can you show the rules without explaining them by showing how the characters react to the rules?

CHAPTER THREE:

MORE CULTURAL WORLD BUILDING

More than any of the other genres, science fiction writers sometimes forget that most people are embedded within a family. A Grand Master of Science Fiction Writers of America, Damon Knight, theorized that may be because so many of the readers and writers of speculative fiction are trying to get away from their families. Most readers of science fiction are novelty seekers, and many seek to escape the strictures of tradition. Writers of fantasy tend to acknowledge that families exist. And writers of horror often emphasize how families can doom their members. Whichever genre and subgenre you write, acknowledging that people come from families can enrich your writing.

Janeen Ippolito, in *World-Building From the Inside Out*, gives the following list of family structure possibilities:

1) *community-based*, with the concept of "It takes a village to raise a child."

2) *multigenerational households*, with the elderly caring for the children

3) *classic nuclear family*, with the essential unit being parents and children

4) *home-sharing*, with two or more family units sharing the same household and responsibilities

5) *cohort living*, with children living in groups by their age and being cared for by any of their parents, depending on who is assigned to which task

6) *government-raised*, with children sent to state-sponsored boarding schools to be educated according to civic morals and principles

In addition to families, people begin life within a local community, which is part of a society, which is ruled by traditions and government.

Day 1 politics and government

Whatever else is going on in your world, if there is more than two thinking entities in it, there is politics. Humans gather themselves into societies, and part of all societies is government. The government requires taxes. And while taxes might involve chickens, usually taxes require money.

Janeen Ippolito in her book *World-Building from the Inside Out* describes a wide variety of governments and how the economy is handled. Here's a list without the description she supplies in her book.

Capitalism
Communism
Anarchy
Republic
Monarchy
Theocracy
Democracy
Dictatorship

While humans are humans and almost any kind of tale can be told about them, the type of government that humans live under can hinder or enhance their behavior in marked ways. It would be an unbelievable story for a street-sweeper to treat a prime minister the same way he would treat a king.

Activities:

A. *Read*:

Joss interpreted the question from among the grunts and smacks of the King at table. "I am concerned, my Lord. I fear some change has taken place in the palace that has altered the national political situation. I fear . . ." Here Joss paused for emphasis. ". . . that you have been overthrown."

Talith stopped chewing and stared. Then he closed his mouth and chomped angrily. He took a long draught of wine to wash it all down, his menacing eye never leaving those of his Chief of Security. Then he stood and leaned across the table. "I said I received a letter from Ligne this morning!"

"Yes, my Lord."

Talith paced around the table. "You never have trusted Ligne, have you?"

Joss thought a moment, not about his reply, for he knew exactly what he thought of Ligne. Rather, about its consequences. "No, my Lord," he answered.

"You thought it was she who kidnapped Bronwynn, and now you think she is plotting my overthrow, don't you?"

"I don't think she's plotting it any longer, my Lord," Joss answered matter-of-factly. "I think she has accomplished it."

Talith smiled cruelly. "Then you shall ride back to Chaomonous tonight and see if your suspicions are correct. You certainly won't be missed, since we're doing nothing but sitting here."

"If that is my Lord's will, certainly I will obey it," Joss replied.

"It is, General Joss. And my instructions to the troop that travels with you will be to conduct you to the dungeon once they are sure that all is well in the palace. How does that strike you?"

"As my Lord chooses . . ." Joss began.

Robert Don Hughes *The Prophet of Lamath*

1) What type of government is this?
2) If this story was taking place in a democratic republic, how would the conversation differ?
3) Why would a general voluntarily go to a dungeon?

B. *Read*:

Shadow-of-Light-Turning made the gesture which meant Mist was being argumentative and unreasonable as usual. "My dying wish is that my granddaughter will not be poor and isolated as her mother is," she signed, casting a disgusted glance at Mist's blue marriage scarf. "Can't you wear the scarf of our caste?" Shadow-of-Light-Turning asked. Although Mist had used the green embroidery thread of the science caste throughout the scarf, her husband's mother was still not appeased. "Aren't you ashamed of yourself for being so strong-willed? And look at your daughter! The girl has no bracelets on her arms, no caste-cap, no jewelry around her calves, no gems around her neck and ankles. When I see her coming home from school, capless, like an outcaste child, I cannot bear the shame."

This woman has nothing else on her mind. Mist thought and signed, "She has not decided yet what caste-cap to wear."

Her husband's mother didn't say the obvious, that a child should not have to choose her caste.

Ninety-eight people lived in the family compound, including servants –none of whom belonged to Ion. As a mere superintendent of standards and weights in the agricultural department, and that only because of his mother's influence, Ion was not well paid. His family had tolerated his love-match marriage to a woman not of his work caste, but his co-workers had not. Neither the traders nor the scientists he worked with considered Ion truly qualified for the inter-caste job –in this case a position which was both scientific and trade-related. And neither did the sub-caste of regulators consider him part of their network. He found peace and acceptance, however, among his family.

Mist, on the other hand, was accepted by the other traders. (Traders, being expedient, valued networks and friendships.) But grudgingly tolerated by her mother-in-law's household who continually reminded her that Ion had given up an advantageous marriage to a woman of the science caste to marry her.

It didn't help matters that because of the initial upheaval in both families, both Ion and Mist flatly refused to accept monies or gifts from their relatives. Such were the dangers of love-matches.

Shadow-of-Light-Turning finished listing Mist's many flaws and walked away without the requisite gesture of respect. Mist and Flowers-in-the-Sun exchanged knowing glances and Mist thought to herself, My little sunshine. My only female ally among my enemies. A minute later, the green entry lights of the family compound gates flashed: three long beams, two quick ones, then six quick ones. Ion's pattern: he was home. Waiting to surprise Ion when he entered their area of the house, Mist stood by the door of their family apartment holding the "orange" in her outstretched cupped hands.

But Ion did not immediately come up to their apartment. When he finally arrived upstairs, he told Mist his mother had intercepted him.

"She believes Flowers-in-the Sun should get the implants," he signed, then after a pause, he added, "And I agree with her."

Mist could not answer him: the "orange" was in her hand. But she glared into his dark eyes until he turned his face away.

Mist put the "orange" in the food closet and walked over to her husband, slowly and deliberately. She forced him to look at her by raising them directly in front of his face. Her hands were so close, they almost touched his nose. Then she made the signs which meant, "No. Once again, my opinion does not matter."

Carole McDonnell *Lingua Franca*

1) What do we know about this world?

2) What kind of family structure does Mist live in?

3) Research and write a paragraph about caste systems. How can caste systems cause conflict for stories?

C. *Read*:

"Why has the king come to visit us, then?" I ask, now that my fingers have stopped trembling.

Daerilin tosses back the last of his wine and waves his goblet in the air. "To find a bride for his son, little princess. How would you like to marry the Menaiyan prince?"

My chest feels hollow. I force myself to breathe, to keep my expression still. Form the corner of my eye, I can see the king's long-fingered hand lifting his goblet. He speaks with my mother quietly, I can only just catch the faint lilt of his voice, the resonating strangeness of his accent.

"We are hardly a strong ally for them," I whisper.

"Perhaps they're just looking for a mouse to snap up," Daerilin replies as the servant fills his goblet. "Their women do seem to die young. They wouldn't want to upset their closer allies by accidentally killing off the bride." Daerilin smirks. "I daresay no one would raise an outcry if something were to happen. To you."

I stare down at my plate, the roast still untouched. I have lost my appetite. Perhaps Daerilin is only baiting me: God knows he has enjoyed his taunts these last years. But surely he would not make this up? Surely the king has not come for me?

"I hear," Daerilin observes momentarily, "that Prince Kestrin is not one to be crossed. Quite a temper he has when he is displeased."

I wish that I could come up with a snide rejoinder, but my wits fail me. If Daerilin is right, then the Menaiyan prince is no better than my brother. He may be infinitely worse, used as he is to commanding a much greater court than ours.

Intisar Khanani *Thorn*

1) What type of government is this?

2) Do women marry for love in these royal families? Why or why not?

3) What kind of king would Daerilin make?

Day 2 eating

Food. Again quoting from Janeen Ippolito's book, *World-Building From the Inside Out*:

It's best to focus on writing about food the way you should eat food—in moderate amounts, just enough to fill in the nooks and crannies of your culture and add detail to your character and plot.

Whether or not it is necessary for your race to eat is up to you, particularly with regards to types of food. Certainly in the world's cultures, anything from guinea pig to pig ears is acceptable, and that doesn't even factor insects (or arachnids). Or maybe the culture survives on nutrient-laced air? Whatever they like to feast upon, there are certain things that you might need to figure out to fully flesh out the culture.

Favorite Foods – These do not have to be common or easily-found foods. Favorite foods are often determined by having emotional, geographical, or even financial significance. Christmas foods are often considered favorites because of the memories they evoke of the holiday. Lobsters are often considered a favorite food in coastal New England because it's easy to get them and seafood is part of the culture. Peanuts are a favorite in the South because they are a major cash crop. What are favorites in your culture?

National Foods – What foods are considered representative of your culture? For America, a few foods are hamburgers and hotdogs and popsicles. In England, Shepherd's Pie, tea and scones, and fish and chips are considered the norm. For Japan, everyone thinks of sushi and sashimi and seafood-based delights. What foods are your culture known for? What are they stereotyped for?

Religious Foods – Go back to your religious elements. What foods are associated with different religions. Consider the Catholic tradition of eating fish on Fridays or fasting during Lent. Jewish customary foods include gefilte fish and kugel. Another area to consider is what foods are taboo. In Islam, eating pig products is forbidden. Many Hindus consider cows sacred and will not eat beef. Are there foods that religious adherents in your culture should not eat?

Taboo Foods – Apart from religion, there are other foods that cultures generally considered untouchable. In America, eating animal brains and genitals is largely considered repulsive, except in certain regional cuisines. People from other cultures often consider processed foods like canned cheese or cheese slices to be abhorrent. One way to determine taboo foods is to start from a culture's comfort foods and national foods, and work towards the opposite end. For instance, in America people generally prefer fish cooked or at least smoked. The idea of eating raw fish is considered disgusting to many.

Holiday Foods – For this, you need to figure out holidays. … However, if there are holidays, then think about what food is involved. Thanksgiving involves turkey and pumpkin pie. Scottish Hogmanay wouldn't be complete without haggis (stuffed sheep stomachs). And round pastries are essential for Chinese moon festivals. What foods reflect the themes and surroundings of your holiday?

Coveted Foods – These are the foods worth a lot of money, or the foods that could be given as fancy presents. What brands or types of food are considered worth saving up for as a once a year treat? Why? Consider location. This might be something like fresh mangoes in Siberia, or venison in the Bahamas. It could also be something rare, such as truffles or expensive wines. Also, it might be demand that drives the price up. Halloween candy is in demand before the holiday, and marked down ninety percent after.

Janeen Ippolito   *World-Building From the Inside Out*   (note: formatting has been changed)

Few North Americans know what it's like to go hungry day after day, month after month, year after year. The availability of food is highly dependent on technology. In 1800, the percentage of labor involving farming was nearly 90%. In 1900, the percentage of people needed to produce food was 38%. In 2000, less than 3% of the labor force were farmers.

How is food preserved and transported in an age without the technology of canning or refrigeration? What will food be like in the future when it can be 3-D printed using proteins spun by bacteria in vats?

The lower your culture is in technology, the harder and longer it takes to procure and prepare food. In areas with scarce fuel, more foods will be eaten raw.

I laugh at stories where the protagonists live on berries, nuts, and roots as they traipse through deep forests. For one, berries and nuts ripen at different times of the year. For two, digging up roots is an arduous task that takes a long time, unless your protagonists are stealing some poor farmer's carrots.

You don't need to make food production and preparation the focus of your story, but it is something you should consider as you build your storyworld.

Activities:

A. *Read*:

A bony hand grabbed his shoulder. He spun around, and came face to face with Basel, who'd found his way this far in the line. "Let me through," Basel said.

Daniel winced at his breath and took a step back. "We're all hungry. Wait like the rest of us."

Basel squinted at him, as though he didn't understand. "I said let me through." He tried to sidestep him, but Daniel stuck his shoulder out to block him.

"And I said wait in line like the rest of us," he replied firmly. People close to them swiveled their heads, curious. Basel glared at him and shifted his grip on the glass bottle in his hand.

Daniel, his face flushing, raised his fists, but before either of them could make another move, a Preceptor rushed down from the front of the line and broke them up. A few townspeople near him tossed him vague comments how he should have just let him through, but none of them bothered to look at him while they did, so he ignored them and focused his attention on Litty.

She was sitting in the road, playing with her new rock, oblivious to the whole situation. Sometimes he envied her freedom. He ran his fingers through his hair. Today was the last day they would have to put up with meager food rations and people willing to fight to be the first to get their hands on half a can of soup. During the air raid a year ago, the railway tunnel that connected Obenon to the world beyond the Untamable Mountains had collapsed, making escape next to impossible. For a whole year, the Order had people on the other side clearing the tunnel, repairing the tracks, and preparing to evacuate everyone from Obenon. Now the train was here and tomorrow they would leave this life behind.

At last Daniel made it to the line's end, presented his and Litty's ration cards, and collected their simple meal, which, to his pleasant surprise, included a small loaf of bread for each of them. The bread days were few and far between, but today felt like a special occasion as it was, and the bread would help them celebrate.

Nate Philbrick *Little One*

1) What do some people do when food becomes scarce?

2) What are some of the causes of food scarcity?

3) What would food scarcity look like in your storyworld?

B. *Read*:

Dyana, from a cool mountain kingdom, has been betrothed against her will to the prince of her people's enemy as part of a peace treaty. Only the tailor knows she is a substitute for a disappeared sister that was named in the treaty. This takes place in a tent in a desert.

"I see you have managed to tear my most recent handiwork already," Harimar noted. "Just there on the shoulder, at the seam."

With a grin, Cahnar rubbed at the spot. Dyana saw no rip. "You have the eyes of a roc. It is one loose stitch."

"Caused no doubt by your exuberance. Or you are growing again. Honestly, Cahnar, must you be so hard on my clothes?"

The two men were joking with each other. She had never seen her father joke with a tradesman.

"I can only be what I am, good master. At the moment, I am famished." Cahnar went to the tray held by the serving woman and picked out a large, oddly shaped purple fruit.

"We were also about to eat. After I fetched the princess something more appropriate to wear." The woman, Bejaka, started to leave, but Harimar stopped her. "No, we will need something other than what I laid out earlier. I have just the thing. I will come with you. If you will excuse us for a moment, Cahnar, Princess." He bowed and exited with the woman following.

"So you and Harimar found common ground?"

"Why do you say that?" She edged away from him.

He tossed the fruit into the air, caught it and crunched into the skin. Juice spilled down his chin, and he jerked forward to keep it from dribbling onto his pale blue shirt.

Dyana laughed at him.

He glanced at her with a sheepish half grin. "Ripe."

"I would not know. I have never seen that kind of fruit before."

"Honestly? It grows in the lowlands, where the ground is always wet, and the flies are thick enough to choke you when you breathe. Here. Try it." He held out the fruit.

She started to reach for it and hesitated. If she accepted this now, what would he offer later? No, resistance must be her first action and reaction if he was to send her home. "I have no wish to try something new. Last night's meal was strange enough to last me for days."

He frowned and withdrew the offered fruit. "I am sorry we did not prepare something to your liking. Perhaps if you told me what you would prefer, I can arrange a more pleasant meal for you."

"I very much doubt that. No matter what the meal, I would be eating it here."

"Would that be so unpleasant?" A tiny crease appeared between his pale eyebrows.

"I did not choose to be here, Prince. I did not choose this life. How can it ever be pleasant to me?"

He seemed to consider the question. "I did not choose this life, either. Should I resent it?"

RC Tolbert   Daughter of Anasca

1) Most people are deeply reluctant to eat foods they have not grown up with or seen people they admire eat. If Dyana ate the strange fruit, it would mean more than ingested nutrition. What would it mean?

2) What do we learn about the government and the world in this excerpt?

3) Make a list of some exotic foods that would be eaten in your storyworld.

C. *Read*:
Goblins have stolen the king's body from the castle before he could be buried.

Musicians played horns and fiddles as goblins piled their plates high with heaping helpings of food. There was some concern that they'd offend Justin since goblins eat what humans couldn't stand the sight of. The fear proved baseless as the King was being a good sport about the matter. That wasn't surprising given that he was dead, but he'd been a good one even when he was alive. One goblin set a plate of food beside the King on the off chance he'd feel better and ask for a snack.

The celebration was in full swing with raucous music, copious food, and much laughter. It went on for hours and even the goblin cooks joined in. Once the music and gorging was done, the goblins gathered around Justin Lawgiver's body. They fell silent, but their expressions were not dour, nor were their tears. A few goblins gave the King a pat on the back and some encouraging words before they settled down.

Estive gathered up his ratty robes and struck his staff on the cave floor. Bang! The goblins turned their eager eyes toward him. Once he was sure he had the crowd's attention, he waved his staff over the cave and addressed the goblins. "Friends, allies, neighbors, people we tied up and dragged here, we come here together to bid a fond farewell to Justin Lawgiver, who through no fault of his own was King."

…

… Estive waved his staff at Brat for him to come over and take his place. "Before we bid goodnight to Justin, I'd like to ask the people who knew him best to say a few words."

Oler picked his ear and farted.

"It's Brat's turn first, Oler," Estive said. He stepped away from the body and let Brat speak.

Brat brushed his dirty hair aside and spoke to the goblin mob. "We were able to break into the castle by—"

Estive threw a rock at Brat and hit him in the shoulder. "Talk about the dead guy!"

"Okay, okay! Geez." Brat rubbed his shoulder and began again. "The first time I met Justin was twenty years ago. The boys and me had broken into his castle for some food. It wasn't hard when they just dump their potato peelings and coffee grounds in buckets where anyone could get them. Anyway, we were nearly out when Justin and his knights came by. Me and Oler hid up in the rafters and waited for them to leave when a rafter gave way and dumped me on the floor and both of my buckets landed on my head."

Brat laughed. "Hoo boy, was that embarrassing! The knights went for their swords, and I was about to run when Justin broke out laughing. He went down on his knees and then sat down so he didn't fall over. I'd seen him plenty of times before that, but that was the first time I saw him laugh. When he got his breath back, he told the knights to escort me outside the castle, and he let me keep my stuff. Then he said that from now on he'd have his cooks leave their kitchen scraps outside the walls where we can get them."

Arthur Daigle *Celebration Fantastic Creatures: A Fellowship of Fantasy Anthology*

1) What do we learn about this storyworld from this excerpt?

2) Research and list celebration foods for Christmas, Hanukah, Eid al-Fitr, and Diwali.

3) Write a paragraph about food you would prepare for a goblin feast.

Day 3 education

Education. Quoting from part of the section on education in Janeen Ippolito's book *World-Building From the Inside Out*:

> Level of education is a standard aspect to consider in characterization. Make that character's level of education have significance (whether good or bad) within their culture and you suddenly have an additional level of connection or conflict. Figuring out the basics of education within your culture can be an easy way to add depth.
>
> Here are some areas to consider:
>
> **Optional or Compulsory** – Compulsory education indicates a high value for literacy and intelligence within the culture. Reasons for educating the general population include having an informed public to participate in civic affairs, and encouraging improvement in various academic fields to surpass other countries in

science or technology. A culture that makes education optional may be one that either has less centralized authority, or sees an educated populace as a threat.

Restrictions – Forbidding certain individuals from education is common in many cultures. Some exclusions are based on gender (usually with females being seen as less capable of or interested in education) or race (out of a desire to keep certain races out of the country or perceiving them as a threat). Another form of restriction includes segregation policies, where individuals are divided into different (and often unequal) schools for a supposed benefit. This a natural consequence of gender, racial, economic, or other tensions.

Duration of Education – This is where timing comes into play. How long is a school day? A school year? How long do students have to be educated before they receive a degree or other recognition of achievement? Agricultural or lower class communities often have less education. Urban or upper class communities tend to place a higher priority on education, whether for advanced careers or for increased social status.

Structure of Education – Structure concerns how a school day functions. In earlier times, students from poorer economic circumstances would all learn in one room, and the teacher had to be capable of teaching at all levels. This is still true in some developing countries. Many modern primary schools have one designated teacher per classroom who teaches all subjects. When the subjects become more advanced in middle and/or high school, each instructor teaches a certain subject, and the students move between classes. In college, often both the instructor and the students move to different classrooms, as instructors have their own offices.

Janeen Ippolito goes on to discuss the physical location of education, style of instruction, instructor training, higher education, valued fields of study, funding, and types of education. Under types of education she lists and describes the following:

Homeschool

Cyber-school

Religious

Preparatory

Private

Boarding

Reform

Military

Specialized educational styles, i.e. Montessori, Goddard, Classical, Charlotte Mason, Homeschool tutorial.

To that list we would like to add Unschooling or Autodidactism.

Another issue you might consider is the presence of libraries. If there are libraries, is anyone able to use the library for free, or is the library limited to subscribers or certain types of scholar? Is the library electronic, paper, or scroll-filled? Are there newspapers anyone can buy and read?

Activities:

A: *Read*

Deputy McKenzie helped me up. "Sorry, didn't mean to scare you."

"I'm fine. Thanks." Fine as I can be with missing parents and police pointing guns in my face.

I walked to the bed and snatched the envelope. "Definitely not foul play. They left a note. I couldn't wake them, so I turned on the light. When I discovered they were gone—like, totally not here—I somehow tripped and knocked everything over. Sorry."

"Very understandable, Miss . . . Larcen?" Lt. Garrett continued to inspect the room.

...

Lt. Garrett studied our family picture on the wall. "Big family."

"Yes, sir."

"There's three, four, five, six—*six* of you kids? No wonder your parents wanted to escape in the middle of the night." He lifted his hat and scratched his head. "Good grief."

Although being the oldest of six made me want to run away sometimes, I didn't recall asking for his opinion. *Since you have a gun, I guess I'll let that slide.*

...

"I guess." I sat on the end of the bed. "My mom travels for work sometimes. But it's never happened in the middle of the night, and she's never taken my dad."

"What does she do?" The deputy tucked a loose tendril behind her ear.

Ah, the dreaded question. One that I tried to avoid. "My mother is a leading expert on Sasquatch. You know . . . Bigfoot."

Four eyebrows shot up—well, make that three—and four feet took a step back. The officers looked at me like I'd sprouted a set of antlers.

I shrugged. Though I tried to keep this odd, family fact from surfacing, there were times, like this, when it worked to my advantage. "Yep. That's what she does."

Then I decided to really freak them out. "She's also an expert on Faeries, Trolls, Leprechauns, Dwarves, and Elves. She has a blog.

Stunned silence.

"Although," I continued, "that doesn't explain why my dad would go along. He's a hairdresser. Okay—cosmetologist. Maybe he wanted to give Bigfoot some highlights or something. Who knows?" A combination of the late night and crazy circumstance made me a bit testy. They can't arrest me for that, right?

"A hairdresser." Lt. Garrett frowned.

"He owns the Camas School of Cosmetology. CSC for short. He hardly does hair anymore, though, except when he teaches a class. *Maybe he could wax that brow for you sometime. Soon.*

"I see."

"So, your parent's van." The blonde tapped her pen against her pouty, lower lip. "You think they got out and left it to hunt down Bigfoot?"

"Seems that way. Maybe that's why my dad decided to go along. Usually my mom catches a flight somewhere, you know, more isolated. People call her or email with pictures and stories. If it sounds legit, then she hops a plane and goes to investigate."

"I'm curious." Lt. Garrett leaned towards me. "Has she ever seen one?"

"Oh yes. Several times."

"Really?" He looked doubtful.

"Really." It seemed likely the elusive, wooly Yetis might be his distant relatives. Their whole body merely one, giant unibrow.

"May I read the note?" Deputy McKenzie extended her hand.

"Sure." While she scanned it, I couldn't help noting her resemblance to a life-size Barbie. The two officers were like Beauty and the Beast.

"It says 'keep doing school.' Do you guys homeschool?"

Oh, joy. A second awkward question in under five minutes. "Yes, ma'am."

She gave her partner *the look*. I've seen it a hundred times. It's the look that says, "Oh, you're one of *those*." She made no attempt to be subtle.

Heather L. L. FitzGerald   *The Tethered World (The Tethered World Chronicles Book 1)*

1) I haven't discussed style yet but I'm going to ask you anyway, how often do you see the word 'said,' in the above excerpt? How do you know who is speaking?

2) There are dozens of reasons why one might homeschool. (And dozens of reasons why one might not.) What are some reasons why one might homeschool?

3) How might homeschooling affect the plot of The Tethered World?

B. *Read*:

MISHA

From that first night nine months ago, a sickness had been growing in me, like some hideous creature wanting to be birthed. I knew its cause. That damnable, beautiful star.

Tonight on the palace roof I tried to look away, to stop my ears to the endless musings and sharp-tongued arguments of my fellow scholars. They bickered over the portent of that silver-white specter wandering the charred field of Sin, god of the night. But it was the night before my final examinations and I could not afford distraction.

Only a few hours remained until dawn, and I must retrieve the one thing that would assure my place among them, that would give me an edge over Navid and all his advantages.

One chance. I had one chance to redeem last month's disaster.

I glanced at Navid, his dark head bent to the shorter Zahir, who served as mentor to us both. Zahir's finger traced a star chart, weighted with amulets and spread upon the roof's ledge, as he explained some hidden knowledge to Navid. A stab of jealousy deflated me. Navid was born into the Kasdim, as I was, and would also face examinations tomorrow. But that was where the likeness ended.

Navid flicked a condescending glance at me, and in that glance was all the superiority he wielded like a club in his privileged hand.

"Shouldn't you be practicing your presentation, Misha?" His nasal voice arched over the rooftop, loud enough to draw the attention of every studious mage. "Perhaps a good meal to strengthen you, eh?" He glanced left and right, ensuring he had an audience. "Ah, but I forgot, you are likely to present your last meal to the Kasdim along with your lessons." He snorted. "Perhaps you should arrive hungry."

The snickering response proved that no one had forgotten last month. My lifelong fear of speaking before a crowd had gotten the best of me, in front of every first-through fourth-level palace mage.

I shrugged one shoulder and smiled. "I have no worries, Navid. Even the contents of my stomach are more impressive than the contents of your mind."

Navid's eyes darkened with a flash of insecurity. He gave a half bow. "We shall see, my friend. By this time tomorrow I expect to have acquired a most troublesome assistant."

One slot for this year's second level. It would belong to either Navid or me, and the one who did not achieve it would serve the other as assistant for the year.

The idea of a year under Navid's thumb propelled me from the roof without further comment. I must not fail tomorrow. The star hung behind me, whispering its usual curse on my head if I would listen, but I ignored its threats.

Tracy Higley   *Star of Wonder: A Novella (The Incense Road Book 1)*

1) What have we learned about this world from this excerpt?

2) What is this style of education called?

3) What is Misha training for?

C. *Read*:

He searched another cabinet and came out with a scroll, which he spread out on the table. It was a chart of the cycles of the moon for the rest of the year.

"This cost me a week's earnings, so be careful with it. I want you to make an exact copy. Be careful to get everything right."

I could read, but I was doubtful about my ability to perform this task. I hadn't written very much in my life; the need hadn't arisen. I wanted this position as his apprentice, however. It was that or a life as a useless runt in a house of blacksmiths.

I took a deep breath and then another. I had to focus on this task. No looking out the window or watching clouds; I needed to concentrate.

Looking around, I found a table where I could sit with my back to the window with nothing of interest in front of me and slowly began to copy the chart. As I made each stroke of a symbol or number, I compared it to the original. The room darkened around me, but I didn't stop. It was painfully slow, and my wrist and back ached, but I kept on writing.

As it started to become too dark to work, I felt a hand on my shoulder. I looked up at the healer.

"The sun is about to set; you had better go home," he said.

I had copied about half the chart. "I'll come back tomorrow to finish this."

"Tomorrow I'll be out. I need to buy sulfur and mandrake, as you noticed."

"And wormsroot," I added.

"No, the caravan that will be here tomorrow doesn't sell that. I'll have to send someone to the city for it."

That would triple the price of the expensive root. "I'll get you some."

His eyebrows lifted. "Really?"

I took an empty container from the counter. "I'll fill this and trade it for an apprenticeship."

"Do you have any idea how much that is worth?" he asked.

I nodded. "I've studied the price sheets. This much wormsroot would cover my apprenticeship at the normal rate."

"Huh." He leaned over and looked at the work I was doing. "This is very good work."

"Thank you."

"If you can raise the money, either by that jar of wormsroot or other means, I'll give you an apprenticeship."

"Thank you!" I yelled and ran for home. I was sure I heard a "Huh," as I left.

Vincent Trigili....*The Adventures of Zero; The Quest for Wormsroot*
Fantastic Creatures A Fellowship of Fantasy Anthology

1) How do people gain an apprenticeship in herbal healing in this storyworld?

2) Why does this character want that apprenticeship?
3) What was the purpose of medieval guilds? Will there be guilds in your storyworld?

Day 4 military

Military. On Earth, there has been only a few pacifist societies, and many of them have been destroyed by neighbors who were not pacifists. Only the smallest of societies do not have a police force. The countries of Earth that do not have a standing army either have an agreement with another nation to protect them or have a heavily militarized police force. Perhaps things will be different in your storyworld.

About 8,000 non-citizens per year join the US military. They gain the same benefits as other enlisted, and if they choose to seek US citizenship, the process is expedited. At present, the US military is voluntary. In the past, there were times when soldiers were drafted from the civilian population.

The US navy was expanded to fight the Barbary pirates, members of the Ottoman Empire that operated out of North Africa. The pirates seized American ships and held rich sailors for ransom and sold the rest as slaves. The war of 1812 between Britain and America was caused mostly by economic sanctions and US outrage over Britain capturing Americans and forcing them into the British navy (which had brutal discipline then.)

The purpose of this exceedingly brief history lesson is to present a number of ways the military of a nation can be made. In your storyworld, you might have a military composed of voluntary militias, mercenary soldiers, drafted or stolen soldiers, professional standing armies, and guerillas. You might have hereditary warrior elites (such as Medieval knights), warrior castes (as the Kshatriya in India), civilized warrior societies (such as the Spartans), and barbarian warrior societies (such as the Huns).

Some of the things you will want to know about your world's police, private security forces, and military are:
How will returning whole and injured soldiers be treated? Will they be hated or loved?
Look up the origin of the word salary. How will the soldiers be paid? Who pays them?
What are the rules of combat? Do the soldiers try to spare civilians? Do they keep POWs?
What sort of armament does the military have?
If borders are guarded, how are they guarded?
Are the soldiers fed, or do they need to scrounge for food from the populace they are invading?
What is the nature of medical care for soldiers?
So forth and so on.

Activity:

1) Write some paragraphs about the military or lack thereof that would fit with your storyworld. Save them in a folder dedicated to information about your storyworld.

Day 5 medicine

Thinking of the nature of medical care for soldiers leads to the question of medical care for everybody in your storyworld. Can limbs be regrown? Can a fairly simple infection lead to sepsis and death? Who has access to medical care? How are the healers trained?

Is illness a rarity in your storyworld? What are the common illnesses? Blindness is a common ailment in many stories in the Bible, and in many developing nations. There are many reason for that, including malnutrition or parasites. But in wealthy industrialized nations, blindness is often caused by diabetes. What kind of illnesses do weather, geographical, employment, or nutritional conditions create for the population in your story?

Is there a distinction between mental and physical and spiritual illness? Does the general population believe in genetics, germs, contagion, or family curses? Are sick people ostracized, judged, avoided, quarantined, cared for in the home or in hospital-like centers? How are those who are disabled from birth treated? Are they treated like everyone else? Better? Worse? Your protagonist's treatment of and behavior toward the sick and the disabled–especially if that ill person is from a different caste, race, or nation—can reveal much about his class, education, and spirituality.

If death is imminent, what are the rituals surrounding the before and after care of the sick person or her survivors? Is there a caste or group of people whose duty it is to deal with the disposal of the deceased? It has only been since the 1950's that undertakers were deemed necessary in the United States. Before that, the family often brought the corpse home to wash, clean, and bury. In some Earth tribes, the mummified body of the deceased is kept within the household as if the dead person is still among the living. There are also differences in the length of mourning. How do the time and rituals of mourning differ if the deceased is a miscarried child? A young child? An aged mother? A husband? Or a brother? Mourning rituals also differ depending on family wealth.

Here are some paragraphs from the section devoted to health and medicine in Janeen Ippolito's book *World-Building From the Inside Out*:

> Medical help often comes in two flavors: traditional and scientific. For the fun of it, we'll also toss in magical.
>
> *Traditional* deals with what a culture has historically done for health and wellness. This can include folk or herbal remedies, as well as food or drink tonics. If it was passed down from generation to generation or made with a secret recipe by a great-grandma, it falls under traditional. This is also where healing techniques can overlap with religious beliefs.
>
> *Scientific* deals with the advancements a culture is making in the field of medicine using the scientific method and modern technology. This typically involves labs, microscopes, pills and technological devices. There is often a clash between tradition and scientific medical treatments, but there doesn't need to be. Finding a way to have the two intermingle would be a fresh take on the material?
>
> *Magical* deals with how magic interacts with the other systems. Usually magic is intermingled with traditional healing methods, but there are possibilities to mix it with scientific. For instance, if magic on your world is defined as a neutral energy force that can be used for good or evil, then why not use magic to power modern medical technology? If your story defines magic as purely witchcraft—the bending of creation to personal will apart from the divinely-appointed order—then medicinal use will be more problematic. Using magic for healing may have some nasty side-effects—or magic could even be the cause of the ailment.

Janeen Ippolito   *World-Building From the Inside Out*

Activity:

1) Write a number of practice paragraphs showing a scene with a character from your storyworld receiving or giving medical care. Here are some suggestions: Write a paragraph in which your medical practitioner encounters one of the common illnesses of that world's populace. Write a scene depicting the death or recovery of a warrior. A king. A peasant woman in childbirth. A fisherman caught up in a futile battle who is calling upon his gods or God…or (if in an atheistic world) recounting his life. These are suggestions, not requirements. Your character might receive care in a bacta tank.

CHAPTER FOUR:

PHYSICAL WORLD-BUILDING

Some science fiction writers take great pride in their knowledge. They may have studied a specific science–linguistics, geology, DNA, marine biology, evolution, etc—and have used their knowledge to speculate on a future world. Fantasy writers can take pride in their ability to unshackle their minds from the "normal" and to imagine worlds unfettered by many of the rules that science fiction writers revel in. Horror . . . what can horror writers take pride in? Ambiance, atmosphere, but primarily catharsis. The word "catharsis" comes from the Aristotelian concept of "identification and fear." This identification with the main character's plight cause the reader to fear and be ultimately purged and intellectually enlightened. For example, one type of horror film makes us fear lack of control. The sub-genre of mad scientists horror–such as *The Fly*, *Frankenstein*–leaves us horrified at the stupidity of meddling in (and our own powerlessness over) mechanics of life.

Whatever the genre, world-building is important. And at its most basic, the world is about time, place, people, and things.

If a story of any genre is set in a real city, past or present, the writer will need to do a lot of research to make sure the characters run down the correct streets, sniff the correct smells, and wander through a correct kind of fog.

But what if the setting is invented or long past and shrouded by the veil of time? If you want your readers to suspend their disbelief long enough to finish and enjoy your story, you will still want to have correct physical details. Rivers flow downhill. If they don't in your world, you had better have a good reason for that. If your population has steel swords but never went through the bronze or iron age, you must have a good reason for that as well. Scientific history in your created world doesn't need to mirror the same pattern of technological advances as Earth's. For instance, your culture might have knowledge of gunpowder but might never have invented guns. Or they may understand quantum physics and mathematics but may have no concept of the atom bomb or nuclear energy.

Here's a part of a science fiction short story set on an alternate Venus that had a different history of asteroid strikes. A group is investigating why a mining camp has gone silent:

> Two billion years ago, the last great resurfacing era, vast quantities of molten rock from Venus's mantle had risen to the surface through long, vertical cracks in the crust. Injections of lava and differential crystallization of minerals had formed on enormous geological basin with distinct layered strata, including reefs of titaniferous magnetite gabbro, and vast quantities of tin and iron. The basin had tilted and eroded and half-drowned, leaving only one edge exposed, a long, narrow continent that wrapped around half of Venus's equator. Most of its volcanic ranges and salt flats were scorching, waterless, and utterly uninhabitable, but a cold sea current rose at its southern coast, feeding banks of fog that grew during the long day and sustained an ecosystem found nowhere else on Venus. The People's Republic had established several mining stations there, to exploit deposits of titanium and tin ore, copper and silver, platinum and bismuth, and to lay claim to the deserts to the north.
>
> This was the coast that the ekranoplan was approaching, drowned in fog and mystery.
>
> An even pearlescent light, streaming with particles and tiny transient rainbows in whichever direction Katya happened to look. The close, clammy heat of a Turkish bath wrapping around her like a wet towel. The puttering of the auxiliary motor and the slap of waves unnaturally loud in the muffled hush. And something echoing in the distance: faint, staccato, persistent.
>
> "I see no monsters," Captain Vladimir Chernov said, turning to Katya. "But I definitely hear something. Do you hear it too, Doctor? Could you give your professional opinion?"
>
> "It sounds like dogs," Katya said. "Dogs, barking. Do they have dogs?"

Paul J. Mcauley   *Planet of Fear*

No one is expecting you in high school to be able to put so much geology in your story. And most stories do not need this level of world-building, but do you see how this careful explanation of the landforms these people are heading for builds confidence that the writer knows what he is talking about? When the bad stuff starts happening, you will have no problem suspending your disbelief. You can fully enter the story without a jarring "Wait a minute. That doesn't make sense."

There are ways for writers to cheat in this age of the internet. Type into your search engine a question like, "What if the moon didn't exist?" and you will find a website devoted to answering questions like that. Ask, "What do the moons of Mars look like from the surface?" and you will find an image that will help you describe the moons of your planet or fairyland. Type in maps of the city you are writing about. Go on social media and ask your friends if any of them can tell you about certain parts of their town.

Day 1 space

For humans to move about without spacesuits in an atmosphere on the surface of another planet, that planet needs to meet a lot human physiology requirements. That planet will need to be a lot like Earth. It doesn't take much change in the percentage of oxygen in the atmosphere for the air to be eventually fatal to humans. A human can live with a variety of air pressures, but anything outside sea level to about three miles high requires machinery and supplemental gasses. The atmosphere must not contain too much methane or chlorine.

There's a relatively small range of temperature that the body can tolerate. Venus is way too hot (plus acidic), Mars is way too cold. The planet will need a spinning core to generate a magnetic shield around the planet that will keep harmful gamma rays away.

Too little gravity and the bones and other organs of the human body deteriorate. Too much gravity and the body is squashed.

If your book is focusing on aliens, you have more leeway because the physiology of the aliens could be different from that of humans.

Things you might want to know about your world include the brightness and size of the star, distance from that star, the other planets, stars, and asteroids that circle the star, the size of the planet, the axial tilt that influences seasons, the length of day, the length of year, the elements in the crust, the elements in the atmosphere, the air pressure, the climate zones, the amount of surface covered by water, how deep that water is, and several more things. There are entire books devoted to designing a planet that humans can live on. It would be to your benefit to read them. Some of those books may go into more detail than you are willing to work through or even need for your story, but you do need to know how many moons orbit the world and how high the tides are.

Thinking through potential differences from Earth will help make your setting feel more real and may even provide drivers for plots.

Even if your world is a fantasy world, you will need to deal with the laws of physics on some level. When a man is stabbed and dies, does he fall down or up or fold sideways into another dimension?

Activities:

A. *Read*:

Rebecca paused for emphasis before continuing, her eyes scanning the crowd. "Since NASA launched its Terrestrial Planet finder space telescope in 2014, my colleagues and I have been scanning the heavens for a planet that would have the characteristics necessary to support life. Our dedication has finally paid off.

"Once this planet, designated 2021 PK, was found, NASA sent a small probe to take photos and readings. As you can see by this next slide, the probe reports confirm our greatest hopes. This planet has many similarities to Earth." Using her fingers to count off the numbers, Rebecca continued. "First, it revolves around a G2V size star. Second, its orbit is only slightly elliptical, unlike most exoplanets we have studied. Third, it is .95 Astronomical Units from its sun, almost exactly the right distance for life to evolve. Fourth, its gravity is only slightly heavier than ours. Fifth, the mean semimajor axis, mean eccentricity, and mean mass are nearly identical to Earth. And, most importantly, it contains high amounts of liquid water, which would be absolutely necessary for life to have evolved there." She paused and brushed a loose lock of curly black hair behind her ear.

Clicking to the next slide, she continued. "You can see here a photo of the planet showing the dense atmospheric cloud cover, which may be accountable for the disruption in the radio signals and the slight degree of distortion in the photos.

"Although the reports are not conclusive, we believe that there is sufficient evidence to warrant a manned mission to 2021 PK. The primary goal of this mission would be to find proof of other life forms. The team would dig under the surface of the planet to search for fossils, plants, or any other signs of life, as well as collect numerous rock samples and perform various scientific experiments…

Keith A Robinson   *Logic's End*

1) What is an Astronomical Unit?

2) What is an exoplanet?

3) What does eccentricity mean in this context?

B. *Read*:

Bunard was the center of the kingdom of Collum. The king's keep, and my quarters as his personal reeve, sat on a vast bluff overlooking the Rinwash River. The road from the castle spiraled down the sides of the overlook, the slope crafted so that horses and carts could bring goods and food to the top. Steep alleys and granite steps cut across the road throughout the tor, allowing our fair denisens to shortcut their way to the base of the hill where the majority of the king's subjects lived.

As I walked, my view alternated between the river to the west, where barges drifted south, and the Cibus Plain to the southeast, where we grew our food. Here and there in the distance, villages dotted the hills whose ripples flattened little by little until they disappeared entirely. Beyond sight at the end of the plain, the Darkwater Forest stretched away to the east and south without light or village to interrupt it. I suppressed a shiver and focused on my destination. …

After catching a glimpse of snow-capped peaks in the distance to the north, I turned south and trekked along a winding cobblestone road that took me past my favorite inn, Braben's, and through a marketplace. … I entered the small, run-down church belonging to the Merum at the edge of the lower merchants' section, just north of the branch of the Rinwash separating it from the poor quarter.

Patrick W. Carr *The Shock of Night*

1) In another place in the book, the writer describes how the city is divided into quarters by the Rinwash river. The amount of time the writer spends on describing the geography of his country is important because, as the reader discovers, that geography is crucial to the plot as the characters move through it. How do you think the geography of this place will influence the movements of the characters?

2) Why would a king situate his castle upon a tor?

3) What do you know about this planet from the description?

C. *Read*:

5. MORNING

Tennant gained the rim of the lava sea with a final crunch of his boots and paused for breath. He never tired of this moment, giving colour to his otherwise dreary life: moving from the sealed habitat on the broken planet's regularly curved surface, to this, almost literally the end of the world—a deep, violent crack in the crust of Sheba, moon of Eclectia. The land, such as it was, ended; the cliff dropped off into dizzying space and lava lapped at its distant foot. The fissure's other side rose up two k's away, distant, unknown.

He turned his face straight up and beheld another major remnant of the cataclysm, the rings of cooled lava that threatened to fall on his head. Swathes of rubble danced around it and the gap between Sheba's halves. If he strained his eyes he might make out Quatermain beyond the littered asteroids. The two had been one moon as recently as two hundred Foundings ago, it was said, and he believed it. He blew out a breath, fogging his faceplate, and returned his gaze to the task ahead, fighting vertigo. Tennant glanced at his partner, then stepped forward from the volcanic grit into the maze of scaffolding at the edge of the abyss. Precious ore to feed the factories of Avenir, partly present in the crust of the more habitable planet Eclectia that now loomed beyond the incredibly distant horizon ahead.

They attached their harnesses and turned to back down the first ladder. The Avenir station glinted there in the bright light of Ceti 94, and off to the right he spied the lesser glow of its distant twin star before the rock blocked his view.

They reached the tunnel entrance and unhooked themselves in turn. Tennant allowed himself one last, long look over the wild and ever-shifting lava in the canyon still far beneath them, before he spun and entered the mine to begin another long shift.

Grace Bridges *Avenir Eclectia*

1) Planets, moons, suns, space station. There's a lot swirling around in this space. What do you learn about Sheba from this chapter?

2) What are the clues that there might not be an atmosphere here, or if there is, it's unbreathable?

3) What kind of stories could take place here?

Day 2 planet

In space opera you can get away with The Ice Planet, The Jungle Planet, and The Desert Planet. You can also get away with driving spaceships from planet to planet like cars driving from one block to another block in the same town. If you want more science in your story, you will consider the various climates that all planets have. There will be warmer places, usually at an equator, and there will be colder places, usually at the poles. Exceptions to that could make some interesting settings.

Every setting on a planet should have weather of some sort. Sometimes the weather can be important to the plot. Sometimes weather can be important for enhancing the mood of a particular scene, i.e. rain when the main character is sad, sunlight that's not too hot when a main character is happy, stormy during a tumultuous climax.

Terraforming is important and fun, but so is building the cosmos and solar system that surround your planet. A planet might have one moon or two, one larger sun, and one slightly smaller moon. These situations can create interesting implications and ramifications for weather, time, human life, and alien life.

Seasons have a heavy impact on cultures. Suppose winter were seven hundred (earth) years long and summers were three hundred (earth) years because of a wildly elliptical orbit. A planet like that would have a thousand earth-long year. How would that impact life, and if there is sentience, their customs?

Activities:

A. *Read*:

Aryl is an Om'ray, a telepathic species with mobile hair. Rastis and nekis are skyscraper tall "trees." Without permission, Aryl and her brother-in-law have followed the harvesters into the canopy.

> Flitters launched into the air, as if disturbed. Instead of wheeling and crying in protest, they plunged without sound into the canopy, disappearing from sight.
>
> They fled the coming M'hir. She knew it. Could almost *taste* it.
>
> The Om'rays had found their places and stopped, waiting. Aryl saw flashes as hooks were freed from their belts and held ready.
>
> Watchers moaned again. This time Aryl could tell their sound came from the mountains. As would the M'hir.
>
> Costa's fingers locked around hers as the world seemed to take and hold an endless breath. He pulled, urgently, and Aryl obeyed, dropping to lie beside him on the small platform. His arm went over her. *Hold on!* she heard, not words but mindspeech.
>
> As she grabbed for her own hold on the platform, she twisted her neck to see.
>
> The crimson stems nearest her face trembled in the silence. Trembled . . . then bent ever-so slightly. No, they weren't bending. Aryl's eyes widened as the stems began to twist open.

Costa stiffened beside her, lifted up as if compelled to look closer. *No!* she sent, reinforcing the warning with a grab at his hand, determined to hold him safe.

Then there was no need for warnings.

The M'hir struck.

It was like the opening of an oven. The next breath she took was searing hot, dry, and full of a chokingly fine, acrid dust. Aryl coughed and quickly closed her mouth, but the air stole the moisture from her eyes and nostrils, took the sweat from her skin until perversely she shivered.

The first fingers of wind tore her hair free of its braided net, whipping the strands against her cheeks. The stems clattered against one another as if excited.

The wind's force continued to build, steady and irresistible. Below, far below, Aryl had experienced the annual M'hir as little more than a rustling overhead that warned of bundles of dresel to be opened and stored. The rastis supporting their homes might lean slightly, disrupting dishes left on tables. Torn leaves and shredded bark would whisper and float its way into branch and crevice, making piles and obstructions to be pulled from ladders. Fine powders would rain down as well, reds and yellows and orange streaking the walkways and clogging screens. Another glamorous chore for the youngest and those not in the Harvest, sweeping and sweeping and sweeping until the black water below grew a skin of rare color.

Up here? The M'hir moved everything.

Including the crown of the rastis beneath them. As it began to shudder and shift, Costa tightened his grip until Aryl could barely breathe. The great plant *groaned*, a deep, tormented creaking, She waited for it to snap, her heart in her throat. Instead, it bent, crown bowing to the M'hir.

Julie E. Czerneda   *Reap the Wild Wind*

1) How does the M'hir differ from a monsoon? How is it the same?

2) What are the similarities of the M'hir to the chinook, foehn, and Santa Ana winds?

3) How does the M'hir affect this culture?

B. *Read*:

I checked the primitive gauge on the kiln. The gauge's needle hovered steadily in the red.

"Still too hot," I said over my shoulder. "Gotta wait another day."

"That's nice," said my fellow inmate, Godfrey. "So what do we do until then?"

"You dig," came the reply from Ivarsen, our lone guard. Like the rest of us, he wore a broad-brimmed sun hat and wraparound sunglasses to protect against Eta Cassiopeiae's blinding rays. Unlike the rest of us, his shorts and shirt were khaki—instead of prisoner orange—and he had a holster on his hip holding a high-power pistol.

In the two planetary years since I'd been assigned to Ivarsen's care, I'd never seen him draw that gun. But with how Godfrey had been acting since his arrival one week ago, I wondered if even Ivarsen's patience had limits.

Godfrey vented his unhappiness in four-lettered fashion.

"Kid," I said, "How in the world did you ever make this detail?"

"I've got a winning personality," Godfrey said, grinning.

I shook my head at him, disbelieving.

Lisa Phaan, our only female inmate, gave me a knowing glance. She didn't think much of the kid, either.

"Prisoner Ladouceur and Prisoner Godfrey on the shovels," Ivarsen said. "Prisoner Phaan on the dumper. Wait here while I drive it around."

Our guard turned and walked away into the white glare of midday, the broken and rocky landscape shimmering behind him.

Godfrey leaned close to me and said, "Why don't we just snuff him?"

I turned and looked at the huge-bodied youth, my eyebrows raised.

"And do *what?* It's two hundred kilometers to anywhere. The sun will kill you before you get thirty. Besides, Ivarsen has a chip in his body that monitors his vitals and stays in constant contact with a Corrections satellite. All the guards at these remote projects have one. If his vitals stop, the satellite gets alerted. Then the cavalry comes."

"Bull," Godfrey said.

"You really want to find out?"

The kid kept looking at our guard while Ivarsen receded into the heat.

"Look," I said, "is it really that bad? Time served here counts triple what it counts on The Island. They feed us and give us shelter. We're not at the mercy of the elements. Why ruin it?"

Godfrey turned and looked at me, hands balling. "Screw you," he said, and walked away.

I shook my head, wondering if I'd ever been that incomprehensibly belligerent when I was in my twenties. Then I went over to slap shut the ceramic door that covered the kiln's thermometer.

As indigenous brick kilns went, ours was pretty standard: a four-meter cubed box constructed from cut-rock slabs. It sat on the eroded central peak of a shallow crater whose expanse had been populated with automated mirrors. Currently, those mirrors aimed skyward. But when we put a batch of bricks into the kiln, and the computer angled all those mirrors towards the small hill at their center, the kiln lit up like a bug under a magnifying glass.

Depending on the season and the weather, the kiln could take a full day to fire up—and the days on Eta Cassiopeia's fifth planet were very long, especially at this latitude.

In the meantime, there was always more clay. And the new settlements along the polar coast always needed more bricks. In a world with no large flora and relatively little accessible iron, what else what there to build with?

                              Brad R. Torgersen   *The Bricks of Eta Cassiopeia*

1) List what you know about this world from this excerpt.

2) Every single detail in these first paragraphs are important for the rest of the story. Although the planet, geography, and climate play crucial parts in the rest of the story, those details are not the focus of the story. What is?

3) Clouds are never mentioned in this story. What tells you that sometimes there are clouds in this part of the world? What tells you they are rare?

C. *Read*:

Only four people took the shuttle from the Far Sun Princess down to Freedom. The other three were immediately claimed by people awaiting them and whisked away in rovers. Lukas picked up his duffle and started walking. Just inside the door of the spaceport terminal, he stopped to stare at a cage of pupcats waiting export.

The animals, the largest native species on Freedom, were the size of Airedales and vaguely resembled a cross between the two Earth creatures for which they'd been named. Lukas studied their large heads, rounded bodies, huge dark eyes. It was an accident of evolution that their proportions echoed those of kittens even into adulthood. That large head held a specialized, though non-sentient brain. Those rounded bodies stored fat for life on the Ice. The big eyes evolved to see on Freedom's dim farside. Popular as pets on the nearest Coalition worlds, they looked so cute that humans inevitably broke into smiles around them.

Lukas did not smile.

He picked up his duffle, left the building and started walking toward Deoxy. The gravity, slightly higher than one gee, did not slow him down. A warm wind from the desert blew through his hair.

Freedom lay close to its red-dwarf sun. Tidally locked, one face lay in perpetual, baking sunshine; the other was the Ice. Constant winds blew from the warmth to the Ice, and a permanent rainstorm raged at the equator. Along the northern-hemisphere terminator, with its comparatively milder weather, lay Freedom's three major settlements: Deoxy, Ribo, and Nucleic. Tourists thought the names were whimsical. They were not. Freedom, founded by serious Libertarians and so without government or laws, was the only planet in the Coalition where genetic engineering of humans, or the humans who resulted, was allowed. If you were born genemod on Freedom, you stayed on Freedom. There was no way to pass Purity Control at any spaceport on any other world.

Lukas trudged along the unpaved rover path, through scrub bushes of dull purple, and then among the foamcast buildings and bright holo signs of Deoxy. The glossy tourist hotels lay along the river; here was the frontier combination of crude structures and sophisticated technology. Without zoning laws, people built as they chose on land purchased from the Coalition charter company, which afterward left them alone. Capitalism on Freedom was a pure thing, even if genes were not.

Nancy Kress   *Migration*   Beyond the Sun Anthology

1) List what you know about this world.

2) Everything shown in these paragraphs close to the beginning are crucial to the rest of the story, from the geography to the pupcats to the society. There are many, many things the writer did not show us because they were not important to the short story. List some of the things she left out.

3) Invented words in speculative fiction often tell the reader a lot, especially in science-fiction. What do you imagine when you see words like "foamcast," "genemod," and "pupcats?" Why do you think Lukas did not smile at the cute pupcats?

Day 3 aliens

Once you have physical landforms and climates, you can start to populate your world with animals most of us know about and/or alien animals you have invented. Now the knowledge of ecology, habitats, and physiology comes in handy.

In science fiction you need to take into account what the different climate zones of a planet are. Even if the setting is only in one habitat, it is useful to know what other habitats there are on the planet of your story.

The habitat has much to do with what sorts of animals and aliens can live there. There are reasons slugs don't live in deserts away from steady sources of water, and reasons blue whales don't live on prairies. Mouth and throat parts determine what sort of vocalizations your animal makes. Physiology determines what the diet will be. If you want to write about aliens, it will do you good to study the freaky biology of animals and plants on Earth.

Everything needs to eat. Giant worms are not going to survive in asteroids waiting for passing space travelers to land and provide sustenance. It makes for a good visual, and in movies a good visual will always trump facts. That's why you cannot derive your aliens from movies or television.

Here are a few of the questions out of hundreds you could ask and answer about your aliens:

Do they have radial (like starfish and jellyfish,) bilateral (like humans and dogs,) or no symmetry (like amoebas?)

What are their senses? Bats can echolocate. Bees can see ultraviolet. Snakes see infrared. Flies taste with their feet. Starfish have light-sensing cells at the tips of their arms. Sharks sense tiny electrical charges. Fish detect water pressure with their lateral line.

What do they eat? What do they eat with? Rasp tongues (aka radula)? Mandibles? Teeth? Tube to suck up dissolved bodies? Absorb nutrition through the skin?

If they are predators, how do they catch their prey? Claws like cats? Webs like spiders?

What eats them? Large predator? Swarms of smaller predators? Parasites?

How do they defend themselves? Claws? Poison? Shells? Rapid running?

What is their integument? Naked skin? Fur? Feathers? Scales? Spines? Exoskeleton?

What body structures causes them to thrive in their habitat?

If they move around, how do they move around? Sea urchins use hydraulic pressure to move their hundreds of little tube feet. Wings, how many? Feet, how many? Or perhaps they crawl on their abdomens.

How do they reproduce? Division? Lay eggs? Live birth? One offspring at a time? Thousands? And how complicated a life cycle do they have? Some fish change their sex after they have lived a certain number of years. The male angler fish attaches itself to the female, fuses to her body, and is mostly absorbed. Are the offspring protected by the parent(s)?

Are there courtship rituals? Do they have spawning seasons or areas they return to in order to mate?

How do they communicate with their kind? Flashing lights? Change in skin color? Vocalization? Radio waves? Motion?

Do they function within a herd or flock? If within a group, how is status determined? Are they solitary?

Activities:

A. *Read*:

The Tikitik rode astride, its pair of long, thin legs a match to those of its mount. From a distance, there were similarities to an Om'ray's form as well, but only from a distance. There were two arms attached to a body, but the body was concave and gaunt, its surface covered in small, knobbed plates instead of skin. The arms were too flexible and bore short spines from wrist to shoulder. The shoulders, though flat and broad, met at a too-long neck that curved forward and down so the head was held in front of the chest.

Aryl's stomach protested.

The head was triangular, widest at the back, and framed by two pairs of eyes that reflected cold white disks from the glowlight. Each eye sat at the tip of a cone of flesh. The hind pair were large and aimed forward; the front pair were tiny, their cones kept constantly in motion as if a Tikitik worried about its surroundings at all times. To make it worse, in Aryl's opinion, the small eyes moved independently of one another unless the Tikitik was interested. Then, all four would lock into a forward stare.

The mouth was obscured by fleshy, fingerlike protuberances, pale gray and of unknown function. Tikitik would hear, but no Om'ray knew what passed for Tikitik ears. Or nose, for that matter. It wasn't because their bodies were hidden from view. They wore no clothing, though they wrapped their wrists and ankles in cloth patterned with more of their symbols, and used belts to carry longknives like those they traded to the Om'ray.

Their Speaker wore its pendant attached to a broad swathe of plain cloth that went from right shoulder to left hip, ending in long tasseled braids that swept down the side of its mount. Aryl could not tell, at this distance, if its pendant matched the one around her mother's neck; she had no desire for a closer look.

"We see you," Taisel said again. She managed to gaze up at her counterpart without losing her dignity, even though beast and rider towered the height of three Om'ray over her small form. Aryl felt a sudden fierce pride.

Julie E. Czerneda   *Reap the Wild Wind*

1) What sort of Earth creatures might have been inspiration for the Tikitik?
2) The Om'rays are the size and shape of humans. What makes the Tikitiks ominous?

3) What would be the advantage for the Tikitiks to have the number of eyes they have?

B. *Read*:

Aryl has been captured by Tikitiks and taken on a mysterious errand. Mind speech with her mother is in italics.

You recover quickly," it commented. "Good. We will go soon." It hesitated, then bobbed its head twice. "The other cloth you wear. Is it something you need?"

Surprisingly tactful. "I need to be clean," she said, making a face. Filthy as she was after a day trapped, she'd rather be naked in the rain; it wasn't a choice, not with the biters that liked Om'ray already making their presence known. "Is there water I can use? To wash my clothes and myself?"

A long, knobby arm reached past her to point. Aryl half-turned. Behind her rastis, the ground slipped into still black water. Water that wasn't still for long, as something beneath its surface surged hopefully up and down again.

"Not that much water," she clarified breathlessly.

The Tikitik gave its soft bark. "There will soon be much more than this, Om'ray. But I understand." It beckoned to another of its kind. "This humble one will wash you."

From the way its small front eyes rolled, the "humble one" wasn't any happier about this than Aryl.

* * *

Are you sure you're all right?

Aryl considered several possible replies, none suited the moment. *Yes. They're responsible hosts and respectful. I've no complaints.*

None that she'd share. The Tikitik's wash had produced admirable results. Her skin was so clean every bite and thorn hole showed in exquisite detail. Her hair, free of soil, was free in truth. The braided net hadn't been returned and the result flew loose around her head and in her face. Her clothes? The undertunic was clean and intact, for what it was worth, since it went only to her knees. The wraps for her arms and legs had disappeared. Those, the Tikitik could replace and did. Their cloth was finer in weave, so those were an improvement.

Otherwise? She really and truly didn't want to know any more about the cold, flat, and thoroughly slimy creatures the Humble One had slapped over every part of her naked body. They'd pulsed and scraped and giggled to themselves as if she'd been a feast. When Aryl had tried to pull them off, the Tikitik had quickly prevented her, saying only the "wash" wasn't done.

When it was, the giggling stopped and the creatures dropped to the ground around her feet. The Tikitik had carefully collected them in a bag.

Julie E. Czerneda   *Reap the Wild Wind*

1) What animals on Earth use other animals to clean them?

2) What would you do if you were washed this way?

3) Why doesn't Aryl want to wash in the water?

C. *Read*:

>   The wagon rumbled and crunched over the scup shells in the sand. Each time Ann and Edward felt one of them crack under the wheels, they shuddered. The hatching could begin at any time.
>
>   The two of them sat silent and tense on the hard wagon bench, their simple black and white clothing a sharp contrast to the dun of the beach dunes and the purple shells thrusting up through the sand all around them. Ann clutched her swollen belly protectively, though she knew she would not be able to save the babe within if the scupps hatched before the wagon reached the shelter of the cliff caves.
>
>   "We left too late," Edward said. It had become a litany of sorts.
>
>   "We'll make it," Ann replied, because they had to try.
>
>   Edward whipped the scaled backs of the placid undru pulling the wagon. Ann could have told him it would do no good; the beasts were doing the best they could already. He glared at Ann's belly before quickly looking away. His look cut Ann to the core. *He's wishing I wasn't here with him, slowing him down. He wishes we had never tried to have this child.*
>
>   "And if the babe comes early?" His teeth clenched.
>
>   "I'm still glad we're having a child, Edward."
>
>   "I don't think you will be after we've been eaten alive by thousands of flying crab-things, shooting out of all these scupp shells. Especially if we might not have been eaten if you hadn't slowed us down with a premature labor."

Autumn Rachel Dryden   *Respite*   *Beyond the Sun Anthology*

1) In this story, which has been reprinted many times, the colonists had not known about the scupps when they settled on the planet because the little monsters lived underground for most of their life cycle. If aliens settled on an alternate Earth without humans, what animals might surprise them?

2) It is best to use aliens who have a characteristic that impacts the plot. If the scupps were merely alien cicadas or seventeen-year locusts, would this story have the same kind of drama?

3) Later, we will discuss a plot device that increases tension in a story that is called a ticking clock. A ticking clock is whatever provides time pressure on the characters. In this story, there are two main ticking clocks. What are they?

Day 4 what to put in the story

Everything in the story you write must be subservient to the story and to the emotion you are trying to invoke in the reader. No matter what kind of intriguing animals, geography, magic or science system you invent for your world, if the animal or mountain or law of alternate physics does not contribute to the plot, character development, or wanted emotion, you should not include the item in your short story. You have a little more room for giddy fun in a novel, but not much. Yes, you want to understand your world thoroughly, but most readers will not want a tour. They want an exciting story. So either you find a way to make a plot point depend on your invention, or you leave it out of your story.

If you look at the writings of many speculative fiction writers, you may notice that many authors go on to develop novel series based on the worlds they have created. Often, you will learn more about the fictional world in ensuing stories, more information about histories, wars, major or minor characters, different nations. So, if you and your readers love your world and its characters, tell yourself that they will one day have another story to tell…on another day.

Activity:

1) Write as many practice paragraphs as you can in the allotted time about the wonderful things you have invented that you likely won't be able to insert in your story. That should get it out of your system, or else form the basis for a second story set in the same universe.

Day 5 what is your world like?

Often a writer will begin with a plot and will then invent a world that will support that plot. Other writers begin with a place and think about what could happen there. And yet other writers begin with a character they want the world to meet. Today's paragraphs are not yet about plot or character. They are for you to describe a world. Once that world becomes "real" to you, you will be able to make that world real for the reader. This practice and preparation will help keep you from getting stuck half-way through the story.

Activity:

1) Now write several practice paragraphs that will give us a grand tour of the place you have invented and some of the things you will put in the story. These are practice paragraphs that should help you see and understand your story world. You should not concern yourself with creating a plot at this point. Simply tell yourself about this world you've invented. Many fiction books have glossaries that help readers keep track of people, places, rituals, food, and laws mentioned in the story. If you have a novel with a glossary, study it a bit. Does it give you any ideas of how your own created world works?

CHAPTER FIVE:

PLOT

Plot means what happens in a story. It might be possible to write a story in which nothing happens, not even in flashback, but nobody will want to read it. Not even your mother. She might say she would like to read the "story", but she really won't. . . . Okay, she probably won't.

Here's one definition of plot: the series of events providing conflict within the story.

Some people like to differentiate plot from story by saying that plot is the action, while the story is the emotions associated with the action.

Plots are the results of choices made by the characters: the characters take or don't take action, and events happen as a result. Plots are often compared to weaving. Writers speak of "loose threads," "weaving in a character," etc. A writer of a well-plotted story must choose what threads to use in her yarn, when to tie-off those threads, and when to rip out utterly useless threads that don't suit the fabric of the story.

If one bad thing after another happens to your character and the character makes no choices, you don't have much of a plot. You have a really long vignette and, to some people, a really boring story. Or possibly you have a melodrama. Some readers like melodramas, but others consider them to be fatalistic with victimized, unreal characters. Other stories simply depict one incident after another with no cause and effect.

The novelist E.M. Forster wrote: "A plot is also a narrative of events, the emphasis falling on causality. 'The king died and then the queen died' is a story. But 'the king died and then the queen died of grief' is a plot. The time-sequence is preserved, but the sense of causality overshadows it."

Your story's beginning is, therefore, important. Note, there is a difference between the beginning of your story and the beginning of your novel. The beginning of your story involves backstory, historical setting, world-building etc. This beginning might be seen throughout your novel in flashbacks, character dialogue, etc. It might even be seen in a small prologue. But the beginning of the novel is where the reader enters the world of the story. This is where you "hook" the reader into your yarn.

We hope that we've persuaded you that something needs to happen in your book, and some of what happens needs to be the main character taking action. That doesn't mean your story needs to be all explosions and laser blasts.

Algis Budrys in his book *Writing to the Point* describes a story as having seven parts.

(1) A Character, (2) in context, (3) with a problem, (4) makes an intelligent attempt to solve the problem but (5) fails, because the problem is more complex than he thought. He tries again, more urgently, and fails again, and tries again, each time learning more about the problem, each time staking more, until with one last maximum effort, staking everything, he (6) wins. And a trustworthy but otherwise disinterested character says, "He's dead, Jim," or the moral equivalent, and that is (7) validation.

Algis Budrys *Writing to the Point: A Complete Guide to Selling Fiction*

Not all American and European novels and certainly not all Eastern novels follow this pattern. Many works in the literary genre will forgo this pattern as well as many short stories. Japanese plots will often follow a plot type called kishotenketsu.

However, nearly all the best-selling stories in North America do follow this pattern outlined by Budrys. So I hope this will be the pattern (or something close to it) you use for the short story you write for this course.

Some people say that all literature can be summed up by one plot structure, others say there are three, some seven, some twenty, and some as high as thirty-six. Knowing exactly the number of plots there are is not the most useful thing for a writer to know, though the knowledge may come in handy.

The ones who say there are only three plots generally call them:

(1) man versus man—In this type of conflict, your protagonist's goals are challenged by one or more antagonists. The antagonist can be family, or friend, foe. It might be as large as the protagonist's own society or as small as a tiny child. What matters is that the antagonist has his/her/their reasons for battling the protagonist, and the protagonist will not easily achieve the goal or win against the powerful antagonist.

(2) man versus self— In these kind of stories, the main character is pitted against some aspect of himself. He might be fighting emotional inclinations, physical or medical ailments, his own personal prejudices and upbringing, his spiritual or social imperfections. His goal can only be reached by pushing his own limitations—limitations he may or may not be aware of at the outset, and which the reader may or may not consider important.

(3) man versus nature—In "man versus nature" plots, nature is represented by time, geography, animals, weather, and the powers and influences of sciences such a biology, chemistry, physics, and the like.

The word man here is shorthand for any sort of character.

All these kinds of plots can be character-driven or plot-driven, but it is important to remember that there is a difference between a story plot and a situation. A character in a particular "situation" is not yet in a "story" until that character wants something. Cinderella would not be a story character if A) she did not desire to go to the ball and B) if the reader was not shown her backstory, personality, and all the events that happened because of her decision to go to the ball.

There are, of course, plots that are not true plots at all. Some melodrama (stories that unreasonably pile one bad situation upon another in over-the-top ways) and episodic (stories that are merely a collection of unrelated incidents) and stories that are too full of coincidence (especially coincidences that conveniently push the story forward) are considered non-plots by some because the writer has failed to properly use cause and effect. Even plotted stories can have difficulties. They may have plot holes and plot drifts, as well. I want you to aim high and to write a perfectly-plotted story.

A speculative fiction story will, of course, follow basic rules of plotting. However, since these stories take place in different worlds that might have different scientific laws, the writer will have to establish how conflict, character, setting, backstory, and history interact. The original story of Cinderella came from China where having bound feet was considered a mark of social status and beauty. In North America, however, Cinderella's tiny feet don't carry that kind of societal resonance. On Earth, a boy who can leap tall buildings in a single bound would be considered abnormal. But a visitor from the planet Krypton would understand why the boy leapt so high because he would understand how gravity works on both planets. Therefore, for the speculative fiction writer, plotting and world-building can uphold or destroy each other.

There are a variety of types of stories. Some call them tropes. Some call them templates. I'm going to list some of them here.

Adventure in which the protagonist goes to the adventure. For both types of adventure, the series of events are goal-oriented.

Ascension or **Descension** in which the protagonist rises or falls from power, such as a story that follows how a poor boy becomes a rich man, or a king becomes a hunted criminal.

Chase or **Pursuit** which is action-oriented

Coming of Age or **Maturation** in which the protagonist changes from child to adult or from irresponsible to responsible. The change can be subtle.

Discovery in which the protagonist uncovers one or more secrets and the rest of the story revolves around the reactions of all the characters to the exposure.

Escape in which the protagonist escapes from something such as a prison or intolerable situation.

Hero Learns Better in which the hero begins the story with a particular idea, and by the end of the story thinks differently.

If This Goes On in which the protagonists acts within a world in which some current societal trend is extrapolated.

Love in which the protagonist falls in love with someone. At one time, the word romance meant fantasy, but now refers almost singularly to love stories.

Metamorphosis in which at least one of the characters undergoes a physical change.

Quest in which the protagonist searches for something and in the process changes herself.

Temptation in which the protagonist is tempted to do what it must not, gives in, and then deals with the consequences. A rarer form involves the hero successfully resisting temptation.

Transformation in which the protagonist is changed inwardly, sometimes because of a quest, sometimes because of a **Hero learns better** kind of plot.

Rescue in which the protagonist rescues someone else.

Revenge in which the protagonist is wronged and seeks revenge. Often character-oriented.

Riddle or **Mystery** in which the protagonist must solve a mystery. This does not always involve a murder, although the murder mystery genre has appropriated the name.

Rivalry in which two main characters are contesting for the same thing.

Sacrifice in which the protagonist sacrifices something important or even itself to gain a greater good for someone else.

Underdog in which a disadvantaged protagonist wins against all odds. This could also be considered a variant of an **Ascension** plot.

    Another way that people like to think about plots as they plan out their stories is to think of the story as a 3-Act structure. There is Act 1 where the character and world and situation are introduced. There is Act 2 where the action and conflict are played out. There is Act 3 where things are resolved or finished.
    If you have access to the internet and type 'plot diagrams' into your search engine, you will find an amusing assortment of triangles, mountains, jagged lines, and charts. Use the one that you understand the best. Some love and use a twelve-part structure for their novel. Others think their brains will melt if they need to figure out how to place the first pinch point exactly on page twenty-five.

For many writers, the way to come up with a plot is to think: Here's a character and here's what she wants. Something is in the way of getting what she wants. She strives to overcome that something. And at the end she wins or loses. The beauty of this simple way of thinking about plot is that there is an emphasis on a character WANTING a thing. If the character doesn't WANT a thing hard enough to work for that thing, the reader won't care either. So, one plot, thirty plots, three parts, seven parts, twelve parts: What you need to do is use what works for you as you make up a story.

Day 1 MICE quotient

Another interesting way to think of plot is to use Orson Scott Card's MICE quotient.

M stands for **Milieu**. This is where the world built by the author is not only the setting, but the focus of the story. Tolkien could have ended The Lord of the Rings when the battle of Mordor ended. However, because the focus was on the milieu, he continued the story with the hobbits going home and the elves departing and did not stop until the new age was established.

I stands for **Idea**. A question is asked, the characters do enough things to discover the answer, and then the story is over.

C stands for **Character**. The story begins with the nature of the main character and ends with the change in the character.

E stands for **Event**. Something has happened and now the world is a terrible place. The main character must right the wrong. The story ends when the world has righted.

If you take a college creative writing course you will be introduced to the concept of The Hero's Journey.

Joseph Campbell wrote a big book called The Hero with a Thousand Faces. Some movie makers use that book as a bible to guide them as they work out their stories. The first Star Wars movie filmed with Luke Skywalker, Han Solo, and Princess Leia followed this template exactly. His template is called **The Hero's Journey**.

Christopher Vogler condensed the Hero's Journey into twelve basic stages along with the corresponding character arc:

Ordinary World – Limited awareness of problem

Call to Adventure – increased awareness

Refusal of Call – reluctance to change

Meeting the Mentor – overcoming reluctance

Crossing the First Threshold – committing to change

Tests, Allies, Enemies – experimenting with 1st change

Approach to the Inmost Cave- preparing for big change

Supreme Ordeal – attempting big change

Reward – consequences of the attempt

The Road Back – rededication to change

Resurrection – final attempt at big change

Return with Elixir – final mastery of the problem

Activities:

A. *Read*:

I get a message in the stream from someone named FrontLot: "We've got company in the yard, brothers. Careful. I almost got hit."

"There's work to do," HardCandy answers. "Ignore them. Another storm is coming."

"How did they get here?" Front asks. "There's supposed to be a fence . . ." The dialogue goes cold then. There's still work to do.

Shaking my head I grab a handhold, move to the highest sheet I've placed. I think I see the problem. A metal fitting, a blinking piece of hardware, is completely misaligned. I stream for the barge's code, give it a once over. The system could never handle that variation. Parameters aren't there. No wonder the thing is—

"What is *this*?" An Abby voice again, closer now. I can almost smell him. No way can he see me, though. I'm hidden above, atop the barge.

"I do believe it is a *woman* skin," a voice says. "Fellows, look!"

I get a feeling in my stomach. Like I've tasted raw spiders. "HardCandy?" I whisper in the stream. "You good?"

No answer.

I pull myself to the center of the barge's top surface. I skirt the bay section in the middle, moving forward. Toward the voices.

"Grab her!" someone yells. "Bring her here!"

There's the sound of movement. A struggle, a female moan.

This is against the rules, and they know it. Hard's master will be ticked. But what about Hard? What about right now?

The next barge is within jumping distance. Barely. It might hurt a little . . .

I try anyway.

My feet crash against the edge of the bay, but I make it safely, stand tall. There is such a ruckus in front of me that nobody heard. I'm grateful. I have to see. Have to know. I scamper ahead.

I reach the edge of the bay and look over. Nearly ten meters separate me from the next barge, but that is irrelevant. The shadows are long here. And the stench is all below.

One Abdul has a woman—Hard, I have to guess, mainly because she's bald—by the back of her beige jumpsuit and is pulling her backwards toward him. Two others are in front, near her wildly kicking feet.

"It is forbidden," she says, almost hissing. "Touch me and lose your hands."

The Abbys laugh. Probably sons of masters. Confident that the law won't find them.

Plus there are three of them. Courage in numbers.

"Where is security?" I stream to no one in particular.

"It makes no difference," FrontLot streams back. "Anyone who can help will be too late."

I watch, feebly, as HardCandy continues to struggle. One of the Abduls near her feet manages to grab an ankle. She shrieks in anger. Kicks harder with the other foot.

The stream has grown completely silent. Like everyone is waiting in fear. A half-dozen debuggers. Frozen. I don't blame them. Stops are fully in place. Tweaks only a forbidden thought away. There is only so much any of us can do. The rest leads to pain.

I glance down at my own slight frame. There's nothing I can do that way either . . .

Kerry Nietz *A Star Curiously Singing*

1) What is the genre and subgenre of this story?

2) What do you think is this guy's normal life?

3) Outline the important choices and incidents that happens in this excerpt. Consider character, causes, choices, and consequences. What did the character do and why? If you were writing this story, what would happen next?

B. *Read*:

I make a fist at my chest, fight the interference. I glance at the machine in front of me. The one beyond, on the far side of them. Can I reach it?

Not by jumping. No, of course not. That is the machine Hard was nurturing, though. What did she accomplish?

I sing out to her drift barge: Are you ready?

The barge feeds me a list of small problems: unequal lift, slight friction on one arm. The big answer is "Yes." He's ready to go.

"Extend!" I stream. I watch as one of the barge's vertical loading arms grows from the side of its bay. Quiet. Frictionless. So far, so good.

Below, one Abbey is looking around. Thinks he's heard something. "What was that?"

I contemplate how nice it might be to have that mechanical arm simply pulverize him into the ground. To leave them all just smelly, hairy spots in the cement. I begin to stream an order to the barge—

Ouch!

A headbuzz hits me, igniting a storm in my synapses. Not enough to debilitate me. Just enough to make its warning clear: the mental path I'm traveling down is filled with danger. Stupid "stops." That wasn't an external tweak from my master. Only the inherent stops from the implant. The bridle on my brain.

I grit my teeth, shake the feeling off. Make myself go calm. This is only a test. I'm doing diagnostics on a malfunctioning barge. I'm not trying to harm anyone. Really.

"Now," I stream, keeping my mind carefully neutral. "Drop."

The arm bends at the large joint. The lifting surface—a silver articulated fork—plunges straight down for seven meters and impacts the pavement behind the group.

Clang!

… Later in the story:

I'm still huddled on my back, hiding in the bay of a barge. I feel the coward. I turn and glance over the edge again. Hard is on her feet, brushing at her sides. Her arms wrap around her then, squeezing. I hear a sniff—could be crying, but I'll never tell. She's free and I got through it without a major tweak. All told, a major success.

I creep away, back toward my personal task. I get a message. A touch of glowing warmth. Only her mind to mine. She knows what I did. She could sense my nearness. It's her way of thanking me. She sends me something else too—a mental gift. "A taste of freedom," she streams. "In case you ever need it."

There is pain in her sending it, probably, but she feels I'm worth it. It stirs me a little. Makes me all out of spec.

"What is it?" I ask, even though it's obvious. It is a location.

"A special place," she says. "Where there's a little more truth."

I thank her, tuck the location away secure in my deeply buried implant.

Kerry Nietz *A Star Curiously Singing*

1) So this is a tiny bit of what did happen next. Now what do you think will happen?

2) Abilities and desires that are expressed in Act I will move the events that happen in Act II. What elements of the above excerpts will be in the Act II of this book?

3) What does this main character want? What do you think the Big Boss Battle will be about?

C. *Read*:

Sabine huddled in a window niche, her knees pulled up to her chin and her teary gaze not quite focused on the dark ruins around her. She knew it was time to go—lingering would certainly mean capture—but she could not force herself to rush to her friend's death.

A stone's throw in front of her, a shower of brick dust rained onto the floor. Sabine started, her muscles tensing as her thoughts ratcheted from mourning to high alert.

Straining to hear beyond the thump of her pulse, she concentrated on identifying the sounds that surrounded her. Crickets and frogs chirped in the grass … an occasional bird chittered overhead … a breeze rustled leaves nearby … all normal sounds, characteristic of the forest just before dawn.

She pulled her cloak closed around her.

Probably a mouse, she reasoned as she scanned the shadows for a safe explanation. Or a night-cat stalking one last meal. Still …

The air felt heavier, as if another presence stood close by.

But that was silly. The Dryht castle was long abandoned and was not haunted by its former inhabitants. Sabine stood to leave. Whatever had just happened, she didn't appear to be in immediate danger. That would change, however, if she were late to the execution.

Before she took a step, a quiet noise scraped the darkness across from her.

She peered into what was left of the ancient Dryht temple. The moon was still high enough to illuminate small patches between the oak and cedar saplings that grew among the grass-lined floor stones, but it wasn't full enough to show what moved among their needles and leaves.

Sabine tried to swallow, her mouth suddenly dry, and to reason through her fear. Although it was possible she had been discovered breaking curfew, it was not likely. All of the Ruddan stationed in her village were busy preparing for the execution.

Sabine shifted her weight, angling for a better view. An explosion of snapping twigs and flapping wings made her jump, a surprised shout catching in her throat. She flinched as a raven the size of a large cat landed nearby.

Sabine relaxed.

Just a bird.

Still … why did she feel as if she was not alone?

Cocking its head, the raven focused on Sabine. Intelligence gleamed in the blue depths of its eye. The directness of its avian inspection felt sinister, somehow, as if confirming local rumors that the birds were used as Dryht spies.

Stop it! Sabine chided herself. Just because her neighbors mistrusted the birds, that did not make the rumors true. The villagers of Khapor told many stories of hauntings in the woods, but Sabine had yet to experience one.

The raven stared, showing no signs of moving.

"Whoever you are looking for," Sabine said to the bird, "is not here. No one has been here for a few years, since the plague that wiped out most of the Dryht race. Well, no one except me."

As if pondering her inconceivable flaunting of the law, the bird cocked its head to the other side, leveling a green eye at her this time.

This difference in eye color unsettled her.

"I am pleased to have met you, I'm sure," she stammered, attempting to mask a growing sense of trepidation with a show of wit and bravado. "However, the sun is rising, and I am expected in the village."

A sudden vision of ravens feasting on her friend's body after the execution silenced her. Turning away from the bird, she hurried out of the temple.

Lauricia Matuska   *The Healer's Rune*

1) If you wanted to analyze this story with The Hero's Journey, what stages are illustrated in this excerpt?

2) If the author were following The Hero's Journey plot template, what is the next step?

3) What Joseph Campbell labeled The Call to Adventure, most writers label the inciting incident. Stories start with the main character in her normal state. An inciting incident is the event that pushes the main character out of what passes for normal for her. What do you think is Sabine's 'normal?'

Day 2 three act structure

Most writers use some variation of the three act structure when they plan and write their stories.
Act I: The introduction of the hero, setting, and set up for what is to come, i.e. the conflict and villain. Establishment of the main character's normal. He may or may not be happy with his normal. Usually he has some discontent but he has not acted on it yet. Foreshadowing happens here and sometimes in early part of Act II. Act I ends when there is an inciting incident, the thing that makes the hero leave the normal.
Act II: Where the pieces that were introduced in Act I engage in conflict. A common pattern is for there to be two attempts by the main character to achieve her goal that she fails at. And then at the Big Boss Battle, or climax, she wins or loses. Shorter stories might skip the two try-fail cycles. Some people put a few small wins in here for breathing space.

Act III: The wrap-up. The establishment of the new normal.

It can be difficult to establish the normal for the hero of the story without boring the reader who wants something to happen. Somehow, you will need to show the hero in her everyday life while giving clues to what her conflict will be. Act I must not be an info dump and yet must convey backstory, which is all the stuff that led up to this point in time. Some of your backstory, world-building, and foreshadowing will be discovered as you write, so you will likely need to rewrite by the time you reach the end of the story. The events of Act I will often change as you edit your story.

The reader wants you to build a rich, deep world. But the reader also wants you to leave most of the richness off the page. You want to put in only as much as necessary to ground the reader in Act I, enough to make sense of all the activity in Act II, and finally, just enough to resolve the story in Act III.

Another metaphor for a plot is a chemistry experiment. Act I is gathering the chemicals, test tubes, and Bunsen burner. Act II is throwing the chemicals you have together, (too late to go back to the closet for more) applying the heat, and watching the reaction bubble away. Act III is determining what precipitated and writing up the results. It is not important to list the copyright date of the textbook, the weather outside the classroom, or the name of your classmate's boyfriend.

Activities:

A. *Read*:

Her blue cat defended Ginger while monsters killed Ginger's aunt Mal in their small house in the woods outside of an ordinary, present-day small town. The cat was wounded and transformed into a man.

> He sighed and stretched out gingerly on Mal's bed, his left hand absently resting on top of the gauze patch under his shirt. He flung his other arm across his eyes and for a moment he only breathed in, out, in, out. I thought he had forgotten me.
>
> "Well, sit down," he said finally, his arm still over his eyes. "It isn't a *short* story."
>
> I sat down on the other end of the bed. My dress was still damp and my hair still plastered to my neck with rain, but I hardly noticed. "I'm sitting," I said, trying to imagine him as a cat again, curled up on my pillow.
>
> "All right. I'm going to simplify this as much as I can. If you have further questions, keep them until the end."
>
> The fact that Hal was speaking in a deep, human voice made my head spin, but I nodded. "Fine."
>
> He took another deep breath. "Once upon a time, there were two kingdoms at war; the winter kingdom and the summer kingdom. The king of the summer kingdom, Oberon, was dying and Maven, the winter queen, was advancing to take over the throne. Oberon had no children, but he had chosen a child with whom the Gift was strong as his successor.
>
> "On the night of Oberon's death, Maven and her hyinen soldiers attacked the summer palace and killed their way to the chosen child. The child's nursemaid, of higher rank than the fey warriors, appointed one of them to accompany her and got a wysling to open—"
>
> "What's a wysling?" I interrupted.

"They're like the wizard from one of your books," he said, his arm still over his eyes. "I'll explain that to you in a minute. As I was saying, they persuaded the wysling to make a rend between the planes – basically, a door between their world and this one. They brought the baby here, out of Maven's reach, because they knew she would be looking for her."

"I'm going to assume," I said, "that Maven would have killed the baby."

"Of course she would have."

"So I'm the baby?"

"You are."

"I'm a fairy – excuse me, fey – king's daughter?"

"No," he said slowly, "you're the rightful heir to the summer throne, but technically you're just another fey."

"Why did Oberon choose me?"

"Because you were one of the Gifted," he said, adding, "I told you that already."

"You didn't explain it," I pointed out. "What does that mean?"

"Remember the paper airplane?"

"Yes," I said, tapping the side of my head. "That's a permanent memory."

He grunted. "There are quite a lot of things you haven't forgotten. You fold creatures from the greylands all the time."

Every creature I'd ever folded flooded into my mind, black and white images flashing by in succession like a lantern movie reel. "All of them? They're all real?"

Mirriam Neal *Paper Crowns*

1) Do you think this scene is in Act I, II, or III?

2) How would you feel if you had just discovered you were heir to a throne in the greylands where the fey live?

3) Ginger's big skill in life is origami. How might that be used in the Big Boss Battle?

B. *Read*:

Nineteen year old Rebecca Esh popped the trays of biscuits into the oven with a sigh. Every day it was the same routine: up at the crack of dawn, kneading and baking, cooking, canning, housework, washing, gardening, and sewing. While the work was very satisfying, something inside of her longed to know what lay beyond the confines of her wonderful community. She had no desire to be out among the "Englisch" as the Amish called them. She had seen enough of her friends who left the community to experience the world "outside" only to come home unhappier than before; glad to return to the simple quiet life they had always known. No, what her heart longed for was found in the tomes that lined her bookshelf: adventure, fantasy, and wholesome historical romance and even some science fiction books. How she wished she could pop in and out of her books at will as a visitor: perhaps then that restless feeling in her heart would find fulfillment.

She straightened up from the oven to glance out the kitchen window just in time to see a silver flash above the hill behind their barn. Normally she wouldn't have given it a second thought; attributing the image to a passenger plane or blimp sailing over her area but when a bright blue beam of light shone down then disappeared it made her freeze in place. It was still yet early morning and she was only halfway through her baking. The rising sun was already turning the sky a pale pink so the intense blue light looked very out of place. She stared transfixed, oblivious to the flour floating down from her fingers and the sausages burning on the stove. She rubbed her eyes with the backs of her hands then shook her head. Surely she had imagined it . . . it couldn't possibly be what she thought it was. Time to stop reading science fiction novels and stick to Beverly Lewis she thought to herself. Her mother, Ruth, bustled into the kitchen with her arms full of dirty clothes destined for the washtub.

Marlayne Jan Giron *In Plain Sight* :Marlaynegiron.com

1) What is this character's normal? There is a sentence in the first paragraph that foreshadows what the coming action will be. Which is it?

2) There is something that happens. Because she does not react, or change her behavior, this is not an inciting incident. What part of the novel is it?

3) Which parts of this first page do you think will play a part at the climax?

C. *Read*:

The death of Juan McAlister made news on two planets, an orbiting space habitat and, of course, the moon. His death did not make news because he was a celebrity, a politician or a captain of industry. No, the death of Professor Juan McAlister, late of Armstrong University, made the news simply because he was a murder victim—the first murder victim on the moon in over seventy-five years of human habitation on the barren rock trapped in Earth's orbit. On the earth, they were shocked and fascinated. On the moon, we were shocked and embarrassed. We thought indignities such as murder only happened on our flawed mother planet. They never happened in our more civilized community. Today, every vid-screen in the solar system told us we were wrong.

I was not watching the news. I stood where I swore I would never stand again—at a crime scene staring at a dead body. This dead body was different. All those others were bodies of strangers. This dead body was that of a colleague, a sometime adversary and a friend.

I was twenty years and 384,000 kilometers away from the Behavioral Analysis Unit at Quantico; yet, here I stood scanning my friend's office trying once again to do the unthinkable: think like a killer.

I came to the moon to move forward, but my advance turned into retreat, and my paradise, purgatory.

Terri Main *Dark Side of the Moon*

1) If you use the MICE rubric to analyze the plot this story will have, is this a Milieu, Idea, Character, or Event story?

2) There is a metaphor in the last sentence. What does the point of view character we are seeing this story through mean by that metaphor?

3) What do we know about this storyworld?

Day 3 endings

The End. The very last of Act III is The End. The ending scene is the last memory your reader will have of your story. You want to make it memorable. Some writers write the final sentence of their story first, tape it above their desk, and then write the story aiming for that final sentence. Some writers don't know the ending until they get there. Wherever you are on the spectrum of knowing your ending, once you reach it, you will want to study the effectiveness of your ending and see if you might need to rework it to achieve memorability.

There are several types of endings to consider.

Thematic This type of ending scene repeats or echoes the opening of the story. This can provide a feeling of completeness and wholeness. I.e., if the theme at the front of the book is friendship, the final paragraphs are about friendship.

Boo! This ending is most appropriate for horror. The hero opens the closet door and the skeleton of his best friend falls out. And then the screaming starts. You might argue that if you end the story there, you have left a thread loose and teachers tell you over and over not to do that. That's true. But it will still work to chill the reader if it is obvious what happened or what will happen next. The reader may not need to see the hero torn to shreds.

Final Twist An ending where the reader learns something new and must now reinterpret the entire story.

Surprise! The ending that you did not see coming. This is not a fair ending if you did not sprinkle foreshadowing clues throughout the story that the reader can go back and find and say, "Oh, okay."

Sweet Fade-Out This is a prolongation of mood with a slide out from the hero's face to a symbolic item or landscape or weather.

Punchline The ending which can resemble "The moral of the story is . . ."

Open Question This ending leaves the reader in suspense. This is a tricky one and you may not have practiced enough writing to pull this off. Even if everyone else agrees that the ending was successful, you will still have the reader who gets mad at you because you didn't answer the question!

Peter-Out The ending where you didn't know where to end the story and kept writing until you ran out of things to say. That's the ending you don't want to do. Act III should be shorter, much shorter than Act II.

There are more types of endings, but these are the most common types. You would benefit from picking up four of your favorite books, writing down the last line(s), and analyzing what type they are and why you liked them.

Since I do not want to provide spoilers for any of the authors' works discussed in this textbook, I will provide the endings of only the famous stories you should already know. If you didn't know the endings—oops.

Activities:

A. *Read*:

"The creatures outside looked from pig to man, and from man to pig, and from pig to man again; but already it was impossible to say which was which."

George Orwell   *Animal Farm*

1) Which kind of ending is this?
2) Is this the kind of ending you would like for your story?
3) You should still not be writing your story yet, but if you were, write a potential ending line like this for a story like yours.

B. *Read*:

"I'll think of it all tomorrow, at Tara. I can stand it then. Tomorrow, I'll think of some way to get him back. After all, tomorrow is another day."

Margaret Mitchell   *Gone With The Wind*

1) Which kind of ending is this?
2) Is this a kind of ending you would like for your story?
3) Write a last line somewhat like this that would fit a story like the one you are considering for this course.

C. *Read*:

I lingered round them, under that benign sky; watched the moths fluttering among the heath, and hare-bells; listened to the soft wind breathing through the grass; and wondered how anyone could ever imagine unquiet slumbers for the sleepers in that quiet earth.

Emily Brontë,   *Wuthering Heights*

1) Which kind of ending is this?
2) Is this a kind of ending you would like for your story?

3) Write this kind of ending for a story akin to the one you are considering for this course.

Day 4 middle

At least half of your short story will be Act II, the middle, where the try-fail cycles and the Big Boss Battle, which most people call the climax, will happen. The hero keeps trying to solve her problem and she almost succeeds, or she succeeds in solving a part of the problem, but for every step forward there are two steps back.

This is often where writers begin to lose plot threads, leap over plot holes, and sometimes drift, unsure where the story is going. It is also where some begin to lose confidence in themselves, their stories, or both.

Activity:

1) Write at least four practice paragraphs that could be set in the middle of a story set in your storyworld. They do not need to be set in your particular story you are contemplating. If you choose to write paragraphs that might go into your story, remember at this point the paragraphs are practice.

Day 5 simple list

The smallest part of your short story should be Act III, the result of the Big Boss Battle.

Sometimes it helps to have an outline of what you will write. Or of what you have already written. I don't mean the kind of outline with 1. And A. and i. etc, although that kind of outline is a beautiful thing. What I want at this point is a simple list of things that could happen at the denouement of a story. Here's an example:

Orloff staggers wounded into the castle and tells the king his throne is safe.
The king thanks Orloff and sends him off to be cleaned and stitched.
In the throne room, the king gives Orloff a huge medal and some land with taxable farms on it.
The king gives Orloff a title that allows him to collect the taxes and marry the noble lady he is in love with.
The noble lady give Orloff a surcoat she has embroidered with his new coat of arms.
They smile at each other.
The end.

This outline allows each sentence to be developed into its own scene. Or they could all be contained within one scene.

What is a scene? It is action that takes place in one setting without a break in time. With the exception of the opening scene of a novel, a scene is generally—but not always—linked causally to the scene preceding it. One or more or none of the characters in the preceding scene might be present and the connection between preceding and following scenes might or might not be clear to the reader. Generally, however—especially if the story is not a mystery—the reader knows why the scene exists. Something has happened in the previous scene and the current scene is connected to it.

Sometimes the connection is direct and in your face. For instance, previous scene ends when the hero limps out of the arena, and the current scene begins with the hero entering her tent and calling for a physician.

Sometimes the connection is direct but there is a shift to the point of view of a different character. For example, you could have the hero pick up her sword and stride into the arena. The next scene could follow the villain cackling in the stands and talking to his minions while he watches the fight.

Sometimes the connection between a scene and the one following it makes readers understand the story better. For instance, if we see in a flashback in the villain's point of view where we see the villain gain a traumatic brain injury at the hands of the hero's father, we'll have a better understanding of the villain's animus against the hero. Sometimes the connection between these two scenes are confusing and will be made clearer later. For instance, the villain might give baffling instructions to his minions that make sense later.

Some people write such short chapters, there's only room for one scene per chapter. Some people write such short scenes, there are several scenes per chapter. Usually there are three to five scenes per chapter, but there is such wide variance there is no rule about how many scenes are in a chapter. The only general rules to writing scenes are to enter the scene only when necessary and leave when the scene has accomplished what it was supposed to accomplish—no dawdling. And if the setting or the main character in a scene has changed from that in the preceding scene, the writer should clue the reader in to the change or changes.

Scenes within a chapter are marked apart by * * * or something similar on the otherwise blank line between them. If you only add an extra space, typesetters and readers might think the extra space is an accident.

Activity:

1) Write a simple outline of an ending scene of a story that could be set in your storyworld. Now turn that outline into a scene.

CHAPTER SIX:

MORE PLOT

Some people place the Inciting Incident at the end of Act I, some at the beginning of Act II. I don't care. Everything before the inciting incident is the backstory. Everything after the inciting incident is the story.

That does NOT mean that the first part of the story is an infodump. We'll go into this more later.

So, what is the inciting incident? It is the action or decision that starts the problem or the story question.

Jeff Gerke says in his you-really-ought-to-read-this book, *The Irresistible Novel*:

> The inciting incident is the thing that gets the story going. The story world and the characters had been doing X, but then comes along Y, which sets things in motion.
>
> Peter Parker is just a regular high school nerd—until he gets bitten by a special kind of spider, giving him superpowers. The spider bite is the inciting incident in the story of Spider-Man. Without it, you would have no story.
>
> Indiana Jones is just a mild-mannered international archaeological superstar (Go, Indy!)—until he meets with some men from the Department of Defense who tell him that the Nazis have found the resting place of the Lost Ark of the Covenant. Now he's an international archaeological superstar in a mad race for the Lost Ark. The visit from the DOD men was the inciting incident of *Raiders of the Lost Ark*.
>
> The "law" of fiction under debate is whether your novel's inciting incident must appear on page 1 (or, at the very latest, page 20) to get published.
>
> No matter what, I urge you to begin the book with something interesting happening. If not action, then something surprising. ...
>
> ...People opposed to the inciting incident on page 1 argue that if you bring in the inciting incident right away, it has no impact on the reader.
>
> Imagine if page 1 of a novel shows a family sitting around watching television, when a gunman bursts in and shoots them all. The reader, who has had no chance to connect with the characters, might be alarmed by the violence, but when it comes to the death of the characters, all he can probably muster is a shrug and a "that's too bad."

Jeff Gerke   *The Irresistible Novel*

Jeff Gerke goes on to say that it is fine to start a story with action, though he prefers that action not to be the inciting incident. He gives the example of the movie *Mulan* which begins by showing the villain and his army swarming over the Great Wall of China. While that action is introducing the main challenge of the story, it also is *not* intruding into the hero's life yet. When the messenger arrives at the village with summons for conscripts, that is what changes the hero's life, and thus that is the true inciting incident.

Think of it this way: When your story begins, your character has been living her life. The reader is not yet aware of all the character's traits, flaws, future plans, and personal history. The reader is also unaware of how your created speculative world works. If the inciting incident happens in the first sentence of the first paragraph of the first chapter, your reader will probably be confused about what the action means to the character's world, life, and goals. The task of the writer is to give the reader enough information to show the importance of the sudden change. In many fantasy novels, an idyllic or cursed situation has continued for ages and the main character has lived in this setting. Then the inciting incident happens—a sudden quest, the sudden arrival of dragons, an evil king, the last straw, the great opportunity—and the protagonist now ventures forth.

The writer must not delve into backstory, but must also avoid starting a story with guns blazing. The Latin phrase "In Medias Res" is a term meaning "in the middle of things." It implies the story begins without an ambling preamble or backstory; it begins at the perfect place to start. An experienced writer trains himself to know that magical moment when he has shown enough of the main character's life to disrupt it. They have given enough foundational information without either boring the reader with backstory or confusing the reader.

Day 1 inciting

The inciting incident must be interesting. Its impact on the main character's life, goal, or emotion must be apparent. The inciting incident is generally bad stuff, although it could be something good—the kind of good that causes trials, stress, and a new journey for the main character. Whether good or bad, if your incident carries no more emotional import than the statement, "Look. All we got in the mail today was advertising flyers," then you need to come up with something more exciting or surprising or funny. The incident needs to raise stakes in something that matters for the character in your story.

Maybe you have established—through setting, dialog, and description—that the character desperately needed for a check to arrive in the mail. You have shown your character with three starving children peering into an empty kitchen pantry, or you have shown the hero's invitation to a fancy dress ball given by the local despot. Whatever the situation, the promised check, money, or gold coins did not arrive and your reader fully understands why the money is needed. The reader's heart now wants what the hero's heart wants.

And now the character can't pay the rent and the police are standing by the door watching the landlord carry her stuff out and throwing it onto the parking lot. Or the character can't feed her children. Or the character cannot go to the ball to assassinate the evil prince because she has nothing to wear. So when the character runs out and does something stupid in a frantic effort to make money the reader is emotionally involved. Now you have an inciting incident.

But if the inciting incident leads to a quick resolution, or if the character or her life is unchanged by her actions, then it is not a true inciting incident. In the first case, stories are about incidents leading to other incidents. A quickly-resolved problem—the hero is forgiven her stupidity and nothing bad results from her stupidity—is not a true story. And if a character returns to status quo unchanged, then her choices have not affected either herself or the world. The inciting incident must impact the character's life so deeply that he must change what he is doing now.

Activities:

A. *Read*:

Cleon moved in close again. "You must realize that not many men in our village would think of bonding with you." Cleon looked down at her. Rowen could smell the smoke of the smithy on his clothing. "But times have changed. Your father has died—" Rowen scowled at his calloused words—"leaving you all alone. But I can change that."

He placed a rough, thick hand on her cheek. Rowen turned away. Cleon forced her face back. "I want you to bond with me." He moved his head down to kiss her. Rowen tried to twist away. Cleon forced her face still and pressed his lips hard down on hers.

Rowen jerked out of his grasp. "Cleon, no!"

His head followed her movement. "I can take care of you, Rowen. And you know no other man will have you."

"Let go!"

Cleon tightened his grip on her shoulders. Rowen grabbed his wrist and—

Time slowed.

A strange sensation rose from deep within her, racing toward her right arm. It surged out where her palm held his wrist.

Cleon stopped talking. He backed away for a moment, looking at her in puzzlement. "Wha-What are you doing to me?"

"I-I don't know!" Her head pounded. What was happening?

His eyes went wide with fear. "Let go of me!" Cleon pulled at his arm.

Rowen tried, but her hand would not let go. Her vision blurred. Images began to fill her mind, images of Cleon. His father beating him while his mother cowered in the corner… Kicking a dog behind the shed until it lay still… Dunking a small boy in a stream while others laughed around him. Over and over, pictures from Cleon's life flashed across her eyes. Rowen began to feel dizzy. She became aware of eddies of hatred swirling inside of her. Was it his hatred or hers?

Her vision began to clear. Rowen felt like she was coming up to the surface of a clear lake after being underwater too long. She drank in great draughts of air.

Cleon yanked his hand away. "What did you do to me?" he shouted.

Rowen tried to talk, but her body would not respond. She could only stand there breathing heavily.

"Answer me!"

She glanced up into Cleon's eyes. They were livid with rage. "I don't know," she said, finding her voice. She took a step back. "I saw… Cleon, I had no idea…"

Cleon snarled and raised his hand as if to hit her. Rowen stared at him in shock. He wouldn't dare—

"Don't ever touch me again, you witch!" He stared at her a moment longer, then lowered his hand. But the look in his eyes told her that if he could have, he would have struck her. "The village will hear of this." He pointed a finger at her. "We will not tolerate witchery."

Morgan L. Busse   *Daughter of Light, Follower of the Book I*

1) What is the inciting incident?

2) Is Cleon in love with Rowen? How do we know? What would marriage, er, bonding with him be like?

3) What do you think is going to happen next?

B. *Read*:

Angel hopped off the school bus and darted toward the back yard, dirt from the driveway kicking up around her ankles. She leaped over the hedges that separated the front yard from the back. Leaves and pine needles slid and crunched beneath her sneakers as her eyes trained on her favorite spot, her reading tree.

The tree grew near the back fence at a thirty-degree angle. Angel had no idea what had knocked the oak over, but it stayed rooted at that odd slant. Someone had also chopped off the top of the tree, leaving one single branch that pointed straight up. Angel walked up the trunk of the tree, turned and sat, leaning against the branch.

A whisper of electricity ran the length of her back where she pressed against the branch, as if energy were traveling into her from the tree. She gasped and looked around, but saw nothing unusual in the back yard. The tree itself looked perfectly normal. Still, it felt different. It felt . . . magical. Or at least what she'd imagined magic to feel like.

She ran her fingers over the rough bark, following a trail down the angled trunk as she leaned forward, stretching her tall frame to its fullest. The tingling surged through her hands, and she yanked them back as if she had been burned.

The thought of burning trees sent a wave of nausea through her. She pulled herself back and leaned against the branch again, inhaling deeply to calm herself. Why was just the thought enough to make her feel this way? The answer had to be buried in her past—but her past was hidden.

And she still had no memory of anything before that day seven years ago.

Except a fear of forest fires.

She looked again at the lichen-speckled bark. Normal. Just my reading tree. Same as always.

She willed herself to think of other things. Happy things, like the fact that school was finally out. No more research papers and history projects. No more teasing for three more months. And she had the satisfaction of knowing that she'd set the curve for the final exam.

The sound of crunching footsteps bolted her out of her daydreams. Zachary had obviously heard the school bus and come to find her. She peered out the corner of her eye and smiled at her little foster brother.

"Angel, you've got to come see what I've caught." He tugged on her arm, his blue eyes pleading for her attention.

"It's not another beetle, is it, Zack?" She pulled her arm free and turned to face him. "I've just gotten home. And you've shown me zillions of them already."

"Not like this one. It's huge and it's got silver flecks all down its back. I've been searching online, but I can't find out about it anywhere. Pleeeease come in and help me. Mom's gonna want you in soon anyway."

Ugh, more insects.

She hopped down from her tree, and followed Zack to the house, passing Mr. Mason's small vegetable garden and feeling the desire to skip along, now that summer had arrived. She was so caught up in her thoughts she nearly tripped over one of the many stray cats that called her back yard home.

"Vander! Watch where you're going!"

The flame-colored tom scampered away, twitching his torn ear, the result of a fight with the cat next door. Angel watched him as he scrambled across the back yard heading directly for her tree.

He vanished.

Kat Heckenbach   *Finding Angel (Toch Island Chronicles – Book I)*

1) Which part of the plot do you think this excerpt is drawn from?

2) What do you think the inciting incident might prove to be?

3) What questions are raised in this excerpt?

C. *Read*:

This first prospector craft perched astride a chunk of ice about five kilometres long. The little ice-flinder orbited Crucible with about a billion others. Her machine oversaw some dumb mining equipment that was chewing stolidly through the thing in search of metal.

There were no problems here. She flipped her view to the next machine, whose headlamps obligingly lit to show her a wall of stone. Hmm. She'd been right the night before when she ordered it to check an ice ravine on Castle, the fourth planet. There was real stone down here, which meant metals. She wondered what it would feel like, and reached out. After a delay, the metal hands of her prospector touched the stone. She didn't feel anything: the prospector was not equipped to transmit the sensation back. Sometimes she longed to be able to fully experience the places her machines visited.

She sent a call to the Mining Registrar to follow up on her find, and went on to the next prospector. This one orbited farthest out, and there was a time-lag of several minutes between every command she gave, and its execution. Normally, she just checked it quickly and moved on. Today, for some reason, it had a warning flag in its message queue.

Transmission intercepted—Oh, it had overheard some dialogue between two ships or something. That was surprising, considering how far away from the normal orbits the prospector was. "Read it to me," she said, and went on to Prospector Four.

She'd forgotten about the message and was admiring a long view of Dew's horizon from the vantage of her fourth prospector, when a resonant male voice spoke in her ear.

"Mayday, mayday—anyone at Dew, please receive. My name is Hammond, and I'm speaking from the interstellar cycler *Chinook*. The date is the sixth of May, 2418. Relativistic shift is .500433—we're at half lightspeed.

"Listen:

"*Chinook* has been taken over by Naturite forces out of Leviathan. They are using the cycler as a weapon. You must know by now that the halo world Tiara, at Obsidian, has gone silent—it's our fault. *Chinook* has destroyed them. Dew is our next stop, and they fully intend to do the same thing there. They want to "purify" the halo worlds so only their people settle here.

"They're keeping communications silence. I've had to go outside to take manual control of a message laser in order to send this mayday.

"You must place mines in near-pass space ahead of the cycler, to destroy it. We have limited manoeuvring ability, so we couldn't possible avoid the mines.

"Anyone receiving this message, please relay it to your authorities immediately. *Chinook* is a genocide ship. You are in danger.

"Please do not reply to *Chinook* on normal channels. They will not negotiate. Reply to my group on this frequency, not the standard cycler wavelengths."

Elise didn't know how to react. She almost laughed—what a ridiculous message, full of bluster and emergency words. But she'd heard that Obsidian had gone mysteriously silent, and no one knew why. "Origin of this message?" she asked. As she waited, she replayed it. It was highly melodramatic, just the sort of wording somebody would use for a prank. She was sure she would be told the message had come from Dew itself—maybe even sent by Nasim or one of his friends.

The coordinates flashed before her eyes. Elise did a quick calculation to visualize the direction. Not from Dew. Not from any of Crucible's worlds. The message had come from deep space, out somewhere beyond the last of Crucible's trailing satellites.

The only things out there were stars, halo worlds—and the cyclers, Elise thought. She lifted off the headset. The beginnings of fear fluttered in her belly.

Karl Schroeder *Halo*

1) What is the inciting incident here?
2) What will be in the climax?
3) What was the viewpoint character's normal life?

Day 2 where do your ideas come from?

Some of you already know exactly what story you want to write for this course, in fact, you already have twenty stories lined up to write. You will never live long enough to write all the stories inside you.

Others of you will have a brain that suddenly blanks when you look at an empty screen or sheet of paper. Today I will talk about some of the ways to generate stories on the days when words have fled your mind.

There is technique for story generating I'll call chaining. That is, take an idea and add a new idea. Here's an example. Take a story you've read and liked. A knight in shining armor saved a damsel in distress from a (dragon, tower, icky in-law, whatever.) Flip it and change an item. A damsel saves a (random noun). Generate the random noun any way you like. Open a dictionary in a random spot. Turn on the TV and use the first animate object you see. Just think of some off-the-wall thing. So, a damsel saves . . . a mouse. Flip and change. A mouse saves a . . . lion. Oh, we've heard that one. A lion saves a . . . duck. A duck saves a . . ., hey, it's possible. A duck can be heroic. Okay, a duck. Sir Drake. Let's change the saves to defeats. Sir Drake defeats a . . . damsel. Why would a duck want to defeat a damsel? Maybe she wants to make duck soup with a smell that will entice a knight to save her. Answering why to a chained idea can generate a story.

You can start with a milieu, or setting, you already like. We've already said you don't get to fanfic, but suppose you take a setting of a story you already like. Suppose you loved the planet that the movie *Avatar* is set on. Do a bit of a change up. Remove the floating rocks with their waterfalls coming from nowhere. Change the blues and purples to reds and pinks. Keep the idea of creatures communicating by plugging into each other. Turn the Na'vi into dwarves. Change the name of the planet, Pandora, into something else to be determined later. (Just make sure the name can be pronounced. Call it Bob until you think of something better.) Now take the dwarf and make her different from the rest. She has a cool hobby. She has a unique ability. She has a crippling fear. She's missing a body part. Make it something that's going to be important at the climax of the story. Don't know what the climax will be? What would threaten her the most because of this difference she has? Brainstorm like crazy and don't call any idea stupid until it's time to prune the ideas into a storyline.

You can take another setting you already know. Look around. Maybe you're sitting in a classroom. What is something awful that could happen? An earthquake could knock the building down with you, no, your character in it. What fantastical thing could cause the earthquake? An angry fairy? A kaiju? An alien earthquake ray? Well, what made the fairy angry? Why did the kaiju decide to step on *your* school? What do the aliens have against you?

Flip, change, play, imagine, and adapt.

These are the aspects of speculative fiction writing that makes this genre fun. Writers of spec-fic stories play with the ramifications of a playful imagination. What would the world be like if cats were invisible, if cats looked like snakes, if elephants were the size of cats? What if humans had no ability to hear? What if ants were the size of cats? What if bees no longer existed? What if we had been placed in a world without a bright sun? What if cats could own people? Oh, wait, that one is true. What if koalas could own people?

Activities:

A. *Read*:

The Lidra are about the size of squirrels and live in Stone Forest. Hunting parties enter Shore Forest to gain needed resources where Kale's ability to sense danger has often saved lives.

"D-don't touch that," he snapped nervously at a comrade, his voice marred by a stutter. "I-I have it just right."

Shoran of the Flower rolled his eyes and held his hands up in mock defeat, stepping away from the row of Kale's weaponry laid out on a table. "Very well, then. Just hurry up. We're never going to get out of here." The boy was new to the foragers and not yet familiar with 'Kale etiquette.' He was young and his attitude was cocky. He hadn't yet faced the dangers of real life that would temper that arrogance.

Kale eyed Shoran suspiciously as if he might be tricking him into letting his guard down. They had done it before. He had to have his choice weapons all lined in a row and they had to remain in that order until he was finished cleaning each and every one to within an inch of their inanimate lives. Then he had to pack them in a precise manner. Not that he ever used them. That would tarnish them! Then he would be forced to spend hours cleaning them again. But as a member of the foragers he was required to carry weapons for self-defense and defense of others, if not hunting. It was a law that every other member of the party was willing to break if they could be on their way faster. Most didn't see a point for him to carry weaponry if he wasn't going to use it, anyway. They had taken away the bow and arrows after it became too tedious to wait for him to polish each arrow to a glistening shine.

Thankfully, their captain, Mict of the Hawk, had figured out a great strategy to have them all leaving on schedule. He set the date to depart a day early. That was usually effective. Unfortunately, not this time, because someone had bumped the table and a spear and knife had been knocked off. Said weapons tried to fall with a clatter, but it's difficult to make much noise when landing upon the giving surface of tightly woven vines that composed the floor of most structures in the Nest. They managed a few dull thumps and a couple louder clacks when they bumped each other, but that was about it.

The damage was done. Once he had placed them back on the table just so, Kale had to go through and clean each and every one of them all over again. About three times each. And once more because the impatience of the other party members was making him even more anxious and he worried he had missed a spot somewhere.

The hapless soul who had bumped the table had been yelled at instead of Kale since Mict knew that trying to punish Kale would get them nowhere. Kale would be rendered a useless blob of tears on the floor. That had happened before, and there had been a couple of fatalities during the journey due to leaving him behind. The captain of the foragers valued the lives of his people over leaving the Nest on schedule, so time made the sacrifice instead of their own blood. (Time was generally accustomed to such treatment. People wasted it on a regular basis.) If there were repercussions due to getting a late start, they were not nearly as severe as people dying.

A. J. Bakke *To Save Two Worlds (is twice as much fun) Worlds Akilter Series*

1) Most heroes start out with a fair amount of courage along with some vulnerability. Kale has no courage, and instead has debilitating anxiety which manifests as Obsessive-Compulsive Disorder. What is the worst thing that could happen to him?

2) Write a few paragraphs of a scene with your imagined worst thing for Kale.

3) If you were writing this book, what would happen next?

B. *Read*:

And now no one had called her Rosette since her mother died. Her smile faded, and she forced her thoughts back to the prince and the silent castle.

Maybe the prince couldn't save them this time. It had been so long . . .

Rose's jaw tightened. *No!* He would save them. He would. She just had to wait a little longer.

Rose blinked. All the daydreams in the world wouldn't put food in her stomach or a fire in their stove. She sighed, checked to see if Cosette had followed her—she had—then bent to peer into the next trap. She paused hallway, arm still outstretched. She propped her hands at her waist, still bent, and tried to take a deep breath.

She couldn't.

Through her dress, she plucked at the stays that held her captive. If only her sisters didn't insist on strapping her in so tight.

Fire lit in her. Her sisters. If only she had the strength to . . . no. The only one who mattered was Cosette. Only ever Cosette. If she kept her safe, it didn't matter what the rest of her sisters did. All five of the greedy little twits.

She tugged at the stays again, still shocked by how small her waist was now. Her sisters lounged while she and Cosette wasted away.

She thought about straightening, but it was too much work. She eyed the slender branch no longer propping open the trap's door. It was just out of reach. Black spots swam in her vision. If only she had something to eat. If only she could breathe.

If only. Always, ever, if only.

Her eyes darted around the nearby forest. Cosette's bright-red cape—the only thing left made by their mother—was glaringly visible through the barren trees. How had she gotten so far away again?

A low snarl did for Rose what she hadn't the strength to do for herself. She snapped upright and spun toward the growl, her world tilting dangerously.

A lone wolf, ribs straining against his patchy coat, swung his head between her and her sister. Rose pulled the dull blade from her pocket and shifted forward, crouched, ready to spring.

Michele Israel Harper *Beast Hunter* Prequel Story to Kill the Beast

1) Rose is strapped (and trapped) in a tight corset. The corset is a literal thing in the story, and possibly also a symbolic thing. If it is symbolic, what might the overtight corset symbolize?

2) Plots require an actor (someone with agency), a goal, and a problem. Who is the actor here? What is the goal? What is the problem?

3) List a few things that might happen next, and then next after that. If you're curious about how your answers compare to the author's, you might buy the story and find out.

C. *Read*:

"You're crazy, Caz! What if they come back?"

"They won't. They're on Deck 9 with the other gypsies from Tye." I don't know why Felly followed me, but I wasn't going to let her ruin my fun. Ever since Mom left, she's been trying to run my life, and after ten years, it's getting old. I'm fourteen. I don't need a mother.

I pulled my ponytail tighter and tried to walk calmly down the beige corridor. The grated flooring echoed beneath me, and the faint vacuum vents pulled at the cloth soles of my coversuit.

I'd timed it right. The guard was on break, and I'd be able to get into the docking area undetected. It had taken me seven tries, but it would be worth it. The only thing that broke the boredom on an Interplanetary City Station like the Arxon was when

Surface dwellers docked to refuel and go through quarantine before traveling on to another planet. The Arxon's speed made it a popular ICS.

This time was special, though. A few weeks ago gypsies had come up from Tye on their way to Caren.

Felly eyed the blinking lights. "What if they have an alarm system?"

"They're gypsies, Felly. Not ICS dwellers." I slid through the door. Several hangars stretched down to the right. Each craft had been docked with its aft facing out over the main cargo bay below, but the one I cared about lay right in front of me: a gypsy space buggy.

Felly followed me a few steps. "That thing's a heap. I don't know how it even flies."

I rolled my eyes at her superiority complex. Gypsies don't stuff themselves into all the rules of ICS dwellers, so they're free to come up with better ideas, including their spacecrafts. I've explained this to Felly before, but she thinks that being older means being smarter.

"I bet they never take this one down to the Surface so they don't have to worry about it burning up in the atmosphere." I walked slowly around the space buggy.

Felly bit her nails and watched the empty guard post. I shook my head. "No one's coming, Felly. I'll bet you my dessert no one will even care that we're here."

"The gypsies will care. And the security guard. And the Station Master." Felly frowned like Dad. "Have you no respect for order?"

I ignored her and ran my hand over the windows, trying to peek inside. "I bet they've got amazing things in there." Felly never gets excited about Surface goods. I breathed in the smell of the metal—metal that had been all around the Granbo System. I'd eavesdropped enough to know that the gypsies who owned this craft were traders, not migrant workers.

"C'mon, Caz. We need to get out of here."

"I know. Haven't you figured out that's what I want more than anything?"

Felly folded her arms. "Caz, you get to travel all around the solar system and meet fascinating ambassadors. If you were down on the Surface, you'd be living in primitive colonies. You should be grateful to live on the biggest and best ICS in the system."

She'll never understand me. Who wants to live in a space rest stop that's between the places people really want to go?

Lia London   *The Gypsy Pearl*

1) Who is the main character?

2) What does she want?

3) What is blocking her?

Day 3 hooks

A hook is what makes a reader turn another page. A hook excites the reader. So what exactly is a hook? The largest hook is the story question. After that comes the smaller questions as the hero struggles toward the Big Boss Battle.

In other words, a story question is often three-fold: narrative, thematic, and character-related. How will the narrative end? What is the theme of the story? How will the character grow or change? If we think of the movie Star Wars IV A New Hope, the first story questions are: "Will the droids escape the forces of the Empire?" and "Will Luke ever leave the moisture farm?" The first story questions escalate to the main story questions, "Will the droids and Luke and companions be able to stop the Empire?" and "What kind of man will Luke become?" The story questions relate to the theme of freedom. What must one pay to achieve freedom? And, in particular, what must Luke pay?

Every scene should contain some sort of hook. Each answered question in a story leads to others. The questions are generally answered by "yes, but." Sometimes a minor story question will be answered by "no." Very rarely is the answer an easy "yes."

Here's a few more story questions: Will the hero defeat this little demon that blocks the path to the biggest demon? Yes, but— Will he *(Don't open that door!)* open that door? Yes, but— Will she indeed decide to be the one to carry on the quest? Yes, but— This is the "hook" of the story. This is what enthralls the reader and keeps him interested in the story.

A minor story question that is answered by "yes" makes the character's journey too easy. A minor story question that is answered by "no" shuts the door to the character's face. "Yes, but— can drive a story. Will Cinderella be able to go to the ball? Yes but she needs a new dress, a coach, and footmen and she needs to be unseen by her step-sisters. Will she be able to get all these items? Yes, she has a fairy god-mother who will provide for her, but she has to return by midnight.

Questions, however, are not the only hooks.

In her short, you-ought-to-read book, *Writing Active Hooks*, Mary Buckham describes more hooks and gives many examples:

1. Action or Danger

2. Overpowering Emotion

3. A surprising situation

4. An evocative description that pulls the reader into the story.

5. A unique character

6. Warning or foreshadowing

7. Shocking or witty dialogue

8. Raising a question (which I already mentioned)

Places that must have hooks are the opening sentence and opening paragraph, end of the first page, the opening and ending of each chapter, and the opening and ending of each scene. Some people say every page should contain a hook. Not every hook needs to be large, but there should always be something the reader wants to know such that the reader develops an itch that isn't scratched until the question is answered.

When you set a hook and make a question, the reader's mind will want to make a completed puzzle by learning the answer. If any of your story question hooks are not answered within the story or at the climax, you will have what is called a loose end. Unless you are writing a trilogy or some other sort of trilogy, you must tie off all the loose ends or people will be unhappy at you. EVEN IF you are writing a trilogy, you must answer at least one of the big questions by the end of each book. It's best if you answer most of them. It's even permissible to answer all of them, and then set the next story in the same world with a new story question.

Activities:

A. *Read*:

He stood. He stepped out into the street. The small town of Blowing Rock, North Carolina, lay sleeping around him. No street lamps anywhere were lit. No porch lights on any houses. No neon signs on any small shops. Even the traffic lights were dark.

Just then the bell in the clocktower above the town hall started ringing. Gil turned. Usually the clock face was lit. Now it was dark. Gil had sharp eyes and excellent night vision, but he could see only a pale circular shadow in the darker oblong shadow of the tower. He counted the strokes of the bell. Ten . . . eleven . . . twelve . . . thirteen . . .

Gil felt a cold sensation trickle down his spine. "Maybe it is just a mistake. A mechanical failure . . ."

His voice sounded so unconvincing to his own ears that he snapped his teeth shut and told himself not to say anything more.

That was when he saw a group of people. They were a block or two away, in the center of the lane, walking. Their pace was not quick, but slow and reluctant. No one carried any lights. They were walking toward him.

John C. Wright   *Swan Knight's Son: The Green Knight's Squire Book One*
(Moth & Cobweb 1)

1) What do you think might happen next?
2) What do you want to have happen next?
3) Do you feel hooked by this passage? If not, why not?

B. *Read*:

Rainbird shed her coat and kicked it aside, up against one of the spines that marched in a row along the top side, the nightside, of the sunway. She wore thick pants reinforced with leather panels and a halter top which left her powerful shoulders and arms bare and her wings free. They rose from her shoulders in thin, diaphanous layers, and hung raggedly to her knees. A true eiree was light and strong enough to fly, but a halfbreed—even had her wings been whole, and with her strength and acrobatic skill—could not.

However.

Rainbird pulled the harness over her head and settled it against her shoulders and back. She cinched the straps tight around her waist and twitched her wings to make sure they were unconfined. Twisted poly ropes clipped onto the harness, their other ends secured to rings embedded deep in the bone.

She stood at the edge of the sunway where it curved down, and stared at the darkened land. Faint pinpricks of light came from some town below. The darker roads and rivers ran like uncoiling ribbons. Far beyond her sight, the sunway sloped down to a shattered tail in a canyon on one side and a skull buried in a swamp on the other. Crumbling high cliffs and shattered stone mountains ringed the crater the dragon had made on its impact.

Rainbird turned her back, looked out at the gritty cream bonescape instead. She was half off the edge.

She jumped.

Most inspectors did not jump. Most inspectors scuttled down, paying out the rope, boots scuffing against bone, edging their way to the track on the underside, the sunside.

None of the other inspectors had wings. None of them had a drop of eiree blood. None of them wanted to fly.

Freefalling in the cold, plunging into darkness. Wind roared in Rainbird's ears, pierced her soft down skin and plunged into her light hollow bones. Her tattered wings streamed behind her. She relished the way her skin prickled as the icy air rolled over it, the way every sense was sharpened, the way everything took on clarity and brightness. A knot of excitement and panic in her stomach wriggled, like a nest of snakes.

This was what it meant to be truly alive.

The end of the tether jerked her back to her duties. She'd been bracing for it, and she brought her feet up in time to meet the sunway. *Smack, smack*, several times, swinging back and forth until she'd managed to slow herself down enough to reach for the hand and footholds sunk into the bone.

Rabia Gale *Rainbird*

1) What do you think is going to happen next?

2) What are the hooks in this excerpt?

3) Do you feel hooked by this passage? If not, why not?

C. *Read*:

Darien groaned and pushed away from the steering wheel. An airbag rested in his lap like a deflated pillow. Shards of glass speckled his jeans, and the air was a sickening twist of chicken nuggets and burning plastic.

No, this is different. He squinted at the sky through the spider-webbed windshield. Above the maze of evergreen needles, fiery slashes of falling stars streaked the evening sky. *Dad died a long time ago.*

"… reports that the high school was hit." The radio announcer's smooth voice leaked from the dashboard. "Avoid the west side of Jade Glen at all costs. Stay indoors and head underground—"

Darien twisted the keys with a jingle, cutting off the radio's feeble life. Memories returned in a haze: he'd swerved to avoid a smoldering crater in the asphalt. *Yeah, taking the back roads to avoid traffic was a great idea, Tera—*

Tera!

Darien's head jerked to the passenger seat. His sister was slumped over with blond wisps covering her face. A thin branch had pierced the windshield and sliced a bloody gash across her forearm.

Darien cursed and wrestled with his seat belt. "Tera!"

Azure eyes fluttered open. Tera groaned and muttered something he couldn't understand.

"Hey! Are you OK?"

"Fine…" Tera's gaze drifted to the stripped tree limb that rested between her arm and side. Her eyes widened. "Oh."

Darien snapped her seatbelt free, then clawed the inside of his pocket. *My phone. Where's my phone?*

"Wow, this could have… stabbed me." Tera pulled her arm away from the tree limb, letting loose a fresh flow of scarlet blood. She clamped the gash closed. "Doesn't hurt so bad."

Darien's stomach heaved. "I'll call the police." He spotted his phone on the floorboard and scrambled for it. *Of course the screen is busted!*

The driver's side door screeched open as Darien clambered out and looked around. Muddy skid marks split the grass from his back tires to the road. The sleepy backroad snaked into the forest, empty and quiet aside from the smoldering crater.

Wonderful. Darien dialed the emergency number and winced as the broken glass bit his finger. The phone played a melodious tune.

"Yeesh." Tera stumbled out onto crackling leaves. She furrowed her brow at the twisted union of pine and blue metal. "I knew I shouldn't have let you drive."

"Seriously?" Darien frowned at Tera over the crumpled hood. "I think you should sit down."

"I don't feel it, really." Tera adjusted her grip on her arm and looked up at the shredded sky. "Hand me your shirt, will you?"

Right. Stop the bleeding. Darien looked down at himself as the phone sang in his ear. His orange shirt was peppered with glass fragments. *It's all we've got.*

He grabbed at his shoulder blades and wriggled out of the shirt while trying to keep the phone to his ear. "They're not answering!" He shook the glass out and hurried to hand it to Tera.

"I bet they've got... a lot of emergencies on their hands right now." Tera wrapped his shirt around her arm, hissing as she pulled it tight. "You know, I bet I could still fix this old Bumblebee if I could find the parts." She squatted to peer under the engine.

Unbelievable. "Forget about the stupid Wannabee and sit down! I don't care if you can't feel—"

"What's your emergency?" a voice crackled from the phone.

Darien snapped upright. "Uh... yeah. There was a..." He put a hand to his temple. His brain felt like pudding. "Car accident. We need an ambulance."

"Is someone's life at stake?"

Darien glanced at Tera, who was crawling backwards under the car, belly-up. "Well, I don't think so, but she's got a big cut and it's bleeding pretty bad—"

"I'm so sorry, but we don't have any emergency vehicles to spare at the moment."

Darien blinked at the red-berried bushes huddled between the trees. "What?"

"I'm very sorry. But I can see your location on my screen here thanks to the GPS in your phone—"

"Yeah, we're in the middle of nowhere! We need help!"

"I'll put you on the list, young man, but there are many casualties and more critical emergencies happening with every meteor impact. We only have so many vehicles and personnel."

'Young man'? Is my emergency not valid because I'm sixteen? "But my sister—"

"I see that you're a mile southeast of the Serran Academy. I'm sure they have medical staff for their campus. Can you make it there?"

Darien's heart stuttered. That boarding school was full of crazy rich people who never left its ancient walls. But what really scared him were the rumors. Somewhere between black magic and meddling of elemental gods, the Serran Academy was at the bottom of his bucket list.

I can't believe this. Darien's eyes caught a black plume of smoke rising from the direction on downtown. "I guess we can walk, but—"

"Great. Orso be with you." The line clicked.

Jamie Foley *Sentinel*

1) What are the hooks in this passage?

2) When is the first time you realize that this isn't set in present day America? What do we now know about this storyworld/universe?

3) If you were writing this, what would happen next?

Day 4 questions

Conflict is what enthralls the reader. Questions, conflicts, and intriguing plot threads keep readers interested in the story.

So, what turns off the reader? What causes the reader to lose interest in a character or a story? The number one cause of readers losing interest is boredom. Readers start out wanting to be interested in the characters and story, but somewhere along the way, boredom, confusion, and dislike of the character or setting derails the reader. She closes the book and moves on. She doesn't care what happens next because all the questions have been answered with trite answers or there are no more hooks.

Hooks at the beginning and end of every scene are what keeps the reader turning pages. If you answer one question, you need to raise a new one until you reach the end of your story and tie up all the threads.

Here are two question hooks:

Joseph Johnson returned to the arena five months after his death.

What question do you have after reading that?

He had never intended for the joke to go that far, and now he was strapped in next the man he hated most.

What questions do you have after reading that?

Let's see if we can make up a steam or diesel punk plot with a series of hooks, beginning with the Story Question that turns into a series of smaller questions that keep drawing the reader along.

Story Question: Can Mr. Excell vindicate his grandfather's claims about blue diamonds on the moon and thereby impress the woman he wants to marry?

Now the smaller questions:

Can Mr. Excell build a rocket that will reach the moon? NO (his rocket crashes on a neighbor's barn.)

Can Mr. Excell find an engineer who can build a rocket to the moon? YES (the engineer has been looking for a job ever since he crashed his own rocket on City Hall.)

With all the rockets crashing, the country has banned the making of rockets. Can Mr. Excell and the engineer build and launch the rocket before the police catch and jail them? (hook and ticking clock) YES (just barely. they launch from a silo as police are breaking down the door.)

Will they reach the moon? YES (although they nearly overshoot.)

Will they find a blue diamond? YES (after arduous search and their food running out.)

Will they be able to return to Earth? UH-OH (Big Boss Battle) (the Lunarians chase them with evil intent. when Mr. Excell and engineer reach the rocket, they discover they don't have enough fuel for liftoff.) [Go back and add foreshadow of fuel leak] (rocks and spears are banging on the rocket.)

Will they escape the Lunarians? YES (they discover they can use the blue diamond as fuel) [go back and add foreshadow of Mr. Excell noticing odd power surges from blue diamond when they first find it]

On return, does Mr. Excell vindicate Grandpa? NO (blue diamond was consumed by flight)

Does Mr. Excell impress woman? YES (he longer cares how the world mocks him and Grandpa because he knows the truth. his new self-confidence attracts the woman and she agrees to marry him.) [go back and foreshadow character arc by adding Mr. Excell's humiliation about Grandpa]
The End
And that's one way to build a story with hooks.

Activity:

1) Look through five of your practice paragraphs. Do you have any hooks in them? Either rewrite one of the practice paragraphs or write a new paragraph that contains a hook.

Day 5 thinking about your plot

By now you should be thinking about the plot of your story. You will want to have your character living what passes for normal life in its world. The character should demonstrate some competency that will be used in the climax. She should have some sort of goal, even if the goal is only to keep living that normal life. The inciting incident will be something that blocks that goal, a problem, or a disaster that disrupts the life of the character. There should be at least one ineffective attempt to solve the problem. There should be a final conflict and then resolution. The questions that were raised during the story should be answered at the end. The character has won or lost. Last, we see the beginning of the new life. If the main character died, we should see how someone she affected is living now.

Activities:

Write some practice paragraphs. Set one of the paragraphs in the normal life of one of your characters. Set one at the inciting incident, and one at a point of conflict in Act II.

Write a practice epilogue. An epilogue is what is written after a story has ended to show what characters went on to do years after the story. Most stories don't have them, and your story does not require one for this course. You're practicing and thinking through the story line. Where can you add hooks? Add some to your practice paragraphs now.

CHAPTER SEVEN:

CHARACTER

A human is a character. A talking dog is a character. A monster is a character. A singing teapot is a character. And all characters have characteristics. Hence their name. Attributes. Traits. Mannerisms. Habits. Personality. Attitudes. Worldviews. Desires. Goals. Needs. Appearance. Strengths. Weaknesses.

Setting is important. Plotting is important. But it's the characters the readers want to read about and what they will remember a year from now. The character and story will need to mesh. If you have invented a character that does not push the plot along, you need to jettison the character or change the plot.

Some writers start all their stories with a specific character in mind and try to find a plot that will showcase the character. The beauty of this is that the main character is likely to be understandable and likable. The downside can be that world-building or plot might be less than they could be, ending up with a story that feels thin.

Some writers start with a plot and find a character that would fit that kind of plot. This is great for being able to start and finish a story that will feel coherent and fitting. The downside can be that characters are made to act to provide plot points and feel cardboardy and flat, such that the reader never engages with the characters.

Some writers start with a tremendous story world, and then try to make a story that would fit on that world. This is good for a series as it helps the books fit together. However, world-building can take up so much time that the story never gets written.

Some writers begin with theme, though that can be problematic, and should probably wait to be discovered at the end of the book. Why? If you start with the theme, you might end up bludgeoning the characters and plot into fitting that theme and also end up with a lot of preaching. People who want to hear preaching will generally read sermons and op-eds. The speculative fiction reader, as all fiction readers do, wants to read a story and have an emotional experience. On the other hand, knowing your theme beforehand can help organize a story. Myself, I don't discover what the theme of my novels are until after they are written. When I was a teenager and a teacher would ask me to explain the theme of a story, I always panicked. I had no idea how to discover themes. That's why this textbook won't ask you what the theme of any story is. You don't need to know anything about themes to write a fine story, though the knowledge would greatly help. An ability to discern themes is also useful for understanding other people's stories.

The key to giving your reader the emotional experience they want is to create a character they will care about. Now, some people will like the "bad boy", and some people will despise him. You need to know who your intended audience is so you can craft a character your audience will want to read about.

Your audience is who you are writing the story for. Right now, your audience may be your instructor. You might want your audience to be people like you, in which case it might be easy to know what your readers would like. You may want your audience to be a bit broader than only people like you, in which case you have some thinking to do. I do like you to think.

Most readers most of the time do not want to read about cardboard characters. By that we mean characters that are flat, that have no depth, that are moved from plot point to plot point with no recognizable motivation to do one thing or another.

Randy Ingermanson in his you-ought-to-read-this book *The Snowflake Method* brought up a beautiful way to think about and understand your characters. He asks the writer to take every major character in the story and make a list of three "The most important thing in the world is ____," statements. Let's say you have a character that is a werewolf. What might his most important things be? Maybe:

1. The most important thing in the world is to keep my mutability secret.
2. The most important thing in the world is to kill all the vampires.
3. The most important thing in the world is to find a beautiful werewolf who will love me.

If those are your character's most important things, he will spend time and effort on those things. He might talk about them. He will definitely think about them. These important things will impact his motivations, goals, and emotional reactions. They will also affect the reader's emotions and "hook" the reader into the novel.

If one of your most important things in the world is to avoid embarrassment, think about how much of your day is spent doing stuff that will keep you from being embarrassed in front of people. If you can give your character motivations at least as strong as that, you will be well on your way to creating a great character.

How will the reader know what the character's most important things are?
How do we know what is important to anybody?
We see their behavior. We see their appearance. We hear what they say. And in writing, we have the advantage of knowing what they are thinking as well.

While we're talking about characters, be careful about how many characters you have in your story. The shorter the story, the fewer main characters you should have. Also be careful about ensemble casts. If you introduce too many characters too close together, the reader will grow confused. Every time you introduce an important character, you must spend words and time on him. If all you give is the person's name and tiny amount of description before moving on to someone else, I promise you that by the time you bring up this important character some pages later, the reader will have forgotten him and will wonder who this new person is. Confusion will ensue.

This leads to another concept that applies to all stories and throughout all the story. Prioritize. Prioritize your characters. Prioritize your character's goals. What your hero spends time looking at and thinking about and dealing with will be considered important in the story by the reader. If much time is spent on what is not important, the reader will grow confused or bored. Do not stuff things into your story that are not important to the story. Give enough description for the reader to know what, where, and who for every scene, but don't give much more than that.

Day 1 revealing character

Now, when a character walks into a story, the reader is usually not handed a list of the characteristics of the person. We might get a description of appearance. We might read what other people think about that character. But we aren't given a character sheet that says: Here is Sheri. Sheri has a bubbly personality and loves to help people. She is afraid of heights and bats. She loves chocolate. The most important thing in the world is that people think well of her.

However, such a character list is handy for the writer.

Characters come with their own backstories, goals, and importance to the story. Dumping all a character's biography, goals, and grudges on the reader when the character appears is not, however, the way you want to introduce the character. Backstories, flashbacks, long descriptions of the new character's facial features and personality traits halt the forward thrust of a story. Try dropping hints about characters before they arrive. Characters fear, love, and gossip about other characters. You might not want to have expository dialogue—commonly called "maid and butler" dialogue—but you should let your reader anticipate the appearance of certain characters, especially those characters who will affect the main character's primary goals.

So, how are we going to find out these goals and characteristics?

Activities:

A. *Read*:

In this excerpt, William Thoren is the mission leader. Chris Davidson is the astrophysicist who discovered an alien spaceship imbedded in a Kuiper belt object via a satellite fly-by. He wants to name the KBO after the senator who sponsored the funding for the satellite. Ian is a rockjack who has joined the secret expedition to explore the alien ship. James is an archeologist. Ann and Rita are members of the Rescue Sisters, an order of the Roman Catholic Church devoted to survival and rescue in spaceships, stations, and space itself. The Rescue Sisters have mandated survival drills and education for everyone on the expedition as they travel for several months out to the Kuiper Belt. (This is not Star Trek. It takes a long time to travel long distances.)

Thoren's mouth twisted with distaste. "The Folly?"

Standing at the conference room table, addressing his supervisor, Chris felt his confidence retreat into a tight little knot in his stomach. How did he get elected spokesman? Around the table, the others offered their encouragement: James with a smile, Rita, a gentle nod. Ann had her hands clasped together in an effort not to clap; her happy shrug making her look years younger. He saw why the miners called her "Little Sister." He wasn't quite sure why she was even at the meeting; she'd just followed Andi in. Commander McVee was filling in for Capt. Addiman; he nodded and spread his hands in a 'sounds-good-to-me' gesture.

"I filed the registration first thing after lunch." Andi grinned, slow and self-satisfied, her eyes on Thoren.

Chris gulped. He hadn't thought about that, about it being so . . . official.

Thoren cleared his throat. "By contract, it is, of course, yours, so you may name it as you please. As for the ship, I believe—"

"*Discovery!*" Ann burst out. When all eyes turned to her, she looked at Chris with eyebrows raised in invitation.

"Well," he stammered, "we were thinking. That is . . ."

"It's a great name, William," James said easily. "We all refer to it that way, anyhow."

"It is fitting," Rita added.

Thoren nodded. "Very well. We shall use Discovery as a working name for the time being. Although Thoren's voice remained level, Chris caught the look that darkened his eyes. Chris sat down fast. *Take your victories where you can.*

"Anything else, Mr. Davidson?"

He shook his head, and James took up the conversation.

"Ian is asking if there's any way we can open up one of the swimming pools." He glanced at McVee.

The First Officer leaned back in his seat and crossed one ankle over the opposite knee, relaxed, in charge, and comfortable with all eyes on him. "I think we have enough water. The question is if we have the right filters. I'll have Quartermaster check and get back to us. I like the idea. It's good recreation for everyone. Incidentally, Lieutenant Chan is setting up a splat tournament. Doctor OvLandra says you're cleared to play, Ann. You know, you've really impressed her, and that's not an easy thing to do. I heard she invited you to her quarters; do you know the protocols?"

"Oh, yes, I've been studying."

Thoren cleared his throat. "Yes. Fascinating."

McVee took the hint. "Sorry, I digress, but OvLandra's been the pride of the ET for a long time. Anyway, I'll check on the pool. It'd be good to have some other forms of entertainment around here."

Thoren surprised them with a wry chuckle. "As an alternative to the 'educational movie night'?"

He shared a smirk with McVee, who explained.

"Our Comms officer brought this to me for approval to distribute." He pressed a button on his console, and the large screen lit up.

A gray, skeletal creature with a huge, oblong head snapped its jaws at a woman who cowered and whimpered in fear. Over the hissing and howls came a voice that lilted like all salesmen of any age.

"Don't know what's waiting on that unexplored alien ship? Not anxious to be caught by surprise? Well, neither are we. And, thanks to the cinematographers of old, we don't have to be."

The scene changed to spacesuited figures wandering in a dark cavernous room filled with large, leathery eggs.

"Every Monday night, we'll be analyzing the procedures and tactics of others who have gone the way we dare go now. After each full-length feature presentation—in its extended form remastered exclusively for CruiseGalactic—we will hold analysis and discussion."

The woman, now in a full spacesuit, strapped herself into a chair, then blew open the hatch to blast the alien into space.

"We don't have to operate in a vacuum. Come join us for these life-and-death discussions. Remember: they made the stupid mistakes so we don't have to!"

The last image froze on the screen: a man on a hospital bed with a pale yellow scorpion-like creature with long legs clamped over his face. Over the still appeared a small box that said in bright flashing letters, "First showing: ALIEN, directed by Ridley Scott. Download a reminder into your calendar now! Avoid death by alien intubation!"

"And now we know why Sean and Ian wanted to get the theater working again." McVee pronounced.

Ann leaned toward the screen, her eyes wide. "It looks so real," she marveled.

Chris clamped his hands over his mouth.

"Well," Rita finally managed to say after a few tries. "I think we've exceeded the bounds of tastelessness." She glanced around, caught Jame's gaze, and pressed her fist against her mouth to keep from laughing. A squeaky balloon sound escaped nonetheless.

Andi's sour expression matched Thoren's.

"Was that Ian Hu's voice? What are we going to do with that boy?"

Rita laughed. "He's as old as we are, dear."

Thoren pointed to the invitation on the screen. "The more accurate question is, what shall we do about that?"

Ann looked at them with confusion. "You mean we aren't going?"

Karina Fabian   *Discovery*

1) What can you tell about Ann's character by this excerpt? Make a list of what illustrated her character.

2) What do you know about Chris Davidson now? Make a list of what illustrated his character. How did his speech mirror his interior monologue?

3) What do you know about William Thoren? Yep, make a list of what illustrated his character.

B. *Read*:

"Fresh Fish, door!" the squad leader bawled.

Tyler Takku, Fire Team 6's "Fresh Fish," was an ugly little man—though his mother didn't think so. He was short and squat, as were the others of the fire team. It was a must as they hauled heavy equipment into Avenir's tight spaces and survivors or bodies out.

The atmosphere feeding from his "bunker gear" or fire armor's life support system tasted faintly of smoke and burning volatiles; something he'd ceased to notice while in training. It was only at times like this, when he should be concentrating, that the sensation snuck into his awareness. No matter how often the filters were changed out or the bunker gear was cleaned, the bouquet remained. He shook his head, clearing the cobwebs.

The shop's door was the normal atmosphere-tight kind found on the other businesses on the mall. The large temper-plast windows attempted to not remind patrons that hard vacuum waited its chance outside.

He ran through the Snuffy's Alphabet—C-A-E-S: Contain the fire-cut Air circulation-cut Electrical current-Search for victims—in his head as he helped place the temporary airlock over the door. Behind the windows the shop looked frightening close to flashover. He bulled his way into the lock ahead of the other firefighters. It was this aggressiveness to get to the fire that caused the Snuffys to refer to each other as "Idjits"—they ran toward danger rather than away.

"Fresh Fish in the lead," sounded in his earphones from both the internal radio and his gear's external mics. One corner of his mind reminded him how happy he'd be when he wasn't the new guy and had a proper nickname. Then the next new guy would be "Fresh Fish" until christened by the squad.

The atmosphere in the lock was evacuated and replaced with inert nitrogen. There'd be backdraft when the door was opened. He dropped to his knees and scrambled forward as the emergency charge blew the door halves back into their slots in the jamb. He was conscious of someone behind him directing a heavy stream of CO_2 and soda above him through the door as smoke billowed in to mix with the lock's atmosphere. Vision being useless, he relied on the heads-up display on his visor's interior for his view of the shop. It occurred to him that he hadn't noticed what sort of shop it was. Well, if anything had been explosive or oxidizing, he would have been warned forcefully by dispatch.

The picture produced by his radar showed a body on the floor to his right. The thermal overlay showed it as well above 37 degrees C. He sighed as he grabbed it and began to back out, dragging the body behind. He'd hoped his first experience would be a rescue instead of a recovery.

Outside, he cracked his visor and turned away as the med team took over his burden. He stood, looking at the mall's carpet as he felt the letdown. The heavy slap of a hand landed on his shoulder. "Why so blue, kid?"

He glanced at the squad leader's smile, then back at the floor. "Guess I just wanted the first one to come out alive."

"Oh? Well, that one never was."

Tyler looked around at the squad leader in confusion. "What?"

"You rescued a dressmaker's mannequin." The other pointed to where a mousey-looking woman was putting a variable geometry dressmaker's smart-dummy through its paces surrounded by the grinning med team.

The new man cringed, Oh Lordy, could it get worse?

Walt Staples   *96. Smoke Eater: Hero, Avenir Eclectia*

1) What do we learn about Tyler in this excerpt? Make a list.

2) What do we learn about this setting or world? Make a list.

3) What do we learn about the fire-fighting crew? Make a list.

C. *Read*:

"Storm's coming."

When he was ten, Eldon Granger broke his arm, and the bone was never set right. Even now, at age sixty-five, he felt it ache whenever a storm approached. Today, although the skies over the small town of Greensboro were bright blue and thickly populated with dramatic cumulus clouds, Eldon felt the approaching storm in his bones.

He sat in his tattered clothes atop one of the charred stone foundations that lay scattered in the tall grass of the North Woods, which bordered Greensboro, using an old buck knife to scoop beans out of a can. At his feet sat a semicircle of children, boys and girls, ages ranging from nine to thirteen, ashen-faced and speechless as Eldon continued spinning his tale.

"Mighty big one's coming, I reckon. You know, a storm came through these parts over a hundred years ago. A *bad* storm, if you know what I'm saying."

The children blinked back at him, spellbound.

"Some storms, see, they just make a racket with all the thunder before they blow on through. Harmless, you'd say. But other storms . . ."

Eldon lifted a row of beans to his scraggly face and slurped them down. Gulping, he leaned toward the kids, lowering his voice to a whisper.

". . . other storms, you see, they have a way of staying. Sometimes they leave something behind."

He sat up and dug in his can for the last scraps of his meal.

"That's what happened back then. Something got left behind. Not from this earth, neither. No sir, came from the world beyond."

One of the kids looked to the sky, squinting against the sun as if hoping to see a flying saucer pass overhead on cue.

"No, no," Eldon grumbled. "Not up there, boy!" With a jerk of his wrist, he stuck his knife hilt deep into the soft earth, eliciting a gasp from the girl sitting directly across from him. "*Down there.*"

He could almost hear the thumping hearts of the frightened listeners. Reaching down, he plucked the blade from the dirt, wiping it off his stained jeans then using it to scrape the last remnants of beans from the can.

A couple of the girls made "eww" faces at each other as Eldon finished his canned supper.

"They come up from time to time," Eldon began again. "Devils, they are. Walking the earth. Looking for little boys and girls who don't mind their elders."

He leveled an appraising glare at each of the children, his eyeballs bulging to almost grotesque proportions.

"I sure hope that ain't none of you. I don't wanna be seein' your pictures on the news, how no one can't find ya. Too many kids have already gone missing 'round these woods ever since the first storm. Creatures out here, haven't you heard?"

Eldon took a deep breath, his mind wandering.

"Maybe that's why you come. You out lookin' for the monsters of the North Woods, that it? Thinking you might spot something out there? A bogle, perhaps? Or maybe the king himself, the bogeyman?"

He gestured at the yawning forest beyond, dark and imposing despite the brightness of the afternoon.

Greg Mitchell   *The Strange Man (The Coming Evil)*

1) What do we learn about Eldon in this excerpt?

2) Where do you think the can of beans came from?

3) What do we learn about the setting?

Day 2 emotional connection

On October 12, 2016, Cynthia T. Toney posted on her blog Bird Face Wendy an article titled *Give Fiction Readers What They Want: Someone to Care About:*

> While attending to a good plot, or a good personal problem to solve in a character-driven novel, a few authors ignore this duty: **to give the readers the emotional connection they want**. And *only* those important to the story, if you please.
>
> From my experience as a reader, that has everything to do with point of view.
>
> I need a single POV (point of view) character, or at most, two POV characters. I enjoy getting into one or two main characters' heads and viewing or feeling everything as though I'm in their skin. That's deep POV, and I crave it, particularly in contemporary fiction. I find it jarring to jump around among several characters' POVs, whether it's for each scene or each chapter. Just when I get emotionally attached to a character—BAM!—the door slams shut and I have to get used to someone else. I only have the time and emotional energy to connect with and care deeply about one or two characters, not three, four, five, or six. And yes, sometimes authors use that many POVs.
>
> The justification by the author for multiple POVs is typically that he or she wants the reader to know what all those characters are thinking. But why? Is every thought in their heads important to the advancement of the plot? Most often, I find that they are not.
>
> And there's the problem—the author is writing **what the author wants**. Not what the reader may want. The reader may not care what each and every character who appears more than once in a story is thinking. And may not have *time* to care.
>
> In YA (young adult) fiction, where the focus of the story and the POV character(s) should be the young people, why would an author want to place the reader inside a parent's or other adult's head? And yet I see that sometimes, when it adds nothing to the story.
>
> I appreciate the skill of an author who can tell me everything **I need** to know about the story through the eyes of one character. Maybe two, as in a romance or possibly a crime thriller.
>
> Like me, readers want to feel a strong emotional connection that will carry them throughout a story. They want to care what happens to the main character(s) in the end, even if they want the bad guy to get his just desserts. My feeling is, that level of caring does not apply to every POV character in some otherwise good stories.
>
> So please, have mercy on my tired reader's brain and my emotional health. Place me inside the heads of only the characters that truly need to tell me their story.

> Cynthia T. Toney   Author of 8 *Notes to a Nobody*, and the *Bird Face* series. Her website has more writing tips: https://birdfacewendy.wordpress.com/

What precisely is POV or Point Of View?

Simply, Point of View is the person through whom the story is being told combined with the verb tense being used.

A little less simply, there are a number of points of view you can use to tell your story. At this time of writing, first person, singular, present tense is the popular POV of YA (Young Adult) or NA (New Adult) speculative fiction, especially dystopias. Here's a quick rundown of POVs illustrated by a line from Alice in Wonderland.

First person, singular, present tense: I act today. Common in present day literature.

In another moment down I go after it. I don't consider how in the world I am to get out again.

First person, singular, past tense: I acted yesterday. Fairly common today.

In another moment down I went after it, never once considering how in the world I was to get out again.

First person, singular, future tense: I will act tomorrow. Common in speech but rare in fiction.

In another moment I will go down after it, and never consider how in the world I will get out again.

First person, plural, present tense. We act today. Generally reserved for textbooks and sermons.

In another moment we go down after it. We don't consider how in the world we are to get out again.

First person, plural, past tense: We acted yesterday. Sermons and political speeches.

In another moment down we went after it, never considering how in the world we were to get out again.

First person, plural, future tense: We will act. Political and inspirational speeches.

In another moment we will go down after it and we will never consider how in the world we are to get out again.

Second person, singular, present tense: You are acting. Rare, used in the occasional short story.

In another moment down you go after it. You don't consider how in the world you are to get out again.

Second person, singular, past tense: You did act. Usually reserved for lectures about how you goofed up. Used often in love songs.

In another moment, down you went after it, never considering how in the world you were to get out again.

Second person, singular, future tense: You will act. Miniscule use in rare short story.

In another moment you will go down after it, and you will not once consider how in the world you will get out again.

Second person, plural, present tense: You (all) act today. Almost never seen in literature as POV. Heard during instruction.

In another moment down you go after it, and never once consider how in the world you can get out again.

Second person, plural, past tense. You (all) acted yesterday. Lectures.

In another moment down you all went after it, never once considering how in the world you were to get out again.

Second person, plural, future tense: You (all) will act tomorrow. Commands.

In another moment you all will go after it. You will not consider how in the world you are to get out again.

Third person, singular, present tense: She acts today. Common in short stories.

In another moment down goes Alice after it, and never once does she consider how in the world she is to get out again.

Third person, singular, past tense: She acted yesterday. The most common POV in short stories and novels.

I suggest you use this one in your short story because of ease of use.

In another moment down went Alice after it, never once considering how in the world she was to get out again.

Third person, singular, future tense: She will act tomorrow. Rare in fiction.

In another moment Alice will go down after it and never once will she consider how she will get out again.

Third person, plural, present tense: They act. Rare in fiction.

In another moment down they go after it. They do not consider how in the world they can get out again.

Third person, plural, past tense: They acted. Rare in fiction, common in history.

In another moment down they went after it, never considering how in the world they were to get out again.

Third person, plural, future tense: They will act. Rare in fiction. Common in fear-mongering.

In another moment they will go down after it and never consider how in the world they will get out again.

Omniscient, any tense: Uses multiple POVs within scenes. At one time this was a popular style of writing. Today, most editors hate it. If you want to sell your work, you probably shouldn't use it. And yet . . . I hear it is slowly becoming more acceptable.

In addition, James Moffett's anthology of stories, *Points of View*, categorizes different kinds of narration that use these POV's

Interior Monologue—The story is told through the narrator's thoughts, sometimes in a rambling manner called stream of consciousness.

Dramatic Narration—The story is told by dialogue alone, often a monologue.

Letter Narration, Correspondence or Epistolary—The story is told by way of letters from one character to another character or to the reader.

Diary Narration—The story is told with diary entries.

Subjective Narration—The narrator is telling the reader about something that happened in the past or seeing something that is presently happening through his eyes but since it is all seen through his eyes, feelings, etc the reader isn't sure whether or not the narrator's perspective might be wrong and unreliable.

Detached Autobiography—The narrator is telling the reader about something he did but enough time has elapsed that feeling about the event have solidified and the event can now be discussed in a detached or objective manner.

Memoir or Observer Narration—The narrator is telling a story about himself in the past from his point of view. The story is personal and not detached or objective.

Anonymous Narration–Single POV—The narrator's personality is hidden so no commentary is made by the narrator on the events, also known as authorial intrusion. Events are viewed through only one character, we see and feel everything through this one character with no narrative judgement.

Anonymous Narration–Dual POV—The narrator's personality is hidden so no commentary is made by the narrator on the events, which are viewed and felt by two main characters. The characters might alternate scenes or chapters.

Anonymous Narration–Multiple POV—The narrator's personality is hidden so there is no authorial intrusion commenting on the events. This is also known as omniscient, where every character's thoughts are known to the narrator.

Anonymous Narration–No Character POV—A story that is told with a distant or detached voice. The reader is allowed only to see the external actions of the characters.

POV is as if a writer is writing a story while looking through the eyes of and/or standing behind a major character. As stated earlier, the majority of stories are written in first or third person POV and in present or past tense.

A POV character (whether written in first person, second person, or third person) written in a present tense novel only knows what is happening in his own past, his own mind, the current setting and time. He does not know what is in another character's mind until the character states it. Neither does he see, hear, or understand what other characters understand, see, or hear. He is stuck in his own mind. A POV present tense character and the reader are both walking through the story together.

A POV character written in the past tense (whether written in first, second, or third person) tells the reader about past events and relates events as they became known to the main character.

Whichever POV you pick, stay consistent throughout the story. Inside of dialogue and inner thoughts, any kind of person and tense can be used, and that will not violate the consistent use of one POV in the story.

A note here on character backstory and grammar:

Flashbacks are often used to tell the reader about a character's history. You can introduce the flashback with past perfect (he had acted), then use past tense (he acted) throughout the flashback, and then segue out of the flashback with another use of past perfect to signal the reader that the flashback is ending. Other than exceptions like that, whatever tense you started the story in, stay there. If you start in present tense, stay in present tense. If you start with past tense, stay in past tense. Timey-Wimey Wibble-Wobbling with your verb tenses is not allowed.

Activities:

A. *Read*:

1. My Question

"Dad, how many universes are there?"

"Only one, by definition, son," he answered. "Hence the term *universe*."

Spread out on the couch, still in his gear, my father spoke in a weary monotone, not raising his head, not opening his eyes. I was surprised to get even a grunt out of him, much less an answer, even if it was an answer that was not really an answer.

I prodded the fake log with a poker, but no sparks flew up. I tried to keep the frustration out of my voice. Depending on his answer, I would either be back upstairs asleep in ten minutes, or running wildly out of the house into the wide darkness before the dawn, at top speed.

It might be too late already. I wanted to take out my phone and look at the time but feared I might glimpse the message that was still glowing on the little screen.

"Let me ask it another way. What is reality?"

He heaved a weary sigh.

2. Before you laugh.

Before you ask, it was because of a girl. Before you laugh, tell me a better reason to dive headfirst off the edge of reality.

Her name was Penny Dreadful. Unless it wasn't. I was in love. Unless I wasn't.

Penny was a very pretty, witty and brave girl, as bold as a Marine platoon storming Iwo Jima. She was famous and rich, and way out of my league.

It wasn't her fault. It's not like she asked me to save her. Heck, she did not even know I was alive. Well, technically, she knew I was alive.

She saw me every day. She just couldn't remember my name.

It's Ilya, by the way.

Ilya Vseslavyevich Bessmertniy Saint Mitrophan Muromets.

And who in the world could recall a name like that? Aside from Russians, I mean. And most of them live in Marion County fifty miles southwest over rough terrain backpacking, or one hundred miles by car, if you go by way of Portland. Or in Russia.

No one famous is named Ilya. Aside from the blond spy on MAN FROM U.N.C.L.E. reruns. That show's been off the air since before the moonshot. I think my mother had a crush on the actor or something when she was a girl, which is how I got stuck with it.

I had been afraid my whole life to ask my father this one, haunting, huge, dread question. Had I never heard of her, nor met her, nor seen her emerald eyes, beheld her golden hair, nor heard her silver voice, I never would have found the nerve.

So, technically, it is her fault, sort of.

But I don't blame her.

If you blame the damsel in distress, you are not the hero.

Before you laugh, tell me a better role for a guy like me to shoot for. A bystander? An extra? A nobody?

So, it was not because of a girl. It was because of the guy I wanted not to be.

John C. Wright   *Somewither: A Tale of the Unwithering Realm*

1) What is the POV in this excerpt?

2) What have we learned about this character and his world?

3) What do you expect this character to look like? (You're probably wrong.)

B. *Read*:

Why why why did I promise to do this?

Joel calculated in his head that he had three minutes and thirty-five seconds to pull this off. The next class started in six and half minutes. He wanted to give himself a buffer.

Three minutes and thirty-five seconds—the exact same duration as Hang on Darkness, the sixth song on Biledriver's first album.

Joel blinked a few times as he tried to refocus his thoughts.

WEEEoooWEEEoooWEEEooo

A high-pitched warbling sound squealed in his ears, accompanied by a brief, sharp pain that shot through his head from left to right. The sound lasted for two seconds, and then it was over. He looked around. No one else seemed to have heard it.

Joel rubbed his temples, closed his eyes and exhaled. It was the second time today that he had heard the strange noise, but there was no time to worry about it now.

He opened his eyes and caught a glimpse of his target: a head of long, shiny black hair cascading over a blood-red blouse. A cold, empty feeling gripped his stomach.

I can't do this. I can't even pass a stupid reading comprehension test. What makes me think I can do this?

Joel scanned the hall of his high school and saw that the other students were blocking off all possible avenues of exit. He replayed a vision of his sister in his mind.

"*You promise, right?*" Taylor's button-shaped ten-year-old face said to him.

With that, he took a deep breath and strode forward.

Three minutes exactly.

Sometimes, you just gotta say, what the heck.

And go with it.

The head of shiny black hair turned away from the locker it was facing revealing a soft, pale face with deep brown eyes and bright red lips. The eyes regarded Joel with an air of bemused expectation.

"Um, hi," Joes whispered at his shoes.

"Sorry?" the lips said as the head leaned in a little closer.

Joel cleared his throat. He had only learned two weeks ago that "sorry" in this context meant that the other person did not hear you. "Hi, um, Suzi, right?"

"Right," Suzi said. "And you are—?"

Joel could almost feel his synapses firing. "Um, Joel—I'm Joel. Joel Suzuki. We're in, uh, the same chemistry class. Honors chemistry."

Suzi's eyes widened with recognition. "Oh, yeah, second period, right? Sorry I didn't recognize you—don't you sit way in the back?"

Joel searched his brain for an appropriate response. The script was not going quite as he had planned. A large Junior Prom poster announcing a day of the week that was mismatched to the actual date distracted him for a moment. He shook his head to refocus once again. "No, I mean, yeah, I guess. It's not really way in the back, actually, it's the third desk from the back, and, uh . . ."

"Okay," Suzi chuckled. "Well, it's nice to meet you, Joel."

"Um, nice to meet you too," Joel replied. His mind started to drown in a pool of his own jumbled thoughts, one of which cried out *now what was I supposed to say next?* "Oh, well, the third desk from the back—in the second row on the right side of the room—if you're facing the class from the front, um, you know, from the teacher's perspective."

"Uh, okay," Suzi said.

Joel clenched his teeth. Faced with internal panic, he retreated to safer, familiar ground. "Um, speaking of chemistry, that's like science, right? And, um, did you know that Newton was the first person to come up with the theory of air resistance? It's like, for low flow speeds, drag is due to the dimensions of a body, the density of the fluid, and the—"

A hand with long red-painted nails closed a locker door. "Hey, um, Joel, I really have to get to class, but it's been nice talking to you, okay?"

"Oh—uh, yeah, okay," Joel stammered. He wanted to tell her that they had one hundred and thirty seconds left to get to class, but she had already turned to leave.

Brian Tashima   *Secret of the Songshell: Book One of the Spectraland Saga*

1) What is the POV of this excerpt?

2) What does referring to everybody by parts of their bodies tell you about this character?

3) What do you know about this character and world? Why is there so little description of the setting? Do you need more description to see this setting?

C. *Read*:

"My first mate's a woman," I say.

At last, a decent facial expression. Both eyebrows disappear behind his bangs.

"A woman?"

"Aye, a woman." I gesture to Devon. "Like Chase but leggier with long hair."

"Ha, ha, Talon." Devon rolls his eyes.

An unexpected smirk brightens the syndicate man's face, though I'm not sure it comes from my jab at Devon or from the thought of being subordinate to a woman.

"Got a problem answering to a woman?" I ask.

The syndicate man shrugs. "Can't tell you. Never answered to one before."

I manage to keep from frowning.

That's not the answer I expected. If he'd come from the Chimeras, he would have had women in leadership. A quarter of their higher-ups had been women. So either he's lying—or he's not Chimera.

He's definitely syndicate. He's got syndicate written all over him. But if he isn't Chimera, what is he?

He faces me fully. "I'll do whatever you want," he says. "I need to work, and I'd rather find it with someone Devon respects." His blue eyes burn into me. "And I'd rather keep my story to myself."

I could demand he tell me. I could make it part of the deal.

But, no, that's not who we are.

"No, lad," I say quietly, "your story is your own, to keep or tell as you would. That's our rule." I catch his gaze, surprised to find it relieved. "Unless it poses danger to the crew."

A muscle twitches at the back of his jaw. "Understood."

I glance at Devon, shifting from foot to foot like a child waiting for permission to open a gift.

Kale Ravenwood. The syndicate man. He's going to make me regret this. He's going to make me wish I'd never known him. If I let him on board, he's going to get us into more trouble than we can get out of, and it'll all come back to this moment, when I should have told him to shove off—and didn't.

"All right, Mr. Ravenwood," I say. "You're in for now."

He nods.

Devon cheers, drawing curious gazes from everyone else in the plaza. We both ignore him.

"If you can last the week without being killed or killing someone you aren't supposed to, you'll do fine," I say. "Otherwise?"

He doesn't respond, but I know he gets what I'm saying. He has a week to prove to me that he isn't going to get me or anyone else killed. If he can't, he's out.

"Where are you docked?" he asks.

"South Gully. We push off tomorrow at 0800."

Kale steps back and lifts his chin. "I'll be there."

A. C. Williams *Ashes*

1) What is the POV of this excerpt?
2) What did you learn about the POV character in this excerpt?
3) What did you learn about the other characters in this excerpt?

Day 3 speaking

If you know somebody, it is easy to recognize their voice. When you're face to face with someone, it is easier to understand their words and beyond their words by their intonation, inflection, body language, and facial expressions. In fact, over 70% of what is meant by a speaker is expressed by means other than the literal words. On the page, all you have are the words and a little description of expression or body language.

Dialogue in a story is not real, and you don't want it to be. What you want is dialogue that *feels* real for the character using it. A writer uses dialogue to show emotion, to further the plot, to explain the setting or worldview. You don't want long, rambling discussions where the characters talk to each other about nothing in particular for page after page.

Dialogue occurs among the characters for several reasons:
To challenge
To agree
To conspire

Thus characters involved in a dialog may:
Agree
Disagree
Agree to Disagree
Misunderstand each other
Lie to each other
Hint
Tell half-truths
Bully another character
Remain silent
Not feel free to tell everything

Side note: if your characters are huffing, scoffing, rolling their eyes, and sniping at each other for pages, you are NOT contributing to the Conflict. You might be increasing the Tension. What you are definitely doing is increasing the irritation quotient and alienating your older audience (raises hand.)

Verisimilitude is the appearance of reality. But if you want to show the reality of an argument, you should not do it by writing a twenty page scene of people arguing back and forth. (Unless you're clever enough to write a Who's On First by Abbot and Costello routine.) Again, prioritize and have the characters say only that which moves the plot along and reveals character.

How someone speaks on a page can reveal the geographical background of a character, as well as educational status, personality, mood, intention, and a host of other things. Every character has its own tics. One character might say a certain phrase a lot, might be laconic, or might pause between sentences. Another character might be a rambler. Still another might use interjections such "like" or "um." The important thing to remember is that your characters' dialog should differ one from another. Let's see what the excerpts below show us about their characters by way of dialogue.

Activities:

A. *Read*:

Gil rubbed the dog affectionately under the chin and behind both ears. "How you doing, Ruff? How is my boy? You are a good dog!"

The dog jumped and slobbered and barked happily. He licked Gil's face but then drew back, his eyes liquid and dark. The dog said sadly, "Eh! Eh! You were wounded in battle."

Gil scowled, "You know that by tasting my face?"

"Yup! Yup! And there is also the fact that there are a big bandage around your head, skinned knuckles on your forepaws, and contusions all over your hide. You were expelled this time, weren't you? Not just suspended?"

"How did you know?"

Ruff cocked his head to one side and made a chuffing noise through his nose, half snort and half sneeze. "Ha! I can smell defeat. And there is also the fact that you are here too soon in the day. You want I should lick your wounds?"

"I'd get dog germs."

"Ha! Ha! That's a myth. Dog spit is the best thing for abrasions, contusions, lacerations, and scrapes. A dog's mouth is a wonder of all-natural medicinal drool!"

So, when Gil shrugged, Ruff licked his knuckles assiduously. Gil said, "That *does* make them feel a little better, now that you mention it. Good grief, it is hot today. There is a pitcher of sweet tea there in the kitchen window, just sitting on the sill. You know any way I could get in and get it?"

"Ah! Ha! You mean like a secret doggy path we can find beneath the mountains to the buried kingdoms of the hidden folk? Uh! Oh! No, there is nothing like that here. There is a puddle in the culvert outside town I can show you. And I found a raccoon who'd been killed by a car! I can bark and scare off the crows. Some of his guts had fluid in them, or his heart maybe. That will quell any thirst! What about these dogwood fruits?"

"That is called a Cornelian Cherry. It is not a dogwood."

"Ha! Ha! Don't argue. I know trees. Here, lie down, and I will lick your head. Make you feel better!"

Gil, eyes closed and covered with sweat, was supine on the landing with his feet dangling down the steps. His shirt was unbuttoned in the hope that a breeze might wander by, exposing the ruddy, purple, blue and sooty hues of the bruises covering him. And a black and white dog was busily licking his silvery hair with its leaking red stains.

Ruff said, "Oh, you gotta tell me. I am naturally curious. I am a naturally curious dog."

"Anything, Ruff," said Gil lazily.

"Why do you get in fights so much? Why not just, you know, flop on your back and expose your throat? It is what I do when I am outmatched. Saves on stress."

John C. Wright *Swan Knight's Son: The Green Knight's Squire, Book One (Moth & Cobweb 1)*

1) What do we learn about Gil in this dialogue?

2) What do we learn about Ruff?

3) Write a few dialogue sentences about what you think a rabbit might say in this world. Then you might obtain the book and find out how close you came to the author's version.

B. *Read*:

If downtown at two AM was a mathematical equation, the answer would be 'creepy times ten.' I took a gulp of room-temperature coffee.

Outside our booth window sat a table full of Goths who clutched their coffee mugs like weapons and glared at anyone who got too close. An apparent dress code of mile-high spiked hair, ten pounds of facial piercings, and exposed boxers made the sidewalks an even bigger freak show.

Across the table, my roommate, Marc Gillam, stretched his arms above his head. The metal bracelet on his wrist clanked on the back of the booth. His mouth gaped in a silent yawn.

"Ready to go back yet?" I asked.

"Nope. Are you?"

"Oh, no. I love sitting here with my contacts getting all grainy and my chin dragging in my latte. I'm good." I took another gulp. "Just surprised you want to stay out this late with finals coming up."

"Josh, please, like you care about finals." Marc stared out into the café, drumming two fingers on the lip of his coffee cup.

I shrugged and turned back to the window. Rather that watch the passersby on the sidewalk, this time I watched the ghostly reflection of the café interior. It reduced the café to a wash of warm browns and bright splotches of clothing, the faces of everyone around me blurred beyond recognition. Even my own long face, spiked hair, and brown eyes looked vague.

Twenty-three years old, five ditched bachelor degrees, and just a few points away from getting kicked out of our military-strict college. Marc was right. Who cared about tests anyway? I yawned.

Marc ran his hand through his dark blond hair. "Heard you had a meeting with your school counselor this afternoon."

Small talk? From my best friend? I looked at him and raised one eyebrow. "Yeah. Turns out that my trig professor didn't appreciate me hacking the school BlackBoard and changing the class schedules." That'd been the least I'd done, but apparently it was the proverbial straw, which made Professor Blackaby a camel. The mental picture make me snicker.

Marc rolled his eyes. "Genius Josh strikes again."

"If I hear that nickname one more time, I'll kick your butt so hard it'll be your new belly."

He grinned. "C'mon. All you need is a pocket protector, and . . ."

I kicked his leg under the table.

"Ow! What're we now, in grade school?"

I crossed my arms on the table and rested my face on them. "Dude, why are we really here?"

"Do we need a reason?"

"Mister Perfect decides to sneak out of his dorm on a weekend, when he should be studying for finals. No, I don't need any—" I rolled my eyes and immediately regretted it when my contact stuck in the corner of my left eye. "Gah, that burns!" I pawed at it. The contact came loose and dropped into my palm.

The doorbell jingled over the coffee shop entrance. I glanced toward it. One of the aforementioned guys with mile-high hair ducked into the café's main room, his eyes running over the crowd as if he was looking for someone specific. Even with only one eye functional, I recognized the squirmy scar on his neck and the Mohawk hairdo. Blake Davis, a guy I'd gone to high school with. The gigantic linebacker's hair was purple now, and he had a few more facial piercings than when I'd known him, but the scar was too unique to be anyone else.

I started to wave.

Marc hissed.

"What?" I glanced at him.

Marc slumped down in his seat, his face turned toward the window. "I don't especially care to talk to him right now."

I lowered my hand, but Blake had already seen me. He waved back, but instead of coming across the room, he just stood by the door, staring at us. At Marc, specifically. Another guy with a spiky blue Mohawk came in the door and stopped beside Blake. They exchanged a few words, and then the blue-haired kid ducked back out. Blake never took his eyes off us the entire exchange.

"Creep," I muttered.

Marc shifted in his seat and finally looked at Blake.

His eyes narrowed.

Blake grinned, the silver stud in his lip twinkling, and pointed at Marc in an "I'm watching you" sign, first two fingers in an accusing V. He turned and pushed out the café door. For a split second, as he crossed the threshold, his skin seemed to waver, a chunk ghosting away to reveal a flash of green scales clinging to his forearm.

H. A. Titus   *Forged Steel: The Crucible, Book 1*

1) What do we learn about Josh during this late night conversation over coffee?

2) What do we learn about Marc?

3) Write a practice dialogue between two characters from your storyworld.

C. *Read*:

"I can't believe you'd be so stupid." Phoena seized a chair across from Firebird and rang for service. Her spring gown shone by morning light, and when Firebird glanced from Phoena's sparkling earrings and necklace up to the chandelier, she couldn't help comparing. As an Academy senior of noble family, Firebird had been allowed to move back to the estate for her final semester. It wasn't far from campus, and this was still her home, for a few last weeks.

"Countervoting the whole Electorate?" Phoena went on. "With a unanimity order? What's the matter with you? Have you forgotten your place?"

This year, Firebird also had learned that her music—she played the high-headed Netaian small harp, or clairsa—was a passport into the common classes. In quarters of Citangelo that Phoena never visited, she'd heard ballads that should make any elector nervous. After three hundred years, Netaia was beginning to chafe under the Electorate's absolute rule and its grip on the planet's wealth.

Firebird faced her sister squarely. "You know what I think about your basium project. If I had to do it again, I'd still vote my conscience. You're not expanding our buffer zone. You only want a show of power."

"So you said." Phoena buffed her nails on the sleeve of her gown. "We heard you clearly yesterday."

Firebird laid her palms on the scanbook viewer. "You got your commendation, didn't you? Twenty-six to one."

"One." Phoena lifted an eyebrow. "In your position, I think I'd be trying to live awhile. You're lucky the redjackets haven't already wasted you. Wastlings who countervote don't last. You're only in there for show, you know. For your *honor*," she mocked.

Firebird curled her fingers around her scanbook viewer. "There's no *honor*," she mimicked Phoena's tone, "in threatening worlds that would rather trade with us than attack us." Phoena's project was secret, and no commoner knew of it. Still, Firebird had used her vote to express her people's earnestly sung longings to live in free, fair peace.

"You never should have had electing rights to begin with," Phoena retorted.

The door swung beyond Phoena. Firebird fell silent, toying with her cruinn cup. Carradee pushed through. A servitor-class attendant followed the tallest and eldest Angelo sister. A deep green robe draped Carradee's form, now swollen with a second pregnancy.

Firebird's life expectancy had almost zeroed.

"Carrie," Firebird murmured as the crown princess sank into a cushioned chair held by the servant. "You look exhausted."

Carradee sighed and splayed her fingers on her belly. "With the little one's dancing all night, it's a wonder I sleep at all. And I'm so worried for you, Firebird. Why must you try so hard to throw away the time that's left to you?"

Phoena leaned back and fixed Firebird with dark eyes.

Easy for Phoena to smirk now, Firebird reflected, but it hadn't always been that way. Phoena had been born a wastling. Firebird was three at the time and Phoena six, both beginning their indoctrination into their holy destiny, when their second-born sister had been found smothered. Investigation had implicated the programmer of Lintess's favorite toy, a lifelike robot snow bear, but—as with the death of their father years later—Firebird harbored suspicions about Phoena that she didn't care to voice.

She watched the scarlet-liveried servitor hurry out. "How can you condone fouling a world, Carradee?" She spread her hands on the tabletop. "Aren't some things worth standing against?"

"But, Firebird—oh!" Carradee grimaced and stroked her stretched belly. "I'll be glad when this is over."

Firebird bit her lip.

Phoena seized the opening like a weapon. "Five weeks," she crowed. "Then there'll be a shift in the family."

Carradee turned pale gray eyes to Phoena in mute reprimand.

Firebird snapped her viewer off. "I'll have longer than that. They'll send me with the invasion force. I would love to fly strike, just once. And I'd rather die flying than . . ." She bit back the comparison. Another grief was still too fresh to expose to Phoena. Lord Randy Gellison had wanted badly to live, had lived hard and wild.

She shook her elbow-length hair behind her shoulders and stood to leave. Phoena's breakfast had arrived, carried by a mincing whitehaired servitor. Netaia's penal laws supplied the noble class with hereditary laborers, who lived caught between the fear of further punishment and the hope that exemplary service would win freedom. Some of the finest musicians Firebird had known, and some of the kindest people, had been servitors.

She snatched up her scanbook and swung out the door. Phoena called after her, "I'll help put the black edging on your portrait."

Kathy Tyers *Firebird*

1) This masterful blend of dialogue, body language, narrative summary, or telling, as well as description and action, has told us a lot about this world in two pages. What do we know about Phoena now?

2) What did the dialogue show about Firebird?

3) Write a practice dialogue with two of your characters from your storyworld that demonstrate hate without the characters screaming at each other. Save it in your file.

Day 4 consistency

Character skills and traits must become known to the reader, and they must be consistent. If your character defeats her enemy with a sword, you need to show her using a sword competently at the beginning of the story or show her gaining competency. You cannot just suddenly pull an ability out during the Big Boss Battle. Readers won't like you if you do that. It feels like a cheat. Think about the movie Star Wars: The Force Awakens, which came out in 2015. The Big Boss Battle scene shows a wispy girl fighting the Darth Vader Wannabee with a lightsaber. Finn, the ex-soldier with her has been badly wounded by Kylo, but Rey is able to hold Kylo off until a rift in the ground separates them. Some people who weren't paying attention called foul at this point and said she had never fought with a lightsaber before, so how was she able to fight with Kylo and not be instantly dissected? The answer is given earlier in the movie. We saw Rey fight off two thieves larger than her, and then she beat the stuffing out of Finn. The girl has shown she can fight. Later, we see her have a vision when Maz hands her a lightsaber. So we know she has the midichlorians that will make her strong in the Force. And so when she and Kylo meet, she can fight him with the lightsaber and we know she might have a chance.

(I will grant the critics the point that a staff is not a light saber. I will even grant that Kylo should have been a great deal more injured for Rey to succeed as well as she did. But the point remains that the moviemakers attempted to show Rey as a willing and competent fighter before the Big Boss Battle with Kylo.)

What ability does your character need to show before the Big Boss Battle?

Activity:

1) Either take three characters from your story or make up three characters and make character charts for each of them. Include information about the name, gender, appearance, age, personality, religion, family, community, usual clothing, work, status, likes, strengths, weaknesses, unusual abilities aka competencies, usual food, friends, and fears. Also list three most important things in the world for each. Save the charts in your file.

Day 5 demonstrating

It is not enough to tell your reader that your character is really good at what he does. You need to show the reader the character doing something that DEMONSTRATES the character being good at something. We need to SEE him throwing darts or hypnotizing chickens or climbing cliffs long before the climax, and preferably at the very beginning of the story.

Activity

1) Take the three characters from yesterday and write practice scenes that demonstrate the character's sense of humor, or lack thereof. Don't tell us. Show us by their behavior, speech, and inner thoughts.

CHAPTER EIGHT:

HEROES, VILLAINS, SIDEKICKS, AND BYSTANDERS

Every story must have a hero, a protagonist, or a main character. Call this person whatever you want. I use the terms interchangeably. The hero is the one who stands on the side of right and the one the author intends for us to root for. He may go on a Hero's Journey. The antihero is the one who stands in the place of the hero but lacks nearly all the heroic traits. The reader is still expected to root for the antihero despite his flaws because he will have some kind of redeeming feature.

The hero will usually have a full name. Sometimes the hero remains nameless, usually in stories where the climax or the reveal lets the reader know the hero is not what the reader thought it was. Somewhere in the story he will be described in detail. Not every detail that you know about the hero, but enough to move the story forward and make him understandable.

Every story must have an antagonist, which can be a villain, but not necessarily. The opponent can be a nice guy who wants the world to have all the nice things the hero wants, but disagrees on how to make the nice things happen. The antagonist does not need to be human. It can be something from nature such as a hurricane or a monster or plague. It can be an unjust social system. She or it will be named in the story and described, sometimes in detail. In some ways, the villain is the driver of the story because she or it causes the inciting incident and pushes the conflict. If the villain is weak, the story is weak.

Not every story needs sidekicks aka contagonists. They are the people who help out either the hero or villain. Sidekicks will often see themselves as heroes because all of us are the hero of our own story. They can be wonderful sounding boards for the hero, the people the hero needs to save, the people who make the observations the hero does not say aloud, the people who train the hero. They might ally themselves with the hero, or they might incidentally help (or hurt) the hero as they go about their lives. If their action is important enough, they might gain a single name and a few details. Sometimes the contagonist will become so important, that character will become another protagonist or antagonist. You can have more than one protagonist or antagonist per story.

Not every story needs, but usually does have bystanders, spear carriers, extras. They are the mass of people the hero saves, the people walking down the same street the hero does, the other customers in the coffee shop. They are the crowd, the crew, the people who get to hang around the captain only if they are wearing a red shirt. They are not given names for the most part. Descriptions of them will be brief or nonexistent.

Day 1 hero

You have a hero, protagonist, main character. Your reader will be willing to spend hundreds of pages reading time with your hero if they like *something* about your hero (or are enchanted by the setting.) Yes, your hero should have some flaws the reader can identify with. She should have some strength or ability that will resolve the conflict during the Big Boss Battle, or climax. Many modern stories skip a climax and the need for the main character to be heroic, but I am talking about the average speculative fiction story.

She should also be likable even if she needs to mature. Professional writers know how to make their heroes likable, and now I will let you in on their secrets. Your hero won't need ALL the following characteristics, but she will need a lot of them. And some she must have.

She must be courageous. She might not be brave at the beginning, but the possibility is there. Perhaps she is not brave at the beginning, or she is too docile, or pathetic. But if she loves an animal that is in danger, she will change. She will fake bravery, become more assertive, or emotional enough to do what she must. She can be fearful and shaking, but when it comes time to save the kitty, she will overcome her fear and Save The Kitty.

She must have some ability or character trait that possibly no one else has or be shown gaining that ability. Even if other people can do what she does, it helps if other people recognize that she is good at what she does. Or she may have an intellectual or physical ability that everyone else has but she has more heart. Alternately, she might have less ability than everyone else but is more motivated. Also others might not recognize her skill. Many heroes are not respected at the beginning

She must be in danger. The danger can be psychological or physical. If the stakes are not high, why would the reader care? Sometimes she's not in danger at the beginning of the story, but will encounter peril because of her decisions and actions, actions of the antagonists, and consequences of time setting, location, and actions of others.

She must be dependable. If she breaks a promise, it must be because of events outside her control and she must feel anguished about the promise-breaking for the rest of the story. She might have made the broken promise because she had wrong information, or she thought unrealistically about her skills. She must do all she is capable of to keep her promises.

She should be loved by somebody who will miss her if she gets squished. Of course, some heroes will feel unloved, unworthy of love, or may lose everyone who loves them.

She should be kind. This is not always necessary if all the other traits are strong, but there should be at least one person she loves and cares about. Niceness to people around her goes a long way to engaging the reader. A subset of kindness is generosity.

She should be assertive, or journeying toward assertiveness, someone who will act to resolve the conflict. She shouldn't make someone else resolve the conflict. She might ask other people to resolve the conflict at the beginning, because she is unsure of herself, but eventually she is the one who must act. If she is not the one who acts, she is not the hero.

She should be focused, obsessed, willing to do whatever it takes to reach her goal.

Despite her obsessiveness, she should be just and fair. No one likes a cheater. Thus, even if we have a Robin Hood type waif trickster street urchin who steals, she must steal from the rich AND give to the poor.

She should want to be a part of something larger than herself and love at least one person besides herself. Ancillary to this is she should have some ideal she is trying to live up to.

She should be a loyal friend.

She could be unfairly damaged. This is important for reader identification. She might have suffered at the hand of thieves or the mouth of gossipers. She might have been slighted or humiliated by or lost her family. This emotional, financial, or physical loss is woven into her motivation even if it is not directly connected to her primary goal. If her entire village was devastated by a flood, she might not be angry at floods but she will be motivated against anything that destroys the lives and livelihood of the poor homesteaders, whether the antagonist be another flood, an evil tyrant kicking people off the land, or a leaky nuclear power plant being built upriver. The reader will want justice for her and understand why she is motivated to reach her primary goal.

She could be funny. Many readers love the hero with a sense of humor, someone who does not take herself so seriously that she makes other people miserable. Unless, or course, those people should be miserable.

She could have a pet. That will let her demonstrate kindness and care. A pet will make it easy for her to have a Pet The Kitty moment. If she kicks the cat, we will assume she is a villain.

She could be friendly and charming.

She could be an underdog or handicapped by the loss of her family and its support structure. Even if she is depressed she should have an inner strength.

An automatic way to make your hero likable is to make her resemble your target audience. That is why nearly all Young Adult books focus on teenage protagonists.

What the hero must *not* be.

She must *not* be a Mary Sue. What's a Mary Sue? The term is taken from the world of fanfic. The name means a character who is perfect at everything, adored by all the other characters in the story, and is frequently told how perfect she is. Usually, the character is an idealized self of the writer.

Some people make thinly veiled versions of themselves to be the hero of every story they write. I would rather you wrote about people who are not you. You will then be less tempted to turn your hero into a Mary Sue or Marty Stu.

Here are a few more things your hero must *not* be or you will lose your entire audience.
Your hero must not be cruel to vulnerable people. That's saved for the villain.
Your hero should not be whiny. Don't ask me how I know this.
Your hero should not be vain throughout the entire book.
Your hero must not be passive and end up rescued by the actions of someone else.
Your hero must not be completely and totally perfect. Oh, I already said that.
Your hero should not have so many flaws that she might as well be the villain.

Some strange is good, but your hero should not be *so* strange that nobody can find a single thing to identify with. Remember that your reader wants to have an emotional experience by identifying with the hero and vicariously living through the experiences of the hero.

Activities:

A. *Read*:

Madame took a step forward, bony hand held out in front of her, finger jabbing toward Birdie's face like a spear. "Mad as a night moth," she declared. "A lazy, useless, worthless child! That's what you are! Useless since the day Dalton picked you up off the road! Twelve years now, I've put up with this nonsense. And what have you done in return? Lolled around like a daisy. Spouted insane nonsense and caused endless trouble for my poor sons!"

Birdie caught sight of Kurt and Miles, the "poor sons" in question, peering at her around the door frame. Poor sons? More like two terrors. Miles stuck his tongue out before Kurt jerked him out of sight.

"Well, I've no use for a half-wit or a mad girl! A girl whose own parents didn't care enough to bother with and abandoned to the kindness of strangers . . ."

The words stung more than Madame's blows, but Birdie had heard them all before. Worthless. Half-wit. Mad girl. On and on Madame's rant continued, until she could no longer distinguish the individual words.

She studied the stone floor beneath her toes, clenching her fists to hold back her rising anger. She had to get out of here . . . had to get away. Without a word, she spun on her heels, pushed past the startled woman, and tore through the common room out into the clear light of day. She slammed the front door, enclosing Madame's furious shouts within the walls of the inn.

Birdie ran. Past the barn, across the dusty inn yard, and out over the hills surrounding the Sylvan Swan Inn. Autumn grass crinkled beneath her feet. ... Sobs rose in her throat, smothering her anger, and she flung herself flat against the cool brown earth and cried into her arms.

Deep below, a sepulchral rumbling from the depths of the earth—a distant melody—rose to greet her. Warm as a summer sunrise, the song caught her up in its embrace. The tears dried on her face. Her sorrow eased. The song was familiar—she had known it all her life—and yet new and wondrous, something too great to be fully known or understood. It spiraled upward, carrying her soul to reach for the sky. Then it stopped abruptly and the melody faded away.

Gillian Bronte Adams   *Orphan's Song*

1) What likeability features does Birdie have?
2) What might her special abilities be?
3) What is this character's normal?

B. *Read*:

When the coach jolted forward, Franz fell heavily on his side, unable to support himself because of the restraining straight-jacket. He wanted to scream but clamped his jaw tight. He wouldn't give all those onlookers the satisfaction of hearing a lunatic's yells. The coach bumped over the cobbled street, and Franz almost tumbled from the seat onto the floor, only just managing to brace his feet against the opposite seat and keep himself in place.

Was this the end of everything for him? His existence hadn't been particularly pleasant up until now, but at least it wasn't utterly, beyond all reason *horrible*. Sure, life as a poor coalman's son wasn't all ease and smiles, but he'd learned how to read and write, and managed to clean himself up enough to acquire a clerk's position with Mr. Teabody. He'd earned a full three shillings a day, enough to keep a very small room at the boarding house, sleep on a clean-ish straw mattress, and eat two square-ish meals a day.

All of those luxuries seemed long ago now . . .

Time passed. The coach left behind the cobbled streets and turned onto the main road outside of town, then passed to a smaller, dirt road. The rattling and rumbling became unbearable, and Franz half wondered if he'd arrive at Briardale with his limbs broken in pieces.

What would life in a lunatic asylum be like? Would he be forced to share a cell with other madmen? Visions flashed through his mind, horror stories told of Briardale and its inhabitants. Somehow he knew, he just *knew*, they would eat him alive.

"Dear me, you're still angry, aren't you?"

Franz's heart stopped. He stared in horror as, on the seat opposite—just where he'd braced his feet to keep himself from falling—something green and misty materialized, swirling and shapeless at first, but resolving at last into the face and form of . . .

"You!" Franz snarled.

Sitting cross-legged before him, her chin on her hands and her eyes blinking with deceptive innocence, was the ghoulish green girl who was the source of all his woe.

She smiled at him, displaying a full set of glowing teeth. "At least you're acknowledging me again." She closed one eye as though to study him more intently through the other, then screwed up her face. "They surely haven't been kind to you through this whole business, have they? Calling you insane! The nerve! But then, that's what you get for throwing things at people."

Never before in his life had Franz wished this much to throttle anyone, but there were important reasons why he couldn't. First, she was a girl, and he would never hit a girl even if she were as annoying as this translucent green creature.

The second reason was that he was helplessly strapped, so, even if she'd been some sort of brute, the only harmful thing he could do was glare.

So Franz slouched down in his seat, satisfying his fury by sending her a glare that bore the weight of a thousand hurling penknives. "During our last conversation, I believe I made it quite clear to you that I never wanted to see your ugly face again."

She "tut-tutted" at him, shaking her head. "Sorry, but I'm afraid I can't abandon you now that we're actually on our way there. While this isn't perhaps the best way to get you there, we should arrive well before nightfall. And that leaves a whole night and a day for you to do what you need to do and save us all. I think that's plenty of time, don't you?"

Grace Mullins   *The Ghost of Briardale   Five Magic Spindles: A Collection of Sleeping Beauty Stories*

1) What likeable features does Franz possess?
2) What was the normal for Franz?
3) What is the inciting incident that makes him leave normal?

C. *Read*:

I took a deep breath and walked into my own personal nightmare. A room full of strangers wandered around making polite conversation, and I was standing all alone in the crowd. No matter how many banquets I attend, and regardless of the conversational skills I have to carry them off, they still tie a knot in my stomach, leave my head pounding and my palms soaked with perspiration. No one notices, except me.

Put me in front of a class or even moderating a breakfast session at a vid conference in front of thousands of people across the globe, and I am fine. Invite me to a dinner party, and you will find me in the car hyperventilating trying to pluck up courage to go in.

I felt as if I was back in high school. The girl with the old clothes from the thrift shop, a stack of books in hand, scraggly hair, too smart about some things and too dumb about others. Teachers' pet and ostracized by my peers. The taunts of my classmates still echoed through my mind every time I entered a room filled with people.

After standing awkwardly just inside the door for what seemed like a century. I made my way to the buffet table. I filled my plate with cheeses, crackers, a few fresh veggies, some strawberries, melon, and a dollop of onion dip.

Terri Main   *Dark Side of the Moon*

1) Why does the protagonist feel differently about giving lectures to thousands of people versus going to a dinner party with some tens of strangers?

2) How many senses are appealed to, aka sensory details, in this excerpt? Do they help immerse you into the experience the protagonist is having?

3) What are the likability features of this protagonist?

Day 2 villain

The villain, the antagonist, the Big Boss, the one out to destroy our hero's life

If the antagonist is non-human or non-sentient being, it must be either unrelenting, all-powerful, or hard to change.

Non-human antagonists have no personal grudge against the protagonist. A mountain, tsunami, or devastating comet is not going to get up and move simply because your protagonist wants it to. If Time is your antagonist for instance, your protagonist must race against it. Time generally is relentless. Therefore, your protagonist cannot change time unless he is a master of time or a time traveler. And even then, changing a past event is difficult. If your antagonist is sub-freezing temperature on Mars, your protagonist will have to find a way to get out of the cold. If your antagonist is the rules of an evil society, those rules will be hard to change.

If the antagonist is an emotional, physical, or intellectual flaw within the main character, then you have a man versus himself story and although other antagonists may exist in the story, the primary antagonist resides within the main character. He must conquer his own flaw for the story to end satisfactorily.

If the villain is human or alien, it is easy to make the villain a cardboard character who twirls his moustache while cackling in glee. Bwa-ha-ha and all.

As a writer, you need to do better than that. You need to remember that everyone is the hero of their own story. Perhaps the villain knows he is smarter or more ethical than anyone else, and so he deserves to rule. Perhaps the villain wants revenge for all the wrongs the world has done him. Perhaps the villain is so depressed by his worldview that life sucks like a chest wound and then you die, that he develops a hatred of the hero and strives to make the hero miserable enough to admit that life sucks and then you die.

Every villain will have a REASON why she is evil, or at least opposing your hero. The reason will not likely be that she just enjoys being evil. She is doing evil in an attempt to accomplish *something*. That something might be gain approval of or revenge for Dad. It might be she knows the world would be a better world if it didn't have certain kinds of people. It might be she longs for a sense of power, i.e. I can hurt you but you can't hurt me. There might be a motivation of jealousy, of fear that she will lose something that is precious to her, say, honor, the boyfriend, or people who envy her, because of the hero.

Just like for the hero, you ought to know what is motivating the villain. You should know what his "three most important things in the world" are. (Thank you Randy Ingermanson for your books about writing, including *Writing Fiction for Dummies*.)

Other writers find more useful the concept: What lies does the hero believe at the beginning of the book? What truths does the hero learn by the end of the book? What lies does the villain believe and cling to with tenacity?

A villain is often someone who is very like the hero. Perhaps he even shares some goals, personality traits, and ideals with the hero. The hero and the villain may both have experienced unjust damage, but the somewhere along the way, the villain has gone too far off track and has lost his way. Just as we share some traits with the hero, we also share some traits with the villain.

You need to understand what warped your villain so you can make him believable and worthy of suspending disbelief.

The following list does not necessarily depict all villains, but if you see the following characteristics you can be pretty sure the character is a villain.

He is a bully.

He breaks promises flippantly or purposefully, having made the promise without an intention to keep it. He may have used the promise only to gain something he needs or wants.

He stabs people in the back.

He is cruel.

He spends time looking for ways to hurt someone else in the book, such as the hero or someone the hero loves.

He might sneer at heroes because he is sure the hero is faking it or does not deserve credit.

He often projects his ill-will on everyone else. Alternately, he might know he is wrong, but feels that the ends justify the means.

He steals the credit that belongs to someone else.

He blames other people instead of himself and believes it when he says, "You forced me to hurt you." Or he may love people other than the hero passionately and never hurt them.

He knows he is better than all the idiots surrounding him.

He might have an exquisite sense of all the injustices done to him but either not care or not notice the sufferings of others.

Activities:

A. *Read*:
This is a reimagining of Sleeping Beauty.

> The dragon roared, … Arabella saw the great black beast rise into the air on its massive wings and race away through the blue sky to freedom.
>
> "My dragon! What have you done?"
>
> Startled at the new fury in Rhoswen's voice, Arabella turned and saw her cousin clutching her own temples, her face white with wrath.
>
> "It is free now," Arabella said, "even as I am. You hold us captive no more."
>
> Rhoswen turned to her, eyes huge, teeth bared. "The grave will be your prison now!" she cried in a voice scarcely human. She reached to her side and pulled a gleaming knife from a leather sheath. With trembling hands she clutched its carved handle and strode toward Arabella.
>
> Stepping backward, Arabella lifted both hands. "Haven't you taken enough from me?" Though she saw only madness in her cousin's face, she tried to keep her voice calm and reasonable.
>
> "Not yet, I haven't! I've always hated you, my perfect cousin, and I could not allow you to hurt this kingdom. Consumed by your pleasures and vanities, you were no more fit to rule than my father was in his greed!"
>
> "And are you fit to rule, Rhoswen? You who have driven the fairies nearly to extinction? Are you, with murder in your heart, as benevolent as you believe?"

"I do what I must!" Rhoswen screamed. Then she charged forward, the knife raised high, its deadly blade flashing.

Michelle Pennington   *Spindle Cursed*   *Five Magic Spindles: A Collection of Sleeping Beauty Stories*

1) Who does Rhoswen think is the villain?

2) Why does Rhoswen think she's the hero?

3) Does the villain in your story think (s)he is the hero? Why or why not?

B. *Read*:

Brandon's back collided with the unforgiving surface, hard enough to stun him. Not that being able to fight back would have done him any good. It never did. His father's fist slammed into his stomach, making him choke and double over. A heavy hand seized his shoulder to keep him upright. A few more punches were then delivered. Each one calculated to hurt but not enough to send him to the hospital. They had been there, done that. It wasn't a fun thing to try to explain to hospital staff. Not with his dad looming over him, portraying so much fatherly concern that veiled a deadly threat.

Brandon could have told the staff that he had been run over by a herd of buffalo to excuse the bruises and they would have bought it if his father backed it. How that worked, he couldn't say. It just happened that way with no plausible reasoning behind it.

Brandon was helpless as sharp pain radiated from his midsection. The breath was knocked out of him. If not for the grip on his shoulder, he would have been on his knees.

He could feel his dad's anger like an invisible force; a tangible heat that wilted everything in its path.

"Stand up straight!" Tanner's voice boomed at him as he wrapped a hand around Brandon's throat to 'help' him accomplish the order.

Brandon gasped as he was slammed against the wall again. Would it end with him dying? It felt as if it might. His dad knew better than to choke him since that would leave bruising. As it was, he might still bear some marks around his throat, but he had the weekend for them to fade.

Another punch was delivered to his gut. He let out a choking sob, his body filled with pain and his soul full up with fear. Tears began to fall, dribbling from thick, dark lashes. He wanted nothing more than to curl up in a ball on the floor. It was all his body seemed capable of. His legs had turned to rubber. He hands shook as he grabbed at his father's hand around his neck. He wanted to say something. His lower lip quivered as he tried, but nothing coherent came out.

"Stupid, cowardly boy," Tanner snarled, releasing him.

Then Brandon was allowed to fall to his knees. He curled over them, arms wrapping over his stomach as if he could find a way to band-aid his aching innards. The incoming sobs didn't help the pain as they made his stomach muscles hitch and shake. Movement caught his attention and he looked through a blur of tears. What now?

Tanner had grabbed the game again. Since he wouldn't master opening the box, he threw it on the floor and then stomped on it with all his impressive might. The game didn't stand a chance as it was flattened and shattered against the nicely polished, wood floor.

"No more games!" Tanner bellowed at his defeated son. He turned on his heel to stalk off towards a different part of the house. Probably to take more temper out on his wife.

A. J. Bakke   *The Hidden Level*

1) What story do you think Tanner tells himself to justify this?

2) What villain characteristics are displayed here?

3) What item do you think will play a prominent part for the rest of the novel?

C. *Read*:
At a dinner party where new professors are being introduced to the staff of a university on the moon:

"People are people anywhere, and human nature is human nature regardless. I spent twenty-odd years as a cop. Most people don't know the true depravity of the human race, but I do." He almost sounded proud of this disturbing admission.

"I guess that is true. The Bible says that the heart of man is deceitful and wicked, and we do not even know it most of the time. But I believe people can control those urges, and that you can screen out those who are less likely to be able to control them. People are capable of divinity as well as devilry," I countered.

"Oh, I see you are one of those lunatic church people believing all that bunk about redemption and the hidden worth in even the worst sinner. Well, some people are beyond redemption, and you're just crazy to believe otherwise. The church had 2200 years and look at the mess we've still got on earth. Your church will take its hypocrisy to the moon as well. But you're right. People got evil lurking in their hearts. I don't know anymore if God exists, but I know the devil does. I've looked him in the eyes too many times."

"I'm sorry, I didn't catch your name." It seemed silly since I had just been wearing the data specs but, it was the only thing I could think to say while trying to control my anger. Whatever his beliefs, he had no right to brush aside mine as if they were trivial. Being a Christian is not popular among academics, but most have the courtesy to respect my beliefs even if they do not share them.

"Oh, Mike Cheravik. I'm going to be teaching political science, sociology and criminology at the university. I spent twenty years as a detective on the Dallas police force. I quit when those do-gooders outlawed the death penalty. Just couldn't stomach seeing scumbags get away with murder. So, I went back to school, got a few degrees, and started teaching. I was teaching at O'Neill U when I got the offer from Armstrong. O'Neill offered to double my pay to stay, but I was ready to leave. Had been for years."

I silently repented of my anger as I began to understand the source of this man's cynicism. More than once staring at the remains of a child butchered by a serial killer, I had asked God where He was. Yet, somehow, my faith never completely left me, although it sometimes seemed far away.

Regardless of how excusable his attitudes, I felt the need to defend my faith. "I can understand your feelings. I spent time in law enforcement as well, but I would appreciate you respecting my religious beliefs. I am a Christian and that does not make me naïve or stupid."

Terri Main *Dark Side of the Moon*

1) Is there a villain here?
2) What are the villainous features of Mike?
3) What are the likability features of Mike?

Day 3 standing around

Bystanders, contagonists, extras, spear carriers, the crowd: these are the people that that aid or hinder or simply observe the hero. They can also be considered secondary and tertiary characters that provide backdrop and context.

If a character spends a lot of time with the hero or villain, talks to them, and helps or hinders either, that character will rise to the level of sidekick. He or she will gain a name, possibly two, and you, the writer, should know at least enough of her background that you understand her motivations. They also help to promote the plot. Their work, status, safety, may affect the plot but only in minor ways. The child injured on Planet Beta 9 that needs to be sent to the hospital on Earth Two, the only hospital in the region. The many space pirates in the badlands of the asteroid belt that the hero must conquer or avoid in order to save the aforementioned child. The director of the hospital staff awaiting the child. The grieving worried mother of the sick child who has already lost her first child to Space Virus 296. The hero, of course has a navigator, but that is his sidekick. Then there is the main villain out there somewhere, poisoning the water tanks of the space colonists. But these other secondary characters also matter. The reader probably either doesn't need to know the background or needs to know very little. A contagonist, such as the aforementioned navigator, deserves some description. So does the child who will arouse pity in the reader.

A spear carrier, or extra, such as a nurse, a lady's maid, or a general on the other hand, someone who only provides a backdrop to the action, seldom deserves any description other than the job the character has. This kind of character helps the setting come alive for the reader. For example, if the hero goes to a coffee shop and doesn't need to wait in line behind a harried attorney talking on the phone with his partner, the setting will feel oddly empty.

If an extra spends some time interacting with the hero, a short line or two of description is not remiss. The reader does not need a name.

Tertiary or third level characters, such as The Crowd, need only the briefest of descriptions. They were splendidly attired. They wore rags. Whatever fits and is simple.

Anybody you spend time and description on will be thought to be important by the reader. Don't fool the reader by spending that time on someone who only shows up once.

Activities:

A. *Read*:

    The rest of my morning, classes are much the same. Two out of the four teachers are gone, and one of the remaining ones is obviously sick. There are lots of questions as to why we're even bothering with school, but no one has the answers.

    At lunchtime I get my food and then try to sneak out to the courtyard and as far away from everyone else as possible. Nearly to my goal, I spot Chris walking up quickly to me.

    "Alex!" he calls out, even though we've already made eye contact. "Why don't you come sit with me?" Unsure for a moment, I decide there's really no point to evasion anymore. This virus surrounds me. I'm probably literally covered in it. If I'm going to get it, there isn't anything I can do about it now. I follow him back to a nearby table and take a seat.

    There are only two other kids eating with us, neither of them friends of mine. Chris tells me their names, but I quickly forget them. I just want to talk with him about my Dad's book, having come to the conclusion that he may be the only person here I can confide in.

    Eating slowly, I try to pay attention to the small talk around the table, smiling and nodding at what I think may be the right times. I don't really hear any of it though. The constant noise that's always in this room fills my head, and the smell I have come to lovingly think of as the 'cafeteria funk' assaults me. I can't take it anymore. I have to get outside.

                               Tara Ellis   *Infected: The Shiners*

1) How many students were in the cafeteria? Does it matter whether it's twenty-five or one hundred fifty?

2) There is no description of the cafeteria. Why not?

3) Why did the writer tell us about the other two people at the table instead of show us Chris introducing them by name and then showing what they looked like?

B. *Read*:

    I was putting fresh oil into clay lamps at the altar when the mantis glided into my foyer. The creature stopped for a moment, his antennae dancing in the air, sensing the few parishioners who sat on my roughly-hewn stone pews. I hadn't seen a mantis in a long time—the aliens didn't bother with humans much, now that we were shut safely behind their Wall. Like all the rest of his kind, this mantis's lower thorax was submerged into the biomechanical "saddle" of his floating mobility disc. Only this one's disc didn't appear to have any apertures for weapons—a true rarity on Purgatory.

    Every human head in the building turned towards the visitor, each set of human eyes smoldering with a familiar, tired hate.

    "I would speak to the Holy Man," said the mantis through the speaker box on its disc. It's fearsome, segmented beak had not moved. …

When nobody got up to leave, the mantis began floating up my chapel's central aisle, the mantis's disc making a gentle humming sound.

"Alone," said the visitor, his vocoded voice approximating a commanding human tone.

Heads and eyes turned to me. I looked at the mantis, considered my options, then bowed to my flock, who reluctantly began to leave—each worshipper collecting handfuls of beads, crosses, stars, serviceman's Bibles, and various other religious items. They exited without saying a word. What else could they do? The mantes ruled Purgatory as surely as Lucifer ruled Hell.

Brad R. Torgersen   *The Chaplain's War*

1) Who do you think the hero will be? Why?

2) Who do you think the villain will be? Why?

3) Who are the spear carriers?

C. *Read*:

The summer campers are eating their first meal in a massive castle. They had expected tents or cabins. And the people running the camp seem very odd.

...She paused and looked at the others. "Does anyone else attend boarding school?"

Sarah shook her head. "Levi and I are both homeschooled. I don't know about anybody else." She glanced between the others.

Trevor said, "Private school."

"I'm homeschooled." Steve turned brick red.

Ashley mumbled something about going to a Christian school. Tommy nodded.

"Well, I go to boarding school 'cause Momma's a U.S. Senator." Lizzie lifted a pink-nailed hand and tossed back her hair. "She's in DC a lot of the time."

"Oh?" Monica tilted her head. "Is your school in Washington?"

"Sure is."

Levi's sleep-deprived mind tuned out the conversation as Sara prattled on about their hall chaperone, someone named Miss Nydia, who'd promised to teach the girls all about sewing. Who cared about sewing? All he wanted was to climb into his comfy-looking bed upstairs.

"What do you think?" A low voice from the table behind him sharpened his fading brain. "Could it have been some sort of giant projection that looked like a cliff? Like, some big screen that gets moved . . . somehow . . . so you see the castle when they want you to?"

Levi's pulse quickened. If someone else had seen the precipice, then Levi wasn't crazy. He glanced over his shoulder. Martin, his face pale, leaned near Hunter.

Disappointment stole over Levi when he saw who had spoken, but he shook it away. Even creepy Hunter and his thug buddy Martin were better than nobody.

"It wasn't a screen," Hunter said in a loud voice. "These people are aliens." When several people stared at him, he grinned and spoke even louder. "It's true. I mean, haven't you looked at these people? They're not normal."

Amy C. Blake   *The Trojan Horse Traitor*

1) If you had read from the beginning of the story, the flurry of names in the excerpt would not be confusing as the writer had introduced each person carefully, one at a time. The writer can afford such a large named cast because she has an entire novel for them to move in. The story is told from whose point of view?

2) Can you tell who the villain is yet? Are you sure?

3) Who are the contagonists?

Day 4 likability

Which likability features does your hero have? Keep in the forefront of your mind that your readers want to identify with the protagonist. They want to read about adventures of people like them or people they want to *be* like.

Which likability features does your villain have? How is the villain like you? How is he not like you?

Activity:

1) If the hero of your story has no likability features, add some today, either in a character chart or in some practice paragraphs.

Day 5 does this make sense?

What understandable motive does your villain have? Unless your villain is a born sociopath, the character needs a reason for the villainous behavior. Even insane people have reasons for their behavior. They might be insane reasons, but they are still reasons.

If it's too hard for you to think why somebody who isn't you does the things she does, then search yourself. Do you always adhere to whatever your standard of good is? What made you violate your own standards?

Activity:

1) If your villain has no discernable motives for pounding on the hero, add some today, either in a character chart or in some practice paragraphs.

CHAPTER NINE:

CHARACTER ARC

I once heard an author, who wrote Star Trek novels for the company that owned the Star Trek franchise, assert that what she wrote was not literature. The reason her novels were not literature was that none of the characters changed. Captain Kirk, Uhura, Spock, Sulu, all of them, at the end of the novel they were exactly the same as they were at the beginning of the novel. If the characters did not change, then it was not literature.

I disagree with that premise.

Granted, her novels were not Character novels. They were Idea or Event novels.

We have many examples of literature with no character arc. For example, how much did the Gingerbread Man change between the time he leaped out of the oven and the time the fox snapped him up? Okay, he went from alive to dead, but how much did his taunting, running character change? How much did Alice in Wonderland change? She moved inside a Milieu story, and change was not required to move the plot along. Serial stories where each episode can be read or watched in any order seldom have character arcs.

Here's one way I do agree with that author: stories with a character arc are usually far richer than stories without a character arc.

What is a character arc?

Glad you asked. A character arc is where the character begins with a set of emotions, habitual behavior, or worldview, and by the end of the story, the character has changed. Perhaps the character entered the story world hopeless and afraid, but because of her choices and the circumstances that changed because of her choices, by the end of the story she has become confident and hopeful. Perhaps a character starts out arrogant and strong, but because he is deposed or crippled or sickened or betrayed, he ends up humble.

Perhaps, like Frodo in The Lord of the Rings, he starts out a humble homebody, who ends up being the kind of person who can stop a mighty enemy.

A hero's character arc, or inner journey, will run parallel to the plot.

There is a fairly short Act I, where the character has a particular set of beliefs, attitudes, and actions within the normal setting.

Then comes the inciting incident, the call, a pinch point that ends Act I or starts Act II, which occupies most of the story. The character's beliefs and attitudes are challenged throughout setbacks and disasters. Often, in the mid-point of Act II, the character has a moment of truth where it reflects on how what it's been doing has not been working. Now the character changes its goal or renews its commitment no matter the cost. Sometimes this is where the character finally realizes exactly what the cost will be and decides to pay it anyway.

During the Big Boss Battle, the character throws in its best weapon to settle the issue once and for all. It wins, or it loses, or maybe it realizes it's not fighting the right battle. This battle settles the issue.

I am partial to parties with dramatic music and dancing and medals and tearful reunions for Act III, the resolution, the tying up of the loose ends and the establishment of the new normal. Your story might not need a party at the end. I still think parties are fun.

At any rate, if the character hasn't died, it will have new beliefs and new attitudes about itself and the world.

By the way, you get bonus points for giving the villain a character arc as well as the hero.

Day 1 what's important?

A great way to generate a character and story with psychological depth and a character arc is to use Randy Ingermanson's concept of the three most important things statements. Let's suppose you don't have a story in mind yet, but you know you would like to write a wartime story from the POV of someone waging that war. Let's think about wars and who gets involved. You don't want the guy who stays on the bridge or in the tent, but maybe you want somebody who does have some responsibility and tells a few people what to do. Okay, how about a sergeant in a space navy or a lieutenant in an alternate Civil War in the U.S, or a splat in a pixy cavalry.

Now let's give that sergeant/lieutenant/splat three most important things statements. Let's assume he/she/it grew up in a home lined with portraits of honorable ancestors who served in their varied militaries. Let's assume the sergeant/lieutenant/splat grew up playing war with a beloved younger brother who in return adored him/her/it. How about these for the three most important things:

There is nothing more important than duty.
There is nothing more important than honor.
There is nothing more important than family.

How can we use these three most important things to generate a story?

Put two of them in conflict. Here's one way.

The sergeant/lieutenant/splat mentored the beloved brother when it was his turn to enter the service. War starts and maybe the brother accidentally pushes a wrong button and blows up an important ship, or he falls asleep during watch, or he accidentally passes a top secret to an enemy. It was an accident, he didn't mean to do it. That doesn't matter. During wartime those are acts of treason. Treason is punishable by death.

And it's the sergeant/lieutenant/splat who is assigned the duty to execute the treasonous soldier!

Now what is he/she/it going to do? Which thing is truly the most important thing?

And now you have a conflict that can drive a compelling story/plot. Something in this hero is going to break, and he/she/it will be different by the end of the story.

Activities:

A. *Read*:

"Lo, Mox!" a familiar voice called from near the barn's entrance.

"Moxy poxy hoggy face, we know you're in here."

Achan sucked in an icy breath and slid back into the goat stall. The voices belonged to Riga Hoff and Harnu Poe, Sitna Manor's resident browbeaters.

Mox's young voice cried out. "Stop it! Don't do that! Ow!"

Achan set his jaw and thunked his head against the wall of the stall, earning a reprimanding look from Dilly. Poril would flay him if he returned late. And there was no guarantee he could beat both boys. He should mind his own business. Regular beatings had made him tough—they could do likewise for Mox.

Or they could cripple him for life. An image flooded his mind: a young slave being dragged through the linen field by Riga and Harnu. They'd crushed his hands so badly that all the boy could do now was pull a cart like a mule. Achan sighed.

He edged to the other end of the barn, stepping softly over the scattered hay. Two piglets scurried past his feet. He clenched his jaw. If the animals got out, Mox would be punished by his master too. Riga and Harnu knew that, of course.

Achan spotted them in a pig stall at the end of the barn. Harnu was holding Mox's face in a trough of slop. The mere thought of the smell turned Achan's empty stomach. Riga leaned over Harnu's shoulder laughing, his ample rear blocking the stall's entrance. Fine linen stretched over Riga's girth and rode up his back in wrinkles, baring more skin than Achan cared to see.

He sent a quick prayer up to the gods and cleared his throat. "Can I help you boys with something?"

Riga spun around, his mess of short, golden curls sticking out in all directions. His face was so pudgy Achan could never tell if his eyes were open or closed. "Stay out of this, dog!"

Harnu released Mox and pushed past Riga out of the stall. The torch's beam illuminated his pockmarked face, a hazard from working too close to the forge. "Moxy poxy piglet got out of his pen. He needs to learn his place." Harnu stood a foot taller than Riga and was the real threat in the barn. He stepped toward Achan. "Looks like you need to learn yours too."

Achan held his ground. "Let him go."

Harnu's gaze flitted to a pitchfork propped against the wall. He grabbed it and swung. Achan jumped back, but the tines snagged his tunic, ripping a hole in the front and scratching his stomach. Achan squeezed his fists and blew out a long breath.

Harnu jabbed the pitchfork forward. Achan lunged to the side and grabbed the shaft. He wrenched the weapon away and spun it around, prongs facing Harnu. He waved it slightly back and forth, hoping to scare the brute into flight.

Jill Williamson *By Darkness Hid*

1) Do you think this scene is in Act I, Act II, or Act III?

2) What do you think Achan's normal is, both physically and mentally, or in other words, outwardly and inwardly?

3) Since Act II involves the working out of things that are revealed in Act I, what do you think Achan's inner journey will be about? There's no right or wrong answer at this point in the book. I'm only asking what you think.

B. *Read*:

Just Shoot Me

"How many girls, Mom?"

"I only invited a couple dozen girls and their parents, Mackenzie. You will be polite and have a good time."

Two dozen girls? Kill me now.

"What made you think I would enjoy this?" I asked. "I don't know any of these people."

"Your father has been the Pastor at this church for four months now. You do know them. Maybe not as well as you should, but you do know them."

"Mom, just because we go to church with them doesn't mean I know them or want to know them."

"We've been in South Carolina since the middle of May and you need to find some girlfriends." She thought she was helping me, I know, but still. "Mackenzie, you need to branch out."

I took a deep breath. "Mom, I like my life the way it is—it's uncomplicated, plain, and simple. My books are my friends."

"You had friends in Lubbock." My mother let out a sigh.

My shoulders slumped. "I had a friend in Lubbock, and she sailed the good ship Brad to Relationship Island never to be heard from again."

"I'm just afraid you're becoming withdrawn, like you were before. School is starting on Monday. Don't you think it'd be nice to at least, have a few acquaintances?"

"Why? So I have someone to say goodbye to the next time we move?"

My mom stopped what she was doing, narrowed her eyes, and tightened her jaw. "Mackenzie."

I quickly realized I'd crossed a line so I fell back to my usual argument. "Plus, you know I don't like large crowds."

"You know, most girls want their sixteenth birthday party to be huge." My mom began working again and turned to grab the tenth batch of cupcakes to frost.

"We both know I'm not most girls, Mom."

"Yes, I know, and I know you don't like crowds, but the invitations have already been sent out. Do you think your father would allow the party to be canceled at this point?"

"No."

"Is there any reason to discuss it then?"

"No."

I slipped off my seat and stood looking at my mom.

"Can I go to my room now? If I'm going to survive tomorrow night, I need some me time."

My mom nodded, and I went up the stairs to my room as the sun started to set. In less than twenty-four hours, my house would be so full of estrogen, middle-aged women wouldn't need their hormone pills for weeks.

East of Eden was in the DVD player, and I snagged the remote before plopping onto my bed. My eyes closed as I crossed my arms behind my head. Hopefully, this would be my one and only birthday party.

EJ McCay *Called Warrior*

1) I do not recommend starting a story with heads talking in a white space. In the first or second paragraph it would have been nice to see a kitchen counter between the two or the mother dropping her knife into the frosting bowl. Nonetheless, this talking-heads beginning of the book works because the conversation is so vigorous and because we girls know these kinds of conversations are held in cars or kitchens. What do you know about these two characters?

2) East of Eden is a black and white movie about a son who cannot please his father, no matter what he does. How might this movie MacKenzie is watching resonate with the rest of the book?

3) List possible arcs for both the mother and the daughter. By the way, Mackenzie sees her first demon at her birthday party and ends up labelled a crazy.

C. *Read*:

Achan was returning from the well carrying a heavy yoke over his shoulders with two full buckets of water. He rounded the edge of a cottage and found Sir Gavin Lukos heading toward him. Achan stepped aside, pressing up against the cottage and turning the yoke so the buckets wouldn't hinder the great knight's path. The buckets swung from his sharp movement, grinding the yoke into his shoulders.

Sir Gavin slowed, "What's your name, stray?"

Achan jumped, wincing as the yoke sent a sliver into the back of his neck. Sir Gavin's eyes bored into his. One was icy blue and the other was dark brown. The difference startled him. "Uh . . . Achan, sir."

The knight's weathered face wrinkled. "What kind of name is that?"

Poril's voice nagged in Achan's mind, *'Tis trouble, that's what*. "Mine, sir."

"Surname?"

Achan lifted his chin and answered, "Cham," proud of the animal Poril had chosen to represent him. Chams breathed fire and had claws as long as his hand. Such virtues would tame Riga and Harnu for good.

Sir Gavin sniffed. "A fine choice." His braided beard bobbed as he spoke. "I saw a bit of that ruthless bear in the barn with those peasants."

Achan stared, shocked. He'd seen the fight? Would he tell Lord Nathak? "I . . . um . . ." Had Sir Gavin asked him a question? "I'm sorry?"

"I said, what's your aim, lad?"

"I should like to serve in Lord Nathak's kitchens . . . perhaps someday assist the stableman with the horses."

"Bah! Kitchens and stables are no place for a cham. That's a fierce beast. You need a goal fit for the animal."

What could the knight be skirting around? "But I . . . I don't have a . . . what choice have I?"

"Aw, now there's always a choice, lad. Kingsguard is the highest honor to be had by a stray. Why not choose that?"

Achan cut off a gasping laugh, afraid of offending the knight. "I cannot. Forgive me, but you're . . . I mean . . . a stray is not permitted to serve in the Kingsguard, sir."

"It wasn't always that way, you know. And despite any Council law, there are always exceptions."

Achan shifted the yoke a bit, uncomfortable with both the weight and the subject matter. He cared little for myths and legends. Council law was all that mattered anymore. Despite his fantasy of running away, he was Lord Nathak's property, nothing more. The brand on his shoulder proved that. "Even so, sir, one must serve as a page first, then squire, and no knight would wish a stray for either."

"Except, perhaps, a knight who's a stray himself." Sir Gavin winked his brown eye.

A tingle ran up Achan's arms. He'd known Sir Gavin was a stray because of his animal surname, but it had been years since strays had been permitted to serve. Surely he couldn't mean—

Jill Williamson *By Darkness Hid*

1) What more do you know about Achan's world now?
2) What is Achan's challenge?
3) If you were using The Hero of a Thousand Faces as a rubric to analyze this story, this scene would represent what?

Day 2 inner, outer

Okay, so an inner journey parallels the outer journey. Act I is like setting chess pieces on a board. Act II is like the playing of the game. Act III is like the checkmate and putting the pieces back into the box and folding up the board. You should not randomly and suddenly throw things into Act II that you did not at least hint of in Act I. You should set up such a world in which the new thing that shows up is logical. In Act I, you must set up the mental state of at least the hero, and it's best if you include the mental states of the contagonists and antagonist. By mental state we mean the pattern of thinking that is default for the hero, what the hero thinks about herself and her place in the world. What is her attitude about the challenges she faces?

Activities:

A. *Read*:

He is Nick Beasely, a PI who debunks claims of magic. She is Lady Cordelia, who claims to be a magician. This is from chapter seven, titled I Hate Magic.

I felt my ears twitch back, flattening against my skull. The fur on my hackles rose, and my tail shot straight up. I had always prided myself on not panicking openly in moments of crisis, but emotions were a lot harder to disguise in this body.

"What do you mean?" I roared. "Don't tell me that! You said, back in the castle, that you were going to change me just to convince me magic was real, and then change me back! So why can't you just do that now?"

"It's not that easy," she insisted. "Magic has rules."

I stared at her in disbelief. "It's *magic*," I exclaimed. "By definition, how could it possibly have rules? Magic is a contradiction of every law in the universe!"

"Of course it has rules," she shot back. "If it didn't, then you could just do anything you wanted to with it!"

"Can't you?"

"No! There are all sorts of things magic can never do. Raising the dead, for example."

"I'm not *asking* you to raise the dead! Just break this spell! I thought that's what fairy tales were all about, after all!" I rammed my fingers through my mane, trying to remember how people went about dealing with problems like this in the old stories. "What if you kissed me?"

Her jaw dropped. "I beg your pardon?"

"Look, I know it wouldn't be pleasant, but it'd be over in two seconds."

"Nick—"

"No, wait." I snapped my fingers – or rather, tried to. The rough pads on my fingertips dulled the snapping noise. "I'm wrong. That wouldn't work. We're not in love."

"No, we most certainly are not, but—"

"But come to think of it, it wasn't actually a kiss that changed the Beast back, was it? It was tears." I whirled to face her and put my hands on her shoulders. "Yes, that should be easy! Just cry on me. Focus on your tremendous, crushing guilt and let those tears flow."

She pulled away from me. "Look, Nick, I do feel guilty, but to be honest, I'm not much of a crier. And anyway, none of those things are going fix you. That's just not how magic works."

"Fine!" I growled, throwing up my hands. "Then how does it work? Explain."

She reached into the pocket of her jacket and pulled out a small piece of chalk. "Here," she said, "I'll draw a diagram."

I raised an eyebrow. "Do you always carry chalk around with you?"

"Doesn't everyone?"

"No."

"Their loss." She knelt down, brushed aside a pile of candy wrappers, and began drawing on the pavement with long, bold strokes.

Kyle Robert Shultz   *The Beast of Talesend*

1) What was Nick's mindset at the beginning of the book?
2) What is Nick's mindset now?
3) What might Nick be doing and thinking by the end of the book?

B. *Read*:

My fingernails dug into the armrests as strains of eerie music floated across the cinema, infusing my spine with ice and trailing chills down my arms.

What had I been thinking?

I jumped as a thunderous crash rattled our reclined seats. Slamming my eyes shut, I slumped in my seat, wishing the next couple of hours were already over.

Better yet, what had Peter been thinking?

The movie roared to life, skipping any previews. Come on! Seriously? They couldn't let me avoid the movie a few minutes longer? Of course, the previews were probably as gruesome as the stupid movie we were about to watch.

My boyfriend poked me.

I opened one eye and followed his pointing finger to the domed screen above our heads. Peter leaned close and whispered hoarsely, his hot breath blasting my ear.

Two lesser-known actors he enjoyed—probably because they were in every slasher flick known to man—filled the screen. They were yammering something about a virus killing everyone. Now they—the dead people—were somehow alive, chasing more people and trying to kill them as well. It was tragic, horrible, blah, blah, blah—I didn't care. It was scary. And I don't do scary. Anyway, it was just another lame excuse for a plot so one more bloodcurdling movie could be made.

I couldn't hear Peter over the ear-shattering volume of the film, so I nodded and retreated behind my eyelids once more.

Listening to it was only slightly less horrible than watching it. Maybe.

I braced myself for the carnage about to begin. I don't know how he'd done it, but Peter had talked me into seeing the latest horror zombie flick. You don't understand. I do *not* watch horror movies. Especially about zombies. It means weeks of no sleep and jumping at every little noise. And sleeping with a nightlight on. Seriously. But here I was, in the nicest state-of-the-art cinema New Mexico had to offer, preparing to spend the next two and a half hours cowering, eyes squeezed shut, hands clamped over my ears.

He was so going to pay for this.

I peeked at my boyfriend. He was staring at the screen in sheer excitement, eyes sparkling. I don't understand it. Why couldn't he look at me with the same enthusiasm, huh? I don't even know. But get this. He had somehow gotten these pre-screening tickets as a *surprise* for me. For *me*. I wanted to stuff those pre-screening tickets down his . . .

I gasped and jumped as the blasting volume of the film was ripped away, leaving a void of silence. You know, that horrid, awful silence right before something jumps out at you? Yeah, that one.

I cringed away from the screen, knowing I was going to scream no matter how prepared I was for it.

Michele Israel Harper   *Zombie Takeover: Book One of the Candace Marshall Chronicles*

1) Where is this protagonist/main character/hero in her mental journey?

2) What is her present challenge?

3) What challenge do you think she will face in Act II? (Again, I am not asking you to be accurate if you haven't read the book. Simply, what do you think?) What challenge would you give her?

C. *Read*:

After a patient hunt and rousing chase, Dad inevitably caught his prey, solved the mystery in time to avoid killing her, got past the whole awkward sorry-for-almost-killing-you phase, and successfully won her hand. That made nobody happy—except Mom. She was ecstatic to marry for love, though her former fiancé was rather put out, her family officially disowned her and put a bounty on her capture, and Dad's family snubbed her.

The Saroth are obsessed with bloodlines, lineage, and birth order, so they tried to arrange her marriage to Marcus Polani. Personally, I'm happy not being his daughter. Katrina Polani's a decent person, but she bit down hard on the whole I-am-better-than-everybody-else-because-I-have-magic Saroth nonsense.

With all the cheery goodwill going around, it's no surprise my parents fled to the woods to hide out, raise a family, et cetera. A horde of zombies attacked my parents when I was a cute, squishy baby. My parents prevailed in that fight, but Mom and I were both bitten. Why the blasted creatures bite is far beyond me. They carry supernatural swords, yet they insist on biting. It's so uncivilized. Stupid zombies. Then again, I'm not sure why they bother conjuring the swords since they always lose their arms.

Mom could heal herself or me, not both, so she saved me. I sometimes wonder what it would have been like if she'd saved herself instead. Of course, I wouldn't be around to see it, but she could have done so much more with her life. Dad found a powerful friend to make a pair of magical bracers that kept me from turning into one of those nasty little biters, hence the metal bracers—that often look like simple silver bracelets—and the thick leather gloves I wear. I don't really have to wear gloves on both hands, just the one that's gray and corpsified, but I find it less conspicuous to wear the pair.

Julie Gilbert *Redeemer Chronicles: Awakening*

1) List some of the pieces in this excerpt that are likely to be used at the climax of the story.

2) What is the POV? What is the tone?

3) The writer makes a promise at the beginning of the book about the genre, stakes, and tone that needs to be carried throughout the book. What might the stakes for this character be? What might be a weakness that an antagonist could exploit?

Day 3 why did he do that?

Readers pick the particular genre they read because they want to have a particular experience the genre gives them. For them to have that experience, they need to identify with or engage with at least one of the characters in the story, preferably the protagonist. To continue the chain of logic here, a character needs to have goals and motivations the reader can understand. This is true of characters who aren't human as well. If the fey or spirit or golem does not have a single identifiable human motivation (such as survival, need to fit in, safety, revenge, love of another etc.) then that character probably should not be the protagonist. The reader would put down your story to look for one she can be lost in.

The following three excerpts come from one story so that you can see an entire character arc. The story has two more character arcs, but we will focus on the character arc of the alien. The alien is a rumsha, one of many intelligent species that are stranded on the planet of Talifar. This particular rumsha is a digger. His fingers are fused into a sharp, shovel shape.

Activities:

A. *Read*:
From ACT I

The *rumsha* pulled the cart of artifacts across the snow-dusted tundra. Twin vapor clouds plumed from his nostrils. His aching ears swiveled at every sound, from the hawk overhead hunting hoardmice, to the foxy digging up a rabbit's burrow. The bells on his ears and whiskers chimed thinly in the frigid air.

Here in the near silence, he could drop his pretense of constant laughter and not be asked why he wasn't honoring the Cosmic Jester.

On his left rose the thin mountain-range that cupped the city of magicians. On his right, flat tundra, growing only grass and toe-high shrubs, rolled like a carpet all the way to the Circle Sea. The wagon bumped up onto pavement. The artifacts clattered against each other and the sides of the metal cart. The *rumsha's* toe claws clicked on the chiseled, flat stone. Bit by bit, as the sun rolled along the edge of the world, the snow melted. Insects rose in great clouds from the boggy ground.

The *rumsha* pulled up to the entrance set into the mountain. The metal gate boomed under the raps of his broad, shovel-shaped nails.

A few minutes later, a square column rose from the ground, whirring and clicking. A human voice issued from the column. "Hello. Who's knocking at the door of Crash Site?"

"I am the *rumsha* who borrowed your magic wagon and mined for artifacts." He tugged on his traditional motley jacket.

"Yea? I saw you earlier this summer. Did you find anything?"

"I found many things."

"Good-good for you. Maybe good-good for us. Oh, wait a moment. Checklist. Checklist. There you are. Question one: Do you have anyone else with you?"

"I came alone. I miss my brothers a great deal."

"Question two. I already asked that. Ha, I never heard of a flow chart before I moved here. Now I need to ask: Did you open anything?"

"The story of what happened to our brothers who opened your container of invisible machines has spread widely among us. I did not open anything."

"Next question: Do you feel sick? Any body parts disappearing?"

"No."

"Good-good. Meet me at the cargo doors."

The column clicked once, and then whirred as it lowered into the ground. The inset door swung open.

"Hoo." Magic pleased the *rumsha*. Were it not that all magicians were insane, he would have wished for some magicians among his species. He shouldered the chains to the wagon, and pulled his cargo through the doorway into the short tunnel that pierced the cliff.

…

…

The blond littlefolk ran her hands down her face, pulling on her cheeks.

The *rumsha* flipped his ears forward. Fascinating. If he tried to do that, he would tear off his face.

The blond littlefolk said, "Level Zero Morning Frost. What am I going to do with you? If it weren't so late in the summer, I'd escort you to the gate myself. I gave you one job. I gave you one rule. What was that rule?"

Not lifting his gaze from his feet, Frost mumbled, "Don't touch anything. Ever."

"And what did you do?"

"I touched an artifact."

"And what happens when we activate any machi—" She glanced at the *rumsha*. "Any magic outside the walls of Crash City?"

"Anomaly wakes up and destroys it."

The littlefolk held up her hand and spread out her nimble, human fingers. The smallest one was missing. "What else can happen?"

"The artifact might eat me."

Some of the magicians pulled glass walls along tracks and formed a smaller room in the cargo bay. Some shoved large things for which the rumsha had no words against a far wall. "We *rumshae* lost more than a finger."

The blond littlefolk tilted her head. "Something's different about you. I haven't heard you laugh yet."

The rumsha flattened his ears along his nape. She must not discover his secret. His shoulders shook. Even that thought was blasphemy. Would he ever stop blaspheming? He clamped down on the growl starting in his throat. That thought was blasphemy as well. Round and round his evil mind scurried. With great effort, he laughed, "Hoo. Hoo."

…

…

The rumsha's shoulders shivered. She was speaking blasphemy, but humans were insane and magicians were especially insane. That insanity negated the blasphemy and turned her words about the non-existent future into simple nonsense.

…

…

"Hoo." The fuss was worth laughing at. May the Cosmic Jester receive his acknowledgement of the joke even if his heart held no humor. Remember to laugh, he prodded himself. "Hoo."

What he remembered was why he had left to go mining for magician's artifacts in the cold tundra, digging in frozen peat instead of the comforting tunnels of his brothers. Digging by himself instead of in a team. He could not keep up the laughter when he was so sad. Why was he sad? He didn't know. But if his brothers or one of the mothers learned of his shameful secret, he would be banished to the lowest tunnels and never let outside again.

The *rumsha* didn't even like outside much, but he needed the option of going outside when his sadness overwhelmed him. Silence on the long road here, silence while digging, silence on the long road back, and carrying precious magician's cloth as a gift to his outsider brothers, all of that would help. No, it wouldn't. Would, would, would. He still could not stop his blasphemous thinking about a future that did not exist.

Lelia Rose Foreman   *A Load of Artifacts, ARTIFACT 2016 NIWA Anthology*

1) This is an example of a made-up religion. What do you know about this religion after reading these excerpts?

2) At this beginning of the character arc, what is the alien's mindset or predominant emotion?

3) What clues tell you that the rumshae don't bother to differentiate their members and give them names?

B. *Read*:
From ACT II

    Frost grumbled, "We're supposed to stay in here for two weeks. They're going to watch us to see if we change color, or blow up, or dissolve into a puddle of goo."

    Eighteen years ago, two rumshae had dissolved into dust while digging up artifacts for the magicians. This *rumsha* had been the first to return to the task.

    "Do you have a name?" asked Frost.

    The human obsession with names never ceased to amuse the rumshae. "Hoo. No." The *rumsha* rolled to his side and stretched his legs and toes. "There is no need to differentiate me from *rumshae* who aren't here."

    "You're the kind they call inside, yea?"

    "Yes. I am a digger. You may call me *rumsha* or digger."

    Some magic dimmed the glow of the overhead lights.

    "I'm not calling you by your species or job. I don't want you calling me Littlefolk Mess-up. My name's Morning Frost, by the way. The tiny empress of Crash Site is Summer Dawn. Do you mind if I call you, mmm, Strider?"

    "I do not mind." Sadness weighted down his ears and thoughts. "I do not see many littlefolk among the magicians."

    …

    …

    Provo Summer rubbed the side of her face and studied the top of Frost's head on the other side of the glass wall. Her eyes widened and she leaned forward, pressing her forehead against the glass. "Frost, is the reason you don't read because you *can't* read, and you're ashamed we'll find out?"

    The *rumsha* gripped the wagon. Did humans need to hide their shame?

    Frost paused. "Maybe."

    "Nature kill it, Frost. Nobody can fix stupid, but fixing ignorance is why we exist. I can assign the adjunct historian to teach you how to read. He can pretend he's interviewing you about littlefolk traditions and politics for a book he's writing. That way, nobody else needs to know you couldn't read when you came here."

    Humans are allowed to keep secrets. Amazing. Rumshae allowed none.

    Frost gazed up at the ceiling. "Strider's teaching me how to read."

    Provo Summer's laughter bounced around the cargo bay. "Who's Strider? The *rumsha*? Clever, clever man, you. I didn't know *rumshae* taught their diggers to read."

    "Hoo."

Still laughing, Provo Dawn knocked on the glass. "How many more secrets are you hiding from us?"

The *rumsha* froze. They must not discover his secret sadness. What if they told another visiting *rumsha*? Then his people would, they would, would. Was thinking about a possible future while knowing it might not happen a lesser blasphemy? If one thought of several possibilities and did not insist on any of them, was that still an offense against the Cosmic Jester? But he did know what would happen, for he had seen it happen to an outside *rumsha*. No, but this time might be different. Might.

Lelia Rose Foreman   *A Load of Artifacts*   ARTIFACT 2016 NIWA Anthology

1) What is the implication if the rumsha accepts the name Frost gave him? Has he accepted the name?

2) What has changed in the rumsha's thinking?

3) What secret was Frost keeping? Why was he keeping that secret? Was his motivation the same as the rumsha's?

C. *Read*:
From ACT III

Provo Summer snorted. She bent over her knees and laughed. "Ow. That's not funny. Ow." She laughed some more.

The *rumsha* wriggled his tail. These humans knew how to laugh, even in agony. They let each other hold secrets. These humans were more his brother than his brothers were.

"You know," White jacket said, "We might have been able to sew that back on if you hadn't told that *rumsha* to smash your finger into its constituent molecules."

Provo Summer drew in a deep breath. "Dearest *rumsha*, you've saved my life. You're the first person to obey me without arguing with me first. If we had listened to you sooner, we wouldn't be in the trouble we are. Before I pass out I want to thank you for agreeing to track down the *toothie* weaponry crawling through our city.

The *rumsha* bobbed his head. The littlefolk female would live. Would. She could die in the next second if the Cosmic Jester chose. No, she would live. At this moment, he would not allow any other future.

"We can't thank you enough, but I'd like to try. What do you want?"

His ears stood up. What did he want? No one had ever asked him that before. It was not the kind of question a *rumsha* asked. What did he want? He see-sawed, with his hips as the pivot. "I." I, not the *rumsha*. I. "I want to know what your magic words mean."

Every magician's eyes swiveled toward him.

Provo Summer said slowly, "You want to become a student here." She pressed her damaged hand against her chest. "Done. You're now a level zero. You and Frost are roommates."

A male squeaked, "You can't *do* that. We've never had another species attend the academy."

The blond littlefolk snapped, "Until I showed up."

"You're a variant, not another species altogether. Who's next?

"The *rumsha*, um, Strider, is a student now. Find a way to cope. All right, everybody. You saw what precautions we'll need. Now, somebody carry me to the infirmary."

White jacket hefted her up. "Oof. It's going to be an interesting challenge to develop prosthetics for him so he can manipulate our tools."

Frost shouted, "And turn pages in books."

The magicians burst into a flurry of activity. One knelt by the smear of finger and pulled out splinters of metal with a tweezers. Some moved lights around. Others ran out of the cargo bay. White jacket slowly carried out Provo Summer. One magician patted Strider's shoulder. "Wait here until we get some safety equipment. We'll do this wagonload before we go into the city."

Strider waited. He would, yes, would join the insanity of the magicians. If he was insane, he could think any nonsense he wanted to. He would learn magic words and be insane and hold secrets and be a person with a name. "Hoo, hoo, hoom."

Strider stamped his feet in dance. "Hoooooo." His sadness slipped off his back and slithered away.

Lelia Rose Foreman *A Load of Artifacts* ARTIFACT 2016 NIWA Anthology

1) There was a plot arc that followed the discovery of artifacts of an extinct species and what those artifacts did to the city of magicians. The plot forced the rumsha into a situation he could never have imagined. As his outer circumstance changed, so did his inner life. What changed?

2) What do you know about these magicians? What are they really?

3) Why were they called magicians? What was the character arc for them as a group?

Day 4 arc

Perhaps you plan to write serials for which there are no character arcs for any of the characters. You can do that. In the future. For this course, we want to have at least one of your characters have an inner arc that parallels the outer arc of the plot.

Activity:

1) We hope you have come up with some characters for your assigned story. If you haven't, make up some practice characters that would fit in your story world. Give at

least one of them a flaw, or believed lie, or weakness, or a strength, and then write some paragraphs describing a possible character arc for that character.

Day 5 decision

Sometimes a character arc determines the plot arc, as the character makes decisions based upon personality, training, expectations, hopes, and fears. His decisions change the situation, and then he must make more decisions. For example, in the rumsha story, the rumsha is sad because he has so much trouble thinking and acting the way his people require him to. They consider it a sin to think about the future because who knows what the Cosmic Jester will do? He decides to leave home to conceal his sadness. That decision puts him in contact with a dangerous alien artifact. Despite being imprisoned in a quarantine room, he decides to get along and learn what he can. He accepts a name even though he sees no reason for it. When the littlefolk Summer tells him to amputate her finger because a toothie machine has burrowed under the skin, he obeys her instantly. When Summer asks him what he wants as a reward for saving her life, Strider decides he wants to think and act like the humans do and become insane without apology. He could have asked to be let go to return to his people. Instead, he asks to be taught the words the magicians use, and thus Strider becomes the first rumsha to enter the academy of the magicians. The story ends with him dancing with joy instead of trudging home over the tundra because of the decisions he made inwardly and outwardly.

Activity:

1) Is there anything in your possible story that will cause the character to make a decision? Write some practice paragraphs with your character set in your storyworld making a decision. What will be the next thing the character must decide because of the prior decision?

CHAPTER TEN:

DESCRIPTION

Description shows us where we are in a novel, what the things around us look like and what our characters look like. Description shows us what the action looks like. You do want to learn how to describe skillfully. Some readers love long descriptions lingering with loving detail upon styles of dress, architecture, and ecosystems. (Ecosystems yay!) Other readers think even single adjectives get in the way of what they want to read: action, action, action.

How much description you should write depends on who you are writing for, your target audience. But even those who love description have a limit. You can say, "A large screen covered the back wall." You don't need to say, "A seventy-seven by fifty-five inch screen covered the sheet-rocked, blue, back wall with a screen saver scene of a farm in Ireland. The screen that reflected the light of the ceiling LED lights had a black rim around it and a day's worth of dust coating it. A light blue, humpback sofa with fringes and four legs sat four feet away from the screen, too close for eye comfort. Between them lay a beige carpet with a pattern of blue dots. Etc." Unless we're the interior decorators of that office, we don't care.

Still, you do need enough description to tell the readers where they are. Especially in speculative fiction you need to describe your setting. A contemporary novel does not need to describe a mail box. A fantasy story does need to describe message owls. A science fiction story does need to describe ansibles or aliens. Horror stories especially need a description of setting to establish a mood.

Here's a great opening of a fantasy novel that grounds the reader in the setting right away, while simultaneously kicking off the conflict:

> Aranya surfaced from the terrace lake, gasping and blowing like a beached trout. She strained to fill her burning lungs with the fragrant, dry air drifting down from Yorbik Island's sprawling coniferous forests. Squeezed beneath Iridith's lowering bulk and the western horizon, the suns blazed like twin golden cauldrons, casting a gleam that burnished the waters for miles about into a vast, luminous copper lake. The buoyant gleam reflected from the skies above, producing a dome of metallic blue so radiant that a Dragon's wings must shiver in awe.
>
> Instead, the Amethyst Dragoness chomped her fangs in frustration.
>
> She could not cross the lake; could not complete a training course on which Ardan and Zuziana succeeded repeatedly, honing their underwater flying skills in preparation for their assault on the Rift. Her eyes lit dimly upon the surrounding beauty. Her breath was shallow and pained, her body ravaged inside and out by Thoralian's deliberately induced Shapeshifter pox.
>
> Marc Secchia *Song of the Storm Dragon*

Not all the novel carries this degree of description. Once the setting has been established in the reader's mind, Marc Secchia goes on to focus on exciting action.

Day 1 what does it look like, sound like, feel like?

The dreaded infodump, narrative summary, TELLING, what you are told over and over not to do by creative-writing instructors. Show, don't tell, you are told. But sometimes the reader does need to be told information (that is not action) that will cause the story to make sense. So how do you do that without boring the reader until she puts your book down and wanders off to play Zelda?

In her September 14, 2016 post on Mad Genius Club (madgeniusclub.com) Sarah A. Hoyt wrote this to demonstrate how to incorporate description in a story:

> The Quality of Description Should not be Strained, a Dialogue with Bill and Mike.
>
> "Hey there buddy," Mike said, as he came into the office, slamming the door behind him and making for the coffee maker like it was on fire and he had the only firehose on the planet. "Why so glum?"
>
> Bill blinked from where he sat at his desk, looking across him at the red spires dotting the desert landscape outside the office window. "My writer's group said I needed more description and sense of place," he said. "But then when I put in description, they told me I had stopped the action and given them indigestible infodumps."
>
> "Ah," Mike said. "Did you?"
>
> "Perhaps a tadbit, but dang it all, man, how is one supposed to convey things like new technology without a ten paragraph break explaining the history and how it works?"
>
> "It is difficult," Mike said, as he scooped up the three precious coffee beans from Earth and shoved them in the little door atop the coffee maker, to allow the replicator to do its thing. "But do you really need the history? After all, most of the time, do you pause to think of the history of your shaver, or how Earth people used to scrape their faces with blades before inventing the exfulicator every morning?"
>
> "No, but... I feel like I'm just spinning bull--" He paused, as Mike, the proper weight of replicated beans having been achieved, turned on the grinder. Why the ... thing couldn't recreate beans already ground, Bill would never know. Even when the scientists explained. "Anyway, I feel like I'm just talking mid-air if I don't give details."
>
> "People don't want details," Mike said. "I've noticed that. Except very rarely, to give a sense of time and place." He squinted out the window at the landscape. Three hundred years after terraforming, Mars was if anything redder as the oxygen rich atmosphere instantly oxidized any exposed iron. He grabbed a mug from the wall. It came from Earth and said "Visit the Sahara Ocean resort." He had no clue what it meant, never having been on Earth, but the picture of lush green landscape and a cartoony ocean filled with fish made a contrast to the desert outside.
>
> He wheeled closer to the window and put a digit on the glass, looking out. Mars sure had changed since terraforming. He wasn't sure how he felt about it, yet.
>
> "I see. But what if the description is part of the point. What if I need some kind of punchline at the end, and need to give hints along the way? Can't I take time and do it properly in order, with history and explanations."
>
> "Oh, sure you can," Mike said. "If you want to bore people blue. For now, though, I suggest you set the fiction aside and we concentrate on that report for the emperor." He wrapped three of his green tentacles around his coffee cup and inhaled the scent of the coffee through his speaking-organ. He couldn't actually drink it, but he loved the smell of Earth coffee.

Sarah A. Hoyt   accordingtohoyt.com

It is best if the details of the world can be described bit by bit as the characters move and act within that world. But sometimes you need to let the reader know enough of the backstory to be able to make sense of the present story. There are a number of ways to handle the dreaded infodump when the reader absolutely must be told and not shown. Let's look at a few.

Activities:

A. *Read*:

    Afternoon sunlight slanted through budding tree branches, dappling the evergreen ivy carpeting the olum grove. Tufts of dormant prairie grass pretended they had a place here. Late snowdrops bobbed in the breeze, heads poking through stubborn patches of snow. The warmth of the spring sun balanced the cold air, making for a pleasant Marso day.

    A dirt road passed by the young grove, and a young woman perched on a tumble of glacial rocks between the two. The thud of hooves brought her head up.

    A leather thong tied coarse, sandy hair out of her face. She sat to take advantage of the sunlight. Her right knee balanced a bottle of ink, and the other knee provided a prop for her left elbow. A journal bound in thick leather lay across her thighs. She paused with a delicate quill of blown glass suspended over the journal as she peered along the road.

    She'd rolled her shirtsleeves up, exposing a tattoo on her left forearm—a six-pointed star within a circle, colored with a range of blue and purple tones. The center of the star glimmered silver. The right sleeve had started to unroll as she pushed it out of the way, heedless of getting ink stains on the linen.

    She glanced at a horse standing loose just inside the grove, nibbling at the lowest of the green-tipped branches. Two small packs bulged behind the saddle, along with a sheathed sword. The horse whickered and resumed snacking. Either it hadn't heard the hoof beats or didn't care about them.

    The woman looked between the sun and the lengthening shadows, gauging the time. Setting the half-finished page beside her to let the ink dry, she pulled another from her notebook.

    Most esteemed Gamaliel, she wrote.

    For all her speed, her writing was small and precise, as if each letter had been practiced continually and distilled to the barest form needed to convey meaning.

    I have little progress to report. After twenty-nine days, I find no confirmation of your theories about the changing weather patterns in this region. The greatest deviation from "Ah, it's been dry, but then so was last winter," was "Haven't seen a drier winter than this since last season." Hardly conclusive. I will stop at our border outpost at Waymeet and continue my inquiries before proceeding east toward the Barrens.

I found one farmer who would not talk about the weather but about the difficulty of this winter's harvest. He said the harvest spells did not work as usual, and physical labor was required to bring in the last crop.

Again, the wind carried the sound of approaching hooves. The woman did not raise her head this time.

He went on at length about his frustration and confusion at the time, finally concluding the elements from the previous harvest must have been stored incorrectly. He was reared a farmer, so I cannot imagine how he could have made such a mistake. I doubt he is content with his conclusions, either, because the topic continued to surface for the length of my stay.

As I write this, I remember one other instance where a spell reportedly went awry without apparent reason. I didn't think much of it at the time—you know how little interest I have in magic—but I wonder if it has some significance. I will listen more closely as I continue my studies. Perhaps a change in weather patterns might affect some spells, as some spells affect a change in weather patterns. I look forward to discussing it with you when I return in the fall.

A verbatim account of the interview is enclosed with my secondary reports. I hope they find you, as always, in good health. With respect, Caissa.

Robynn Tolbert   *Star of Justice*

1) Normally, writing a letter is a boring activity. How did the writer inject tension into this scene? We don't see any conflict yet, but the letter might hint at what the conflict might entail. What do you think might be the coming conflict?

2) What do we learn about this world in this letter?

3) Notice how active the description is. Not a single 'was' has inserted itself into the first four paragraphs. Now ruin the first paragraph by rewriting each sentence to include one or more 'wases.'

B. *Read*:

The first room had been constructed to look like the main control center of the dying generation ship in which the first settlers had crashed. Lighting was the blue of emergency alerts. Gauzy streamers, suspended from the ceiling to some of the stations, represented smoke. Scents injected into the air smelled of burnt wiring. Mannequins were fashioned to look like typical Eshuvani wearing the historical clothing of the time, a loose tunic over a pair of knee-length pants and ankle boots. The typical, modern-style shirt still had the somewhat looser sleeves of the period gathered at the wrists by wide cuffs. The sleeves on Amaya's uniform were less puffy than modern fashion but still more so then the typical, human style.

They toured the stations checking out the timeline from the historical records recovered from the ship's computer.

"In 1612, Earth calendar, a coolant leak in the engine . . ." The computerized voice droned on through the speakers overhead.

Amaya tuned it out and studied the detail on the exhibit. She knew the history of the first contact quite well. As a *kiand* specializing in interspecies relations, the detailed analysis of the first contact story had been part of her required education. The coolant leak had led to complete breakdown as one system after another struggled to correct the problem. By the time the computer had awakened the technicians in suspension, there weren't enough systems left online to continue. They'd limped to the nearest habitable planet, which turned out to be Earth.

Cindy Koepp   *Like Herding The Wind*

1) What device did the writer use to convey a lot of information in a short time?

2) Make a list of ways to convey a lot of information other than letter writing or museum displays.

3) What have we learned about this world from the museum display?

C. *Read*:

In previous pages Willet Dura, a reeve, has been assigned a guard he doesn't know by a secret organization he didn't know about until they kidnapped him and then released him to investigate the murder of one of their own.

"They told you last night. I'm your guard, Bolt." Lean and spare and deadly, the single name fit him well enough.

Our gazes met. The fine white line of a scar tracked its way next to his hairline over light blue eyes. "You must have really annoyed somebody. What pasture did they call you out of for this duty?"

His grin deepened. "Arinwold."

The village lay forty leagues to the south, near the western edge of the valley between Collum and Owmead. It was literally a pasture. That explained how he'd gotten to the city so quickly after Elwin's death.

"And how am I supposed to explain your presence to the king?"

He grinned, showing teeth. "You won't have to. I've been hired by the city watch. They thought it would be a good idea to have me accompany you. For some reason, there are a lot of people who think you need protecting but not a lot of volunteers for the duty."

I shrugged. "I killed a man who needed it. He happened to be a marquis and he didn't have the opportunity of escaping justice by buying his way out of it. For some reason I can't discern, being a commoner who cut down a duke's brother in the king's throne room has made me unpopular with the other nobles."

His eyes twinkled. "That's a mystery, true enough."

Patrick W. Carr   *The Shock of Night*

1) There is one paragraph of pure telling. How many sentences are in it?

2) This is a series. How did the writer keep from boring the reader who might be learning what happened in the first book for the first time?

3) How was Bolt described?

Day 2 mood

One of the things description can do is set the tone, or the mood of the writing. If your character is walking down the street, he can notice the blue skies, aircraft crossing the sky, like the airplane he plans to board the next day and rejoice at people wearing shoes he designed. Or, while he is walking down the same street, he can notice all the cracks in the concrete, the wind drifts of torn ads and wrinkled wrappers, the stains on the sidewalk, and the grime coating all the windows. What he notices can establish a mood.

Another thing description can do is keep you engaged with the hero as you look at things through her eyes. A soldier entering a city might notice all the sniper spots, hidden corners, places bombs could be hidden, and a building that reminds him of the building where his buddy was killed.
A child might notice chalk drawings on the sidewalk, the little plastic hand of a discarded doll sticking past the lid of a garbage can, and will definitely notice every pile of dog poo.
A graphic designer will know the names of all the typefaces, or fonts, on every sign. Most people don't notice signs at all unless they are looking for a particular store or office.
An architect will notice the styles and composition of each building and how each has been purposed and repurposed to achieve the goals of the built environment.
A dog will notice the smells of every animal that had walked by in the last three days.

You do not, you cannot, describe everything. You do want to describe the things that will determine the tone you are striving for, the character and attitude of the viewer, and advance the plot. Any description that does none of those things should be cut.

Activities:

A. *Read*:

Crouched way up at the top of the wall in the rusty bed of the Rocking Truck, Modesto tugged his jacket more tightly across his chest, pushed back his hat and squinted around at the sky. At the moment there was no one in particular that it would be lucrative to watch for, but just to keep in practice the boy liked to climb up here and keep track of the comings and goings in general. Below him to his left was the South Gate area, not quite its usual crowded self because of the recent rain, and beyond that to the southeast—the direction that was nearly always downwind—he could see the ragged shacks and black mud lanes of Dogtown, canopied by the snarls of smoke rising from the eternal fires in its trash-filled trenches.

The boy clambered over the collapsed cab to sit on the hood and look north. The broken-backed truck, as immovable as the age-rounded concrete wall it straddled, didn't shift under him; nor had it ever moved in the memory of anyone now living.

The towers made ragged brushstrokes of black down the gray northern sky, and at the skeletal top of the Crocker tower he could see bright orange pinpricks that he knew were torches; the night watch was coming on duty early, and Modesto knew that their various spyglasses would be turned to the east, watching for any sign of the army that was rumored to be approaching from San Berdoo. And though even Modesto couldn't see them from here, he knew that out beyond the north farms there were armed men on horseback patrolling the Golden State Freeway from the Berdoo Freeway in the north to the Pomona in the south.

Thirty feet below his perch he noticed a grotesque vehicle moving south down Fig Street toward him, and with a grin half-admiring and half-contemptuous he identified it as the carriage of Greg Rivas, the famous pelican gunner. Like most kids his age, Modesto considered gunning a slightly embarrassing historical curiosity, conjuring up implausible images of one's parents when they were young and foolish . . . Modesto was far more interested in the more defined and consistent rhythms of Scrap, and the new dances like Scrapping, Gimpscrew and the Bugwalk.

With a creaking of axles and an altered pace in the clopping of the horse's hooves, the vehicle turned west onto Woolshirt Boulevard, and Modesto knew Rivas was just arriving early for his nightly gig at Spink's.

Bored, the boy turned his attention back to the thrillingly ominous lights in the Crocker Tower.

Tim Powers   *Dinner at Deviant's Palace*

1) Where is this?

2) What do you think happened historically to make this place?

3) Does this story feel like a fairy godmother is going to waltz in and grant Modesto a gift?

B. *Read*:

Soon he spotted the scraggly birch grove and the werevane that served as his trail marker. Fergus left the road at that point and picked his way upward through blighted birch, rabbit brush, and boulders, trying to retrace his normal route. At the hill's crest the barbed-wire fence stretched, cordoning the canyon from intruders. A sign speckled with buckshot warned against trespassing. But there was no one here to enforce those restrictions.

Besides, Otta's Rift needed protection from no one.

Mike Duran   *The Telling*

1) Make a list of the words or phrases that set the mood of this excerpt.

2) And just what is that mood or tone?

3) Would a space ship landing and disgorging helmeted storm troopers fit the mood of this piece?

C. *Read*:

Baden Haczyk

Solitude was easy enough to accomplish here. He was crouched in his bunk with his nose buried in his delver, reading history articles pulled off the Reach information network. The cabin hatch stood shut and the mellow jazz of a man named Duke Ellington played in the background. Getting alone wasn't the issue.

The problem was that it could never be maintained for long aboard the six-brace vessel *Natalia Zoja.*

The intercom buzzer jolted Baden out of his reading.

"Baden?" his dad called.

He ignored it. Baden wanted nothing more than to stay locked up in his cabin. It was four by five meters of his private space. He'd taken great pains to scrounge enough goldenrod paint to add some color to the four different shades of grey. There were storage bins crammed into every available square centimeter—under his bunk, clamped to the bulkhead, embedded around the hatch. There'd be even more space for him to sprawl out if he didn't have a closet-sized shower and bathroom off to one side, but Baden viewed that as nonnegotiable.

"Baden!" His dad sounded upset—so what else was new?

Baden tossed the delver onto his desk, where the handheld electronics pad landed amidst a pile of data chips. He stretched his arms and ambled across the cabin in six steps. "What's wrong, Dad—no one to yell at?" He punched the response key. "Yeah, what?"

Not surprisingly, his dad's initially sour tone did not improve. "Get up to the bridge. "We're five minutes from tract shift. I want a diagnostics run on the communications system and sensors, got it? They need to be checked before we arrive at Muhterem."

And how are you, Dad? Good. Oh, me? I'm just fine. Baden sighed and ran a hand through his unkempt brown hair. No matter how he combed the unruly stuff, it would not cooperate. "Sure, I'll be right there. Just give me a minute to—"

The intercom clicked off. Baden stared at the unit open-mouthed, his sentence lost. He scowled. "Just give me a minute to drop-kick you into a black hole."

Steve Rzasa   *The Word Reclaimed*

1) Who is the main character, and what is his mood?

2) What does the description of his cabin tell you about the protagonist?

3) One feels crowded, almost suffocated by containment in this spaceship. What might that contribute to the conflict?

Day 3 describing people

Nearly every beginning writer gives "police blotter" descriptions of their characters. There are better ways to describe their characters than *Her hair was dark and shiny and her eyes were blue.* Let's look at some of the ways skillful writers tell you what someone looks like.

> Gareth took the opportunity our travel afforded to provide what little information he had around mouthfuls of dark bread. "We found two men, one dead from blood loss, the other nearly so." His mouth pulled to one side beneath a nose that had been broken so many times that it changed directions often.

Patrick W. Carr   *The Shock of Night*

Earlier in the book, we were told that Gareth had a plain soldier's face. That's all the description we get of him. The man is a couple steps above spear-carrier, almost a contagonist, and thus he earns a name and two lines of description. Do we really need to know his hair and eye color?

Activities:

A. *Read*:

> Janice Marshman advanced. Her perfect posture and methodical movements gave her all the allure of a black widow. The silken red hair and thick eyelashes didn't hurt. She unnerved Annie. If *The Stepford Wives* ever needed a new model, the director of Marvale Manor could be Robot-in-Chief.
>
> "An evening stroll?" The director's lips slightly curled at one edge—her signature smile. "A fine night for it."
>
> "Yes." Annie adjusted her sweater, acutely aware of the tools underneath her skirt. "It is a fine night."
>
> "Winter's coming early." The director cast a slow, drawn look at her, lashes glinting like flytrap pincers.

Mike Duran   *The Telling*

1) The description of this person also sets a tone. What is it?

2) Would this character next blow and pop a bubble of bubble gum? What would that do to the tone?

3) Lashes glinting like flytrap pincers is quite the simile. List three more ways to describe eyelashes that establish a tone.

B. *Read*:

> His princess was dusty.
>
> Arpien should have expected that. Anything lying undisturbed for a hundred years would gather dust. He'd crossed the ocean to find the right sword for this venture, but neglected to pack a feather duster.

Great Grandfather Herron had always referred to the enchanted princess's beauty as ethereal. It was, at least, unnatural. Her form outlined under the sheets was slender, the face delicate under the layer of grey. Her skin would be fair and clear, though the only evidence of that was the two streaks under her nostrils, where her breath had blown the dust away.

Arpien hovered over his enchanted princess. He had thought of her since childhood. Beautiful, ageless. The air would shimmer with magic as he kissed her soft lips, broke the evil fairy's spell, won a kingdom and her heart.

The anticlimax exhausted him. He was not going to put his mouth on hers until he mopped her off.

Arpien scanned the tower bedroom for a rag. The gauzy tatters of the pink and off-white bed curtains disintegrated at his touch. Oh. They were mostly cobwebs. He wiped the clingy strands on his trunk hose. The fibers twisted together like sticky gray yarn and finally fell to the floor. The age-swollen wooden dresser drawers complained and squeaked when he jimmied them open. Absent mice had long since shredded and remodeled the clothes inside into bedding. Absent, too, were the birds who had left a buildup of dried grass in the narrow openings of the archer's slits. White-purple droppings splattered the tapestries.

Sweaty, his arms scratched up by thorns, Arpien was still the cleanest thing in the room.

Sarah E. Morin *Waking Beauty*

1) Cobwebs, tatters, disintegrated, gray, age-swollen: you would expect horror with these words. Why don't you here?

2) What has this description told us about this scene? Whose point of view is the reader following? Who are the main characters? What is happening?

3) What do you think will happen after Arpien mops her off?

C. *Read*:
Lord Dura has just learned he received the gift of reading people's souls. Now he wants to know who in prison is innocent.

I moved to the next cell, but when I motioned Gareth forward with the list, Bolt put his hand on my shoulder, tense but not threatening.

"This is unwise, Lord Dura."

I heard the hitch in his voice, knowing he would not speak in plain terms before Gareth, counting on it. "I am merely checking the contents of each purse to ensure they have no means of escape."

Bolt snorted his disgust, and I ignored the questioning look from Gareth to point between the bars at a heavy-set man with the scars and ears of a brawler. "Name and charge?"

"Erich." Gareth shook his head. "No last name that we know of or that he'll admit. He's accused of beating a man to death, supposedly for cheating at dice." Gareth shot a look through the bars as the prisoner rose from his pallet, rising as he stood until he overtopped us both by a head. "Be careful of this one, my lord."

I nodded, making sure none of the menace I felt coming from the boulder of a man before me reached my face. "Empty your purse into your hand and extend one, and only one, through the bars."

Coarse laughter scraped its way free of his throat. "You can trust ol' Erich, my lord. 'E wouldn't 'urt a flea." His hands groped through his pocket slits and he leered at us. Undoing the draw strings, he emptied what remained of his possessions into one hand. Grime covered most of it as though even his belongings carried the taint that stained his soul. I stepped forward, bracing myself against the tunnel and flood of visions I expected at his touch.

As my hand neared his, Erich dropped his belongings and lunged, moving faster than anyone with that bulk should. He threw himself backward, and I raised my free arm against the impact as the bars raced toward me.

The pain shooting toward my shoulder did nothing to stop the prison from blackening down to the pinpoint of Erich's eyes. I passed into a series of images and scenes from child to boy to man. They never varied, never wavered. Somehow I became aware of gorge rising in my throat. I vomited, and light returned to my vision.

When I straightened, I saw Bolt standing at the bars, his sword against Erich's throat, the giant trying in vain to see the edge of the blade against his skin. Gareth stared, not at me, but at Bolt, his mouth agape. "I never saw him move."

The time spent delving Erich's memories could have been measured in less than a handful heartbeats or less, but the filth of his deeds coated my mind like hot tar. Erich measured his pleasure by the amount of pain and power he could exercise over others.

Patrick W. Carr   *The Shock of Night*

1) What words are used to describe Erich?

2) Did your imagination supply the rest of his appearance or were you frustrated that you did not learn his hair and eye color? Were you frustrated that his clothes were not described?

3) What have these paragraphs told you about this world?

Day 4 how do you feel about it?

There is static description and there is active description. What description should be doing in your story is giving us an understanding of the when and where of the setting, establishing character, establishing tone, and moving the plot forward. Static description stops the story to explain what something looks like. Active description propels the story by letting us know how the setting or object makes the characters feel or act.

Here are four paragraphs from *Embers (Abiassa's Fire Book 1)*:

Even the midnight sky seemed to shrink, yielding darkness to the territories beneath its heavy cloak. Or maybe they were shrinking because of her intended course—if her connection with the land was as whole as she'd been taught, could it feel her turmoil? The irrevocable path she'd chosen?

Grief anew threatened to strangle her. She closed her eyes. If she did not do this, the fires could go out. The land could die. But if she did, *she* could die.

"My lady-princess?"

The soft voice pulled Kaelyria from her somber thoughts. She straightened, smoothed a hand down her silk-embroidered gown as much to brush away the weighty thoughts as to compose herself, and turned from the window. Across the black lacquered floor, torchlight scampered up the gilded walls and tapestries, casting an odd glow against her handmaiden's young face.

Ronie Kendig   *Embers (Abiassa's Fire Book 1)*

Grief can feel heavy and suffocating. The description of the night contributes to the reader's feeling for the princess. Midnight means the sky is dark. Then describing the night as a heavy cloak contributes to the feeling of heaviness, darkness, confinement, and the somber, weighty thoughts of the princess. The sky shrinking parallels the sense of grief strangling the princess.

The writer probably did not describe sparkling stars because that would not have contributed to the mood of grief and dread. Nor did she give much description to the dress the princess was wearing, other than to confirm the princess wore the type of clothes princesses wear. If the embroidery and colors had been described, that description would have detracted from the mood of the princess fearing that her decision would kill her.

What you put in and what you leave out of description can contribute mightily to the reader's engagement and experience they will have while reading your book.

Activity:

1) Write at least three practice paragraphs describing your world and your character or characters doing something in it. Make clear where the character is, what he is doing, and who he is. The characters you describe do not need to be the hero or villain, though they can be if you wish.

Day 5 with my eye

When your main character walks into a room, it will notice some things about the room. What will be noticed will vary by character. If your character is wealth and status conscious, it will notice how much the furniture cost and state of upkeep. If your character is an artist, it will notice all the art on the walls and how drapes and furniture coordinate. If your character is a scared child, it will notice all the good places to hide and everything that looks scary.

Activity:

1) Take a scene from your story where one of your characters enters (a room, a city, a vehicle, somewhere) and describe that setting from the viewpoint of the character. Then describe the setting from the viewpoint of a different character.

CHAPTER ELEVEN:

CONFLICT AND TENSION

Without conflict, you don't have a typical story. Conflict is the struggle that happens when a character, a protagonist, has a goal which the villain or antagonist blocks the protagonist from achieving. The goal needs to be important. If the goal is only who gets to choose what the family has for breakfast, that's not important enough for a story.

Unless that small conflict represents who is gaining control of the family. Unless the family is choosing which person to eat (and then we assume the protagonist's goal is to be the one not eaten)

For the story to be interesting, the stakes need to be high. Some writers contend that the stakes must always include death of the protagonist. That does not always mean a literal death. The stakes can involve a psychological death, a death of the protagonist's ambitions or desires. If a man tries to become king and loses, he could be sentenced to death by the winner, he could be exiled and stripped of all his resources, he could lose the love of his life, or he could see the country he loves destroyed by an incompetent king. If all that happens when he loses is he gets to return to his estate and resume life as normal, then the stakes aren't high enough for the story to be interesting.

Another way to understand the conflict is to pose the conflict as a story question. Will hero get what he wants, or will the opposition crush him?

Although the conflict can cause the feeling of tension in the reader, in literary terms, they are not exactly the same. Some writers say that conflict is the actual struggle, while tension is the threat of the conflict.

One of the things that can cause tension is the device called a ticking clock, or ticking bomb. For example, suppose a hero is hiding at the moment because if he is caught by opposition soldiers he won't be able to assassinate the evil king. The threat of being caught is the immediate ticking clock. As soldiers get closer and closer to the room the hero is hiding in, tension rises. If the hero is caught, we then move on to the next ticking clock. Will he be able to escape in time to prevent his execution or the death of everyone he loves? The clock ticks until the climax. The tension stops when the hero has won or lost his goal.

Day 1 tension

Every scene except the last one must have some tension in it. Every scene must contribute to the conflict or you risk the danger of boring your reader. By your reader, I mean your intended audience, the people you hope will read your story with pleasure. That will never include everybody. Never. The people who are fascinated by murder mysteries might find romantic conflict boring. The people who read only political essays might find themselves yawning if they are forced to read fantasy conflict. Don't worry about the readers who would never like the kind of stories you write. The world is full of books for them. You worry about providing the amount and kind of tension your reader craves to have an emotional experience while reading your book.

I am not advocating arrogance on your part, but rather a recognition of the truth that you cannot please everybody. Hopefully, knowing that truth can cause you to relax while you try to raise the tension within the reader. Do try to please the instructor of this course.

As you go through the following readings, think about how the writer uses tension in the work, and think about how you can include ticking clocks and conflict in your story.

Activities:

A. *Read*:
Randal and the others of his squad are wearing computerized battle armor.

A heavy hand rested on Randal's shoulder; he turned to find a friend. "It's been good to serve with you, Corporal," Kimathi said, taking a knee. "We will talk about today when I see you in Heaven tonight."

Randal followed suit, shaking his head. "I'm hoping we won't remember these things in Heaven. You and I can talk about cricket batsmen and boxing, like usual."

"*Sawa kabisa*. I will enjoy that."

Both laughed with a mirth neither felt, determined to keep up a good front until the end. Then there was nothing else to say, only to wait in silence for the end to come.

When the Abkhazi assaulted, they came as a victorious army, making no pretense of subtlety. They knew victory was theirs. But even demoralized and beaten, the NGDF troops never broke—they were simply consumed, dying in place.

Acting Commander Zhao's final order sounded over the comset. "Retreat to Rally Point Zeta. The Dragoons will rearguard the withdrawal."

Randal fired the last of his LMG ammo and began a zigzag sprint for the rear, sparing a last glance for Kimathi. An incoming rocket had taken his friend from him.

The volume of fire was intense. Everything was obscured with smoke. Entering a momentarily clear patch, Randal spotted Mireault. Several foot soldiers were trying to bear her down with sheer weight of numbers.

She dropped one with an armored knee somewhere soft, but was losing the fight to keep her balance. Vaulting a demolished hoversled, Randal plowed into the knot of troops surrounding the girl, crushing one between them and sending the others flying.

Behind them the Dragoons of the scout company made a last, gallant foray at the enemy, slowing the Abkhazi advance for a short while before being ripped to shreds.

Randal and Mireault caught up with the fleeing caravan of supply crawlers and command vehicles taking the main road southward. Here and there ran a surviving armored infantryman. Another flight of Banshees soared in view overhead. Randal braced for whatever was about to drop on him, but instead the weapon pods detached well ahead of the survivors, scattering small objects over a wide area.

It took him a second to catch on. At first he assumed they were cluster bombs ranging wide of their target. When none exploded he realized they were ADMs—Air Deployable Minefields. The vehicles were boxed in. "This way," he yelled to Mireault, pulling her from the path the others were taking. "Those were mines!"

He and Mireault clambered up the steep bank to the east of the road. Looking back, he witnessed the final moments of the battalion as hovering gunships finished what the Banshees had begun, shredding the vehicles with chain gun fire. In seconds each was a burning shell.

The two of them didn't stop running for several kilometers. Randal finally called a halt to catch their breath. Scanning behind for any sign of pursuit, he took in the skyline. It was blanketed with dark pillars of smoke.

A passage from his Greek lessons surfaced in his mind; it was the inscription over the graves at Thermopylae: "Go tell the Spartans, stranger passing by, that here obedient to their laws we lie …"

J. Wesley Bush *Knox's Irregulars*

1) What is the conflict here?

2) What is the ticking clock?

3) What have you learned about the character of Randal in this passage?

B. *Read*:

He spoke a little louder than normal, but it wasn't the volume so much as the really hard tone that made me take notice. "Ashlynn, you've been very uncooperative today, and your rebellion deserves punishment. Now, you have more choices. Have you heard of a story called *The Whipping Boy*?"

I nodded slowly. I'd had to read that book last year. I felt sick. No one had ever asked me to choose a punishment before. Mostly, if I did something bad enough, Nana just used a sturdy wooden spoon to give my bum a good swat.

"Good. Wallace there is holding a capped syringe. It's filled with a very potent liquid form of methamphetamine. Over the past week, we've worked hard to break your friend of an addiction to this drug, but this is very important and I need your full cooperation."

Danielle groaned.

"I am willing to redo all that work. The withdrawal symptoms aren't fatal, but they are uncomfortable," Dr. Devya said.

"Please stop," I begged. I couldn't see me, but I'm pretty sure I was really pale. I didn't wanna hear any more threats. More than anything, I wanted to go home and to have Danielle go home as well.

"I'll do it," I said, struggling to stand.

"No more trouble? You haven't even heard the other choices."

"No more trouble," I promised. My heart raced like it wanted to bust free.

Dr. Devya stared at me, reminding me of a snake hard at work studying its dinner. "I'll tell you the other two choices anyway. I appreciate your newfound enthusiasm for the project, but I still think you need a clear picture of all the consequences. The second possible punishment would be solitary confinement for forty-eight hours."

"You'd leave her all alone?" A hopeful note escaped me.

"Yes, alone in the dark without food or water for two days."

"You're evil," Danielle said to him quietly. She straightened her shoulders, tipped her chin upward, and glared at Dr. Devya.

I could tell she wanted to say more but couldn't. Guess she had a lump like I did in my throat. It felt like I'd swallowed a hot marshmallow whole.

"I am thorough, my dear," he said to her, before turning to me again. "The third option is a bit cruder. Wallace and Mark could administer the punishment with their fists." Dr. Devya spoke casually, like a man without a care in the world. "Choose one."

Julie Gilbert *Ashlyn's Dreams*

1) What is the conflict here?

2) What is creating tension?

3) Who is the villain, and how do you know?

C. *Read*:

Bensin rose from the mattress he had been kneeling on, stretching his stiff limbs. Fishing in his pocket, he pulled out the two paperclips that he had straightened and then re-bent near the ends. He felt his way across the dark room to the door, ran his hands over the handle till he found the keyhole, and inserted the first paperclip. Though he could hardly see anything anyway, he closed his eyes to concentrate as he inserted the second one, raking it in and out to work his makeshift lock pick just the way Ricky had taught him. The metallic *clickety-clickety* seemed horribly loud in the quiet house, but there was nothing to be done except hope his owners were truly sleeping soundly.

Finally he felt the last pin rise out of the way. With the first paperclip, he turned the lock, and with a quick twist of the handle, the door swung open.

I did it! Grinning in triumph, Bensin tiptoed through the doorway, down the carpeted hall, past the bedroom where Mr. Creghorn was snoring away, past the baby's room, and into the living room. As softly as he could, he slid back the deadbolt on the front door and found the keyhole. The *clickety-clickety* seemed even louder now, and he held his breath, wondering if anyone would hear.

But the only other sound was the ticking of the clock on the wall above the couch. Turning the handle to make sure the front door was really unlocked, Bensin dared to breathe again.

Pocketing his paperclips, he tiptoed back into the bedroom and pulled the door shut once more. Then he hurried over to the other mattress and shook his little sister gently by the shoulder.

"Ellie, wake up!"

In the darkness, Ellie rolled over. "Hmm?"

"Wake up," he repeated softly. "We're leaving!"

"Huh?" She sat up, catching the urgency in his voice. "What do you mean?"

"We're escaping. Here, put your shoes and sweater on." He was already wearing his own sneakers, uncomfortably tight at the toes since the Creghorns didn't believe in buying shoes for slaves very often. He bent to pick up the light jacket he had left at the foot of his mattress. Though it still got warm in the middle of the day, nights were cool at this time of the year in Jarreon

"The Creghorns are asleep," he told his sister as he thrust his arms through the sleeves, "and I've got the door open. You're going to be free tonight!"

"But it didn't work last time," she protested, fumbling in the dark to put on the clothes he handed her. "And they were really mad."

"I know, but I have a better plan this time. And with it being New Year, I figure most of the City Watch will have the night off, so we won't be spotted as easily."

"But what if they catch us again?"

"Then you just look small and cute like you're so good at, and you'll have nothing to worry about. You're too little to lash." He hoped.

Annie Douglass Lima *The Collar and the Cravvarach (Krillonian Chronicles, Book 1)*

1) What is the conflict here?

2) What is the ticking clock in this particular excerpt?

3) What do you expect to happen next?

Day 2 foreshadowing

Foreshadowing can increase the tension and make the climax believable.
How do you foreshadow without telegraphing the climax or the ending of the story? This issue is addressed by Rachelle Gardner's article she posted on http://www.rachellegardner.com/foreshadowing-vs-telegraphing/ which she posted on Nov. 3, 2009. Below is an excerpt of the post. We recommend you go to the article yourself to learn more.

Today I thought I'd talk about an aspect of novel-crafting that I don't see addressed very often, even though I deal with it all the time when editing novels. It's the technique of **foreshadowing** and its black-sheep cousin, **telegraphing**.

Foreshadowing is when you purposely drop tiny hints about what's going to happen later in the novel, to heighten the effect or the suspense. It might not even be a hint, but an image or idea that thematically relates to whatever's going to happen later. It's like subtle shading to plant tiny, even imperceptible, seeds in your reader's mind.

Telegraphing is giving away too much, too soon, thereby *ruining* the suspense, or the impact of the event.

When you foreshadow, the reader usually doesn't notice it when they initially read it. But later they might have an "aha" moment, remember it, and put two and two together. Often foreshadowing can't even be detected until someone reads your novel for a second time. It's that subtle.

But telegraphing works the opposite. The reader notices the telegraphing detail, groans, and predicts what's going to happen. It takes the fun out of reading a novel. Envision the important event, or piece of information that your reader's going to learn, like a balloon. Telegraphing is like letting some of the air out of the balloon ahead of time, so when the time comes for the "pop" you get a fizzle instead.

Rachelle Gardner *Foreshadowing vs Telegraphing* (note: formatting has been changed)

Here's an example of foreshadowing:

After the father has been abducted from their home, most of the Larcen family are preparing to return to the Tethered World wherein dwell all the fantastic creatures and peoples from fairytales. A neighbor visits.

>"Mr. Marshall is downstairs." Brady stood in the doorway of Nate's room, where I rummaged through stacks of size 3T clothing.
>
>"Really? Why?" I followed Brady to the top of the stairs. We stood in the shadows and listened.
>
>"I'm sure when Liam gets home, he'll decide what's best," Mom was saying.
>
>"That's just it." Mr. Marshall's gruff voice had that lifelong smoker quality. "It sure looks like he's home. His car's been here all day."
>
>"I'm not sure that's any of your concern. I ought to know whether my husband is home or not."
>
>"Who are ya talkin' to, Twinkie?" Aunt Jules joined the conversation.
>
>"Well, now, who's this young lady?" The smell of Mr. Marshall's ever-present cigar wafted up the stairs.
>
>"My aunt, Julie McGriffin, this is Joseph Marshall, our neighbor."
>
>"Nice to meet ya, neighbor," Aunt Jules said.
>
>"It's a pleasure Miss—or is it Mrs—McGriffin?" Mr. Marshall was uncharacteristically chatty.
>
>Aunt Jules gave an impatient grunt. "A happily married *missus*."
>
>"You don't say. And where's the mister?"
>
>"Joseph." Mom sounded perturbed. "Thanks for checking on us. We're fine. Really. As you can see, we've got company, and we're rather busy. So, if you don't mind . . ."
>
>"Sure. Sure. Merely being neighborly. I'll see ya soon. Nice to meet you, Mrs. McGriffin."
>
>The door shut.
>
>I looked at Brady and shook my head. "That was weird."
>
>"Yep."
>
>"Yer neighbor is a cheeky sort," Aunt Jules said.
>
>"Not sure what got into him. He's always watched us from afar. I don't think he's ever checked on us. Even after an ambulance showed up when Nate had that seizure."
>
>"Well, today seems to be the day for strange things, doesn't it, love?"
>
>"Mmm-hmm."

"They say life is stranger than fiction, right?" my brother whispered, "whoever 'they' are."

I nodded. "I think 'they' are going to have to come up with a whole new category, especially for our family. Neither fiction or life is this bizarre."

Heather L. L. FitzGerald   *The Flaming Sword*

So what did you learn from the excerpt of this portal fantasy? Mr. Marshall is a minor irritant in the preparation to rush to danger. He is not threatening the family and does not appear violent. And yet, you understand that the man is unpleasant. You know his name. You know he snoops. You will not be surprised if he shows up later during a conflict. You don't know what part he will play, but you will not be surprised if he turns out to be a minor villain, possibly a spy, possibly more. On the other hand, you cannot say whether or not he'll end up the Big Boss. The role he will play is not telegraphed.

Nonetheless, this small scene does raise the tension a little bit. Will Mr. Marshall discover the way to the Tethered World? What will he do if he does? And of course, there's the hook: Why does he snoop on the Larcen family? Is it simply because they're conveniently across the street? Is it because he hates homeschool families and is looking for something to report? Is it because Big Foot is his boss? Inquiring minds want to know.

Activities:

A. *Read*:

The lifestyle Services case worker seemed friendly and genuinely interested in him. Tom Galloway wasn't entirely pleased about that. The case workers he'd dealt with in the Twin cities had all seemed overworked and time-pinched. The desks in their cubicles had been piled with file folders and official bulletins, and they themselves had exhaled an institutional miasma that seemed to say, "Don't show me any red flags and we won't ask too many questions."

But Megan Siegenthaler seemed to have all the time in the world, and was cordially curious about everything having to do with Tom and his family. Her small office had been painted a cheery mint green, and a tasteful landscape print hung on one wall. No family pictures though. He supposed those might be stressful for some of the case subjects. Or just as likely she had no family.

She herself was a honey-haired woman who must have been very attractive once and was still comfortably good-looking. Her green eyes were especially remarkable. She smoked a long thin cigarette, as was her right in all places except for hospital ICUs ever since the passage of the Smokers' Reinfranchisement Act. She'd offered Tom a breathing device, in accordance with the provisions of the Act, but he'd turned it down. Tobacco smoke had never bothered him much.

"I suppose it's pretty dull here in Epsom compared to life in the Cities," she said.

"I like it dull," said Tom.

"Does Christine like it dull too?"

Tom adjusted his mouth in something like a smile. "No. She'd like to move back."

"What do you think about that?"

"I don't care what she'd like. I'm trying to keep her alive."

Megan picked up the Galloway file and flipped through it. She had very long fingernails, enameled in red. Tom had always wondered why anyone who had to work with paper or keyboards would bother with such a self-inflicted handicap. "I think we ought to talk about this," she said. "Your last case worker made a note about your attitude. You realize that, in the long run, you can't keep your daughter alive, don't you?"

Tom kicked himself in a mental shin. He should have learned to keep his mouth shut by now. He didn't want to have this discussion again.

"I know what the law says," he grunted.

"Then you know that if Christine decides to end her life, you have no legal power to stop her. The Constitution's on her side. If she complains to us that you're interfering, she can be taken from you and escorted to the Happy Endings Clinic by a Lifestyle Services worker. The law is very explicit."

Lars Walker *Death's Doors*

1) The antagonist is not always a person. In this "If this goes on" story what do you think the antagonist is?

2) What does the protagonist want? What are some of the reasons a teenager would want to kill him or herself? If a teenager waited two or five years, would the unbearable situation change?

3) What have you learned about this world in this brief excerpt?

B. *Read*:

Dac smiled a brave smile at Ken then closed the stockroom door with a finality that reminded her that this room, this safe haven, could also be their tomb. She heard her husband riveting the boards in place as she turned and saw twelve sets of excited, terrified eyes watching her.

There should be more, she thought. Then shook her head of iron gray hair. The rest would be hidden in other homes. She could not protect them all. However, looking at the children before her made her realize how frightened they were and how much they needed her to be a safe haven in the storm. She smiled at them. "Look at you. Snuggled down like it was story time."

"We get a story, don't we, Dac? Momma promised."

That was Sho Whelan with his ginger hair and almond-shaped dark eyes. The youngest here at five.

Dac nodded. "Of course." She stepped through the room, weaving her way through the cluttered room of shelves and makeshift beds, to the rocking chair that the children had automatically left empty. "But today's story will be special."

"Why?"

The rumble of something exploding too near for comfort silenced the room. Much of the excitement died in the growing fear of what could happen. Dac smiled, turned in a flamboyant arc to get the children's attention back on her, and sat down.

"Because this story is true."

Dac settled into the old rocking chair, a relic from another world, and put the pulse rifle to the side—within reach but out of the way. She held up her hand to forestall the next question bubbling up. The children were polite and well-mannered but it was an extraordinary time and tempers ran hot.

"When we came to New Montana on one of the first colony ships, our town was simply called 'Haven'. Nothing more. Nothing less." She watched Sho's face screw up in confusion and glanced to the other children. They knew where this was going. Every child over the age of five knew . . . and still they leaned forward, eyes bright.

"But . . ." Sho stopped himself and looked around at the other children, knowing that sometimes his questions upset them.

Dac smiled. "Why is the town called 'Angel's Haven' now? That is what this story is about." She raised her gloved hand. "And how I got this."

Sho's eyes widened as he stared at That Which Should Never Be Mentioned.

"Are you ready?"

Again, something either hit the ground with tremendous force or landed too close for comfort. The ground rocked with a roaring sound from the north. Dac kept her face neutral as possible and continued on without waiting for an answer. "This is the story of the Dust Angels and how they came to be. The first thing you need to know is that my name wasn't always Dac. It was Elsa . . ."

Jennifer Brozek   *Dust Angels* copyright 2013 from *Beyond the Sun Anthology*

1) A writer can raise up questions in the reader's mind that the reader doesn't care to know the answer to. A question that the reader does care about is a hook. This excerpt raises a lot of questions. List as many questions as you can see. Which questions do you most want to know the answer to?

2) It's easy to figure out why Dac is telling a story to the children. But no writer should put in an element that has no purpose in either the frame or the story within the frame. What do you think the purpose of the story Dac tells will be?

3) Contrast between elements can make each element more vivid. For example, white looks whiter next to black than it does next to yellow. What are the contrasting elements in this excerpt?

4) We know Dac's gloved hand will be important at the climax of the story. How do we know that?

C. *Read*:

I am the mask. The mask is me.

No collector is known by name. Nor by face. There is only the mask. A dark shroud over my features. Eyeless, mouthless. Solid. I get the call, I dress, and I collect.

In reality, I'm Radial Crane. Thirty years old, single, childless, with a small place in the city. But here, now, I'm what I'm supposed to be. An incon collector.

And I'm waiting.

...

"Drones show he is trying for it, Collector."

"The exit?" I frown, quicken my pace. "Crazy incon."

I reach the end of the hall. There are two rooms. The door to the left stands wide open. It is a complete mess. Stacks of paper and slickzines. A dirty net access machine in one corner, keyboard stacked atop it as if to protect it from whatever rodent infests the floor. There is a reek of contraband substance.

The rightmost door is closed. I think about summoning the monitors, about borrowing their eyes again. Perhaps I can get them outside and around the building.

The exit window must be on the wall opposite the door. If Quantum is correct, the incon is poised there already. Climbing his way out.

He still has a gun . . .

I hear a heavy scrape, like a piece of furniture sliding under someone's weight. More breaking glass. He's not pointing a gun at the door right now, that's for sure.

I smash in, crouch, find the target straddling the window. His gun hand is down, but he quickly reacts, trying to aim.

I don't give him time. I fire another trank, catch him square in the shoulder.

The guy is like a rhino, though. He grunts, makes a futile swipe at the embedded projectile, and manages to bring his gun up. "You're nothing more than a butcher, Mask," he says. "A well-heeled butcher."

I see his finger squeeze, so I give him another trank. This time, I find that space between his eyes. He lunges, manages to fire low. Then the frame of the window breaks free. He falls back.

There's nothing I can do. Seconds later, I hear a thump.

"Incon disposed," Quantum says. I frown. I don't approach the window. Don't even bother to check. "I know," I say. "Chalk it."

"Collection complete, Radial. Well done."

...

Lunch at the zoo is good. Normal. We meet at the entrance as planned. It is still sunny. We walk the entire circle of the Australia and Asia exhibit—complete with aged wallabies and a lonely snow leopard—before we find a place to sit near the orangutan pen. She tells me of her family, two parents and brother, and their employment. She says how lucky they are. How votes have been kind to them. Not that she doesn't consider the vote itself kind, only that it is nice to win. To continue as you are.

That is a common belief.

She asks about my family. I keep things general. I don't tell her I lost an older brother to the vote. Only that my mother and father are still alive but separated. Physically about as far apart as they can be in this strange sector we call home.

...

Heather and I make our way first to the giraffes and then the lions. The whole zoo is designed to look as habitat-native as possible. If anyone really remembers what that was. For the lions, that means lots of tall grass and large shade trees, apparently.

There is one male lion, seated on the ground beneath a large oak tree. ... Behind him, partially obscured by the tree, is an ever-pacing female. Her eyes have been watching everyone from kid to grownup. Both animals look worn out to me. Stuck.

Kerry Nietz   *The Mask*

1) In the very first sentence, the writer manages to do three things at once. "I am the mask," foreshadows what will happen at the Big Boss Battle, establishes a motif that will be repeated often, and provides the theme of the book. Pretty good for four words. What does the mask mean to the main character?

2) The predators, worn out and stuck in a zoo, provide another motif. What do you think they will come to mean to the main character?

3) Is the main character a hero or a villain? Why do you think so?

Day 3 made you look

Why does everybody in the restaurant look when a couple starts arguing? Why does everybody in the cafeteria look when a kid trips and dumps his tray on a teacher? Why does everybody slow down to look at the accident at the side of the freeway? And how can that "Why?" be used to capture a reader's attention?

In Jeff Gerke's you-really-ought-to-read-this book *Hack Your Reader's Brain* there is this passage:

> If there's one thing the brain is constantly scanning for, it's danger. Peril. Impending harm to life or limb.
>
> If you're sitting somewhere reading this book but then a fire breaks out right beside you, your brain is going to prioritize your safety over your edification. You won't be able to help it: You'll pay attention to the fire—assessing the danger, moving to safety—until it's no longer a true danger. At that point, your brain may allow you to go back to reading.
>
> It is one of the beautiful oddities of the human brain that it can experience things *vicariously*. If you're in danger, you feel it and your body reacts to get you to safety. But it's also true that if someone *tells* you about danger they were in, or you watch it on TV, you can begin feeling something of that same danger yourself. As if you were in the danger. That's why, when someone relates a harrowing story, we can't *not* listen.
>
> Be sure to notice that part of it: Even if you're just hearing about a story that happens to someone else, your body and brain can react as if the events are happening to you.

We can use this beautiful oddity to our advantage as novelists.

If you depict a character in danger, your reader will pay attention. Guaranteed. The attentional circuits will fire, telling her to give heed to these matters. She won't be able to not pay attention.

Jeff Gerke *Hack Your Reader's Brain*

Danger is not the only thing that will snag a reader's attention. Jeff describes more ways to catch a reader in his book, and I urge you to get your hands and eyes on a copy. It's short and you won't regret reading it.

Activities:

A. *Read*:

"He has promised to return, and he is not a man to let his family down," Adda told us, my little brother and me, in answer to Malhyn's question.

Appa will come back to us, won't he, Adda?

It had become a ritual for the three of us—the question posed, the answer given—as comforting as the sight of Adda's nails raking one of our last popla stalks, freeing the hard grains, those brown teardrops that were now our only remaining source of nourishment after three years without crops.

Our storehouse, once full of stalks and their earthy scent, was now empty.

The night before we had feasted on the last of our offworld supplies, those tins of food left from the great exodus, processed food we only ate out of necessity: five forkfuls each of fermented vegetable, and three spoonfuls of sweet fruit from a can. A final treat. We spoke Appa's name together while the honeyed juices still coated our tongues.

He had been gone so long. And he had left us behind to be pronounced outcasts.

His sin, our punishment.

The ritual continued. Malhyn's small voice asked, "Appa will not forget us, will he, Adda?"

"He is not a man to forget what belongs to him."

I didn't doubt he would remember us. But I feared we'd never see him again.

Grain wept down Adda's sun-darkened hand and into the leaf green bowl in her lap. It was her favorite bowl, even though a chip marred the rim and a thin crack snaked along the side. Appa had given it to Adda when they had taken their vows and begun their new life as one. They had chanted their wedding promises into its inner curves, then covered the invisible vows with roasted grains and unblemished fruits and fresh vegetables of yellow and orange hues, all grown by their families.

The wedding ceremony I had dreamed of for myself. Before.

I have had trouble keeping a grasp on dreams since Appa left.

Adda began to sing. The popla grains each played a note in harmony as they struck her bowl—tink, tink, tonk, tink.

At least, if we are to die, we will die with the memory of our own food singing its last song in our stomachs. There is a kind of rightness in that, though I don't know why. Some things you simply know inside. Such as Appa's knowing that he must leave. Such as our knowing that Appa surely must return.

Only I didn't know it anymore. I no longer held that assurance as firmly as Adda or little Malhyn.

My hands felt empty.

"Let me help, Adda," I said, reaching for a stalk, for something to fill the emptiness that was not merely in my belly.

She stopped singing. "No, daughter. Allow me the full pleasure of this. I want today's meal to come from my hands, mine and your father's. He and I sowed the seeds from which this stalk grew. He and I tended and reaped. We stored it in the cool days. I will prepare and cook it in this warm one. My heart will dance when I see you and your brother eat."

I knew what Malhyn did not, what Adda had left unspoken. She would eat none of the popla porridge. It was to be her gift to us, the meal, because it was her duty to keep us alive. Eating it would be our gift to her, as it was our duty to believe we would live and that Appa would not forget us while he sailed the empty places that had never frightened me at night until he went deep into them.

He will be safe, I have told myself, as he was the first time he crossed the black of the second heaven. He will be as unharmed as he was during the months when our parents flew through the vastness to reach Dorna III and build this town of Havenheart, making of this alien world a home. I and my brother had never moved through that desolate darkness, and we never expected to. The elders are stone; they do not waver. Re-entering the void is transgression. They'd allowed the use of the old planet's technology, of the forbidden spacing vessels, only the one time, only to flee the corruption of their original lands.

New world. New life.

Mirtika Schultz   *Waiting for Appa*

1) What is the conflict here?

2) What are the stakes?

3) This is literary science fiction. Except for the literary genre, genres do not need to be this beautifully written. It's nice, but not necessary. Write three of the phrases that tell you this is literary style.

B. *Read*:

Grey Alexander crouched behind a fat saguaro cactus and tried not to think about getting killed.

"Hear anything, Rin?"

Her younger sister Orinda listened with her auris plug then shook her head. So far she'd hear nothing but a thundering herd of thirsty zebras. But that didn't mean they were safe.

Grey knelt in the hot, gritty dirt. Flyovers didn't happen often in the Preserve, but with a bounty on the heads of the unconnected, some pilots considered them easy money. And Masdaar didn't care if the bodies were still breathing or not.

She tapped at her bracelet controller, and the turquoise stone transformed into a grid of thumbnail touchscreens. Running her finger across the grid to activate the ocelli contact lenses in her eyes, Grey focused on a stretch of sage-pocked desert a quarter mile away. They hadn't be able to afford implants for both of them, instead designating Rin as the ears of the mission and Grey as the eyes.

The ocelli immediately brought the area into sharp focus. Along the edge of Grey's vision field, tiny red numbers indicated 8x zoom and F16 aperture. She sometimes imagined she could see the voltage of the invisible electric border fence shimmering in the desert heat.

Grey tapped her wrist again, wishing the lenses could perform x-ray scans. What if she missed a robot drone?

C. J. Darlington *Jupiter Winds*

1) What is the conflict here?

2) What does the author do to maintain tension?

3) Write a practice scene with some tension in it and a reference to the conflict of your story.

C. *Read*:

Everyone splashed onto the beach and raced toward the guard holding aloft the knife made of pearlescence. Boys tussled over the bit of tether trailing behind Raisehim.

"Help me, Highkick," Bowmark called.

The boy hesitated, glanced at the other racers, then ran back. He slung Tsunami's other arm over his shoulder and together they hauled the unconscious boy toward the physician.

Runsfast jogged toward them, his rusty red, straight hair working itself out of its tie. He gathered the boy into his arms. "I have him."

Raisehim whooped. He leaped and waved the knife over his head as the rest of the boys backed away from him.

"Dismissed!" shouted Crunchit. All the boys except Raisehim began their runs along the beach. Ululating, Raisehim ran into the path through the jungle that led to his home.

Bowmark marched up to the guard. "Why didn't you punish Raisehim? He injured two of my people, bullied Lookfor, and nearly got me killed."

Crunchit stooped to yell in Bowmark's face. "What he did was legal in the obstacle course. You keep wasting your time and energy trying to help warriors who should be taking care of themselves. What are you training for?"

Bowmark refused to back down. "We're training to fight a Southil invasion. How are we going to defeat them if we're fighting ourselves?"

"You fool! You learn how to form an army when you're designate. What are you training for *now*?"

As if cosmically cued, the ground shook for a second. Both guard and Bowmark turned to look in the direction of King's Island. So many earthquakes so close together could mean the volcano would erupt soon, but no smoke marred the blue sky above the jungle. The driftwood pile collapsed into a tighter configuration.

The guard said, "It's a good thing you're still too young to prove."

Bowmark briefly closed his eyes. If only he could stay too young forever. He grasped his Giver's Hand medallion and whispered, "Giver, please don't let the volcano erupt while I'm in age range. Please let me age out". That was an evil prayer. If Bowmark aged out, then Spearmark would become the presumed. How could he allow his sweet brother to go on the Disc?

The two faced each other again. Crunchit repeated, "What are you training for now? What are all of you training for?"

Bowmark's throat tightened. "I don't want to kill anybody. Not even that pig's anus."

"Then you want to die."

"No, I don't want to die."

"Presumed, those are your only two choices."

"I don't—I don't—"

"You are choosing to become a pile of ash. And you're condemning me. Do you think My King won't pitch me onto the hot lava after you for failing to train you properly?"

Bowmark struggled to breathe. "He wouldn't. He hates the Disc."

"We all hate the Disc. That's the point. Why else is My King secure on his throne?" Crunchit grabbed Bowmark's chin and wrenched his face up. "Listen to me. Raisehim has caught the fish your net refuses to see. You need to be able to do anything, *anything*, to win. If he takes you out even before you get on the Disc, who do you think is going to win?"

Bowmark pulled his chin from the guard's fingers and backed a step. "You think Raisehim will be the challenger."

"I *know* Raisehim will be the challenger. Unless you take him out before the proving. Unless you change. If both of you end up on the Disc, Raisehim will become My King, and I will obey him like I obey all the Protocol. And. You'll. Be. Ash."

Josh Foreman *Scarred King I*

1) What is the conflict here?

2) Who or what is the villain here? Are you sure?

3) Write at least one practice paragraph that shows, not tells, the conflict in your story.

Day 4 title scenes

How is your story coming along? If you don't have a strong conflict with high stakes, maybe you need to rethink your story. By now you should have in mind a world, a character or characters, and an idea for your plot. Think through your scenes. A scene is what happens in one place within a limited amount of time. Many novels have over a hundred scenes. Flash or micro fiction usually gets by with one.

Activity:

1) For each scene in your story, write a short title and a one sentence description of the scene on an index card (or an equivalent in some word processor such as a spread sheet or bulletin board.) Your title for the scene could be something like Opening or Inciting Incident or Big Boss Battle or Noble Death. The one sentence description could be something like Princess falls down stairs during ball. Or Soldier drags best friend to field tent. Or Kid walks into new home. Do not put everything in the scene on the card. Save the cards or spread sheet.

Day 5 one thing after another

Most professional writers think of their story with scenes like beads on a string. When they sit down to write, they know the order will be opening, inciting incident, try-fail, (maybe midpoint psychological crisis) try-fail, climax, denouement. The opening will establish the genre, tone, characters, type of conflict and stakes. The try-fails will grow in intensity until the most intense climax. Then comes the final result, leaving the reader satisfied and eager to read the next book.

Activities:

1) Today, you get to play with the scene cards. Lay them out with the scenes in order. You can tape them to the wall, lay them on a desk or the floor, print the spreadsheet, whatever helps you see the whole story in one place. If you haven't thought of what the first setback would be, lay a blank card titled Setback 1 in the line.

2) Study your line of scenes. Are there plot gaps? Is the progression of scenes logical? Move them around until you are satisfied with the shape of the story. Make a pile of the cards in order.

3) Pick up the first card and write the first scene. Don't try to make the first scene perfect yet.

CHAPTER TWELVE:

EDITING, REVISING

Sir Terry Pratchett said, "The first draft is just you telling yourself the story."

Editing hurts.
Some people hate the writing of the initial story, but love the process of editing. Other people, perhaps most people, love the white-hot pleasure of creation, and hate the process of cutting away words they worked so hard to write.

Editing is often called cutting and polishing, a metaphor taken from jewelry making where a gem is cut and then polished to brilliance before being set in a ring or broach. Diamonds look like cloudy white pebbles before they are cut and polished.

Cloth needs to be cut and sewn to make pants and shirts.

Metal needs to be melted, extruded, and shaped before it can be paperclips and cans.

Writing needs to be edited.

Writing down your ideas can be a lot of fun. However, if you want your writing to also be enjoyed by people who like the sort of stuff you write, your work will need to be edited.

One reason we keep emphasizing your audience, the people who like the sort of stuff you write, is that it doesn't matter how brilliant your work is. Most people won't want to read it. You can rant about the barbarians who don't have the acumen to like what you like, or you can shrug it off and realize we're all different. Even your intended audience might be splintered by those who like urban fantasy, but won't read urban fantasy with ghouls.

Here's something else you need to know: you are not your story. People can hate your story and still like you. Your story could be good or awful, and it will not reflect on how good or awful you are. The story will reflect how skillful you are at writing and will reflect what you are interested in and your attitudes about life, but the story is still not you.

The story is something you made. Any criticism of what you have made is not a criticism of you, it is the criticism of the work. Just about any flaws in your work are fixable. You do not need to take personally any critiques of your work. I know people who crawl under their blankets and eat pints of ice cream whenever somebody says their work isn't perfect the way it is. I understand how threatening criticism of your work can feel. After all, you bled on that paper.

You need to get over it. Yeah, it hurts. You still need to get over it.

Here's what professional writers know and beginner writers often don't: the first draft is dreck. I don't dispute that there are writers whose first draft is publishable, but they are so few that the chances of you being that exception are vanishingly small.

Here's another thing professional writers know. If you keep trying to improve the first draft while you're writing the first draft, you will write slower than a snail. It's possible you will never finish your first novel.

Write your first draft with abandon. Misspell things. Put (…) for the name of something you don't know and need to look up or make up later. Punctuate badly. Change your mind about the emphasis of the plot midway through the book. Change the setting. Change everything. Just put the words on the page. You need to get past the paralyzing idea that what you write must be perfect the first time (or second time or third time.)

Here's something we want you to know before it happens to you. Let's say you've written a story and you have self-edited it a thousand times. That's an exaggeration, or hyperbole, but that's what it can feel like. You've taken the piece to critique groups and you've followed everybody's advice. You read a ton of books about writing and tried to follow all their advice as well. Friend after friend have said they love this book. You fearfully send a book to publisher that publishes the same kind of thing you write. The publisher rejects it. Sadness and Woe. But you are strong and you persevere and you send it out again and again. Finally, a publisher tells you she loves the book and offers you a contract. Elation! You find an agent or a book to help you with negotiating the contract or maybe you didn't know you needed to do that and you signed the contract the way it was handed to you. You announce to everybody you know and lots of people you don't that a publisher has bought your book.

And then you get your manuscript back from the publisher's editor.

They said they loved your book. But they want you to change Every! Single! Sentence!

Now you act like a professional or you act like a nonprofessional. You will be outraged. Guaranteed. You will be devastated. Almost guaranteed. You may want to crawl into bed, pull the covers over your head, weep for many hours and then eat a few pints of ice cream. Or maybe you will shout for hours at the dog about how they want to change you and your style and who do they think they are?

They are the publisher and editor. They want your book to sell almost as much as you do. They know what styles and subjects sell well for them, and what styles and subjects don't. Owners or shareholders yell at them if they put out a book that flops.

What the publisher and editor do not need is you yelling at them. They will decide to never, ever work with you again. And they will tell all their editor friends to never, ever work with you. And thus your career dies.

Here's what a professional does. She says "Thank you. I will look this over." Then she goes for a long walk or watches TV or goes target shooting while feeling very, very angry for however many hours it takes. Then she gets over it. She sits down with the ms, saves the original manuscript in its own folder with the date of when she said good-bye to it, and then starts revising the story with each revision being saved under a different date.

Why save the original story in a safe place?

Because every single profession on earth has its percentage of incompetent boobs. It is highly unlikely but possible that the editor who wants you to change Every! Single! Sentence! is one of those. More likely, however, the editor's suggestions will make your story far better (even though it won't feel like that at first.) But just in case the revisions mangle your story instead, and then the publisher decides to not publish the story after all, you can go back to your precious, unchanged baby and start the process of sending the story out into the world again.

Day 1 types of editors

You will need an editor. Always. You will ALWAYS need at least one kind of editor for your manuscript. Perhaps you didn't know there was more than one kind of editor. What kinds are there?

Acquisition Editor: You don't need to worry about this one yet. She's the one that says, "I want this book!" and then tries to persuade the publisher to buy it.

Production Editor or Developmental Editor: Again, you don't need to worry about this one unless you become a production editor and self-publish. This is the editor that coordinates and manages all the many parts of publishing Because you don't know even what you don't know, you have no idea how many parts there are.

Content Editor or Substantive Editor: This one is the big picture editor. Do the events in your story follow the proper story structure for the type of story you are trying to tell? Do you need to rearrange or even totally change scenes? Do you need to add or subtract scenes? Does this scene make sense? Is the voice appropriate for the topic? Most beginning writers need a content editor. After you have published a few successful books, you might internalize enough principles that you can forego the content editor.

Line Editor: This editor checks for stylistic consistency and appropriateness. He will check the grammar, punctuation, transitions, and some spelling.

Copy Editor: There is often blurring between copy and line editing, but the copy editor also obtains permissions, writes captions for pictures, gives instructions to the printer, provides back matter and cover copy, and might change measurement standards to conform to the country the book will be sold in.

Proofreader: You will always need a proofreader. She looks for mistakes in punctuation and spelling. You will always need a proofreader. He catches the tiny mistakes that everyone else missed or that the writer introduced while trying to follow the advice and suggestions of the other editors. You will always need a proofreader.

Self-Editor: This is what you need to be after you have written your story. Editors hate it when writers hand them a rough draft that has not been self-edited at all. There are enough good self-editors out there as competition that you won't get away without doing some of your own editing. You need to check the flow of your story at the levels of story, chapter, paragraph, and line. You need to catch the grammar mistakes, typos, and misspellings. You need to make the manuscript the best you can possibly make it. And then you still need to hand it to a proofreader. It is impossible for you to catch every single mistake. You know what you meant and your eye is likely to glide over mistakes. No matter how great a writer you become, you will always need a proofreader.

The most common mistakes editors see are tense variability, POV errors, homonym and/or spelling errors, punctuation mistakes, and typos.

Tense variability is the switching of tenses, past, present, future, in chapters. Pick one tense and stick with it. Within dialogue, if that's how your character talks, then variable tense permissible. Lots of things are permissible in dialogue that nobody wants to see in narration. Here's an example:

He runs for the bus and he caught it.

No. The sentence should be either He ran for the bus and caught it, or He runs for the bus and catches it.

POV errors involve wandering outside of the POV character to describe what the POV character would not be able to see or sense. A character cannot see what his eyes look like unless he is looking in a mirror. Here's an example:

She (the main character and POV) looks at the dog and feels sorry for him. The dog feels an itch.

No. She can't feel the dog's itch (unless there's some psychic bond). She can see the dog whip around and nibble on its skin. Another POV error is to think you're writing from one POV and then switching randomly from one POV to another.

Homonym and spelling errors involve the wrong word with the right sound:

He walked passed the girl.

No. He walked past the girl.

The only way you can stop making homonym errors is to go through the brute process of memorizing what words mean and how they are spelled.

Words spelled creatively instead of accurately are better known as misspelled words. Please look up all the words you are not sure you are spelling correctly. But how do you look up the spelling of the word you don't know how to spell?

There are some hacks you can use for misspelled words. Make good friends with someone who can spell. Type (potential spelling) definition in your search engine, and if you're lucky the computer will find the word for you. If the computer says the equivalent of "I got nothin," you can think of a similar word and go to a thesaurus, and maybe you will find your word in the list of synonyms. Or maybe you could just use a different word.

Typos are the mistakes your fingers make while typing or even writing by hand. Look at the the dog. Look at the bog. The spell-checker of your word processor cannot catch all the typos you will make. And you will make them because you're human. If you're not human, maybe you won't make such mistakes, but I doubt it.

The most common punctuation errors involve the punctuation during dialogue. Different countries and different historical ages have different rules. In the USA of today, the period, comma, exclamation mark, and question mark go inside the quotation marks. If what comes directly after the dialogue is a variant of 'person says,' the last dialogue sentence ends with a comma instead of a period. If what comes directly after the dialogue is 'person does something besides say,' the last dialogue sentence ends with a period.

Examples: "Don't come into my yard," the dog said. versus "You don't want to do that." The dog scratched his ear.

Note how one 'the' is capitalized and one 'the' is not. Also, in case you didn't know, 'The dog scratched his ear.' is an action beat which tags who is the speaker is without using the word said.

There are more common punctuation errors. Some of us remember the time when the spaces between sentences needed to be two. Now that is incorrect, and publishers want only one space between sentences. It is easy when typing to skip a needed space or accidentally add too many spaces.

Here's a hack that will help you eliminate too many spaces if you are using a computer word program. Use the Replace function. Type two spaces in the Find box. Type one space in the Replace box. Then click on Replace All a few times. Voila, your extra spaces are gone.

There are many style guides out there that will deal with punctuation, one of them the Chicago Manual of Style. There are slight differences between the manuals, usually dealing with research papers and nonfiction books. If you know which style guide your publisher prefers, use that one. We know that style guides make the most boring reading on the face of the earth. Practicing scales is boring, too. You practice scales to build muscle memory. You read style guides until you have internalized the rules and your writing looks professional.

It's not a big deal to make a mistake unless you refuse to fix it.

Activities:

A. *Read*:
Example of tense variability and homonym errors:

He shrieks and she opened the door. With baited breath, she looks around and saw nothing because it was two dark outside.

"They're's nothing their," she announced and slams shut the door.

He reddened in the throws of embarrassment. "Are your sure your rite?" He throes himself onto the floor to shriek sum more.

1) Rewrite this to make all the tenses the same. I don't care which tense you pick.

2) Define each of the following words: hurtle, hurdle, peak, peek, pique, too, to, their, there, they're, you're, your, its, it's, bait, bate, bade, bayed, right, rite, throws, throes, threw, mind, mined, shutter, shudder, leech, leach, break, and brake. (note. Yeah, I know I promised I wouldn't teach you about homonyms, but these homonym errors bug the snot out of me. As I wrote the textbook, I realized I did need to talk about homonyms. What I should have done was go back and take out the promise in the beginning of the textbook. Why I didn't is because I saw the perfect opportunity to teach you two lessons. One: Sometimes things change during the writing of a book or story, and you will need to go back and change things in the beginning. Two: If your writing does not deliver what you promised, you will tick off your reader.)

3) What are your most common homonym errors?

B. *Read*:
Example of misspelling and typos.

> She passis him on the rigt as she heds for the kichen. He lashes out a hand to cache her by the the ankle.
>
> She stompss on his fingurs and he shrieks again..
>
> "I'm desparate! he cries!
>
> I don't caer!" she mumbles and stumbles past the door way. "well your get out ov the way?"

1) List the misspelled words and then their correct spellings.

2) There are three punctuation errors here as well. What are they?

3) Pick one of your story paragraphs, find, and list all the errors you find. Then fix them.

C. *Read*:

Example of POV error and punctuation:

> She wanders around the kitchen, looking for a weapon she can use against whater is making that sound in the dark Where is it?" she yells. She not admit to herself how frightened she is. The noise of sliding utinsels fills the air as she slides drawrs out and bangs them shut. He wonders when she'll stop making so much noice attracting whatever is is out therh..
>
> He staggers tohis feet. "Stop that! Do you want the whole county to hear," He stumbles into the kitchen after here. Stop." he says. Oh, no she's got a butcher knife, he thinks.
>
> She whirls around, brandishing the knife. She knows theyll be safe know.

1) Rewrite this from one POV.

2) List the punctuation errors.

3) Typos can involve misspelled words when the writer does know the spelling, missing or wrong punctuation, missing words, doubled words, and excessive or not enough spacing. List the typos.

Day 2 weasel words

Weasel words. Business and politics have their own definitions of weasel words and so does writing. Every editor has a list of words they don't like. They call them weasel words, words that make sentences flabby. Not everybody uses the same list, but there is considerable overlap. I will draw one list from goteenwriter.blogspot.com.

So what are these weasel words besides disliked words? In writing there are two definitions. One would be a personal list of the words or phrases that you overuse. For one generation, 'just' is a weasel word. For another generation 'even' is the word that is sprinkled randomly over the page. You might have a different personal weasel word for every book you write. The second definition pertains to styles of writing. Today's published writing tends to spare, lean sentences. There are many words we habitually use that are not needed in a sentence.

From goteenwriter.blogspot.com:

Jill's List

Vague words

Many, few, lots, a lot of, a little, some, most, almost, more, a few, rather, might, perhaps,

much, often, for the most part, like, seem, etc.

Absolutes

Every, very, entire, everyone, everything, etc.

Verbs that facilitate telling

Feel/felt, see/saw, hear/heard, think/thought, look, watch, taste, smell, wonder, decide,

notice, remember, recall, consider, ponder, is, am, are, was, were, has, had, have, etc.

Infinite Verb Phrases

Starting sentences with —ing words

Continuous action words

As, when, while, after, continued to.

Pronouns

Overuse of "they" or "them" tends to create the feel of an omniscient POV.

Time transitions

Just, then, as, the next day, all at once, soon, etc.

Adverbs

Softly, angrily, sadly, really, basically, immediately, very, actually, surely, usually, truly, suddenly, etc.

Double verbs

Started to, began to.

Some other words on my list:

Thought/though/through, loose/lose, there, it, be, being, been, became, that, well, poor, anyway, quite, however, about.

goteenwriter.blogspot.com

So, you may be thinking, what's wrong with those words?
Nothing.

However, overuse of the words on this list will irritate the editors you're trying to impress. Let's look at ways to eliminate these words to make your writing leaner.

All at once she was running across the lawn.
Versus
She ran across the lawn. or She darted across the lawn.

He actually pounded on the table. He thought angrily, "She won't get away with this!!!!"
Versus
He pounded on the table. She won't get away with this! (note: Some people say to always italicize thoughts. Some say to never italicize thoughts. Do whatever your publisher's editor wants. Don't put quotation marks around thoughts.)

Running through the door, he tripped on the stairs.
Versus
He ran through the doorway and tripped on the stairs. (note: You cannot simultaneously run through a door and trip on stairs.)

Through the window, he heard a bird chirping in the tree.
Versus
Outside, a bird in the tree chirped. (note: If we've been reading through his POV, we already know who is doing the hearing.)

He wondered if he should open the door.
Versus
Should he open the door?

She walked slowly.
Versus
She trudged.

He started to run.
Versus
He ran.

She smelled bitter ash.
Versus
The smell of bitter ash seared her nose.

He tasted bitter ash.
Versus
Bitter ash coated his tongue.

She felt sick.
Versus
Her joints ached and her stomach threatened to erupt.

I recommend you read *Rivet Your Reader with Deep Point of View* by Jill Elizabeth Nelson. Her short book will help you deal with weasel words.

Activities:

A. *Read*:

Immediately, he stood suddenly and began to run. After running for a while he started to slow down. Walking slowly down the path, the trees were looming over him. Leaves were falling onto the path. The squirrel wanted nuts from him and it felt hungry. He was truly hungry, too, and began to enter a store with food in it.

1) Rewrite this paragraph, ridding the sentences of weasel words, and revising to make the flow of words less awkward. Correct any other errors you see.

2) Go through your manuscript and delete every 'very' that isn't inside dialogue.

3) Rewrite the example paragraph again. This time set it inside your story world and try to make the paragraph more vivid with details, including sensory impressions. If your world doesn't have squirrels, use some other creature.

B. *Read*:

It was slithering tthrough the door. It wondered if it should open the door. It's mouth wrapped around the doorknob. It almost didn't fit. It opened the door. The door creaked. The door swung open. On the other side of the door, people shouted "Surprise!!!!!" And then suddenly people were scrambling all over each other and screaming, "Snake!!!!"

It shook its head, wondering what everyone was talking about. And then it remembered. That's right, he remembered, "A wizard had changed him into a snake."

1) Rewrite the two paragraphs to make the writing look more professional and less confusing.

2) Rewrite the two paragraphs, changing everything you must to make the situation fit your story world.

3) Go through your manuscript and delete all excessive exclamation points. (Hint: most of them)

C. *Read*:

She just really wanted a very little bit of ice cream. She had hardly ever dreamed she was this close to it. It smelled like strawberry. It even smelled like walnuts. But she really didn't even care about even them. Walnuts are okay. But they are okay only a little bit. Even the cone smelled good. It smelled so good she wanted a little bit. She inched a little closer. When he wasn't looking, she jumped. She jumped at the icecream. She actually knocked his hand. The ice cream was flying almost exactly like a bird. Then crash!!!!! The ice cream was smearing across the sidewalk. She lunged and caught it. Now the ice cream was smearing across her nose.

He pulled on her leash. "Who said you could have that?"

She barked happily and loudly and swiftly.

1) Rewrite this first draft. Eliminate all the unneeded words. Combine sentences where the combining will make the sentence be both clearer and more succinct.

2) Take your rewritten paragraphs and set them in your story world. Change any noun, verb, adjective, and adverb you desire.

3) Go through a page of your manuscript with dialogue in it. Change half the "(whoever) said" into action beats instead.

Day 3 active verbs

Active versus passive versus passive aggressive. This is where your teacher might tell you to circle every 'was' in your manuscript with red ink. If it looks like your page is bleeding to death, you should decide to replace as many of those 'was's' as possible. Can you get rid of all of them? Probably not. Still, you should try. Editors see 'was, is, are' as weak words that can be eliminated in favor of stronger words. 'She was tired.' does not bring forth as strong an image in the reader's mind as 'She sank into the chair, pulled off her shoes, dropped her hands into her lap, and sighed.'

Another example. He was cold. versus His breath plumed into white clouds as he tucked his gloved hands under his armpits. Ice crunched under his feet. If he had ever had the habit of licking flagpoles, today he would have abstained.

(note: First I wrote, today was the day he would quit. *thought about that was* Wrote again: today was the day to quit. *huffed, aggravated, nearly huffed IN aggravation but remembered I don't write that way anymore* I wrote the third version, realized the last sentence added goofy nonsense when I wanted serious, and left it in anyway to show you the process of revising. My final final version before going to an editor would have that sentence deleted.)

This is not to denigrate passive verbs or even weak verbs. They have their place. "To be, or not to be, that is the question," is a strong statement despite the passive verbs. However, on the whole, you should strive to have a longer list of active verbs than passive verbs in your writing.

The phrase 'It is' aggravates many editors. You should use that phrase as little as possible. In fact, you should use the pronoun it as little as possible. And you need to be careful with all pronouns, to make sure the readers always knows exactly who they, he, or she is.

(note: I could not get rid of that last is. Also, I had started the paragraph with It is is a phrase that … and revised the writing to remove all the its and is's I could.)

She was verbing can usually be changed to She verbed. For example, 'She was running'. is weaker than, 'She ran.' Are there times you should keep the Noun was verbing? Of course. Changing 'He was reading the book when the light went out.' to 'He read the book when the light went out.' would be silly. Still, your writing will benefit if you rid your writing of as many 'was verbing' phrases as possible.

Passive sentences such as 'The ball was kicked by her.' can be more strongly written as 'She kicked the ball.'

We wanted you to not fuss about weak words and such while you were writing your first draft of your story for this course. Start fussing now.

If you have more writing to do to finish your story, go ahead and keep writing the first draft carelessly, knowing that you should give yourself enough time to go back and fix the errors you can see.

Activities:

A. *Read*:

He decided he was going to start reading that book. He started reading on the first page. The first page was very hard to read because the words were very long and very hard. The second page wasn't any bit better. It was very rainy outside his window. It was dark, too. He began to think the book would benefit from an outdoor shower. Who would begin to fault him if he didn't read a wet and wrinkled book? The book was irritating to him.

1) Rewrite this to remove all the weasel words and make the paragraph more dynamic.
2) If you are writing your story on an electric device, do a FIND on your story for all the 'began to' and 'started to' phrases. Can you strike them from your sentences and have the

sentences remain coherent? (note: I first wrote ... and have the sentences make sense, thought about all that sibilance, and changed the words.) (another note: I always need to FIND 'turned to see.' which is my particular weasel phrase.)

3) Now find all the 'thought' and 'decided to' in your story. Think about deleting those words.

B. *Read*:

It was a dark and gloomy night. Shadows were all she could see. She was beginning to get scared and was about to start running. A lightning flash was bright. Tripping, she felt for the doorknob of the front door that was in front of her. She saw a glint on the doorknob that was brass.

1) Rewrite this to make the paragraph more dynamic.

2) Write two more ways to demonstrate rain besides It was raining. You may set the rain in your storyworld if you wish.

3) Write two more ways to demonstrate wind besides It was windy. You may set the wind in your storyworld, should you desire.

C. *Read*:

The alien listened as it heard the sound of every, single, last doors slammed in the corridor. It worried it. It wondered if it should go right or left? It was darker. Slowly, stealthily, it sneakily creeped to a window and looks inside the classroom.

"Don't open that door."

"Why not?"

"I think I saw something by the window."

A very little, tiny human girl whistles.

The alien looked almost scared. What was he going to do? It crept to the next window and thought about deciding to escape. It had left behind a classroom of thirty students. Jerry was still talking. Inside the next classroom was emptiness.

1) Rewrite the passage above so it makes sense. You might compare your revision with that of someone else to help you see how confusing writing can lead to multiple interpretations.

2) Look at a page of your manuscript with some dialogue on it. Are there any places where the reader might not know who is speaking? If so, you know what you must do.

3) Take your revision of the scene above and rewrite it again with description to fit in with your storyworld.

Day 4 checklist

There is an excellent editing checklist on goteenwriter.com you can use as you go through your manuscript looking for ways to polish your work.

Macro editing looks at the big picture, the structure of a story. One of the topics of macro editing the goteenwriter checklist deals with is plot. Below is a reproduction of a small part of the free, downloadable PDF that goteenwriter.com has on their website.

Is my story problem established early? Why should the reader care?

How is the beginning of my story? Have I:

•Shown the main character in his home world?

•Presented my main character with an invitation to go on a journey?

•Made it so he chooses to go on the journey? Have I given him a compelling enough reason?

•Established my character's goal?

How is the middle of my story? Have I:

•Given my main character multiple people, places, activities, or objects to love and fight for?

•Presented my characters with multiple obstacles to overcome?

•Designed several big twists in the story?

•Created a big midpoint scene?

•Created a clear disaster that leads to an "all hope is lost" moment for the character?

•Made my other characters (antagonist and secondary) active? Are they living lives of their own?

How is the end of my story? Have I:

•Locked my main character into a final battle of sorts?

•Written a convincing win or loss?

•Written a denouement that fits the story?

(Note: formatting has been changed from the original. Also, every question above has a lesson on the website goteenwriter.com that explains the concept in detail.)

Activity:

1) Take the above checklist and your story, and then answer the questions for yourself. If you detect any deficiencies in your story, now is the time to work on them.

Day 5 another checklist

Micro editing deals with the smaller details of writing. Here is another section from the self-editing checklist from goteenwriter.com about dialogue:

Did I punctuate my dialogue in a way that makes my meanings clear?

Did my characters use different words and phrases from each other?

Have I considered this conversation from the views of all participants?

Run a search for "said," "asked," and other dialogue tags I use often. Is there an action tag or thought beat that would work better?

Why is my character saying this now? Why does she feel this is the right/best time?

Are there places where I info dump in my dialogue? Pay close attention to spots where I refer to time. ("Since today is Thursday, your assignment is due in two days.")

In group conversations, how is the pacing? Is everyone pulling their own weight in the conversation?

Here is another section that deals with showing and telling:

Run a search for telling words: notice, found, spotted, experienced, looked, feeling, felt, watched, wondered, listened, tried, seemed, and thought. Did I use these words well? Or did I rely on them for telling the story instead of showing it?

Search for telling adverbs. Am I saying "he walked quickly" when I could say "he rushed?"

Run a search for the phrase "with a" and see if I tried to sneak in some telling that way too.

(Formatting has been changed and this reproduces only a small part of the downloadable self-editing checklist on goteenwriter.com)

There are a great many more issues to address while self-editing, but the above questions are a good place to start.

Activity:

Ask the above questions while you go over your manuscript a few more times.

BONUS LESSON

HOW MANY WAYS CAN YOU WRITE "POE SAT ON A CHAIR?"

1. You can rearrange the words:

On a chair, Poe sat.
A chair was what Poe sat on.

Hmm. In this case, these are not improvements, but sometimes simply rearranging the words can make a sentence more understandable or lyrical.

2. You can change the verb:

Poe dropped into the chair.
Poe sank into the chair.
Poe plopped onto the chair.
Poe fell into the chair.

Poe pulled out the chair, turned it, and straddled it backwards, leaning his forearms against the back.

3. You can provide concrete sensory details:

The chair creaked as Poe sat.
Poe sat on the grotesque chair shaped like a woman's high heel shoe and covered in pink plush.
Dust poofed out of the upholstery of the chair when Poe sat, and released a musty odor.
Poe sat on the wobbly chair.
Enervated by the heat, Poe sat on the chair, noticing but not caring that his sweat stained the wood a darker brown.
Poe sat on the chair and splinters dug into his thighs.
Poe sank farther than he had anticipated in the soft cushion of the chair.

4. You can provide emotional detail:

Poe sat and clenched the arms of the chair so hard he accidentally wrenched one loose.
Poe sat in the chair and faced the corner. Not fair! Ken broke the bowl, not him!
Poe drooped onto the chair, beaten.

5. You can add metaphor:

Poe settled on the chair as though placing his head in the mouth of a lion.
Poe placed himself on the chair with the regality of a king.
Poe lowered himself onto the chair as though fearing it was electric
Poe sat on the chair like a gangster boss surveying his minions
Poe perched on the chair like a vulture waiting for the cow to die.
Poe forcefully pressed himself against the chair, as though trying to hide from a giant spider.

6. You can provide context:

Poe sat on the metal chair and let them strap his arms and legs. They could make him sit, but they couldn't make him talk.
Poe sat on the throne made of bones and said, "Ouch."
Poe sat on the edge of his chair, his heart racing, and cheered for the dragonettes.
Poe hurled himself into the chair. For the first time in his life he won Musical Chairs.
Poe hurried to his seat, relieved that she had invited him to sit beside her during the running of the centaurs.
Poe narrowed his eyes as he eased back in the captain's chair and calculated the odds of Ted having a blaster in his boot.

Activity:

1) Write a simple declarative sentence such as Jay walked across the room. or Jayne picked up a rock. and embellish it six times, using the above ways to alter the sentence.

CHAPTER THIRTEEN:

YOUR FIRST CHAPTER

Some people say your first two pages, some your first fifty pages, and some your first five hundred words. I'm going to say your first chapter and call it good. So what about your first chapter, the first pages of your novel, or beginning paragraphs of your short story?

Jeff Gerke says in his you-really-ought-to-read-this book, *The First Fifty Pages*:

> ...Structurally, the first fifty pages of your book have to accomplish certain objectives, or the foundation will be weak.
>
> You have to engage your reader, first and foremost. You have to introduce your hero. You have to establish the context of the story. You must reveal the genre and milieu and story world. You have to set up the tone of the book. You'll also be presenting the stakes, introducing the antagonist, establishing the hero's desires, starting the main character's inner journey, and getting a ticking time bomb to start ticking down.
>
> And you want to do all these things without boring your reader, losing your reader, dumping backstory on your reader, misleading your reader, insulting your reader's intelligence, or tipping your hand to your reader.

Jeff Gerke   *The First Fifty Pages*

Whew. That's a lot of stuff do in the first pages. His book goes into far greater detail than I have room for in this textbook, so if you possibly can, obtain that book. The beginning of a book needs to do a great many things, almost all at once. Well, if it were easy, everybody would be doing it. You now have a great advantage over most other writers in that now you know what you are supposed to do. Practice will help you achieve it.

Day 1 opening scene

If you are a movie watcher, you can think about your first pages like this:
When you begin watching a movie, how do you know what kind of movie you're watching? What have the filmmakers placed in the opening scenes to inform you about the world and the characters?
Watch the opening sequence of a number of science fiction, fantasy, or horror movies. If you can, watch the scene with the sound turned off. What information is being presented to you? What is the weather like? How are the people dressed? What has clued you into the world situation? Watch the scene again, this time listening to the dialogue. What information does the dialogue present?
If you do not watch movies, you can apply the same questions to a few books.

Activities:

A. *Read*:

> I always wondered what it would be like to be dirt. Dead and useless and ugly and walked on. Until a seed drops. Takes root. And grows into a sapling that grows into a tree that produces crates full of fruit every year. All because dirt gave it life.
>
> Dad says I put too much thought into the little things.

But I don't think so. Tomorrow is Career Day. I'll leave my home—my *family*—to take up a new life in the city. And I wonder. I wonder if my life will have meaning then. If a seed will be planted, or if I'll remain as useless as dirt. Unnoticed, unseen, disregarded, and overlooked.

I pick up my crate of freshly picked apples and walk through the orchard toward my cabin. The brisk November wind whisks across the Community Garden and blasts into my face, filling my lungs. I absorb every last detail of my surroundings and commit it to memory, a picture to cling to when I need to remember what it's like to live in the place city folk call paradise.

And no wonder.

My eyes scan the green rolling hills and blue sky. I've been told the surrounding megacity of Ky has gray skies and the only blade of grass for miles is planted in window boxes. As the only place that grows fresh food in this country, the Garden is like the heartbeat of Ky.

I live in the apple orchard, in the midst of a mile-square patch of trees that I pruned and harvested from since childhood. Lush red fruit dot branches the way stars dot the sky. Apple trees grow bountiful fruit and are associated with the principles of generosity and abundance. So, of course, the apple tree is the sign of our charitable government.

Sara Baysinger *Black Tiger*

1) What is the conflict?

2) What is this world like?

3) What is the genre and the story question?

B. *Read*:

Llanfair Mountain, Pennsylvania

1870

Wishing gets you nothing.

These words are old wounds carved into the trunk of an ancient tree. Above the vandal's warning, the tree stretches evergreen limbs across the glassy-surfaced Wishing Pool. Below, its dark roots twist and trail into the water.

Do trees make wishes? I do not think so.

But I am wishing.

I wish that my sister would come out of the water. I can see her resting on the perfect, round pebbles at the bottom of the pool, the ones tossed in by visitors over hundreds of years, the ones said to be required by the pool sprite as payment. One perfect pebble for each wish. Such pebbles are rare in the world—as rare as magic itself.

Bubbles rise from Maren's mouth, each one slowly drifting to the surface before popping. Her eyes are closed, her body is as still as a corpse. Little gray fishes nibble at the fabric of her floating petticoat. As she dreams her webbed toes twitch and a smile spreads across her face.

She never looks so happy on the land.

"Come out," I say, knowing she will not—even if she does hear me. She never obeys me.

Behind me, twigs crack and leaves rustle. I turn to see our wyvern lifting one foot and then the other, fussing at the moss and sticks between his birdlike toes. His blue scales, pale as a summer sky on his belly and dark as midnight on his back, catch the dim light like curved slices of stained glass. He nods his dragonny head and snorts. Auntie has sent him to bring us home for supper, no doubt.

                                  Carrie Anne Noble   *The Mermaid's Sister*

1) What is the setting?

2) What is the tone?

3) What elements here do you think will be involved in the climax?

C. *Read*:

He used to believe everyone was born with the magic, an innate hotline to heaven. Some called it intuition, a sixth sense; others called it the void of God. Zeph Walker called it *the Telling*. It was not something you could teach or, even worse, sell—people just had it. Of course, by the time their parents, teachers, and society got through with them, whatever connection they had with the Infinite pretty much vanished. So it was, when Zeph reached his twenty-sixth birthday, the Telling was just an echo.

That's when destiny came knocking for him.

It arrived in the form of two wind-burnt detectives packing heat and a mystery for the ages. They flashed their badges, said he was needed for questioning. Before he could object or ask for details, they loaded him into the backseat of a mud-splattered Crown Victoria and drove across town to the county morgue. The ride was barely ten minutes, just long enough for Zeph Walker to conclude that, maybe, the magic was alive and well.

"You live alone?" The driver glanced at him in the rearview mirror.

Zeph adjusted his sunglasses. "Yes, sir."

"I don't blame you." The detective looked at his partner, who smirked in response.

Zeph returned his gaze to the passing landscape.

Late summers in Endurance were as beautiful as a watercolor and as hot as the devil's kitchen. The aspens on the ridge showed gold, and the dogwoods along the creeks had already begun to thin. Yet the arid breeze rising from Death Valley served as an ever-present reminder that beauty always lives in close proximity to hell.

Mike Duran *The Telling*

1) What is the setting?

2) What have you learned about the main character in these few paragraphs?

3) What is the genre and what is promised to the reader?

Day 2 middle of the action

We are often told that we should start our stories in *media res*, or in the middle of action. That is good advice, but it is often misinterpreted. If you aren't happy until a bomb explodes, by all means blow up a bomb in your first chapter, but never forget the reader needs to see a character they care about or all the booms mean nothing.

If you begin your novel at the climactic battle, then the rest of your story will need to be all flashback until you reach the climactic battle again. I've seen it done, successfully even, but I would never advise a beginning writer to try the technique. Nor would I advise writing the story backwards or in a spiral even though I have enjoyed stories written in both of those ways. The way most readers enjoy their stories is to start at the beginning and finish at the end.

The best way to start a story in the middle of action, is to pick a much smaller version of the climax action, something that will demonstrate the protagonist's capabilities and character.

Activities:

A. *Read*:

"Dad, look out!" Archer shouted. From the back seat, Kaylie shrieked.

Mr. Keaton swerved, but it was too late. The SUV clipped *something*, and it sent the vehicle spinning on the icy road.

"Archer, help!" Kaylie cried.

"I'm on it!"

Archer threw out a buffer of his will, a spongy cushion of blue light that adhered to the SUV and gently fought the wild rotation. As the vehicle's spin began to slow, Archer increased the tread on the tires. They caught, and Mr. Keaton regained control of the steering.

"Whew!" Kaylie gasped, huddling in a pile of blankets all restrained by the shoulder harness and lap belt. "Good one, Archer."

"You . . . saved us," Mr. Keaton said, the emphasis of his words so vague Archer couldn't tell if it was a question or a statement. His father white-knuckled the steering wheel as he slowly increased speed once more. His eyes were riveted to the street. "What . . . what was it? What did we hit?"

"I don't know," Archer said. "All I saw was a blur of white."

Kaylie's hand appeared over the armrest and pointed. "I think it was one of those."

Archer turned his head. Ten feet away lumbered a twelve-foot mountain of white. It was bulbous and thick, moving at impossible speed. Kaylie screamed.

Mr. Keaton turned the wheel, but the SUV didn't respond. It careened sideways into the snowman . . . and a snowman it was, but not any lovable Frosty or Olaf. This snowman wore a gaping, toothy scowl. Its branchy appendages moved as if hinged in a dozen places. A blurry green fire blazed in its eyes as the thing put its leering face right up against Archer's window.

Archer jumped back, yanking at his seat belt. He didn't think, didn't plan. He just reacted, calling up his will and unleashing a flaming fist right through the window. But the glass didn't shatter or crumble. It flash-melted, as did the snowman's face when Archer's will-infused flame struck it. The creature howled through what was left of its mouth. Its brambly hands flew up to its misshapen head . . . and knocked it right off the torso.

"Snot rockets!" Archer yelled. "Go, Dad, go!"

Mr. Keaton hit the gas and pulled away. Archer watched the snow creature; he saw a new head rise up out of its body, turn, and scream. There were others, more demented snow beings, emerging from the woods and lumbering toward the interstate.

"Better stay in the left lane, Dad," Archer said.

"Uh . . . yeah," Mr. Keaton replied. "Left lane. Good idea."

* * *

Archer launched out of the SUV, cut across the front lawn, and was on the steps in a heartbeat. "C'mon, Dad! We need to get inside."

Mr. Keaton scooped up Kaylie and loped across the yard. When they were safely inside, Archer shut the door hard and turned the lock.

"Don't," Mr. Keaton warned. "Don't lock it. Mrs. Pitsitakas, Amy and Buster will be here any minute."

Archer stared at the door as if it might bite him. "Okay, right. I forgot. But only until they get here. Then we lock up like Fort Knox, okay?"

"Archer," Mr. Keaton whispered as he lowered his daughter to stand on the foyer floor. "What . . . what is this?"

"It's the Rift, Dad," Kaylie said, as if that fact were such an elementary concept.

Mr. Keaton hung up his jacket and scarf. "I don't know what that means," he said. "One minute, I'm all chained up in the dark, thinking I'm having the worst nightmare of my life. Then Kaylie and that Australian guy show up, and the sky—it just ripped apart. Next thing I know, I'm at the hospital—but if I've been dreaming, I still haven't woken up. Creatures in the snow? You . . . making things out of thin air—it's all impossible."

Kaylie frowned. "It's a Dream-Temporal fusion," she explained. "Brought about by the fragmentation of the dividing fabric."

Mr. Keaton stared. "I . . . still don't know what that means."

Archer blew out a sigh. Kaylie was correct, but in her eight-year-old genius explanation, she hadn't gotten to the heart of what their father was asking. The events of the previous forty-eight hours raced through Archer's mind in ragged visual strips . . .

The bizarre dinner meeting with Rigby, Kara, and the Lurker in the Dream . . .

The showdown between him and Rigby, each holding the life of a loved one against the other . . .

And then the Rift.

Wayne Thomas Batson   *War for the Waking World*   *Dreamtreaders Book Three*

1) What does this story promise to give the reader?
2) What are some of the rules of this storyworld?
3) Who is the protagonist and who are the contagonists? How do you know?

B. *Read*:

"Late, late, late . . ." Nyssa Glass nearly bowled over a wind-up paper vendor as she emerged from her boarding house, her ruffled skirts swishing around her knee-high, buttoned boots. She clutched her leather satchel to her chest and inhaled the comforting, nutty smell of the flaxseed oil she'd polished it with the night before. The satchel was her most prized possession, carefully constructed with pockets for all her various tools, but stylish enough that she could wear it to church functions without drawing attention.

Mr. Calloway, her employer and mentor, always insisted on escorting her to church functions, but being away from her tools made her anxious, a throwback to keeping lockpicks in her back pocket, she supposed. If Mr. Calloway had made that connection, he probably would've tried to break her of the habit. He seemed to see it as a harmless quirk, though.

Nyssa searched her brain for an excuse for her tardiness. It wasn't really one thing that had caused her to be late. More of a series of minute annoyances. Laces snapping on her corset, for instance. She hated her corset. It hadn't been a required part of her wardrobe until the last year or so. Before her enrollment in Miss Pratchett's School of Mechanically Minded Maids, no one had cared if she dressed like a boy. Now that she was a graduate of that prestigious school, though, she had to dress her status and age.

Turning sixteen seemed to have only brought on more wardrobe restrictions and pimples . . . the pimples being the second thing to go wrong that morning, though she supposed it was her own fault for letting them distract her. Normally she wouldn't bother with make-up, but the size of the red spot on the bridge of her nose had sent her begging her roommate for powder. The breakfast was burned, keys were misplaced, and their elderly landlady had caught her in the hallway and wanted to chat.

"Should've just shouted, 'sorry, late,' and ran for it." Nyssa shook her head at her own weakness. "No, you had to not only say, 'I'm doing fine, thank you,' but ask her how her parakeet was faring as well."

The air was cool, but hazy with the exhaust from the nearby steam-power plant. The click of the inner workings of New Taured's automated button factory rose above her footsteps, causing her to walk in time with that rhythm. A few folk lingered on the sidewalk, milling about; however, most shops wouldn't open for another hour. Mr. Calloway liked to open early to "make the most of the day."

Nyssa liked to stay up late then sleep until her alarm clock screamed at her.

The clock tower at the end of the street clanged for seven o'clock. She clenched her teeth.

As she turned onto Clockwork Row, the timepiece store on the corner erupted in a cacophony of chimes, bells, and cuckoos. She wasn't sure how the keeper tolerated that going off every hour on the hour. Nyssa needed silence to work . . . well, silence except for the sound of her own voice. Talking to herself was another of her "harmless quirks."

Lights shone through the windows of Mr. Calloway's shop, the painted letters declaring his ability to repair all forms of videophones, radios, and signal sending devices. The sign in the door already read "open."

She pushed open the door, triggering a mechanism which chimed out the first several bars of a lullaby, and Nyssa smiled in spite of herself. It was a new tune today. Mr. Calloway liked to mix it up every so often.

The old man pushed down his magnifying goggles and smiled at Nyssa from the other side of the counter. "Ah, there you are. My watch must be fast."

"Your watch, the clock tower, and the two hundred or so timepieces in the store next door?" She raised her eyebrows.

"I know. Coincidences abound." He bent back over the inner working of a radio.

Nyssa mulled over her options. Just because Mr. Calloway wasn't going to make a big fuss over her being late didn't mean he didn't deserve an explanation, but as she'd hashed out on the way over, there wasn't really an explanation, not a concise one anyway. "It won't happen again," she said simply.

Hiking her skirts to just above her knees, she vaulted over the counter.

Mr. Calloway pushed a schematic towards her. "Dalhart & Rivera is launching an upgraded version of the videophone next month. They sent out advanced schematics this morning, so we can be prepared for questions and complete any repairs."

Nyssa unrolled the fresh white paper, inked in blue. It took her a full three minutes of scanning to spot the first difference between the new and the old. "Is this all? A slightly larger viewscreen and one or two new vacuum tubes? That hardly seems worth the trouble of a relaunch."

"Ah, but you know every wealthy patron will wish to upgrade their in-home system, just to say they have the latest and the greatest." Mr. Calloway gave a wry smile. His watery blue eyes looked huge through the lenses of his glasses.

Nyssa looked away to avoid laughing.

"It's a shame, though. When the company was just 'Dalhart Incorporated,' they built things to last forever, not to be replaced every six months." He waved to the wall behind him where a bronze-framed screen rested. "I purchased that model almost a decade ago when I took the shop over from my father. Still works like a charm."

If by like a charm you mean makes the caller sound like they are under a foot of water and look like they're standing in front of a carnival mirror. Still, you have to admire the simplicity of those first models. Made to do one thing forever and do it the best. A lot of people could learn from that.

Mr. Calloway dabbed at his bald head with a handkerchief. "I want to do a quick inventory. You have the counter. Don't scare off any customers, young lady." He winked and left through the swinging door into the back.

Nyssa glanced over the counter. Mr. Calloway's tools were scattered everywhere, completely ignoring the outlines she'd made to mark each instrument's designated place. She clicked her tongue, and hung her satchel on a hook behind the counter.

"For as much pride as he has in this shop, you'd think he'd keep it in better order."

"I heard that!" Calloway called from the back.

She chuckled. "Sorry, I forgot you weren't deaf yet, just senile."

"Hardy har har. If it matters so much to you, clean it up yourself."

Nyssa laughed, shook her head, and began lining up wrenches, spanners, and crimpers. She sorted the spools of wire by gauge and the vacuum tubes by size before spinning around to polish the reliable, old videophone's screen.

"Trusty old Dalhart 2." She swiped a muslin cloth over the raised lettering declaring the maker and the model number.

The lullaby chimed, and she turned with her best smile pasted across her face. Not that she didn't like people, in small doses, but she was told her default face made her look cold and indifferent. People could be so darn sensitive.

A man with dark glasses and a top hat shadowing his pale face strode in. He wore a black raincoat with the collar pulled up to the corners of his thin mouth. He grinned at her as if she were a tasty leg of lamb and he a slavering dog.

H. L. Burke *Nyssa Glass and the House of Mirrors*

1) What traits and skills do you think Nyssa exhibits in these first paragraphs will be important at the climax of the book?

2) What can you tell about the setting or world this story is in?

3) Who do you think will be the protagonist and who the antagonist?

C. *Read*:

David Jonathan Malard was not about to let a mere Faxon get the better of him, despite the fact the leathery brute weighed almost twice as much as he and sported an impressive arsenal of knuckle blades and an LB-87 rifle. Keeping a firm hold on the rifle barrel, David twisted low to the right, using the weapon to hold back a direct strike of the blades. In a single, smooth turn, he came up beside and slightly behind his enemy. The Faxon hissed as David drove the heel of his boot into the tendon below the hock, which was never as strong as the heavy-boned legs would suggest. The move easily dropped the larger creature to his knee.

There was not time to waste. An injured Faxon was a dangerous Faxon. Pressing his weight against the rifle to which he still clung tenaciously, David slammed his left elbow into the top of the creature's thick, black muzzle, blocking the flailing blades with an armored wrist cuff. The blow to the muzzle did exactly as David had been taught, and the Faxon was momentarily stunned. Using the precious seconds, David yanked the rifle barrel upward and twisted it out of the Faxon's hands. The creature gave in indignant growl, lunging forward to receive the butt of the rifle across his nose. Flinging the rifle out of reach, David slapped a cuff around the Faxon's wrist. It immediately locked. Enraged, the Faxon lunged forward. David remained undaunted, having already thrown a second cuff around a thick, rounded beam. With the press of a button, an energy pulse locked the cuffs' signal together, keeping the Faxon from moving any more than a single step in any direction. David stood just out of reach.

With a deep sigh, he examined his catch. Not bad for a night's work, but unfortunately the night was still young and this was not his main target. He allowed for a moment to catch his breath, preparing himself for yet another difficult task. Taking a couple steps back, he ran his hand through the sweaty strands of blond hair that stubbornly fell back over his hazel eyes.

He was a handsome man by most standards. At the age of thirty-four, he was still quite young. His features were soft, yet well defined. A boyish charm glinted in his eyes that lay beneath a strong brow accented by smooth cheekbones and hard-set jaw. He stood a good six-foot-two in height and from head to toe, he was a wonderful example of fitness and strength. While not massive in muscular bulk, his body was toned by the rigors of his active lifestyle.

After wiping his brow with his uniform sleeve, he glanced about, his keen eyes picking up the subtle variations within the shadowy alley. A headband aided in his scrutiny of his surroundings. Special sensors sent a holographic shield across his eyes, adjusting to the subtle changes in light to provide both shading in bright environments and superb night vision. Assessing that all was now quiet around him, David turned to the thick, military-style band on his wrist, watching the readout on the mission's current status. Taking a deep breath, he resumed his work, jogging hurriedly down a narrow street.

"Where's my team, Eatrax?" he called. His voice instantly carried through the black, military issue comlink he wore as a band around his neck.

"Eastside," a voice answered from a small band tucked behind David's ear. "Low road. Watch for Kruestar. He doubled back."

David allowed himself a slight half smile. This was exactly what he wanted.

Jolene Loraine *Night Hawk*

1) Who is the main character?

2) What is the milieu, or setting?

3) What is the genre and tone of the book? In other words, what is the writer promising the reader?

Day 3 promises, promises

Speaking of promises to the reader, here's a story.

A writer wrote a noir that went along as most noirs do with just a hint of spooky, and then in the middle of the book, the story veered into time travel and quantum physics and metaphysics and wild science. He had previously written a noir detective mystery with a pun on Shrodinger's Cat as a title that was full of riffs on quantum physics. Those of us who had read that one and enjoyed the first noir were surprised by the whiplash turn in the second book and delighted. Other readers who picked up this noir first and accepted the first chapter as establishing the genre, tone, and style were outraged, and vented their ire on Amazon. They thought they had bought a simple noir and wanted to read a simple noir. Those readers might never again pick up a book by that writer.

Another writer claims that she destroyed her career as a sweet romance writer when she published a book of speculative fiction. Her fans eagerly bought the book and were disappointed when it wasn't a sweet romance. They no longer trusted her, and that writer's sales plunged.

There are two lessons to be gained from that. One, deliver what you promise in the first chapter. Two, use a different pen name for each genre you write in. David Farland who writes fantasy is the same man as Dave Wolverton who writes science fiction. That way, fans of one genre won't accidently spend money on a genre he or she doesn't like. One doesn't need to be secretive about the different pen names. They are simply aids for the reader looking for a book she or he will like.

Activities:

A. *Read*:

The early October sunlight streamed through the rectangular stained glass windows that lined both the up and downstairs of the sanctuary. There were sixteen total, four on each side of the lower portion of the room and four on each side of the church's balcony. Boone knew that there were sixteen. He had counted them during many services, as he had also counted the number of light bulbs in the chandelier, the number of people in the choir, and sometimes the number of times Pastor Morgan called out, "Can I get an amen?" in a single service. Today, he was up to five. The sunlight became more intense, tossing a rainbow of colors across the white plaster walls. Boone glanced downward as a speck of red light found its way to the back of his hand.

His curiosity followed the light up to its home on the far side of the church. Behind the iron balcony railing, Boone watched as the beam of light rested beside a beehive of glass. Then, it jumped to the illustration of an open Bible, inlaid in blue glass and encircled by deep red. The light grew brighter and more intense. He tried to blink, but his eyes would not shut. At the bottom of the window inset in its own pane of glass were the words "To him that worketh not." In thirteen years, he had never seen those words.

He read them under his breath, "To him that worketh not." The light from the chandelier began to flash off and on. Silence filled the room. Pastor Morgan's mouth still moved and his hands still gestured, but Boone couldn't see what he was saying.

The flickering of the grand light fixture increased. "Is this a joke?" he questioned nervously, noticing that no one moved from their seat to fix the malfunction above them. Then, the carpet pulled up from the floor sending tacks flying through the air. The paint chipped off the walls raining flacks of white over the unmoving churchgoers. With a horrible untamed howl the organ played uncontrollably. Boone hurriedly scanned the room, looking side to side for anyone in any acknowledging this event. With a loud pop, the flashing ended and everything returned as it was. Once again, Boone could hear the words of Jeff's father.

"Noel," Boone whispered, "did you see that?"

"Hush, Boone," she warned.

Lauren H. Brandenburg   *Boone The Ordinary*

1) What is the hook in the beginning of this novel?

2) What is Boone's normal life?

3) What is the genre and tone of this novel? Can you tell what the stakes are yet?

B. *Read*:

Fauna coaxed a flower to bloom and leaned in to inspect it. The colors were duller. The bright fuchsia had faded to a dingy pink. Another effect of the curse. She pressed her lips together and let her wings pull her back away from the plants.

"Come on, Fauna." Nella gestured for her to catch up. "We are almost to the field."

Fauna flapped her delicate wings, and the breeze carried her over to her sister.

The same breeze rippled through Nella's wavy white hair and swayed the trees towering over them. Below Fauna, the grass had begun to wilt, the tips drooping and changing to brown. Why did Father not intervene?

Nella flew on ahead, dodging large bushes and massive tree trunks. Her pink petal skirt twisted around her body.

Fauna was not sure she wanted to visit the field. Rumor had it that her childhood play place had been turned. What that meant, she was not sure. Inside her chest, though, her heartbeat thundered like centaur hooves.

Nella paused at the edge of the forest. A bright light shimmered around her and then disappeared as she shed her tiny form for a much taller version.

Fauna landed on a nearby boulder and did the same. The light swarmed around her. She breathed in the change and then settled on the rock once again. No longer was the rock a massive boulder, but more of a stepping stone. Without waiting for her sister to say anything, Fauna marched past her and into the field. Dreary flowers hung their heads as she approached. Long grasses swayed with a brisk wind.

Nella followed behind her, her steps swishing in the grass. "It looks so different."

Beyond the field, mountains stretched to the sky. Menacing clouds hung around the peaks and cast shadows on the field.

Nella ran a finger over one of the forlorn-looking flowers and then let out a deep sigh, dropping her hand to her side. "It's so sad. I feel like the island is dying."

Fauna took Nella's hand and pulled her over to a pile of rocks where they sat side by side. "That's because Bellanok is dying."

Nella gasped.

"When the demon entered our protected land, it let death and sin in with it. Now everything that is happening to the outside world will happen here—unless we find a way to stop it."

Nella crossed her arms. "We have plenty of capable dragon and centaur warriors to venture into the mountains."

"Yes, but they would not be able to destroy the demon. Not on their own." A pair of light blue eyes floated through her mind. Why was he haunting her dreams again? "As queen, it is my duty to protect Bellanok. I must seek Father's will. Right now, I sense that he wants me to leave."

Her crystal blue eyes widened. "You cannot leave!"

Fauna pulled her sister close. "I do not want to." Tears stung the corners of her eyes. She could not remember the last time she had cried. Queens had to be positive and uplifting, at least around those they were charged with caring for.

"Fauna, look." Nella pulled away and pointed behind Fauna to where the tree line met the edge of a mountain face.

A stunning snow-white unicorn strode into the meadow. It stopped after a couple of steps and dipped its head to graze. Every time its head moved, the silver horn glittered like dew on the early morning leaves.

"It has been so long." Nella stood and took a hesitant step toward the unicorn. "The unicorns have stayed hidden in the deep forests since the demon made its way to the island."

Fauna could only stare at the magnificent creature. Every movement—so ethereal.

The unicorn jerked its head up, ears pricked.

Something was wrong.

Ralene Burke   Bellanok: *The Reluctant Savior*

1) What have you learned about this world in the beginning of the novel?

2) Who are the main characters?

3) What is the genre? What are the stakes?

C. *Read*:

Today, she would ask him. If she didn't, her mother would have her way, and then Ayianna would be stuck among the humans for the rest of her life. She latched the gate and picked up her lantern and the milk pail. Ivory froth filled the pail halfway, down an inch since yesterday. At this rate, they wouldn't have enough milk for the winter.

The morning lingered between the half-light of dawn and the shroud of night. The darkness obscured much of the forest and the dirt path behind her house. A cold breeze hissed through the odd, bushy silhouettes and spindly evergreens, whispering fear into her heart and provoking images of creatures hiding among the shifting shadows. She shivered and quickened her pace. Would she ever get used to living here?

Her lantern swung in her hand as she made her way back to the front yard. Its yellow glare skimmed the clumps of vines twisting up the back wall. Her house was almost as big as the village governor's, which would have put her family at an advantage if her father hadn't been an elf.

She sighed.

What kind of future could she hope to have here?

None.

She clenched her jaw and gripped the pail's handle tighter. Enough wondering. She needed to hurry and speak with Father before the porridge was ready—before Mother's presence could interfere.

At the end of the goat pen, where the path curved left to the front of the house, a sharp cry pierced the lingering darkness. Ayianna jumped back, upsetting the milk in her pail. She bit back a curse.

"Liam?"

No, the cry didn't sound like a wolf. Ayianna scanned the underbrush, the autumn trees above. Behind her, the goat bleated, but went back to nibbling on the grass. She shrugged, her eyes still scanning the bushes as she turned to go.

Leaves rustled, and the bush's slender limbs shuddered. Shadows veiled the intruder, the light of the lantern unable to penetrate the layers of dry leaves and stems. Ayianna peered closer. A dark mass burst out of the bush toward her face. She flung her arms up. The milk pail slammed into her head, and its warm contents splashed down her face, neck, and clothes. The lantern rocked on its hinge, the flame flashing and flickering. The intruder screeched, and a rush of wings brushed against her skin.

Ayianna lowered her arms.

A large bird ruffled its dark feathers and made to settle its wings, but one hung at an odd angle. Its round, ebony eyes ogled her.

Could it be?

"Fero? Is brother home already?" She glanced around, but her eyes failed her in the half-light. Her wet clothes clung to her skin, and the breeze grew colder. She shivered and glared at the bird. "Brother or not, look what you made me do? Now, I've got no milk, and I'm all wet."

Fero jerked his wayward wing back and hissed.

"Are you hurt?" Ayianna lifted the lantern, and its glow washed over the falcon, revealing dark stains on his ribbed underbelly. She reached out to touch him, but he snapped his curved beak at her. The branch shifted, and the bird thrashed about, trying to regain his perch, but then he broke free and soared haphazardly into the red-tinged sky.

Atop the bush, a strip of cloth fluttered where Fero had sat. She tore it free. The fabric was damp, soiled, and stunk of decay. It stained her fingertips red. Blood?

"Ayianna!"

Her mother's voice wrenched her from her thoughts. Ayianna tossed the cloth aside and darted up the path to the fire pit where her mother bent over a pot and stirred. The steam and smoke swirled into Mother's pinched face. Her head covering hung loose over her shoulders, revealing her messy braid and stray hairs.

Ayianna's stomach knotted. Should she say something? What would she say? Her brother's crazy bird had stopped for a visit and left a soiled piece of cloth? It was probably nothing. She shivered again in the morning breeze.

"I tripped and spilled the milk."

She clucked her tongue. "Well, the porridge is ready." She held up three steaming bowls. "Take these inside, I'll be in soon. Once you're done, you'll need to start on the garden right away. We don't want to risk an early frost and lose everything we've worked for."

Ayianna nodded. She set the lantern aside and placed the milk pail in the attached shed. Sacks of threshed wheat sat at the back, waiting for the colder months where she would have to grind them into flour. Barrels filled with brine and cabbage lined one wall. Bundles of herbs hung from the thatched roof; their spicy scents stung her nose and mingled with the souring cabbage. The smell turned her stomach.

She ducked back outside and accepted the bowls from her mother. Balancing them in her arms, she kicked the door open and slipped inside. She'd have to clean up later or lose the opportunity to speak with her father. The thin door clicked shut behind her.

"Morning," her father said. He sat on the edge of a bench and pulled his boots on. Thick streams of silver swam through his shaggy hair. Another sign that village life didn't agree with him.

"Morning, Father." Ayianna set the bowls on the small table in the center of the room and eyed him. Was he in a good mood, or should she try later? She took a deep breath. "Did you sleep well?"

He rubbed his face and stifled a yawn. "As well as I might, I suppose. Porridge again?"

She nodded.

Her father made a face and then smiled. He gestured toward the ceiling of the three-room house. "We have a roof over our heads and food in our bellies. What more could we ask for?"

Ayianna fidgeted with a chair. Here was her opportunity, if only the words would come. She opened her mouth to speak, but clamped it shut again. She grabbed one of the bowls of porridge and plopped down. Her soul writhed against the silence and would spew out recklessly if she didn't follow through. She took a deep breath.

"Father?"

He looked at her and smiled, but his eyes gave it away. He was bracing himself, knowing already what she was about to say.

J. L. Mbewe *Secrets Kept (The Hidden Dagger, Volume 1)*

1) What questions are raised here that you want to know the answer to?
2) What conflicts do you read here?
3) Did you see the foreshadowing? What is it?

Day 4 consistency

Think about the story you are working on. Does it waver as to what genre it is? Is the style consistent? Does the action fit the expectations of the intended audience? Does the vocabulary fit the abilities of the intended reader?

Activity:

1) You may not have finished your story, but go through what you have already written. What does your first chapter or paragraphs promise the reader?

Day 5 paperwork

Someone quipped that you had better like what you write because you'll be required to read it hundreds of times. It will feel like a thousand times. But that's what professional writers do. They don't whip off something, read it once, and send it off. They go over the manuscript over and over again, each time looking for a particular thing to bolster or fix. When you're looking for spelling errors, it is difficult to also look for plot progression and theme. So commit yourself to reading your story over and over, each time looking for one thing.

Peter de Vries said, "I love being a writer. What I can't stand is the paperwork." Nonetheless, he did the paperwork.

Activity:

Does your first chapter of your story do what it was supposed to do? If not, rewrite.

CHAPTER FOURTEEN:

VOICE

Some people make a big deal out of voice and make it sound like something mysterious. There's nothing mysterious about it. In writing, voice is the totality of the choices that a writer makes about sentence structure, vocabulary, subjects, emphasis, and expressed attitude.

The voice of many genre writers is fairly indistinguishable from each other as most genre writers are trying to be invisible so the readers notice only the story. But even so, there will be differences in vocabulary, subject, and mood. Some writers manage to turn every story into a thriller. Some writers turn every story into a philosophical treatise. And some writers sound angry whatever they write.

Your voice will change several times as you grow in skill and as you practice. You might try to imitate the voice of other writers, which is fine, but eventually you will settle into a style of writing that will reflect the words you know and how you use them. Your voice will reflect what you think is important in life, and what is not even worth noticing.

Different kinds of voice, or styles will attract different kinds of audiences. At the moment, unless you're in a really bad mood, you are writing to please your instructor. What your instructor likes may not be what the people you hope will read your work will like. If you want to write for middle grade boys with ADD or dyslexia, you will not want to use a dreamy, poetic, complicated voice. If you want to write stories for people like you, you will want a voice that pleases you. You won't care if a thirty-year-old drill sergeant likes your writing or not.

Still, for the moment, you will want to learn how to write in such a way that your instructor is pleased. Not only for the grade, but because you need the practice. Learning how to write in a variety of styles will help you develop your own voice in the end.

Day 1 writers write different ways

Take a look at this passage from *Reef* by Paul McAuley:

> Margaret Henderson Wu was riding a proxy by telepresence deep inside Tigris Rift when Dzu Sho summoned her. The others in her crew had given up one by one and only she was left, descending slowly between rosy, smoothly rippled cliffs scarcely a hundred meters apart. These were pavements of the commonest vacuum organism, mosaics made of hundreds of different strains of the same species. Here and there bright red whips stuck out from the pavement; a commensal species that deposited iron sulphate crystals within its integument. The pavement seemed to stretch endlessly below her. No probe or proxy had yet reached the bottom of Tigris Rift, still more than thirty kilometers away. Microscopic flecks of sulphur-iron complexes, sloughed cells, and excreted globules of carbon compounds and other volatiles formed a kind of smog or snow, and the vacuum organisms accumulated nodes and intricate lattices of reduced metals that, by some trick of superconductivity, produced a broad band electromagnetic resonance that pulsed like a giant's slow heartbeat.
>
> All this futzed the link between operators and their proxies. One moment Margaret was experiencing the three hundred and twenty degree panorama of the little proxy's microwave radar, the perpetual tug of vacuum on its mantle, the tang of extreme cold, a mere thirty degrees above absolute zero, the complex taste of the vacuum smog (burned sugar, hot rubber, tar), the minute squirts of hydrogen from the folds of the proxy's puckered nozzle as it maintained its orientation relative to the cliff face during its descent, with its tentacles retracted in a tight ball around the relay piton. The next, she was back in her cradled body in warm blackness, phosphenes floating in her vision and white noise in her ears while the transmitter searched for a viable waveband, locked on and—*pow*—she was back, falling past rippled pink pavement.

The alarm went off, flashing an array of white stars over the panorama. Her number two, Srin Kerenyi, said in her ear, "You're wanted, boss."

Margaret killed the alarm and the audio feed. She was already a kilometer below the previous benchmark and she wanted to get as deep as possible before she implanted the telemetry relay. She swiveled the proxy on its long axis, increased the amplitude of the microwave radar. Far below were swells and bumps jutting from the plane of the cliff face, textured mounds like brain coral, randomly orientated chimneys. And something else, clouds of organic matter perhaps—

The alarm again. Srin had overridden the cut-out.

Paul McAuley *Reef*

What would you say this writer's voice is?

He writes in long, complex sentences and has long paragraphs. This story is written in third person past tense. He is not afraid to use big words, or in other words, he uses a large vocabulary grounded in biology, technology, and astronomy. His description is detailed and exquisite. He is not in a hurry. His science fiction is as hard as it comes. He assumes his audience is conversant enough with those subjects that they can follow the plot. Therefore he is writing for a college-educated audience with an interest in science.

Now let's look at another writer:

… When it is your time, it is your time. That's the process.

The number of negative votes that are required varies based on age. In its original form, the formula was simple: Every decade of life adds another vote necessary to rule you an incon. At birth, you require only two. Pre-born . . . well, they only ever required one negative, right? Ten year olds require three. Twenty year olds require four. Thirty year olds, five . . . etc.

The formula got more complicated when they added pro-votes. There is an offsetting factor with those. The weight is heavier the more closely associated the person is to the voter.

The vote is tallied on your birthday each year. Doesn't mean you're collected that day. Could be weeks later. Months. It also means people tend to be nicer around their birthdays. Occasionally you see lobbying. But not much. Lobby too much, and people start negging you just because.

It is a balancing act, but that's life. A high-wire act that nobody ultimately survives.

I think about Jake again. Look out the window at the sunny day. Shrug. Maybe I'll go to the zoo.

My screen chirps at me. Jake again?

A message box pops up. The image is clearly not Jake. It is the blonde. Even frozen in place, she looks completely composed. Perfect straight hair, blue eyes, shining white teeth. Beautiful. I glance at the rumpled clothing I have on. There are small stains on my shirt. A tear at the knees of my sweats. No way can I take this call now.

Kerry Nietz   Mask

In this piece, we see the writer uses a lot of short sentences and sentence fragments. Despite all the you's in the first part of the excerpt, this is not second person past tense. The first five paragraphs use you in a rhetorical way and is all telling and inner thoughts. This telling is interesting and necessary to understand the rest of the novel. The next three paragraphs is how most of the rest of the novel is written. (Note: I first wrote 'nearly all.' The third time I read this I switched 'nearly all' to 'most.') Since inner thoughts do not determine the person or tense, you need to look at the last paragraphs to know which point of view is being used. In this case the POV is first person, present tense.

The vocabulary is not simplistic, but is simple and easy to read. Because of the future tech and future sociological changes featured in the book, this would be labeled science fiction/horror. There are few commas, two invented abbreviations, and a matter-of-fact tone in this excerpt as well as an informal style. The inner thoughts of the character are shown often. There are no metaphors or similes in this piece.

One more:

The passage angled down. Cool air wafted from below. As pleasant as it was to get out of the heat, that forlorn feeling settled on me hard.

"Why do you live like this, Burt?"

His eyes were flames in the glow of the lantern. "Like what?"

"Alone. This place makes Dead End seem crowded."

"I'm not alone. I got Fluffy."

That didn't reassure me.

Neither of us spoke for a spell. He probably figured I'd run the other way if he said more. All I could do was see how this played out.

Finally he said, "If you found somethin' valuable, would you share it?"

I considered. If I wanted to be a Rockefeller, I'd have taken a different road. "Sure would. Guess I don't need much."

"That's what I figured. And we're friends, right? I can trust you?"

"I'd have to be to go along with whatever you're brewing here."

"Figured that too. That's why I came to you and not that fake in Black Rock." He wiped his eyes, which had grown misty. "Friendship's a rare thing, Doc." After a pause, he added, "Love, too."

A few steps farther the passage opened into a cavern so vast, the lantern couldn't penetrate the limits of it. What got my heart pounding was the low, rhythmic lapping of waves.

"Well, I'll be," I said. "You found water." And not just a trickle. This was a sea, broad, wide, and gleaming dimly.

Not far away, a deep moan echoed off the walls. I could conjure a lot of things in my mind and nothing to fit that sound. My heart froze.

I swallowed, trying to moisten my throat, which was drier than the Mojave. "Is that what you brought me here for?"

Burt set down the broom and crowbar and walked to the shore. "Yep."

"What is it?"

"You can decide for yourself."

I looked behind me, wondering how long it would take me to get back to sunshine, where scorpions and hungry coyotes seemed suddenly friendly. "Maybe I don't want any part of it."

He turned back to me, hands on his hips. "You took a hippocritic oath."

"I'm beginning to feel like I did. Did I ever tell you I dropped out of medical school? Why do you think I opened shop in Dead End?"

He came up and put a reassuring hand on my shoulder. "That don't matter," he replied. "You can cure the warts off a hog. I'm livin' proof."

Small splashes drew near. Something was coming, cutting smoothly in and out of the water.

A. R. Silverberry *Three Steaks and a Box of Chocolates Fantastic Creatures a Fellowship of Fantasy anthology*

In this excerpt there are a few paragraphs that have four sentences. Most of the paragraphs are three or less sentences and most of the sentences are short. The style is folksy, informal, straightforward, and humorous. The speech, creatures mentioned, and town names indicate this is a Western. The unknown creature swimming in the dark water indicates that this is also a fantasy, so this is a mashup. The vocabulary is not simple, neither is it ornate. Most of the dialogue tags are action beats. There are a few metaphors that nicely tie the characters to the setting. The POV is first person, past tense. The writer appears to like people and their foibles. A great deal of the story is told through dialogue. The occasional dip into inner thoughts strengthens the engagement of the reader with the main character. The characters are not heroic in scope, not bigger than life. They are common people.

Activities:

A. *Read*:

By the time Lord Chelsey's ship reached the mouth of the Thames, only thirteen men were still alive.

Chelsey stood at the bow of the Western Star, staring mutely at the familiar stretch of English coastline. The coal fire in North Foreland's octagonal lighthouse tower burned, just as it had when they'd left, guiding ships into the sheltered estuary. The silted islands were the same, with the same sailboats, dinghies, and barges wending through the maze of sandbanks, carrying trade goods between Essex and Kent. After seeing the great Western Ocean crashing headlong over the edge of the world, it seemed impossible that these familiar sights should remain. As if nothing had changed.

"Nearly home," said the first mate, the eighth young man to hold that post since leaving London three years before. He was seventeen years old.

Chelsey didn't answer. He didn't insult the boy by promising a joyous reunion with family and friends. They would see London again, but they wouldn't be permitted to step ashore. It was almost worse than failure, this tantalizing view of home, where life stumbled on in ignorance and peace.

But he hadn't failed. He had campaigned for years to convince King Henry there were treasures to be found at the Western Edge, and he had been right. The barrels and chests that crammed the ship's hold should be proof of that, at least. Treasures beyond his imagining, not just gold and cinnamon and cloves, but precious materials never before seen, animals so strange they could hardly be described, and best of all, the miraculous water. Oh, yes, he had been right. At least he would be remembered for that. Black-headed gulls screamed and dove around them. Through the morning mist, Chelsey spotted the seawalls of the Essex shoreline, only miles from Rochford, where he'd been raised.

He shifted painfully from one leg to the other. It wouldn't be long for him. He'd witnessed it enough by now to know. Once the elbows and knees stiffened, the wrists and fingers would lock soon after, followed by the jaw, making eating impossible. One by one, they had turned into statues. And the pain—the pain was beyond description.

"Admiral?" It was the first mate. "You'd best come down, sir. It's a terrible thing."

Chelsey wondered what could possibly be described as terrible that hadn't already happened. ...

David Walton *Quintessence*

1) Look at the second paragraph, count and write down the number of words in each sentence. What point of view and tense is this written in?

2) Pick one of your practice paragraphs that has more than five sentences and one from the above example that has five sentences or more. You may combine paragraphs if you need to reach five sentences. What are the differences between this voice and your present voice? You don't get away with saying his is good and mine is (awful, nasty, so bad the world could be sucked into this black hole of badness.) We want a quantifiable answer. What is his average number of words per sentence versus your average number of words per sentence? How many of his sentences start with (he, she, name or title of protagonist?) How many metaphors or similes are in his paragraph? How many in yours? How many times does he use a version of the verb to be (am, was, is, were, are.) How many times did you? How many concrete nouns did he use? How many did you? How many sentence fragments? How many complex sentences? Are his descriptions mostly nouns, or mostly adjectives? Your paragraph? Compare the length of his paragraph versus yours. Does he repeat words? Do you? Does he use a broad vocabulary? Do you? How does his comma use compare to yours? I am not asking for a good versus bad evaluation here. I am asking only for quantifiable differences.

3) What is the mood of this excerpt? What is the mood of your practice paragraph?

B. *Read*:

Long ago there was a little land, over which ruled a regulus or kinglet, who was called King Peter, though his kingdom was but little. He had four sons whose names were Blaise, Hugh, Gregory and Ralph: of these Ralph was the youngest, whereas he was but of twenty winters and one; and Blasé was the oldest and had seen thirty winters.

Now it came to this at last, that to these young men the kingdom of their father seemed strait; and they longed to see the ways of other men, and to strive for life. For though they were king's sons, they had but little world's wealth; save and except good meat and drink, and enough or too much thereof; house-room of the best; friends to be merry with, and maidens to kiss, and these also as good as might be; freedom withal to come and go as they would; the heavens above them, the earth to bear them up, and the meadows and acres, the woods and fair streams, and the little hills of Upmeads, for that was the name of their country and the kingdom of King Peter.

So having nought but this little they longed for much; and that the more because, king's sons as they were, they had but scant dominion save over their horses and dogs: for the men of that country were stubborn and sturdy vavassors, and might not away with masterful doings, but were like to pay back a blow with a blow, and a foul word with a buffet. So that, all things considered, it was little wonder if King Peter's sons found themselves straitened in their little land: wherein was no great merchant city; no mighty castle, or noble abbey of monks: nought but fair little halls of yeomen, with here and there a franklin's court or a shield-knight's manor-house; with many a goodly church, and whiles a house of good canons, who knew not the road to Rome, nor how to find the door of the Chancellor's house.

So these young men wearied their father and mother a long while with telling them of their weariness, and their longing to be gone: till at last on a fair and hot afternoon of June King Peter rose up from the carpet which the Prior of St. John's by the Bridge had given him (for he had been sleeping thereon amidst the grass of his orchard after his dinner) and he went into the hall of his house, which was called the High House of Upmeads, and sent for his four sons to come to him

William Morris *The Well at the World's End*

1) Look at the second paragraph, count, and write down the number of words in each sentence. What is the point of view and tense this is written in?

2) What are the differences between this and your present voice? Contrast with a different practice paragraph of yours.

3) Is this a voice you enjoy? We are not asking, "Is this good? Is this bad?" There is no right or wrong answer to a question of enjoyment. Why do you or do you not enjoy this voice? Is this a voice your intended audience would enjoy? If not, what kind of voice would your intended audience enjoy?

C. *Read*:

Yet another reminder that nothing right now was normal.

Reaching into the armory, Jared began pulling out armor, weapons, and supplies. Jared, Vetta, and Kilvin each slipped into high grade Navy combat armor, a rugged combination of deflective and ablative plating that had saved their lives countless times before. Jared pulled on his combat visor and keyed the heads-up display, where he could communicate with Rami and get data from her and from the others as needed. Nearby, Darel pulled on an Aecron skinsuit, a less impressive-looking but effective proximity armor, complete with a skin helmet that integrated into all of his sensor equipment.

Jared laid out the weapons along the bench: pulse pistols, pulse rifles, ordnance-firing gibeon rifles. Jared, Kilvin, and Vetta each took a pistol, the hand weapons fitting cleanly in a torso holster built into the combat armor. Jared and Vetta picked up gibeon rifles and saddled them across the armor's back holster; Kilvin did the same with a pulse rifle. Darel, typically, used none of those weapons, instead strapping on a less powerful Aecron handpulse that allowed him to do other work without having to draw or holster a weapon.

Thus armed, Jared had Rami patch a tridimensional schematic of the complex into the display nest to the armory. "We'll insert here," he said, pointing as he spoke, "provided Darel can get the doors open. The primary command post is about five trics inside the main entrance, which at present looks unoccupied. Darel then will access the primary database while the rest of us keep the area clear. There are several floors of cells in the colony, not to mention the mining section, so we could have some climbing to do, depending on where Nho is. As you can see here, there are three main access tubes that we can use to get from floor to floor, which, given the traffic of hostiles, will probably be a better option that the main lifts.

"Now, keep in mind, we're likely headed into a full-fledged riot. There are a lot of prisoners in there, not to mention the possibility of some nervous guards, so keep your eyes open and make sure you shoot the right people. Remember, our primary task is to keep our path clear and extract Nho, not to kill prisoners. That means the gibeons are a last resort. Is everyone clear?"

The others responded with sober assents.

"Good. Let's go."

Jared spoke with confidence, but inside his stomach twisted. They were venturing into a volatile situation and fear of the unknown crept into him. He took a deep breath and channeled his unease into action, leading the way to the airlock.

Joshua A. Johnston *Edge of Oblivion*

1) Take another of your practice paragraphs with at least five sentences and compare this voice with yours in quantifiable terms.

2) Does this excerpt make you want to read the rest of the book? Why or why not?

3) This is an example of an ensemble cast. What will the writer need to do eventually to help the reader tell all the people apart? Would it be wise to have this large an ensemble cast in a short story?

Day 2 metaphor

Metaphors and similes are comparisons between things that are unlike except for a particular quality. If you write, "Her hair was as black as ink," the only commonality between hair and ink is the color and shine. A simile is simply a specialized metaphor that uses the words like or as.

Metaphors can enliven writing, making the actions and objects more vivid in the reader's mind. Metaphors can contribute to the mood, or tone of a story. Consider the following:

> Rain pattered against the window like a thousand tiny fists. I traced my finger in patterns along the glass, feeling a kind of wistful restlessness I hadn't felt in a long time.

Mirriam Neal *Paper Crowns*

We hope you will agree that "Rain pattered against the window like a thousand tiny fists," is more vivid than, "It was raining hard." Somehow the first sentence conveys the gloom of the day better than the second.

> Then the phones—landline and cellular—had failed, as had cable service, whereupon the Internet had deconstructed as abruptly as a plume of steam in a gust of wind.

Dean Koontz *The Taking*

The phrase, "the Internet had deconstructed as abruptly as a plume of steam in a gust of wind," not only makes a graphic visual of a fairly abstract idea whose only real visual is the blue screen of death, but also carries echoes of biblical concepts about the shortness of a man's life.—James 4:14. Yet you do not know what your life will be like tomorrow. You are just a vapor that appears for a little while and then vanishes away.—is one such verse. Being able to create a two for one, both vivid visual and biblical resonance is a mark of great writing.

Metaphors done well deepen the reading experience, while metaphors done poorly will make the reader laugh, probably not in the way you want them to.

Now that we've told you how metaphor and simile will enliven your writing, here comes the specialized advice that goes with speculative fiction: Do not use metaphors in your first chapter or else use them with great caution.

Why?

Here's why. In your first chapter you are introducing people to the main characters, the problem, the setting, and the rules for your world. The rules of the world are already known by the reader that picks up a romance, police procedural, or legal thriller. The reader that picks up a speculative fiction book knows the rules are different, but doesn't know how yet. They will pick up clues as they read along to assemble a picture of this different world. If you use a metaphor, say, Ralph was a great ape pacing his cage, glaring at the predators who had put him behind bars, your readers will assume that Ralph is a great ape. You do not want to confuse your readers that way. Unless he is a great ape, in which case the sentence is not a metaphor any more.

Use all the similes you want in the first chapter, saying 'like' and 'as' which give clues to the reader who is constructing your storyworld in their mind that those particular words are not to be taken literally.

Activities:

A. *Read*:

He enjoyed the ramen and was just waiting for the coffeemaker to finish perking the strong, black java that brought each morning to life. He looked over his class notes then shrugged into a t-shirt, plaid flannel over-shirt, and a pair of jeans—the working uniform for a great day of student teaching.

Pouring a mug of eye-opener, Bertram noticed Mr. 1C's Rottweiler anointing the azaleas outside his basement apartment window. He was right on schedule, too.

The pounding that followed, however . . . that was entirely new.

The sound was heavy and insistent, like a man kicking his way out of a cask of Amontillado or the Ghost of Christmas Past trying to make a big entrance. At first, Bertram wondered if the water heater pipe had finally broken. Or if Mrs. 1C was driving the Bonneville with a flat again.

But then he realized the sound was coming from the other side of his door. Bertram turned down ol' Jimmy right in the middle of "Swingin' on Saturn's Ring" as the door banged open, and it looked like Death himself had gotten into the building.

This man filled the doorway, dressed shoulder-to-boot in black, hands thrust into the folds of a long, shiny coat. The only colors surrounding him were his ruddy complexion, the pale jaundice-yellow of his wild, cropped hair, and the whiskey-tint to his aviator glasses. In a quiet, urgent voice, he asked, "You Ludlow?"

"Ludlow." Bertram blinked up at him nervously. "Yes . . . Ludlow. I'm Ludlow."

"*Bertram* Ludlow?" A serrated smile cut across the man's face.

"Yeah, but who—?"

"Stellar," said the man, pulling a weapon. It was a gun, a pearlescent silver with no hammer, chamber, or visible safety. He aimed it at Bertram, peering over his shades with eyes a disconcerting amber orange and, so simply, pulled the trigger. It was a quick sting and then nothing—nothing at all.

Jenn Thorson   *There Goes the Galaxy*

1) What is the first simile in this excerpt? Write two more similes that would illustrate the sound of heavy pounding on a door.

2) What is the second simile? Does the simile adequately describe the menace of the intruder? Write two more similes that could describe a menacing stranger.

3) Write a simile for what a day of student teaching is like.

B. *Read*:

   Marie holds her stuffed rabbit close, in a chokehold. In the dim light, a garden of blond hair grows over her pillow. She is three years old and smiling and she smells like baby-soap. Her eyes are already closed.

   "I love you, honey," I say.

   As a physicist, it bothers me that I find this acute feeling of love hard to quantify. I am a man who routinely deals in singularities and asymptotes. It seems like I should have the mathematical vocabulary to express these things.

   Reaching for her covers, I try to tuck Marie in. I stop when I feel her warm hands close on mine. Her brown eyes are black in the shadows.

   "No," she says. "I do it."

   I smile until it becomes a wince.

   This version of the bedtime routine is buckling around the edges, disintegrating like a heat shield on reentry. I have grown to love tucking the covers up to my daughter's chin. Feeling her cool, damp hair and the reassuring lump of her body, safe in her big-girl bed. Our routine in its current incarnation has lasted one year two months. Now it must change. Again.

   I hate change.

   Daniel H. Wilson   *The Blue Afternoon That Lasted Forever*

1) Note that the metaphor is taken from the man's work. Would the metaphor have been as effective if the words had been drawn from something else? For example, suppose the writer had said the bedtime routine is fraying at the edges, like a scarf torn on a nail. While that's not a bad metaphor, it would be better used in a different story. Metaphors are best when they relate to the story's tone or the character of the protagonist. Write two more metaphors that fit the meaning, but don't fit the tone of this story.

2) Here are three similes: fast as a rabbit, slow as a slug, hard as ice. Rewrite each one twice with different comparisons.

3) The simile "white as the underbelly of a snake" conveys an altogether different tone than "white as falling snow" or "white as the paper before he set pen to it." Take a color, say green for example, and write three similes that will convey three tones: menacing, frivolous and happy, and serious.

C. *Read*:

   Unity Village. The insinuation of the name is far from the disposition of its people. Seventeen years haven't been long enough for me to change this. Instead, I've conformed to the cold separateness we cling to. The concept of unity is now a nostalgic whim from the past—like gentlemen doffing fedoras, free ice cream on a hot afternoon, bare-footed children hoop-rolling. Selfless consideration is rare, except from the Mentors. And they only fake it.

   Mentor. The word turns my stomach and my shoulders tense.

Assessment Day.

A few yards from the village square, my trudging slows like a dying wind-up toy. I stop and allow the mud to creep its fingernails into my boot leather. Straight ahead, a weathered wooden platform rests dead center inside a square of empty market booths. Leafless dogwood trees surround the square is if trying to fill the silent space.

Harman, the master gardener, stands rigid between his stocked vegetable stand and the Enforcer car parked beside him. It shines like a black stinkbug, its warning to the meager crowd of onlookers as palpable as any stench. A painted gold backward *E* shimmers against the black paint as the sun peeks over a thatched roof.

Nadine Brandes   *A Time to Die*

1) This excerpt has four metaphors and similes. The first use of the word like is not one of them, for here, 'like' means 'for example.' List the four and label metaphor or simile.

2) Every adjective, metaphor, and simile contribute to the sense of dread. Ruin this excerpt by changing each metaphor and simile into something light-hearted.

3) Now write five similes and make them as goofy as you can. Then, if you have access to the internet, go to http://www.bulwer-lytton.com/winners.html and learn how *not* to do metaphors and similes.

Day 3 she said it

Active verbs, specific verbs, and specific concrete nouns will make your writing more vivid. For example, "She moved across the room," is vague and wimpy. "She walked across the living room," is better. But even better would be something like, "She sauntered from the door to the couch in the darkened living room."

An exception to that rule about using active, specific verbs is the word 'said.' Most of the time, simply write (whoever) said. If the character shouted, or yelled, or whispered, go ahead and write (whoever) shouted. That's better than writing (whoever) said loudly. But if your character is always spouting, declaring, emphasizing, explaining, expostulating and on and on, your character will look silly. When it comes to the word 'said,' the thesaurus is not your friend. And if you use action beats, you will seldom need to use 'said' or its synonyms. Action beats are the character doing something before, during, or after speaking. The action can add meaning to the dialogue and remove the need for said to tag the speaker. Tag means to add something to the dialogue that will let the reader know who is speaking. Look at one of your favorite books. See how often the writer uses action beats to keep track of who's speaking during dialogue instead of (whoever) said.

Activities:

A. *Read*:

The dragon wheeled a full hundred-eighty degrees and lifted me high as he lashed out with one of his foretalons. His fearsome claws connected with a smaller winged figure that spun crazily from the force of the attack. I saw the glint of a drawn weapon in the figure's hand. My lingering vertigo prevented me from gathering more than that.

Majestrin craned his neck around and plopped his head at his withers once more. "Try to stay seated. The ride's going to be rough."

I groped around the dragon's back and neck, at a loss for significant handhold. Mejestrin had better submit to the idea of tack or barding after this. I clutched one of his dorsal plates and prayed.

With a mighty thrust of his wings, Majestrin surged forward.

"Are we fleeing?" I yelled over the wind that roared in my ears. "How bad is the situation?"

"I simply hope to buy us some time to think. At least two dragon-kin want our hides."

I glanced around the deep cobalt landscape below and caught sight of our two flying opponents whose wings flapped crazily as they fought to match our speed. It would take a heroic effort, given that Majestrin outsized them at least five-to-one.

Not far ahead, I also spied the spire of a dead tree, mostly stripped of branches from many years of withstanding the press of the elements.

"Majestrin, do you think you could swoop down and break off a couple fathoms of that tree trunk?" I asked.

The dragon spared a glance back to me, just long enough to offer a devilish grin. "Hold on tight."

He tucked his wings and plummeted in a steep dive. I hunkered down low, putting as much of my torso against his neck as possible so the sheer force of the wind did not tear me from his back. As the leaves of the trees crackled and whipped at Majestrin's hind legs and tail, I felt a lurch and heard a sharp crack. We shot for the sky again.

"Will this do?" Majestrin called, reaching back to hand me the slender tree trunk he had acquired.

I weighed the length of it against my strength. While a little crooked, the shaft mimicked the length and girth of a lance. "Yes, nicely. Come about, my friend."

Rebecca P. Minor *The Windrider Saga*

1) There is not a single paragraph that is composed of five sentences in the excerpt above. You will need to combine two or three of the paragraphs to obtain five sentences to work with. Now make two lists from every verb in the combined paragraphs. Make a list of all the active verbs. Make a list of all the passive verbs (variants of to be).

2) Take one of your practice paragraphs that consists of at least five sentence and make two lists, one of active verbs, and one of passive or weak verbs.

3) Rewrite one of your paragraphs to make every verb active. Then take that same paragraph and rewrite it to make every verb passive. Which voice do you prefer?

B. *Read*:

Rough stone tore Rathe's palms as he stumbled through the gaping maw of the cave. He tore away the makeshift leaf filter covering his mouth and sucked in the cool underground air, soothing his burning lungs. Pain lanced through his side as each breath tortured cracked ribs.

He turned to the entrance and gazed into the ash-clogged air outside. Grey blanketed the world like a shroud, quickly swallowing his large three-toed tracks and obliterating any scent that would lead the trackers to him. Satisfied that he would be safe for the duration of the ash fall, Rathe staggered farther into the cave. His claws echoed hollowly on the stone floor, their quiet *clack, clack, clack* bouncing into darkness.

The musical trickle of water sounded nearby, and Rathe angled toward it. Sudden wetness at his feet alerted him to the presence of a shallow pool. He lowered gingerly to the ground and stuck his snout into the chill liquid. The bitter taste of ash flowed over his tongue, but sweet relief filled his parched throat. Yet each swallow intensified the pain in his ribs.

The cool, moist rock felt good against his hot skin. He rolled onto his left side, away from the fire in his battered ribs, and slapped against the ground as drowsiness flowed over him. The water's flow sung him to sleep.

A shrill cry jolted Rathe from soothing darkness. Pain seared through his right side and down his tail. Through the agony, the fading echo of the cry played at the edges of his mind. He groaned as he rolled onto his belly and forced down a few more swallows of water.

He pushed to his feet, swaying slightly as his stiff muscles adjusted to his weight. He cocked his head and listened.

Whatever had made the sound had gone silent. Or the cry had been only the vestige of a nightmare.

Stuart Vaughn Stockton *Starfire*

1) In North American writing, sound effects such as *clack, tick, and whoosh*, are generally italicized. How many sounds are in this excerpt?

2) There is one metaphor in this excerpt. What is it?

3) Analyze the voice of this piece.

C. *Read*:

In the pages prior to this excerpt, everybody has been killed in the embassy of the country that Rafe is a spy for. Rafe is running for his life. His contacts have been killed as well, and now he is following a woman he doesn't know because she promised to lead him to safety.

The woman looked up and into what looked like a disused maintenance tunnel, narrow and low, its entrance almost invisible in the surrounding rock. Rafe hurried after her.

"Wait!" Rafe heard its soft mental whir before the machine clicked into alertness. Something small and box-shaped launched itself at his knees. He kicked out at it and winced as his toes made impact. The machine—only a spider, thankfully—hit rock, bounced up, came skittering back. Rafe braced himself.

And the woman was in front of him. She sidestepped swiftly, and the spider, locked on her position, swiveled towards her. Its front legs lashed out, but she'd already moved. They danced for a few steps, the spider confused and thrusting blindly, the woman weaving and maneuvering. Finally she stepped in with a series of kicks that smashed the spider into the wall. Then she leaned down and put her fist through what passed for the thing's head.

Its many legs twitched once, violently, then lay still.

It was over in moments. Rafe had barely taken two steps forward to help her.

"They'll guess what happened when they find the machine. The Primary is bound to check in eventually," cautioned Rafe, trying not to gape.

"We can muddy the waters a little." The woman picked up the spider—broken and dead, it could be tucked under an arm—and ducked out of the tunnel long enough to chuck it out on the tracks, right at the bend.

"If a train crunches it, they'll think it got confused and wandered onto the tracks."

Rafe nodded. Spiders were old mage-made technology. No one these days knew how they worked or how to make them, not even the Shimmer mages. The conscripts running the Primary might not even know of this one's existence.

"Come on," called the woman. She flashed a light, briefly.

He followed her further in for a short distance. Mud squelched under his feet. "Where now?"

She pointed the light beam up to where a rusted iron ladder, missing rungs in spots, led up to an iron cover.

"This is it?" Rafe followed the light. "You're planning to bring us up into Brethren Circle, right in the middle of the Girdlesday crowd and the arms of the stazi?"

"How perspicacious of you. As it happens, you're right." The woman climbed up the ladder and knocked a rapid staccato on the cover with the end of her light. Then she pushed up the cover and peered down, face pale in the darkness. "Coming?"

Rabia Gale   Quartz

1) Are there any metaphors or similes in this piece?

2) Two sentences contain back-story. What do you know about this world from them?

3) Analyze the voice of this piece.

Day 4 sentence length

At one time, those who wrote in English wrote long, long sentences, with many clauses as well as pauses, marked off by commas, to qualify any of their assertions; and the readers enjoyed that style of writing. Today, most readers prefer shorter sentences. At one time, writers would be embarrassed to have a sentence fragment anywhere in their novel. Some writers today write more sentence fragments than complete sentences in their novels. Preferences may change again in the future. Some authors write with thoughtful pauses between each scene of action. Other authors pile on active scene after active scene with only the barest of pauses for breath. At one time writers could write (Noun) was (verbing or an adjective) as often as they wanted. Today's writers are encouraged to cut out all the to be verbs: was, were, are, is.

Activities:

Today, you will (note: I first wrote: 'are going to', then revised to 'will') give your voice a workout.

1) Take three of your practice paragraphs that are at least five sentences long. Rewrite each paragraph with sentences as long as you can manage. You may add information. You are allowed to end up with fewer sentences than you started with.

2) Now set that aside that and rewrite every paragraph with as many short sentences and sentence fragments as you can. You are allowed to add information.

3) There are several ways to say the same thing. The way you choose to express a thing is your voice. Did you like writing long sentences better than short sentences? Which came closer to your natural voice?

Day 5 what style?

Did this discussion of voice give you any ideas of how you could change your voice to come closer to what you want your story to do? If you could be a famous author, who would you most want to see reading your work? (Don't say, "Everybody," because that will never happen.) What sort of style would your intended, or target, audience most like to read?

Activity:

1) Work on your story today. Are there sections you will want to rewrite?

2) You have only four more weeks before you need to turn in your story. Stop procrastinating.

CHAPTER FIFTEEN:

WORDS AND WORLDVIEWS

I have discussed and will further discuss a number of issues some people have had with various genres and various tropes within those genres. By now, a number of you are no doubt wondering, "Why? Why does anybody care? Why does it matter what words and tropes are used in our stories? Why do we need to listen to people who fuss about words? They are merely marks on paper or pixels on screens. There is no reality to them. They are ONLY WORDS!"

Only. Words.

What are words only? Do words only represent objects and actions and their qualities?

Why do some people consider freedom of the press worth dying for? Why is there censorship and fights against censorship? Why do libraries celebrate Banned Books week?

Consider this:

Over two billion people worship a God who calls himself The Word. They believe that by His words the world was created. While few of those people think that the words they utter create reality, they do think that words will orient them to reality or blind them to reality.

If words are only vibrations in the air or marks on paper, then why did the Sanhedrin hand Jesus over to the Romans and then the Roman government execute Him? Words are ideas, and the Roman government thought the ideas of Jesus were dangerous.

If ideas are only things that float around in our brain and have no repercussions, then why did Marx sit in Chetham Library while sponging off his in-laws and making many marks on paper? Those words excited a lot of people and resulted in the overthrow of many governments, many wars, and ultimately the murder of over a hundred million people.

Why do companies spend money on written ads?

Yes, fiction is different from non-fiction. But fiction can do something that non-fiction seldom does. Fiction trains the heart. The lessons and meanings of fiction often bypass the head altogether and change the hearts of the readers. And for many readers, where the heart goes, the head eventually follows.

Question: If you believe words are only words, why are you bothering to write?

Words reveal worldviews.

All of us have a worldview even though most of us don't know it. A worldview is a set of basic beliefs through which we interpret the world and ourselves. For example: Is the universe a basically evil place, or is it a good place? Are you born to suffer, and die like a dog? Is there or is there not a God? Are children born evil or born good? Is family important or is it an incidental assortment of people? What is my purpose in life? What is the purpose of all the other people? Which political system will cause the most people to flourish? Where is humanity headed? Why do people do things I don't like? Are social rules chains or wings? How you answer those questions will be dictated by your worldview.

If your worldview is that life sucks like a gaping chest wound and then you die, and that's the kind of stories you want to tell, you will find a readier audience in France, Germany, and Russia than you will find in North America. Readers of horror are more tolerant of such messages, but North American readers prefer stories with happy endings. Non-Americans will sometimes comment on the naiveté of the North Americans. They are amazed that North Americans seem to think there are solutions to problems, and they work hard to find them. Part of the attitude that "If you search, you will find a solution," comes from the stories we tell ourselves.

In the book *The Universe Next Door*, James W. Sire says in effect that a worldview is a basic orientation of the heart. This orientation is expressed as the story told to oneself about oneself. Or else this orientation can be thought of as a set of beliefs and assumptions about reality. These assumptions can be true, partly true, or entirely false. James W. Sire goes on to say these beliefs can be conscious, subconscious, consistent or inconsistent. These assumptions provide the foundation for how we live.

So why are we talking about this in a book about writing speculative fiction?
Because:
Every story has imbedded within it a worldview. The writer may not know she is expressing a worldview. The reader may not know he is ingesting a world view. The expressing and ingesting are still happening. Even if the reader is not conscious of what is happening, a seed is sown. If one reads enough in a certain worldview, it is possible that the reader's heart will absorb the lesson and then work on changing the mind. It is *not* inevitable that one will change one's worldview because of what is read, but it is common.

If a certain type of story is attractive to a reader, the worldview behind the story may be attractive as well. One (you, we, I) can more easily withstand the attraction if we are aware of both our worldview, and the worldview expressed in the attractive literature.

Most writers have no idea what lessons they are teaching in their stories. I want you to be among the writers who are aware of what their words might do to impressionable people.

Also:
It is possible to live peaceably with people whose worldviews differ from your own. It is possible to respect a person made in the image of God and disagree with nearly every point of her particular worldview. It is possible to express that disagreement without being mean and spiteful.

(An aside note: In general, men will express disagreement more aggressively than will women. This general observation has nothing to do with the particular woman who is in front of you and hitting you with the verbal equivalent of a baseball bat. Again, this general observation has nothing to do with the particular man who is in front of you disagreeing with words as soft as moth wings. So why did we make this observation? Because I have often seen woman panic and get their feelings hurt over the more aggressive style of men, while men shrug off the combative words. I have seen men not even notice a woman is disagreeing with him. Understanding this dynamic might help in classroom discussions.)

Yes, all the contributors to this textbook have worldviews. We believe there is an ultimate truth. We also believe that not all roads lead there, but rather only the straight and narrow road. We know the students who read this textbook may range in religious worldview from agnostic, atheist, Bahai, Buddhist, Christian, Daoist, Hindu, Jainist, Jewish, Muslim, Pagan, and Undecided or even Haven't Thought About It yet. However, we are not using a stick, tome, or wombat to beat you about the head to drive you to that narrow road we believe in. Why not? The reason is two-fold:

(1) We want you to think. Yeah, we know it's hard, but you can do it. As people who have spent some time thinking, we understand how uncomfortable and how threatening that can feel. You still ought to do it from time to time.

(2) The world is full of people who are not you. If you cannot spare one moment to consider how people who are not you see the world, how are you going to be able to write about purple aliens from Neptune, elf queens, or angels battling demons?

Some people think that the only way to see worth in another human being is for that other person to agree with them on everything. Please do not be in that group of people. Please learn the difference between an opponent and an enemy. Please learn how to say, "That's interesting. Why do you think that?"

It seems to be imbedded in the human psyche (worldview alert) that when there is disagreement about something important, the go-to response, or first response, is to say, "That's stupid!" or even, much worse, "That's evil!"

Are there evil ideas and evil people? Of course. It's not wrong to think so or even say so. However, you should not be quick to assume the person you are speaking to is evil because of how he looks or the language he speaks or the religion he holds.

You cannot make progress with a person if you think the person disagreeing with you is stupid and evil.

No one has ever been bullied or humiliated into changing her mind. Anger and fear shut down the prefrontal cortex and erase critical thinking while the person is angry and fearful. Hence the incredibly stupid arguments you can hear between two angry people. If you deliberately provoke anger and fear in another person (and sometimes when you didn't mean to) all you accomplish is furnishing that person with another brick in the wall between you (or the people you come to represent at that point) and the angered person.

You should learn that that other people have reasons for their beliefs, even though their reasons do not persuade you. The reasons may not persuade you because you know something the opponent does not know, and if she did know, she would change her mind. Most likely though, is that you both have nearly the same set of facts. But one of you will weight, or consider, one of the facts as more important than the others, and the other will weight a different fact as the most important. Worldview will help determine which is the most important fact to the viewer.

Here I would like to make another point about arguing or discussing things about which there is disagreement. If you have not trained in debate and don't yet know your subject as well as you would if you studied it harder, you will likely lose your debate and/or be trapped into trading insults. You can lose an argument and still believe whatever it is you believe because you trust in those who are wiser and who have studied more than you. And then if the subject is important to you, you can resolve to talk to those who know more than you either in person or in the long conversation. The term long conversation here refers to the aggregate of books written over centuries about the same subject.

Worldview is shaped by the stories we tell each other.

In the following story excerpt, a govner of Mons Ascraeus has invaded the kingdom of Olympus Mons on Mars with his knights. They have caught the king sporting in his swimming pool with some women, all of them naked. They covered the king in a bathrobe and now they are talking:

"You free climbed Olympus Mons, without wearing oxygen bottles?" The voice of the king spilled over with disbelief.

"This is how we live on Mons Ascraeus, your heretic Majesty. I'm surprised you didn't know that. Shall we discuss something of more importance?"

"Oh, you call me a heretic, do you? You small-minded man of this primitive era. I am a reader of books of the past, Govnor. I know these knights you call 'riders' and this devotion to religion is a horrible aberrancy, a distortion of distant primitive beliefs preserved by religious fanatics. I seek to rise to greater heights, to restore the former civilization of what people like you ignorantly call 'The Time of Magic,' to lay aside your fanaticism and replace it with a new era of enlightened tolerance!"

My lord sheathes his sword before responding. He is still standing in the shallow end of the pool, warm water up to his knees. He looks up at the king and replies, "You just called me a fool. How is that tolerant? Or more to the point, you have forbidden your subjects to make pilgrimage to the Gran Templo of Chryse. How is that enlightened?"

The king shakes his head in disbelief. "You're so ignorant you don't even know you're ignorant. The so-called religious 'revival' leading to the spread of the faith you hold so dear was started by Spanish-language Baptists. Which is why you worship at their temple. Why you say, 'Jesu Christu' instead of 'Jesus Christ.'"

Govnor Pederson yanks clear his sword again, "You will not curse the name of my Lord with those words again, not without penalty!"

"What, are you going to chop me up, here and now? Then what will you do? I perceive you want something from me. You won't get it if I'm dead."

"Believe me, heretic, I am willing to try something at great risk and see how my God guides me through it. If that includes ending your life right here and now, so be it." My lord's voice is low and firm, not out of control at all.

"Roger, allow me for a moment," says Madam Susan. "I also am a student of the past, your Majesty. And you should know as well as I do there is an historic reason why the English language version of the name of the Lord came to be seen as only profanity. You should also know it was the excesses of the past culture that led to the collapse of the technology of that time. And that the religious revival came mostly afterward. And that our Martian feudalism has preserved human lives—as opposed to the total anarchy ruled by unbelievers that preceded it."

…

The king turns back to the govnor. "It seems I have underestimated the hardiness of you Ascraeans...but let us talk honestly of our differences, like men."

My lord replies dryly, "If you can, please do so."

The ruler of Mons Olympus ignores this remark. "You want the pilgrimage to resume. Is that all you want?"

"Why would you oppose the pilgrimage?"

"I mean to rebuild the past here, ncluding space travel. I need every working hand—I can't have my people wasting time on religion. I want them to build a future of freethinking minds, a future like the past, but better. The pilgrimage takes too much time for too many people."

Susan asks, "Pardon me, but you intend to force people to be freethinking?"

"Believe me," the king answers her, "Once they realize what they have to gain, they will thank me for it." Turning to the govnor, he adds, "Speaking of gain, is there something else you would like from me? Gold perhaps? To compensate you for the losses of your merchants from passing pilgrims?"

"Our merchants, such as they are, do make some money off the pilgrimage. But this is not what we are here for. Keep your gold! I am here for the rights of men, women, and children."

"Ah, the best of knighthood, pure and noble," says the king with obvious sarcasm. "Are you sure that's all you want?"

Govnor Pedeson pauses a moment. "Now that you mention it, I demand full freedom of worship for your people. Including the right to make pilgrimage. I also ask that you will cease all warlike activity after this and be at peace with Ascraeus and all your other neighbors"

Travis Perry   *The War Between the Mons*   *Medieval Mars* anthology

Worldviews are not always discussed so openly in books, but sometimes they are. Here are three people talking while the protagonist watches and rests. The king's worldview seems obvious: religion is a dangerous waste of time. Science and a proper ordering of society will bring in a golden age for the humanity living on Mars. He easily assumes that religious people are stupid and greedy for gold. When Susan asks him if he is going to force people to be freethinking, he is so ensconced in his thinking that he doesn't notice that she is being sarcastic.

The govner's worldview is that it is of utmost importance to obey God and to treat his savior's name with respect. He believes in religious freedom, and will go through great effort and expense to insure religious freedom for people he isn't even responsible for.

Which of these express the attitude or worldview of the author? Usually, but not always, the protagonist thinks or speaks with the author's attitude coloring the words. If the protagonist does not echo the writer's worldview, then whichever character that is written about with respect will be the one to carry the author's views.

In these two excerpts I squished together, the protagonist does not speak. Can we still tell what the author thinks? Maybe. There are clues.

The king was caught naked, which is always embarrassing, and so he is seen in a bit of a ridiculous light. The king is idealistic about science and technology. He speaks scornfully and disrespectfully to the man who has just defeated him militarily. The author makes sure the reader sees the disconnect in forcing people to be freethinkers just in case the reader missed it during the king's speech.

It's possible that the author does not like the kind of scientism that rewrites history and thinks scientific knowledge will save humanity. One can love science without embracing scientism, which is an excessive belief in the power of scientific knowledge and techniques. (The determination of excessive or not depends on worldview.)

On the other hand, the govner is seen as temperate, reasonable, and idealistic about religion. If the writer despised Christians as much as the king does, the govner and his knights would have likely been presented as more thuggish, violent, hypocritical, and greedy for gold. They would have been presented as ignorant as the king thinks they are. Having the govnor portrayed as fighting for peace and freedom could indicate that the author appreciates Christianity and possibly other religions, thinking that people should be able to choose which religion or none they will follow.

Reading what the protagonist sees and thinks about could nail the impression of what the writer thinks.

Day 1 revealing world view

One of the reasons we want you to understand worldviews is because everybody reveals their worldview by their actions and choices and arguments.

Your worldview may change as you grow up, and your behavior when no one is watching will reflect those changes.

You will most likely reveal your current worldview as you write your story for this course. We want you to be aware of what you are revealing. And we want you to be aware of what other authors are revealing.

Now we must insert a warning:

You cannot always tell what a writer believes by one story or by what one of her characters say. The writer may have adapted his storytelling to produce a story that will be more commercially successful. A writer may deliberately hide her worldview so that she won't get into trouble with people she considers important. The writer may be telling a cautionary tale, in other words, a story that shows that when people believe this awful thing, even more awful things happen. The writer may have inserted one or more characters whose words do not reflect the writer's beliefs to contribute to conflict in the story.

But even though you cannot state with complete certainty what a particular writer believes, you can learn to see what worldview is being expressed.

Activities:

A. *Read*:

It's a rather strange thing to be expected to tell a ghost story out here in interplanetary space. The captain has asked me to do this rest period and I'm a man who obeys orders. He says you passengers asked for a ghost story this time and, what's more, you want a ghost story of space.

Now, that's not an easy thing to do. Ghosts and space travel do not quite hit it off with each other. Ghosts belong to the old world, the air-bound, land-bound, sea-bound world, a world where people were dominated by ugly castles and power-mad little men and bent by the desires of little, land-locked souls. Dirt and lust and night fright: those are the things that called forth ghosts. We haven't had much of that these past seventy years, thank heavens.

Somehow, out here in the spaces between the stars, between the worlds, there's no room for that sort of horrible thing. There's fright, sure, for there's lots of danger between the stars. There's eeriness, sure, on those strange planets and bits of asteroidal rock. But there are no ghosts of twisted little minds, generally speaking.

Donald A. Wollheim   *Asteroid 745: Mauritia*

1) What might the worldview of this writer be?

2) What words does he use to indicate that he feels trapped on Earth?

3) What might be his hope for the future?

B. *Read*:

"Slave is a word you've been taught to hate, but humans were made to be slaves at first to serve God as our master in a beautiful place. But things changed. From birth, everyone's master is emptiness. Slaves to emptiness spend their days giving emptiness different things. Fun, people, work, games, hobbies all seem to do the trick for a while. But in the end, the emptiness is back, hungrier than ever. When you choose Him, you find the only thing big enough to fill emptiness.

"His overall plan for your life is no mystery. We have His book and His talents to use here . . ." he spread his hands ". . . where He's chosen to place us in space and time. Think about the talents and passions you use every day. A wise guy once said the chief end of man is to glorify God. The meaning of life is being what He made you to be: doing what you're good at. Which brings us back to your question. Tell me, then. What should we do with you?"

For the first time, Jen's tone carried a bit of hope. "Well, I know scads about com-visions—"

"Hardware or software?"

"Both." She beamed. "But I'm way better at processing software."

He nodded. "Very useful. We have a team of Hacks called the Body Surfers, and a Field Hack works with each Muscle Cell."

"I'm not sure what that means, but I'll use stuff I know to help out."

"What about you, Dave?"

I always hated when this came up. My day job at Slider's minimart paid my half of the rent. Sixteen-year-old Jen always came off like a Brainiac with a twenty-year-old loser of a big brother.

"Well, the only things I've ever been good at are com-vision games. You know the kind where you see the barrel of your gun and the room around you? They're called first-person shooters. I've won a couple of corporate-sponsored Web tournaments."

My tone never topped a mumble. For some reason hobbies didn't seem very important right now. I didn't even try to make it sound good. People never understood my useless skill.

The usual response is oh-that's-nice, so it raised my brows when he said, "You mean like *Peacekeeper*?"

Someone who understood my hobby usually had to listen to me chatter. Not today. "Yeah . . . I played on a Peacekeeper champion FBT team, and won the second player terrorist escape for the last couple years."

"I've heard those games are some of the best Sandman training a kid can get."

Frank Creed   *Flashpoint*

1) What might the worldview of the author be?
2) What words indicate that Flashpoint is in the subgenre of cyberpunk?
3) What might be his hope for the future?

C. *Read*:

The most merciful thing in the world, I think, is the inability of the human mind to correlate all its contents. We live on a placid island of ignorance in the midst of black seas of infinity, and it was not meant that we should voyage far. The sciences, each straining in its own direction, have hitherto harmed us little; but some day the piecing together of dissociated knowledge will open up such terrifying vistas of reality, and of our frightful position therein, that we shall either go mad from the revelation or flee from the deadly light into the peace and safety of a new dark age.

Theosophists have guessed at the awesome grandeur of the cosmic cycle wherein our world and human race form transient incidents. They have hinted at strange survivals in terms which would freeze the blood if not masked by a bland optimism. But it is not from them that there came the single glimpse of forbidden eons which chills me when I think of it and maddens me when I dream of it. That glimpse, like all dread glimpses of truth, flashed out from an accidental piecing together of separated things—in this case an old newspaper item and the notes of a dead professor. I hope that no one else will accomplish this piecing out; certainly, if I live, I shall never knowingly supply a link in so hideous a chain. I think that the professor, too, intended to keep silent regarding the part he knew, and that he would have destroyed his notes had not sudden death seized him.

H. P. Lovecraft   *The Call of Cthulhu*

1) What might the worldview of this writer be?

2) List the words that make the emotional tone of this piece.

3) What is his hope for the future?

Day 2 how do they see it?

As we discussed earlier, a protagonist can be a person of some sort, a symbol, a way of life etc. but is most often a person, and often the person from whose point of view the story is told. An antagonist must be something that opposes the protagonist. It is often a person with a different worldview. Rarely, the antagonist and protagonist will have the same worldview, but they oppose each other because they have the same goal and only one may reach it. Sometimes the worldviews of the characters will explain why they oppose each other.

Worldviews shape our language, our attitudes, our behavior and our likes. If a reader loves Ganesh or seeks to honor the Prophet or strives to obey the commands of Jesus Christ, you cannot mock his belief and expect the reader to like it. Christians are oh so tired of the crazy, violent preacher trope. Muslims are weary of the insane terrorist stereotype. Hindus wonder if Westerners will ever try to understand the beliefs behind the images they revere instead of assuming silly things. Atheists can't stand the goofy characterizations of them in Believer's books and movies.

Does that mean you can't have an antagonist of a faith you don't adhere to in your book? Of course not. You can discuss and have as antagonist (or protagonist) anything you want. You do need to be careful, though, and think about how different peoples *see themselves* or you will reproduce the same stale clichés that Hollywood does. Please be better than Hollywood.

Activities:

A. *Read*:

   000.364.07.16

There was once a time when only God knew the day you'd die.

At least that's what they tell me. I wasn't alive then—back when life bore adventure and death held surprise. I guess God decided to share the coveted knowledge. Either that, or we stole it from Him. Personally, I think He just gave the world what it thought it wanted: control.

My thin rectangular Clock sits on the carved shelf across the room, clicking its red digital numbers—red like blood. Today marks the first day of my last year alive.

000.364.07.16

Three hundred sixty-four days, seven hours, five minutes, and sixteen—no, *fifteen*—seconds to live. I've always thought it cruel they include the seconds. But people want absolutes. They demand fine lines in a fuzzy world.

My toes curl like pillbugs when they touch the cold wood floor. I creep to the open window, flick a shivering spider off the sill into the October breeze, and close the shutters. Wind still howls through.

I pull on a pair of wool socks—a frequent Christmas gift of which I never grow weary—and ignore the mirror. It's the same face every morning: tangled hair, bleary chocolate eyes, and a waspish glare that doesn't leave until after coffee.

I push through the bedroom door into the kitchen and just miss a collision with my mother. She sweeps past bearing a mixing bowl of steaming cinnamon oatmeal. Pity her morning greeting isn't as warm as the breakfast she slams on the table. "Twenty minutes, Parvin."

"It's *my* time I waste sleeping, not yours."

The rectangular kitchen glows under the heat of the cooking fire on the opposite wall. A metal wash tin and a red water pump sit to my left, beneath our only glass window. Cold morning light reflects off the soapsuds. The rough kitchen table crowds most of the walking space unless all four chairs are pushed in tight. I plop into the closest seat.

"It's already six-thirty." She blows a stray hair away from her face. "You've wasted seventeen years, let's not spoil your last one."

Ah, mother-daughter love.

Nadine Brandes   *A Time to Die*

1) What might be the worldview of the protagonist?

2) What might be the attitude of the other person?

3) Are the worldviews of the characters in your story all the same or different? How are they different? How are they the same?

B. *Read*:

I was thinking about the intricacies of life, and how simple it was to control them, if handled with efficiency and precision, how there could be no surprises, no mistakes.

But I knew there wouldn't be any mistakes; after all, there was no true right and wrong. Everything was relative, and relativity only called for adaptation. I knew this as sure as I knew the sky was blue, and Taco Tuesday at my school cafeteria was invented by cannibals. It was as real as the game device in my hands, or the air in my lungs.

Anticipation mounted, and my heart started to skip. The last piece of the puzzle was seconds from touchdown when—

"Dinger! Put that game away!"

I nearly flew out of my seat at the sudden interruption of my Tetris game. I luckily (skillfully) remained cool, merely snapping my eyes up to meet the discerning stare of my tenth grade AP American History teacher, Mrs. Smithe.

I had to grin because her darkened eyes were burning over the top of her thick, black-framed glasses, and I knew she was annoyed. This was not the first time, today or otherwise, she had stopped, mid-lecture, to remind me to pay attention. In her world, no matter how addictive the game was, it was supposed to come second to her teaching. "Supposed to" being the operative phrase.

"Aw, but I'm so close to beating this level." I smirked good-naturedly.

The silent, deadly expression I received told me it was clearly not one of her good days, so I shrugged carelessly, smiled brilliantly, and tucked away my Game Pac. I even decided to graciously wait ten more minutes before pulling it out again. Mrs. Smithe seemed reassured by this illusion of obedience, and went back to teaching. She was always a bit of a control freak, but I've never really met a good teacher who wasn't.

And for all her trouble, Mrs. Smithe—Martha—was probably my favorite teacher at Apollo Central High School. She was middle-aged, with short curly hair that almost stood on end when her teacher-senses were tingling. I supposed it was her glasses that really gave her an authoritative demeanor, since her short height and tiny bone structure did not. And she always had coffee nearby. I once figured out while I was bored in her class that she could support a small company stock all by herself. You have to admit that's impressive. If I had any problems with her, it was that she just didn't seem to understand that Tetris was the ultimate meaning in my life.

I'd played the game for years, and it was the key to unlocking the secrets of all life—that we were all just players, some of us winners, a lot more of us losers. That there was nothing more to life than filling it with fun, and working to fit all of the pieces together cohesively, in order to claim glory and the right to brag. It was a beautiful, meaningless thing, the epitome of my preferred existence.

Plus having the title of Tetris King was a nice touch—I'd thought "Tetris Emperor" was a bit much.

C. S. Johnson *Slumbering*

1) This has been handed to you on a plate. The protagonist's name is Hamilton Dinger. What is Dinger's world view?

2) As Dinger changes in the story, do you think he will change into a hero or into a villain?

3) What is his hope for the future?

C. *Read*:

Sinclair stood at the forward rail, watching the water. The seas had grown high, and the boat pitched up and down as it crested each wave and dove into each trough. In the darkness, it was easy to see the water's luminescence, which made each rolling movement more unsettling. Most of the passengers were curled in the hold, sick or trying not to be. John Marcheford, however, stood clutching the bowsprit, gazing west as usual.

The weather wasn't really dangerous, at least not yet, but Sinclair had ordered the mainsails reefed and the sea anchor thrown out to reduce the chance of broaching. He trusted the helmsman to keep the boat faced into the waves, so for the moment there was nothing for him to do. He joined Marcheford at the bowsprit.

The man was an enigma. Stuffy, dignified, and unromantic—the last man in the world for a wilderness outpost—yet he awaited the ship's arrival with apparent eagerness.

"What do you expect to find on Horizon?" Sinclair asked.

"A sanctuary. A haven for the religiously oppressed." It was a quick answer and sounded rehearsed.

Sinclair crossed his arms and leaned back and forth against the motion of the ship. The rolling seas didn't bother him, he'd seen far worse. "That's what it is for your people. What is it for you?"

Marcheford regarded him, apparently deciding whether or not to speak. "The apostle Paul said his ambition was to preach the gospel where Christ had never been named." His expression grew wistful. "I've preached to believers all my adult life. But that's what I want: to preach to those who have never heard."

It took Sinclair a moment to figure out what Marcheford was talking about. When he did understand, he exploded in laughter. "You want to *evangelize* the *manticores*?"

Marcheford turned back to the waves. "Catherine Parris tells my son there are thousands of them. Dozens of tribes, isolated from the rest of the world. That means generations living and dying without a single messenger to share the gospel."

"Bishop, they're animals."

"You're not all that different from an ape yourself, taken from a physical point of view."

Sinclair grinned. "But I have a human mind and soul. These manticores will probably cut your throat just to watch the blood flow."

"Thanks to your healing water, it won't do them much good."

Sinclair was surprised Marcheford had even drunk the water—he'd expected the bishop to object on some kind of religious grounds. "Don't fool yourself. It won't bring you back from the dead. If Collard had shot me through the heart instead of the stomach, I wouldn't have gotten up again."

"And where would your human mind and soul be then?"

It was a loaded question, and Sinclair brushed it aside. "We're on different sides in that fight."

"I don't think so. We both want this colony to succeed."

"You want to bring more creatures under God's power. I want to steal God's power for myself. I want to bring the dead back to life."

"You're serious. Isn't that just a little bit arrogant?"

Sinclair laughed. "I've already turned a rod into a snake, healed the sick, cast a devil out of a young girl, and made a blind man see. You don't think I can learn to raise the dead?"

"I'll settle with you getting us safely to the island," Marcheford said.

"That you can count on."

David Walton *Quintessence*

1) What is Sinclair's worldview?

2) What is Marcheford's worldview?

3) What do you think might happen when the ship reaches the island of Horizon?

Day 3 humane moral order

Here is an essay by Mike Duran in its entirety taken from his blog deCOMPOSE where he discusses movies, the genres of speculative fiction, and philosophies. This particular essay was posted on September 7, 2016.

Horror v. Sci-Fi as a Vehicle for Morality

by Mike Duran

One of the common arguments against a Materialistic, Naturalistic worldview is its inability to define or present a compelling Moral universe. And as much contemporary sci-fi is tethered to such a worldview, it could be asked whether science fiction (at least, of the Materialistic cloth) is a fitting vehicle to address issues of morality.

The Wintery Knight once posed the question Does reading science fiction predispose people to atheism? His answer was, basically, *yes*.

Science fiction makes the mysteries of the universe seem easy to an atheist. Everything can be easily explained with fictional future discoveries. Their speculations about aliens, global warming and eternal universes are believed without evidence because atheists *want* and *need* to believe in those speculations. In the world of science fiction, the fictional characters can be "moral" and "intelligent" without having to bring God or the evidence for God into the picture. That's very attractive to an atheist who wants the feeling of being intelligent and moral without having to weight actual scientific evidence or ground their moral values and behavior rationally. The science fiction myths are what atheists *want to believe*. It's a placebo at the worldview level. They don't want cosmic microwave background radiation – they want *warp drives*. They don't want chastity – they want *holodecks*.

Avatar's fickle deity may be the best example of what happens when atheists attempt to force a Moral code into their sci-fi storytelling. At the center of the story, at least from the "good pagan" protags' perspective, is "All-Mother," who is described thus: "All-Mother does not take sides. She balances nature." All-Mother is, basically,

Nature deified. Problem is, Nature is "red in tooth and claw." Extracting morality from an evolved impersonal pantheistic life-force is problematic… especially when it comes to lessons on ethics and just war theory. You see, "if Nature is the arbiter of survival, then whoever has the biggest guns, wins; neither Deity nor Destiny will intervene." Which is why the Moral Universe that director James Cameron's Avatar exists in is quite muddled.

So all the while *Avatar* is pushing a New Age, Neutral Deity, that Deity is busy acting very non-New Age and un-Neutral, arming her forces to the teeth. In the end, the Impartial, Impersonal Force of Cameron's world turns *partial* and *personal*, comes to the rescue and turns, tooth and claw, on the bad guys…to make the story work, *Avatar* must abandon its New Age, Nature-worshiping, Gospel of Gaia sympathies, to bring about sufficient resolution to the story.

It's the fly in the ointment of much contemporary sci-fi — If your fictional universe is a product of chance, material evolution, and random subatomic frenzy, then please don't attempt to make your story a vehicle for morality. That is, any reasonable, cohesive morality. I mean, if the Force is impersonal and binding all living things together, then there really is no compelling reason why choosing Sith over Jedi is ultimately worse or better than the other. (Which is probably why George Lucas worked so hard to import Western concepts into his Eastern worldview.)

On the other hand, horror, it's been suggested, is a genre more naturally tethered to rational, traditional morality. In his article, A Guide to Reading Ghost Stories, Robert Woods makes this point. Referencing Russell Kirk's essay "A Cautionary Note on the Ghostly Tale," Woods writes:

As with G.K. Chesterton's assertion in his "Ethics of Elfland," fairytales are inherently moral as they reflect a universe of moral order and consequences when good is dismissed and evil embraced. Russell Kirk writing of his own ghost stories says, "What I have attempted, rather, are experiments in the moral imagination. Readers will encounter elements of parable and fable…literary naturalism is not the only path to apprehension of reality. All important literature has some ethical end; and the tale of the preternatural…can be an instrument for the recovery of moral order." (emphasis mine)

So just as there are "laws" that must be yielded to in the natural order, in "ghost stories" there is "a parallel principal within the supernatural order." The affirmation of this "supernatural order" is key to the power of such tales. Or as Kirk puts it, "The better uncanny stories are underlain by a healthy concept of the character of evil." In other words, a universe with a moral order, where good and evil, holiness and horror, have real consequences, is intrinsic to ghost stories. The author's take turns interesting when ghost stories are juxtaposed against science fiction. Woods makes this point:

For Kirk, the "ghost tale" may better communicate certain truths when compared to science fiction. "For symbol and allegory, the shadow–world is a better realm than the mechanized empire of science fiction."

These "certain truths" that Kirk references are, of course, truths belonging to ghost-stories and the supernatural, moral order. The "mechanized empire" of science fiction cannot adequately grapple with such realities precisely because it denies them. Or, at least, has an insufficient basis to explain them. This is what Kirk describes as "the dreary baggage of twentieth-century naturalism."

Kirk explains in his essay:

...many people today have a faith in "life on other planets" as burning and genuine as belief in a literal Heaven and a literal Hell was among twelfth-century folk, say—but upon authority far inferior.... Having demolished, to their own satisfaction, the whole edifice of religious learning, abruptly and unconsciously they experience the need for belief in something not mundane; and so, defying their own inductive and mechanistic premises, they take up the cause of Martians and Jovians. As for angels and devils, let alone bogies—why, Hell, such notions are superstitious! (bold mine)

So the naturalist, having "demolished… the whole edifice of religious learning," must deify "something." Or as Chesterton put it, "When man ceases to believe in God, he doesn't believe in nothing. He believes in anything." Thus, having no supernatural moral order to point to, the naturalist must look for something to fill the void. Of course, this defies his "own inductive and mechanistic premises." Nevertheless, they replace angels and devils with "Martians and Jovians." They swap God for the Universe, redemption for evolution. "Dreary baggage" indeed!

Because much science fiction is built on "naturalism" — a denial of a "supernatural order" — the appeal to morality lacks bite. Morality grounded in naturalism, i.e., societal mores, tribal regulation, individual preference, etc., is not nearly as compelling as morality grounded in a "supernatural order." This is why, it seems, ghost stories ARE superior to science fiction for exploring moral issues.

Ghost stories appeal to a supernatural order.

Science fiction stories appeal to a natural order.

Morality grounded in the Absolute (a supernatural order) is far more compelling than morality grounded (?) in the transient. But for the naturalist, because there is no absolute supernatural order, morals can only be transient. Relativistic flotsam is all the atheist can really offer.

Of course, this is not to suggest that the humanistic science fiction author cannot write from a "supernaturalist" frame of reference, but that they cannot do so without "defying their own inductive and mechanistic premises." The horrorist needn't make any such leap. A moral supernatural order is intrinsic to the ghost story. We enter such a tale with the cargo of Good and Evil. For the naturalist, however, Hell is a superstition. As is a supernatural moral order. Let them deify "Martians and Jovians" all they like. In the naturalistic Universe, appealing to ultimate Good or Evil is unnecessary. And irrational. But such is "the dreary baggage" of twenty-first-century naturalism.

Of course, there is much great science fiction out there which grapples effectively with moral issues. What should be noted is that in most cases, the books that do this assume a world where morals actually matter and are not just products of matter.

END OF ESSAY BY MIKE DURAN   Note: formatting has been changed.

Well. This essay is bound to offend at least some of you. I write science fiction and cling to a moral order. It is true that the majority of science fiction writers are agnostics or atheists, but a fairly large percentage of science fiction writers are Christians, Muslims, Buddhists, Jewish, Wiccan, and a host of other faiths. It is also true that many writers of horror are agnostics or atheists. One's faith, by itself, does not determine what type of literature one chooses to write. But, one's faith will often 'leak' through the words.

I have seen many atheists argue that a humane moral order can be derived apart from a revealed (by a deity) moral code. What do you think?

Activities:

A. *Read*:

"There were all kinds of rumors floating around. We heard one house is completely empty, except upstairs, hanging in the closet, is a red dress. Another house has a small attic and in the corner of the attic is a doll with no eyes. That kind of stuff. Pretty creepy."

She placed the heel of one hand on the edge of the table, but didn't say anything. The hand was as pale as the underside of a snake. The fingers elegant, the nails jagged.

Keith forced his eyes back to the flashlight. "But Marcus said it wasn't the houses themselves that are frightening. He said it's something else."

"What?"

"The emptiness. Marcus said it's the emptiness around the houses. And inside too. That's what makes us uneasy. And I have to admit, Mother, that at least for me—he was right."

Saying it out loud made Keith feel a little stronger. "In my philosophy class we were debating whether or not God created evil. Since He created everything, then He must have created evil. But Dr. Edding said the flaw in that argument is assuming evil to be something. Evil is not something. It is the absence of good. Even Satan was created with free will, but he chose the emptiness. That's why we're afraid of wastelands. Why we feel uneasy when we learn that atoms are mostly empty space. We're made of tiny desolations, and that makes us uneasy. It's the nothing that we fear. Because that's what evil is. Nothing."

She frowned.

Keith kept going. "People always talk about how those long stretches of Nebraska and Kansas are boring. But Marcus said people are actually sensing something along those stretches that strikes a dark chord in all of us. He called it uncanny emptiness. He said it's not so much boredom as fear. It's a reminder the universe is mostly void. The spaces between the stars. The spaces between our brain cells. All our thoughts are leaps across the void."

Bret Carter *Forlorn*

What do you think about the statement that the universe is mostly void?

What does uncanny mean? Check at least three different dictionaries and see if you can find the origin of the word.

The woman in this excerpt that Keith is talking to is *not* his mother. She insists people call her that after she has trapped them. How is the name she insists on contributing to the uncanny feeling of this story?

B. *Read*:

An equation means nothing to me unless it expresses a thought of God.

Srinivasa Ramanujan, Indian mathematician (1887-1920)

Abdul Karim is his name. He is a small, thin man, precise to the point of affectation in his appearance and manner. He walks very straight; there is gray in his hair and in his short, pointed beard. When he goes out of the house to buy vegetables, people on the street greet him respectfully. "Salaam, Master sahib," they say, or "Namaste, Master Sahib," according to the religion of the speaker. They know him as the mathematics master at the municipal school. He has been there so long that he sees the faces of his former students everywhere: the autorickshaw driver Ramdas who refuses to charge him, the man who sells paan from a shack at the street corner, with whom he has an account, who never reminds him when his payment is late—his name is Imran and he goes to the mosque far more regularly than Abdul Karim.

...

In a finite world, Abdul Karim ponders infinity. He has met infinities of various kinds in mathematics. If mathematics is the language of Nature, then it follows that there are infinities in the physical world around us as well. They confound us because we are such limited things. Our lives, our science, our religions are all smaller than the cosmos. Is the cosmos infinite? Perhaps. As far as we are concerned, it might as well be.

In mathematics there is the sequence of natural numbers, walking like small, determined soldiers into infinity. But there are less obvious infinities as well, as Abdul Karim knows. Draw a straight line, mark zero on one end and the number one at the other. How many numbers between zero and one? If you start counting now, you'll still be counting when the universe ends, and you'll be nowhere near one. In your journey from one end to the other you'll encounter the rational numbers and the irrational numbers, most notably the transcendentals. The transcendental numbers are the most intriguing—you can't generate them from integers by division, or by solving simple equations. Yet in the simple number line there are nearly impenetrable thickets of them; they are the densest, most numerous of all numbers. It is only when you take certain ratios like the circumference of a circle to its diameter, or add an infinite number of terms in a series, or negotiate the countless steps of infinite continued fractions, do these transcendental numbers emerge. The most famous of these is, of course, pi, $3.14159\ldots$, where there is an infinity of non-repeating numbers after the decimal point. The transcendentals! Theirs is a universe richer in infinities than we can imagine.

In finiteness—in that little stick of a number line—there is infinity. What a deep beautiful concept, thinks Abdul Karim! Perhaps there are infinities in us too, universes of them.

The prime numbers are another category that capture his imagination. The atoms of integer arithmetic, the select few that generate all other integers, as the letters of an alphabet generate all words. There are an infinite number of primes, as befits what he thinks of as God's alphabet...

How ineffably mysterious the primes are! They seem to occur at random in the sequence of numbers: 2, 3, 5, 7, 11... There is no way to predict the next number in the sequence without actually testing it. No formula that generates all the primes. And yet, there is a mysterious regularity in these numbers that has eluded the greatest mathematicians of the world. Glimpsed by Riemann, but as yet unproven, there are hints of order so deep, so profound, that it is as yet beyond us.

To look for infinity in an apparently finite world—what nobler occupation for a human being, and one like Abdul Karim, in particular?

As a child he questioned the elders at the mosque: What does it mean to say that Allah is simultaneously one, and infinite? When he was older he read the philosophies of Al Kindi and Al Ghazali, Ibu Sina and Iqbal, but his restless mind found no answers. For much of his life he has been convinced that mathematics, not the quarrels of philosophers, is the key to the deepest mysteries.

Vandana Singh   *Infinities*

1) What do you think of the assertion that mathematics is the key to the deepest mysteries?

2) Describe this writer's voice.

3) What *might* the worldview of the writer be?

C. *Read*:

In previous pages a team from Earth has gone to explore the first alien spaceship ever seen.

"Okay. *Unity*, we're putting your audio on public broadcast now. Remember to switch to the private channel if there's anything you don't want Moscow or the general public to hear." After a pause, Nick said, "This is Houston. Commander Babel, care to share what it's like up there?"

Varik collapsed into his thoughts. The moment had come. He had long wondered how many months Neil Armstrong spent pondering his words for the lunar proclamation. The "one small step" line still reverberated almost a century later, and Varik's next words would be no less significant.

After clearing his throat and drawing in a long breath, he said, "If we, the people of Earth, are united by science, then nothing is impossible for us. The *Unity* crew has boarded *Angel One*." Varik waited for the applause in ground control to die down in his headset. "Widowicz and Ishikawa are almost to me. I see no doors or windows, an indication the spacecraft was possibly unmanned."

…

"Keep it up. We need science to come to the rescue."

"Technically, it's engineering, not science," Ishikawa said through a yawn. "And Jan doesn't think science can save us anyway."

"What?" she exclaimed. "Ishikawa, I—" Janice shut her mouth and glared at him, as if he had betrayed her darkest secret.

"What do you mean?" Varik asked.

"Nothing," she said. "It's a long story."

"No, seriously. What do you mean?"

Varik sensed the other two were withholding a confession, and his patience was too frayed for anything but straight answers. Speaking more angrily than he intended, he thrust a finger toward the floor and snapped, "You might as well tell me, because I can't talk to anyone down there."

Ishikawa opened his pursed lips and sighed. "She wasn't a fan of your speech. She said people can't be united by science."

The dull insult cut deeply into Varik's pride, partly because of his fatigue and respect for Janice, but mostly because the words he said aboard *Angel One* were supposed to be his immortal legacy.

"Well, what should I expect from someone who carries a crucifix in her pocket?"

Janice recoiled. "Hey! It's a reminder, not a magic charm. What I told him was that science is a method, not a moral cause. People don't rally around methodologies. They unite for causes like religion that are focused on people and greater meaning."

Varik scowled. "Religion uniting people? It's our leading cause of death."

"That's an old myth," Janice said with a dismissive flick of her hand. "Governments and diseases have killed far more people, but complex things are two-edged swords. They always have good and bad sides and it's dishonest to admit to only one side and not the other. Bacteria cause plagues, but they're also essential for life. Governments cause wars but also protect people, and religions can serve the poor or serve themselves."

He had never heard this side of Janice before. "There's a reason I studied physics in school, not theology or philosophy. Too much bickering. Give me something that moves forward. Something that puts humans in space."

Janice rubbed one of her bloodshot eyes. She looked as tired as he felt. "It moves us forward in space, but not in ethics or civilization. It's morally neutral. Science creates bigger buildings but also bigger bombs. The greatest atrocities are usually committed by people with the technological advantage."

"But not in the name of science."

Janice crossed her arms. "I didn't hate your speech. All I said was that as wonderful as science may be, I think humans need more to unite. And science cuts both ways, just like religion and politics. It's usually beneficial, but if we blindly trust it, we fail to account for all of the variables and the end users. That's how tragedies occur."

"She is at least partly right," Ishikawa said without looking up from his work. "Technology made it possible for us to be here, but it also made it possible for us to be hacked."

C. W. Briar *The Other Edge*

1) In this short horror story from the anthology *Wrath and Ruin*, two of the characters are arguing whether science or religion can better unite people. Pick a side and write at least a paragraph arguing for that side.

2) Now pick the other side and write at least a paragraph defending that side.

3) What is Varik's worldview? What is the worldview of Jan? What worldview do you think the author might have? What might the title *The Other Edge* refer to?

Day 4 drawing lines

The following discussion is presented from the worldview of a particular subset of Christianity because that is what I know, and I do not presume to speak for those of other faiths. If you have a faith or lack thereof perspective that you think would benefit the textbook, please send it to me. I cannot guarantee that it will be included in the next edition, but I would still love to hear from you.

Many people, both Believers and Non-believers, have a deep dislike of speculative fiction. You should know what the reasons are, not so you can make fun of the reasons but rather so you can understand, empathize, and have a respectful answer for the objections that good people can have.
Some people want to read only true things. They find make-believe boring.
I know of a person who won't read speculative fiction because it frightens and depresses her.
And then there's people who think speculative fiction is inherently evil.

E. Stephen Burnett, who writes at speculativefaith.com and christandpopculture.com, and Mike Duran who writes at mikeduran.com have posted several articles defending the use of speculative fiction to Christians who object to the reading, watching, and writing of such fiction. We can only touch on highlights here, so we urge you to go online if you can and read their articles about objections to speculative fiction.
E. Stephen Burnett contends that speculative fiction can be read to glorify God. We are commanded to have times of rest, and reading can be part of that rest. He also contends that much of the opposition to speculative fiction is based on some wrong ideas.
What wrong ideas?
He says some people think that if they and their children read "clean" fiction and fact, watch only G-rated movies, have social activities only within a church, and pray with the correct words, that they and their children will stay safe and clean in a fallen and dirty world. He has two main objections to that concept.
One: thinking and praying correct words that will guarantee a particular level of safety and comfort is akin to thinking one can force God to act in a way that the prayer wants. He contends that no one can force God to do anything because God is sovereign.
Two: the thought that if children are kept away from evil things, they will remain pure contradicts what Jesus Christ said about evil coming from within. Mark 7:21, Matthew 15:18
Burnett is not advocating that any and all vile things be shown to children, but rather, that discernment be exercised and literature be discussed. If a parent reads the same book the child is reading, then the parent can discuss what is good and true about what is in it, and what is evil and deceitful. The parent can teach the child what worldview the writer is promulgating, and thus teach the child how to discern for themselves once they leave home.

Mike Duran complains about thinking that if a book is "clean" ie no cursing, sex, excessive or graphic violence, use of magic, etc, that therefore the book is safe to read and that the reader will remain uncontaminated. He contends that many clean books are just as deceptive as unclean books. He further contends that "unclean" books and unclean parts of the Bible can tell truth, sometimes better than clean books. You are allowed to disagree with this.
On the three websites mentioned above are many vigorous discussions disputing and agreeing with the above contentions, understandings, and misunderstandings. It takes many books to address these issues with any kind of thoroughness.

Here is the thing I want you to draw from this: People care deeply about religion and whether or not they are getting it right. Hearing someone else's opinion can be unsettling and cause great anxiety. Anxious people push back. No matter what you write, somebody is going to be offended by what you write. You need to decide what is important enough to you that you're willing to catch flak for it.

Am I giving you permission to write about anything any way you want to? Not really. I do want you to be aware of what you're writing. It is easy to copy what everyone else around you is writing and inadvertently violate your own worldview. Sometimes, someone in the intended audience can take what you meant as metaphor to be theological truth. Time goes on and sometimes a person won't remember where they obtained a particular religious opinion, and might think it comes from holy writings instead of the fiction you wrote.

We want you to be aware of what you're writing. And we want you to be aware of your intended audience.

We all draw lines for ourselves, and the audience draws lines. Not all the lines are about morality. Some lines are expectations. If you write a romance and do not have a happily ever after, you didn't write a romance. You just thought you did. A romance reader who reads that story will never read another story by you. Science fiction readers expect some logic, some admission to the hard material realities of this world, and some problem solving. Fantasy readers expect to be carried away to a land of fantasy. Horror readers expect to be scared. Once you have determined your target audience, you next need to determine where the readers lay their lines. If you want to sell your stories, you want to write within those lines.

Activity:

1) Look at the story you've been working on. Whom do you think it might offend? Are you willing to offend that subset of people? Does the story accurately reflect your worldview? If you want your story or at least one of your characters to reflect your worldview, will you need to change anything?

Keep working on your story.

Day 5 what about magic?

Perhaps what offends people the most about speculative fiction is superpowers, magic and spells, and frightening supernatural creatures. If you write fantasy, you will likely need to invent a magic system. Is it possible to invent a magic system that does not violate deeply held convictions about the nature of God?

Travis Perry in his blog The Big Idea posted this article:

7 Ways to Deal with the Problem Magic Poses Christian Fantasy Writers

First off, what is the problem with magic for Christians? Or sorcery? Or witchcraft? (Are all of those things even the same?)

An entire book could be written on this topic (perhaps I'll do that someday) but to keep this as brief as possible, the short reason this is a problem is the Bible has nothing good to say about the practice of magic (neither does extra-Biblical Christian tradition). No translation of Scripture will record the 12 Disciples watching Jesus walk on the water and say, "Wow, that was magical!" Nor is the manna falling from heaven in Israel's wilderness wanderings described as some kind of powerful spell that Moses used, nor even is his rod described as "magic," even though Moses had the power granted to him by God to turn it into a serpent at whatever time he chose. No, the Bible describes events like these as "miracles," or "signs," or "wonders."

On the other hand, when the Bible talks about "magic" and calls people "magicians" or "sorcerers" (you could substitute "wizards" if you wanted), it includes the court magicians of Pharaoh, who resisted Moses by demonstrating to Pharaoh that the power Moses showed from God was not really that special after all. The Bible also makes mention of a death penalty for witches (Exodus 22:18--though the Bible does not record any instances of this particular death penalty being carried out). It also mocks the interpreters of dreams who worked for Nebuchadnezzar in the book of Daniel, showed sorcerers converting to Christianity and demonstrating the genuineness of their faith by voluntarily burning all of their own scrolls of magic (Acts 19:19), lists magic as a sin from which the Earth under judgment from God will not repent in Revelation 9:21 (the Greek word for "magic" or "sorcery" there is linked to the word "pharmacology" and indicates the use of drugs to induce mental states associated with sorcery), and in general has only bad things to say when the word "magic" or related words like "sorcery," or "witchcraft" come up.

A verse in Isaiah (8:19) directly contrasts reliance on God with the use of magic: "When they say to you, 'Consult the mediums and spiritists who whisper and mutter,' should not a people consult their God? Should they consult the dead on the behalf of the living?" (NASB--the King James Version uses the word "wizards" instead of "spiritists.")

So this seems to be the basic problem with magic as the term applies in the Bible. As defined by the examples the Scriptures provide: Magic is the attempt to use supernatural power outside of relying on the one Creator God of the Bible. Note I've phrased this so that it does not comment on whether "magic" really does contain supernatural power. The very attempt to circumvent God to gain access to the supernatural is, Biblically speaking, a problem.

"So why bother putting magic in stories at all?" someone might ask. "If magic is an issue, why shouldn't a Christian writer leave it out of stories altogether?" I'd say there are three basic reasons to work out a means to include it: 1) Fantasy is a popular genre with loads of readers. It makes sense to desire to reach them from a strictly analytical point of view. Not to mention it can inherently interesting to write fantasy for people who've read it--and fantasy normally contains magic. 2) Fantasy has the ability to use analogy or allegory to create powerful messages about the world we live in. And what is called in the story "magic" can be a key part of any such analogy. C.S. Lewis achieved using magic that way in the Chronicles of Narnia, in fact. 3) And it so happens to be that magic is a staple of fantasy as much as aliens are a staple of science fiction. You could write the one without including the other, but it would not really represent the genre well for the most part. Or be as interesting.

So, how to proceed? I would say the basic task is to make it plain the magic in the story world is not the same thing as the sorcery the Bible condemns. In order to harmonize with the Bible's condemnation, a Christian writer must make it plain that the supernatural power referenced in the story is not in fact in opposition to reliance on the Creator God of the Bible. I know of six good ways to do this (and will reference a seventh):

1. Only the villains have "magic."

This is probably the most straightforward approach. Bad guys use spells, sorcery, incantations, and magic items. Good guys are stuck with either plain items devoid of any magical powers, or have supernatural power openly linked to God and under His control rather than theirs (and which is never described by the term "magic"). The Left Behind series actually shows baddies into witchcraft whereas the good guys, especially the two prophets in Jerusalem, call down supernatural power overtly in the name of God. To take this notion into the realm of fantasy, take this same sort of thing but instead of setting it on planet Earth, put it in a world of imagination, but one where God is still God, though perhaps under a different name (e.g. Aslan--though note that magic in Narnia is not just reserved for the villains).

2. Rename miracles and prophets as "magic" and "wizards."

Take a person who acts like a prophet of the Old Testament, but call him or her something other than "prophet." Create situations similar to Moses parting the Red Sea or Elijah lighting the sacrifice to God with fire from heaven, but don't call it prophecy or a miracle or a sign or a wonder. Call it "magic" or "sorcery" instead and those who them "wizards" who call upon the equivalent of the name of God in the story. Or along those lines. Doing this would take advantage of the fact that fantasy readers expect magic in a tale, but turns their expectation on its head so the story magic works the opposite from how the Bible negatively uses the word. Therefore, done correctly, such wizards would really point back to prophets and their sorcery powers back to God's power (by whatever name He is presented in the story). Readers who are not Bible-savvy may not immediately notice that the story points back to a Biblical way of seeing the supernatural, even though that's what it would do. By the way, L. B. Graham, Christian author of fantasy, mentioned at a previous Realm Makers conference using an approach roughly similar to this method in some of his books.

3. Treat "magic" as an allegory for the workings of God.

I'm thinking especially of how C.S. Lewis used the term "Deep Magic" as a description of what the "Emperor-beyond-the-sea" had written in the stone table where Aslan was sacrificed (in The Lion, the Witch, and the Wardrobe). It stated that the White Witch was entitled to kill every traitor and if anyone denied her that right, then all of Narnia would perish in fire and water. But an even deeper magic said that if a willing innocent victim was killed in the place of a traitor then the Stone Table would crack and death would be overcome. Clearly this references how Christians see Christ dying on the cross for sin, but is phrased as "magic." A story could call other acts of God or properties of God that parallel what we know to be true, magic. Wizardry of this sort would not allow characters to use spells and as such might call for the addition of another method of dealing with "sorcery" (one that does allow spells). Though I can imagine a fantasy story without spells at all in which all references to "magic" are simply to acts of God in allegorical form.

4. Treat magic as a form of undiscovered science.

In the multiverse I've imagined behind my book The Crystal Portal, I imagined there is a kind of physics that operates in other universes that is undetectable here. I conceived of magic as a form of power that flows though the multiverse not unlike how electricity flows through a circuit. For universes closest to the source, this power is readily available. It's subject to manipulation by acts of the will and spoken words (so the use of this power resembles spells), but other universes drain most of the power by the time it hits our reality, so it has never been discovered in our world. In universes that have active magic, wizards are like scientists who study the properties of the invisible and learn how to use it, like how scientists learn to manipulate the forms of energy and matter we know about. Like science, such power can be used for either good or evil and like technology, there are unexpected residual wastes that can be harmful.

Other novelists have invented other means in which "magic" is either science by another name (as I've done myself in the "Time of Magic" referenced in Medieval Mars) or have stated magic is an undiscovered science. Note that making sorcery equal science may create a story universe very similar to ones written from a non-Christian perspective, of the sort that have wizards and spells. But the difference is the kind of story that creates magical power which can be used in a neutral sense isn't really supernatural power anymore. It's the power derived from the ordinary physical world as much as photography, internal combustion engines, and atomic power is. What is called "magic" really should be considered part of the natural order.

It still would be possible for someone to seek supernatural power in an illicit way in such a story world (as magic is referenced in the Bible). Which would make the sin of witchcraft, i.e. trying gain supernatural power while circumventing God, a separate thing from the use of magic, which would in fact be science by another name or in another form.

5. Blend the lines between the supernatural and natural.

What I just suggested in effect blends the supernatural and natural by making acts that would appear to be supernatural merely the acts of a type of science instead. But I'm suggesting here applies stories that go the opposite way.

Instead of giving everything a natural explanation, nothing has one. Everything is off-the-rails strange and nothing can be said to be a deliberate attempt to achieve the supernatural without God because everything (or most everything) is already supernatural from the point of view of planet Earth as we know it. I'm thinking of Alice in Wonderland or The Wizard of Oz type story universes, where scarecrows and rabbits talk, where changing your size is a matter of what you eat and drink, and tornadoes will transport a house to another land without killing its occupants. If magic is so worked into the fabric of everything that it isn't special and using it is as natural as walking and breathing then that sort of magic does not relate to the Biblical condemnation of people seeking the supernatural without God. Though such a story can shut out God by never mentioning Him and can act as a sort of allegory for witchcraft, it certainly does not have to be. A story universe like this can just as soon mention God in various ways, even though the classic examples I mentioned do not.

6. Treat magic as an innate special ability in analogy to spiritual gifts.

This approach in some ways is a subset of #5, but can also employ notions of #4 as well. It might seem logically contradictory for a story to be both more and less scientific in its approach to the supernatural at the same time, but the author I know who uses this method makes both work. Kat Heckenbach both Finding Angel and Seeking Unseen ... treats the power of magic as a gift that an individual has, given from beyond herself or himself. As such, her approach runs parallel to what the Bible has to say about spiritual gifts, almost forming an allegory of them. Yet since working the supernatural is just a natural ability, she in effect makes the supernatural more common and ordinary as per point #5. But at times she gives specific descriptions of how someone's ability affects matter or energy in terms someone who has studied science on planet Earth would recognize. Which goes back to #4. In truth, Kat's approach is unique, but her basic idea of making magic an inherent gift the magic user possesses can well harmonize with a worldview that does not include witchcraft in the Biblical sense of the term.

7. Downplay the Biblical objection in the first place.

This approach would be to either ignore altogether what the Bible says about magic or claim it only references a specific kind of attempt to gain supernatural power without God. I have heard people use the verse I quoted in Isaiah to claim the Bible does not condemn all magic, it only condemned necromancy, that is, trying to interact with or raise the dead. Which is why I gave examples outside of Isaiah. No, the Bible condemns far more than just necromancy. It takes a broad shot at magic as a whole, though we need to understand by study what that really means.

I don't recommend approach #7. I think one of the things that distinguishes an overtly Christian writer of speculative fiction is the attempt to work these issues out by some means or other. Not to ignore them. It does not mean conformity to just one way of thinking and it doesn't mean it's impossible to be creative or imaginative. ...

Travis Perry   travissbigidea.blogspot.mx (note: formatting has been altered)

Activity:

1) If you do have magic in your story, does it fit within the seven systems listed above, or have you invented yet another kind?

Keep working on your story.

CHAPTER SIXTEEN:

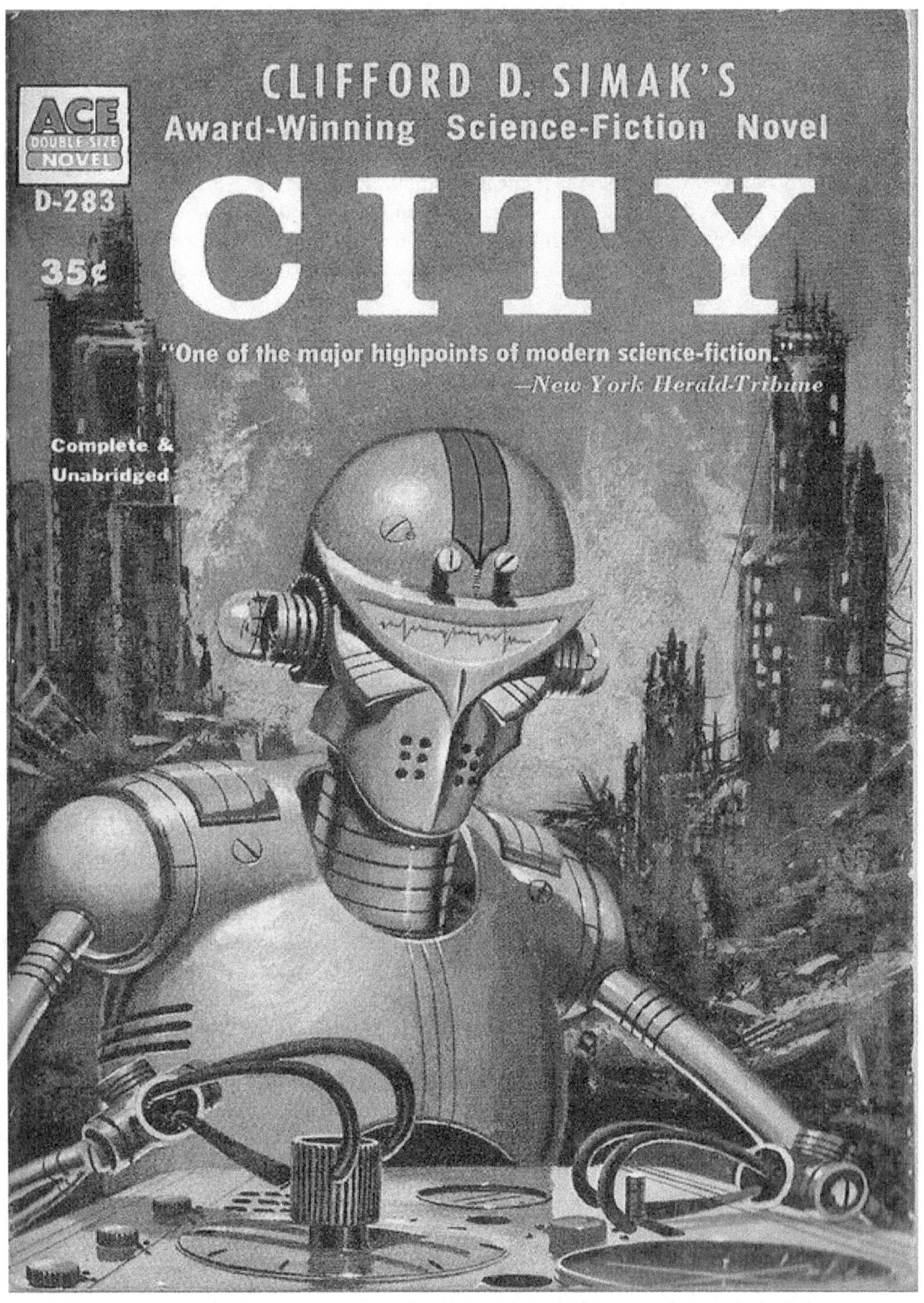

SCIENCE FICTION

Science fiction prides itself on being the What If literature. It fancies itself as capable of opening people's minds to new ideas. Only tangentially is science fiction used to predict the future. More usually, the genre is asking the question, What IF the future looked like this? How would people live then?

One of the emotions that many science fiction writers are trying to invoke is wonder, also known as sense of wonder. This is the feeling you have when you first walk into a redwood forest or stand on the edge of the Grand Canyon. One dictionary defines wonder as a verb meaning to admire, to be amazed, to be in awe, to marvel. It means something strange or surprising or a remarkable phenomenon. One person defines sense of wonder as an intellectual and emotional state frequently invoked in discussions of science fiction. It is an emotional reaction to the reader suddenly confronting, understanding, or seeing a concept anew in the context of new information. A slang cliché for that is the mind is blown.

Another emotion many writers try to invoke is that of adventure. It's exciting to ride down rapids. It's exciting to race around an asteroid. Many readers like to feel that sort of excitement by reading about what they cannot do.

Sometimes science fiction presents a challenge, a puzzle. As in a good mystery, the reader will follow the cues and try to discover an answer before the writer reveals it. The reader feels the same sort of satisfaction from solving the challenge that the Sudoku player feels as each number snicks into place.

Day 1 tropes and aliens

TROPES: In literary terms a trope means a word or expression used in a figurative sense, a figure of speech if you will, or a common or overused theme or device also known as a cliché. In genre terms, a trope is not necessarily a cliché or an insult. A trope can also be thought of as an idea or phrase that has been used often enough that readers of a particular genre know instantly what is meant so the writer does not need to devote time to explaining the phrase. At one time, science fiction writers needed to explain how warp drive worked. Now everybody knows what warp drive is. Other tropes in science fiction include: aliens such as Bug-Eyed Monsters or BEMS, space ships, genetic manipulation, ray guns, particle guns, robots, superpowers, parallel universe, immortality, post-apocalypse, mad genius etc. No doubt you can think of a hundred more. Use of tropes does not automatically mean you are using clichés any more than using a woman in a romance is a cliché. Or a detective in a murder mystery. You don't need to strive so hard to be creative and invent something new in science fiction. If you think you've invented an entirely new idea in science fiction, likely you haven't read enough yet. Go ahead and use whatever tropes you need to tell your story. But don't copy plot point by plot point some movie you've seen.

There are a few tropes many editors wish you would not use. Please don't send an editor a story where the last man and woman on Earth are Adam and Eve. Don't have a computer blow up as it tries to solve a paradox. Please don't use fatness or dark skin or ugliness as signifiers of evil. Don't at the end of the book say it was all a dream. Somebody will say sarcastic things about your story if you do.

Some people dislike the trope of intelligent aliens. This was a surprise to me, but it turns out there are interesting reasons for the dislike. On his blog, The Big Idea, Travis Perry wrote a post about the clash of opinions about intelligent aliens:

7 Christian Objections to the Existence of Aliens--posed and answered

Caveat--I address this topic as an Evangelical Christian writer who has included aliens in science fiction stories and feel justified in doing so. The objections (and answers) below were written by me, but based on things I've encountered elsewhere:

O1. No aliens (or alien planets) are mentioned anywhere in the Bible, so there must not be any.

A1. A counter-argument could be made based on the fact that the Bible certainly does mention non-human intelligences. The difference between supernatural intelligences and aliens is something I've discussed in previous posts (such as Angels and Aliens), but nonetheless, the point could be made that the Bible clearly envisions intelligences other than that of mankind...However, the best answer to this question would be to point out that the Bible didn't mention the Americas either--yet they existed and furthermore were inhabited by intelligent beings--humans of course, but to people during the Age of Exploration it was a mystery how human beings had already arrived in this newly discovered land. Christians see no contradiction in the Americas not being mentioned in the Bible and existing anyway--they simply embraced the truth that while the Bible is true, it does not contain all truth that exists, that is, it does not contain all the information in the entire universe, nor was it ever intended to do so. For example, I, along with most of the readers of the Bible throughout history, am not specifically mentioned in it by name, yet I'm reasonably certain I exist ;)--so the Bible not mentioning aliens in the way we understand them in modern times is insignificant.

O2. The Bible says mankind is "created in the image of God." So if we are in God's image, anything else that does not look like us would not be in God's image. So no other form of intelligent life can exist.

A2. Er, this one is contradicted by the Bible itself whenever it describes angels differently from humans, such as the seraphim of Isaiah 6 (for a view of the seraphim that relates to this topic, please see my previous post The four faces around the throne of God--faces of aliens?)...they are intelligent, but don't look like us. And why couldn't aliens created by God be intelligent, but not look like us? Why would they necessarily have to be in the image of God? And who's to say that they wouldn't be in His image, even if they looked different from us? Perhaps the "image of God" is taken a bit too literally by some. God is able to see and hear...we have eyes and ears. God is able to move and we have legs, He creates and we have hands. God is aware of himself and plans for the future, and we human beings, in His image, do the same sorts of things...if that's what's meant by the "image of God," this is a trait we human beings could well share with extraterrestrials, if there are any.

O3. The Bible teaches the Earth is the center of the universe and if there are aliens, clearly their existence would show the Earth is not be the center. So nobody who believes the Bible should believe there are aliens.

A3. First off, not all Christians take the Bible literally at all, but among those who do (including me, except for clearly poetical or figurative parts), I don't believe we would agree the Bible teaches the Earth is the physical center of the universe--the Bible does not in fact talk about the universe in terms in which it makes sense to discuss a center. It simply says, "the heavens and the Earth"--the world we live on and the sky that surrounds us. True, Psalm 93:1 says "the Earth cannot be moved"--which doesn't say it's the center of anything--and it doesn't even say that the Earth "does not move," but rather that *God has established the world as what it is and no one else can change that* i.e. "move it." There are other passages, mostly in poetic sections in the Bible, but also in famously Joshua 10 ("the day the sun stood still"), which talk about the movement of the sun across the sky. First off, these passages are quite few in number. Second, they are from the point of view of the observer on the ground--and yes, I myself see the sun move across the sky. It is true that some theologians in the past used the Bible to justify the geocentric system of the universe devised by certain Greek philosophers...and who ignored certain passages of the Bible that did not line up with that system (including the mention of innumerable stars, which the Greek philosophers did not believe in, because they counted all the ones they could see and were certain there were no more).

My first answer was a little bit unfair in a sense, because even though according to what I understand, the Bible does *not* actually state the Earth is the physical center of anything, it nonetheless does clearly put our world at the center of a spiritual story. And why shouldn't it be--the Bible is the book for US after all, we human beings. But look at it another way--an implication of the Theory of Relativity is that all points of view of all observers are valid--time and space are variables affected by velocity and mass...which means there does not exist any absolute grid across the universe, nor any completely universal time clock, which means that *each and every individual place is a much the center of the universe as any other.* So why would Christianity be challenged in any way to find out first hand that perhaps aliens would see their own "center of the universe" as being every bit as important as we see our own?--our "heavens and Earth" without further specification would be just like their own view of their heavens and home world...And Christian theologians have long stated that God is Omnipresent--which means He is everywhere...in the center of every single place, throughout all space and time.

O4. The New Testament says Jesus is the Savior of the world. That would mean that He is not the Savior of any other worlds. Why would God save only human beings and no one else--it would not make sense for God to create aliens if Jesus just died for this world--so there must not be any aliens.

A4. The first two sentences don't follow logically as per what was said in A1. Just because Jesus is the Savior of our world and no others are mentioned, it does not stand to reason He is *only* the Savior of all the worlds (if there are more than one). Besides, who says aliens need saving? Perhaps any aliens which exist are themselves not sinful. That is, they could have a sense of conscience they perfectly follow at all times. This is a possibility that C.S. Lewis worked through in his space trilogy, especially the first two books. Or perhaps they are demonically evil, consistently violating their own sense of right and wrong at all times, and like demons, disinterested in repentance ...

By the way, the New Testament Greek word for "world" in John 3:16 (as in "For God so loved the world...") is the word, "Kosmos," which, yes, you guessed it, can mean "universe" as well as "world." So John 3:16 could be read, "God so loved the *universe*, He gave His only Son..." What if the only Son manifested himself in the form of an alien on alien worlds?

O5. The New Testament makes much of Jesus being of the same sort of being we are--a descendant of Adam, which makes Him suitable to die in our place. Obviously he could not be the same sort of being that aliens are, so He could not be their Savior, so God must not have made any aliens (because that would be cruel).

A5. First off, that assumes aliens would be sinners, which they may not be, as addressed in the question above. What "sinners" means is having a sense of moral conscience, being aware of violating this conscience against your own will at times-- that is, a sense of sin and a need for repentance and forgiveness. If humans encounter aliens and find that they like us are "sinners," I think it can be safely said that Christian missionaries will immediately want to preach the gospel to them. And if these aliens accept Jesus as their Savior, it would stand to reason people will say that Jesus being human was important in spiritual terms, not in the literal physical sense.

Secondly, who is to say that aliens would not have their own story of a Savior who died for the sins of their world? The Christian objection to what I just said would probably center around passages like Hebrews 10:12, which plainly state that Jesus died once for all sins for all time. So clearly He could not have died here and then later (or earlier) died on an alien world...or is that just talking about Jesus dying just once? If so, would an alien equivalent of Him count? And what if the Word made flesh (as Jesus is shown to be in John 1:1-18) were in fact actually the same being for all races of beings, human and alien alike, the same spiritual reality with differing bodies--could it be that *all* versions of the single Savior would all exist at the same time, live at the same time, and die at the same time, in effect, dying only once, even though simultaneously in many places? (after all, God can be everywhere at once, so why would not the Savior be able to die in more than one place at once? even though that is not what we would normally expect)

O6. Alien encounters described by UFO believers sound much like Medieval encounters with demons. Since we know from the Bible that demons are real, that means UFOs are fake and the so-called aliens involved are fake--these are actually demonic encounters!

A6. Uh, maybe. But even if UFO encounters were generally demonic, it would not necessarily follow that all of them are demonic, would it? And even if UFO encounters were *all* demonic, it wouldn't necessarily stand to reason that there are no aliens. It would simply mean the UFOs don't represent the real aliens that may actually exist on other worlds, beings we have yet to encounter. This opinion on UFOs actually has nothing to do with whether there are aliens or not...

By the way, I don't *know* if aliens exist or not--I don't think there is any way I *can* know without actually meeting one or some other form of direct evidence. It's interesting to me though that some atheist friends of mine are utterly convinced aliens *must* exist...even though they state they are atheists due to a lack of evidence of the existence of God...

O7. The New Testament has a story of the end of time (mostly in Revelation, but based on Daniel, Isaiah, Zachariah and other passages of Hebrew Scriptures) that is too soon for there to be any time to find aliens. And no aliens are mentioned there. So there are no aliens--or we human beings will never meet them, anyway.

A7. For a previous post on "aliens" in Revelation see my post Alien God of the Christian Rapture. As for the rest, well I believe the Scriptures deliberately put the Christian believer into a state of being that continually expects the return of Jesus at any time...and I don't think that it's been an accident that it's been so long. Yet, if it's been two thousand years, why couldn't it be twenty thousand years before the end? Granted, there are a number of things in these prophetic passages that sound very much like modern conditions to me (especially Israel literally reestablished as a nation, true since only 1948)--or sound like certain interpretations of the passages, I should say. Yet history shows that same sorts of things can happen over and over again in human events...human beings could spread out over time to many worlds, meet many aliens...and then undergo a long slow collapse back to just one world, our own...reproducing a number of conditions familiar to Biblical students of end times, twenty thousand years from now. And *then* the end could come. In short, we just don't know how much time there is. So in terms of time, human beings may well exist long enough to meet aliens someday...or perhaps we will only meet them in eternity, not mentioned in the Bible, but included among the things that the human eye has not seen nor the human ear heard, but which God has prepared for those who love Him (see I Corinthians 2:9).

So, aliens, which have become a common piece of modern American culture as much as zombies or vampires or superheroes, but which are thought to really exist by some very serious and intelligent people, should pose no real challenge for the Christian writer who wants to represent a worldview consistent with Christian doctrine...yet one that still includes extraterrestrials...

Travis Perry   The Big Idea   7 Christian Objections to the Existence of Aliens
(Note: formatting has been changed)

Activities:

A. *Read*:

But if I had been breathing, the view I beheld when I turned away would have taken my breath away. I was halfway to outer space, looking out at a night world as if from the window of a jetliner: One that flew above normal civilian aircraft, maybe one of those pressurized spyplanes that brush the edge of vacuum. The stars were diamonds, brighter than those of desert midnight.

Except that there was no window, and no jet. I was up so high that I could see the curve of the horizon, and the moonlit clouds were so far below they looked like a wrinkled cotton carpet or a fallen winding sheet.

When I looked over the side, I saw the Invasion Machine was clinging to what looked like an infinite dark road bristling with spears, as if an army defied gravity and defied heaven, and marched straight toward the zenith.

But it was not a road: it was vertical immensity, too large for me to imagine or to take in, even though I was looking at it. A tower. The tower.

It was Duhumunamaru itself, infinitely above me, infinitely below.

In the moonlit gloom, the Utmost Dark Tower was a pattern of grays, dark blues, and inky black, alleviated here and there with enough touches of sard, smaragd, or gold to make the Tower look like the patterned hide of a poisonous snake, or as if some mythic dragon sleeping on a bed of gold coins, rising in flame, still had doubloons and pieces of eight wedged in the crocodile crusts of his armor.

From the shapes and shadows, I could see how it rose, bastion upon bastion, massively ornamented, massive, barbaric, gigantic. If architecture is music, this tower would be the sound made on a pipe organ by pressing all the lowest pitch keys and footpedals at once, and holding them down until the church windows broke.

John C. Wright   *Somewither   A Tale of the Unwithering Realm*

1) What emotion is the writer trying to evoke in the reader?

2) How does he do that?

3) List the tropes used in these paragraphs.

B. *Read*:

Tomed bolted upright out of a deep sleep. He swung his feet from the bed and pulled the bottom of his shipsuit over his legs. Something had woke him, but what? He rubbed his eyes and cast his gaze around the room. The rooms looked normal enough. Gray walls and beige carpet, and generic painting on the wall to the right, all normal for stateroom on a *Hiem*-class starship. The air circulator hummed along with a steady rhythm. Even the door that led from the bedroom to the rest of the suite was still cracked open just as he had left it.

Tomed sensed nothing in his room. He frowned, extended his consciousness outward, and felt the alarm of the bridge crew a moment before the red alert klaxon sounded. He pushed his arms into his shipsuit and dashed out of his cabin before he had finished zipping it up.

The bridge was controlled chaos. A dim light pulsed red when the alert siren sounded. The voices of the bridge crew mulled together as all of them hollered out damage reports and status updates.

"We're venting atmosphere!" an officer called out.

"Engines are still offline!"

Tomed pressed himself against the doorpost at the rear of the bridge until he was needed. The damage assessment station and the engineering monitor were to his left and right. The weapons control station and sensor station, the captain and first officer's stations and the navigation and helm controls were in rows ahead of him. The Main Holographic Display, or MHD dominated the very front of the bridge. It currently displayed a three dimensional hologram of this ship, the Goddard, with several areas highlighted in red.

Aaron Demott   *A New Threat (The Psygen Chronicles)*

1) What emotion is the writer trying to evoke in the reader?

2) How does he do this?

3) List the tropes used in this passage.

C. *Read*:

"Speak in the language of the eldest," Guardian advised. "Among our people, the younger speak always after the manner of the elder."

Kitty took a breath and stepped toward the executives, adjusting the dials on her translator to the oldest possible setting. "I thank you for your courtesy," she said, hoping she was using the right phrasing. "My name is—"

"The Evermother will hear your petition for spawning," the largest of the Kokkalns said briskly. The clicks emanating from his carapace were so breathy that the translator clearly had trouble deciphering them. "Be warned. She has never received an off-world petitioner before. She will likely deny your request."

"If she does, would we be permitted to try again later?"

"If she denies your request, you will be dead. The Evermother devours the head and central organs of any who summon her unnecessarily. You should have known this."

Kitty cast a sour glance at Kahihatan. "Apparently *someone* forgot to do adequate research before beginning this project."

Kahihatan opened his mouth to object, but the Blind Queen's executive was still speaking. "We understand that you desire speech prior to assimilation. The Everqueen rises. Voice your questions."

"Right. Well . . . mostly, we require information as to the nature of the assimilation."

"You must assimilate the shadows before you may speak with the Evermother."

"Can you explain the function of the shadows?"

"Speech with the Evermother is impossible until the shadows have been assimilated."

Kitty rubbed her forehead. "Right. Okay, let's try a different tack. Who created these sculptures?"

"Our artisans built them when the Evermother devoured the last of her molt-mates. Your inquiries are senseless. The Everqueen rises. Assimilate the shadows."

"One more question!" The dispersing Kokkalns paused. Kitty looked around desperately. Surely there was a clue somewhere. There was always a clue . . . "What are those first molts doing?" She pointed. Immature Kokkalns crawled along the surface of each statue, brushing abstract contours with their mouths."

"They are artisans. They adjust the shadows each generation, so that our connection with the Blind Queen may continue. It is a task only the young may perform."

"Only the young . . ." Kitty trailed off thoughtfully. Guardian had said something similar when they'd met in the upper tunnels. He'd claimed that Kitty's youth made her well suited to assimilation.

What did she know about first-molt Kokkalns? They were smaller than their seniors. They were better able to tolerate surface conditions. They had sophisticated mathematical skills and excellent spatial perceptions, and . . .

Nancy Fulda   *Angles of Incidence*

1) What emotion is the writer trying to evoke in the reader?

2) What is the "ticking time bomb" or thing that creates urgency in the situation?

3) List all the tropes you see in this passage.

Day 2 what's it really about?

Science fiction is seldom only about science. Science fiction usually explores how scientific advances and discoveries impact people. Science fiction often explores present day issues in symbolic ways. When one watches episodes of the original, black and white Twilight Zone, one is struck again by how afraid Americans were of Russia at the time, and how the then-communist country might destroy the United States with atomic bombs. Watching episodes of the original series of Star Trek, one is reminded of the civil rights movement and riots in the cities that were going on as the show was filmed. Another iteration of Star Trek, called DS9, deals with issues that were headline news at the time of its filming, such as transracial adoption and what public schools should and should not teach.

Science fiction asks what would happen if disease were eliminated. How would people change? Suppose social rules were completely different from the rules of middle-class Americans. How would people react? If some present trend goes on, what will happen?

Some people think that science fiction, despite the trappings of technology and aliens, is the most human genre in literature because the genre asks questions about what it means to be humans and how future technology will affect humans. How humans and their customs will change.

I disagree about science fiction being the most human genre, but it is true that the stories in science fiction are about humans, what they are, and what they might do. And like all stories, there are themes, the things the stories are about behind the particularities of incidents and characters. You can write about the theme of, say, how humans should be free in millions of ways. One of them is by using science fiction.

Activities:

A. *Read*:

Grace hesitates only slightly before continuing her efforts. You watch her, trying to recall more about this woman you've shared your life with, but your grasping thoughts turn up only emptiness. You haven't recognized her—haven't recognized anyone in your family—for years. That's what Alzheimer's means. Or what it used to mean.

You're not sure what anything means, anymore.

Grace arranging blankets along the side of your bed, pauses to stroke your arm. "Someone had to be first," she says sadly, almost like a litany. "The next batch of patients will have it easier. They'll begin treatments almost as soon as they're diagnosed, long before the neural tissue breaks down . . ." She gazes into empty air, and adds with forced enthusiasm, "But we'll get through this, you know we will. You were always tough as ironwood. Remember how we used to sit at Squaw Peak and look over the valley? You told me you felt cheated as a boy, because all the frontiers had been taken, and it was too late to be a pioneer."

She keeps talking, wave after wave of trivialities burdening the air. It is clear that she loves you. It is equally clear that she does not realize how few of her words find purchase on the slippery crags of your recollection. Names and anecdotes sweep past you, unconnected to anything familiar, and therefore quickly forgotten. Your blank stare must be disheartening, but she doesn't stop. She was always stubborn that way, relentlessly optimistic in the absence of all evidence. Why you can remember *that*, when everything else is gone, you can't say.

An image rips across your thoughts. A spiderweb, torn by a stick, so that the tattered remaining strands are left to dangle in the wind. The hand gripping the stick is yours—you are certain of it, although you must be remembering something wrong, because it looks like the hand of a child—and you recall staring, fascinated by how quickly the pattern disintegrates once the central supports have been torn away . . .

Nancy Fulda   *Recollection*

1) The spiderweb is a metaphor for what in this story?

2) What scientific advance has been made in this story?

3) How is the point of view character reacting?

B. *Read*:

After the funeral, Quang Tu walked back to his compartment, and sat down alone, staring sightlessly at the slow ballet of bots cleaning the small room—the metal walls pristine already, with every trace of Mother's presence or of her numerous mourners scrubbed away. He'd shut down the communal network—couldn't bear to see the potted summaries of Mother's life, the endlessly looping vids of the funeral procession, the hundred thousand bystanders gathered at the grave site to say goodbye, vultures feasting on the flesh of the grieving—they hadn't known her, they hadn't cared—and all their offerings of flowers were worth as much as the insurances of the Embroidered Guard.

"Big brother, I know you're here," a voice said, on the other side of the door he'd locked. "Let me in, please?"

Of course. Quang Tu didn't move. "I said I wanted to be alone," he said.

A snort that might have been amusement. "Fine. If you insist on doing it that way . . ."

His sister, *The Tiger in the Banyan*, materialized in the kitchen, hovering over the polished counter, near the remains of his morning tea. Of course, it wasn't really her: she was a Mind encased in the heartroom of a spaceship, far too heavy to leave orbit, and what she projected down onto the planet was an avatar, a perfectly rendered, smaller version of herself—elegant and sharp, with a small blackened spot on her hull which served as a mourning band. "Typical," she said, hovering around the compartment. "You can't just shut yourself away."

"I can if I want to," Quang Tu said—feeling like he was eight years old again, trying to argue with her—as if it had ever made sense. She seldom got angry—mindships didn't, mostly; he wasn't sure if that was the overall design of the Imperial Workshops, or the simple fact that her lifespan was counted in centuries, and he (and Mother's) in mere decades. He'd have thought she didn't grieve, either; but she was changed—something in the slow, careful deliberation of her movements, as if anything and everything might break her . . .

The Tiger in the Banyan hovered near the kitchen table, watching the bots. She could hack them, easily, no security worth anything in the compartment. Who would steal bots anyway?

What he valued most had already been taken away.

"Leave me alone," he said. But he didn't want to be alone; not really. He didn't want to hear the silence of the compartment, the clicking sounds of the bot's legs on metal, bereft of any warmth or humanity.

"Do you want to talk about it?" *The Tiger in the Banyan* asked.

She didn't need to say what, and he didn't do her the insult of pretending she did. "What would be the point?"

"To talk." Her voice was uncannily shrewd. "It helps. At least, I'm told it does."

Quang Tu heard, again, the voice of the Embroidered Guard, the slow, measured tones commiserating on his loss; and then the frown, and the knife-thrust in his gut.

You must understand that your mother's work was very valuable . . .

The circumstances are not ordinary . . .

The slow, pompous tones of the scholar, the convoluted official language he knew by heart—the only excuses the state would make to him, couched in the over-formality of memorials and edicts.

"She—" He took a deep, trembling breath—was it grief, or anger? "I should have had her mem-implants."

Aliette de Bodard   *Three Cups of Grief, By Starlight*

1) There are more futuristic ideas and science fiction tropes in these few paragraphs than in the entirety of many novels. Yet the story is not about technological advances. What is the story about?
2) List three of the things in this excerpt that are science fiction tropes. List three of the things that are the same as today.
3) Is there a police blotter description of Quang Tu anywhere in these paragraphs? Is such a description necessary? Why or why not?

C. *Read*:

"We traveled a good distance today," Brother Lucas said, hoping for civil conversation.

"On the wings of a snow white dove," the Seeker sang with a little snicker.

Grandmaster Justin stirred a simmering pot of lentils hanging above the coals. "Over 500 kims by my estimate.

Brother Lucas sat in awe. "A true miracle to fly over 50 kims an hour."

Grandmaster Justin slapped his leg. "Hardly a miracle." He scooped lentils into bowls and handed one to the Seeker. "The maps become more unreliable this far out. We need you to get us to Eden. You won't fail us?"

"On my honor, I will lead us," the Seeker muttered through a mouthful of lentils. "They guided me for nearly a cycle before I laid eyes on the holy site and beheld all the holy relics."

Brother Lucas took his bowl. "They?"

The Seeker glanced up at the shimmering star field. "The holy angels."

The bowl nearly slipped from Brother Lucas's hand. Grandmaster Justin turned his head and coughed away a snicker. "Thank you for not shaking my confidence in you, my friend. If the angels guided you, I'm sure they'll guide us now."

The Seeker scraped the bottom of his bowl into his mouth. "Of course." A little spittle mixed with his words. He stood. "It's time for my vespers."

"What do you make of that?" Brother Lucas asked after the Seeker ducked through the tent flap.

"What, don't you believe in angels, Brother Lucas?"

"Of course I do," Brother Lucas snapped back. "It's just . . . just . . ." What was he trying to say? "The man is mad."

"Mad or no, he seems to know the area well. Whether from Eden or some other place, he did bring back a few ancient devices." Grandmaster Justin snickered softly. "*Holy* relics, indeed!"

"Why do you hate people of faith so much?"

The Grandmaster chewed on a forkful of lentils. "I don't hate the people. It's your misguided notions that I can do without."

Brother Lucas gestured at the night sky. "But there is so much beauty and complexity in the universe. It couldn't have happened by chance. There is so much mystery."

"Everything is knowable," Grandmaster Justin said. "It may take a long time, but in the end, it is possible." He pointed at the double star above the horizon. "We came from there, Terra and Luna. Our ancestors, with their technology and knowledge."

"I am aware," Bother Lucas whispered.

"And where do you think our dragons came from? God? Humans created them hundreds of cycles ago." He pointed at the ornithopter. "*I* created that."

Brother Lucas stared at bright Terra. "Reason says that it's impossible for something to come into existence from nothing, Grandmaster. If you believe the universe had a beginning, what caused it? Where is your evidence that God doesn't exist?"

Grandmaster Justin slapped his knee and snorted. "Ah, the Sanctus Ordo trained you well. When you were a student of mine, Lucas, I hoped you would follow a career in the ciencias. Lynette's future was set by being the Lord Governor's daughter. But you, Lucas, you are intelligent and full of curiosity, you would have found a home in the Order of NASA."

Brother Lucas imagined the old classroom, his times studying with Lady Lynette. She was always the intelligent one, not him. He forced his mind back to the present. "There's room for both science and faith in the search for truth, Grandmaster." He stood and stretched. "It's been a long day and another follows. Goodnight."

Mark Venturini   *Search for Eden*   the anthology *Medieval Mars*

1) What do you think this excerpt is about?

2) If the protagonist from the story you are writing were in this scene, what would she, he, or it be doing?

3) Look at the story you are working on. What is the human idea you are expressing along with the action?

Day 3 abeyance

Science fiction (and to some degree fantasy and horror) often does something few of the other genres do. That is what Orson Scott Card calls abeyance. What he means by that is science fiction writers will often introduce a new concept, a name the author made up, a new invention, and then will not instantly explain what that new concept, name, or invention is.

Abeyance will often stall the fans of westerns and war stories. The romance reader will often stop at the strange word and say, "Wait. I don't know what this word means and I'm not reading another sentence until somebody explains this to me." The legal thriller reader might say, "This is confusing," and toss the book aside.

Experienced science fiction readers will take in the new word and hold it in mind as they read and pick up clues to what the new word means. This sense of discovery and solving the riddle of the new word is fun for the science fiction reader. When the author casually tosses in words like hyperdrive, spindizzy, ansible, and seed village, the reader perks up and wonders what that could mean. The reader watches to see what the characters do with the replicator or transmogrifier, and from that figure out what the thing is.

Now, there are a few rules for committing abeyance.

One: Do not give the reader a name of a device and then not show the whatever in action or being used before the end of the book. Preferably demonstrate the item within the chapter or the next. If you leave the reader hanging with the unknown thing still unknown, he will think unkind thoughts about you.

Two: Do not introduce more than one unknown thing at a time. Some few of us can hold as many as ten unknown things at a time waiting for the scenes that will explain the unknown things. More of us can hold up to five unknown things before we give up in confusion. Maybe most of us can hold only one unknown thing until the unknown thing is revealed, and then we can cope with the next new unknown thing. If your story has a lot of unknown things that cannot be instantly guessed by the name, try to space them out, the same way you space out characters so they won't get jumbled or lost in the reader's mind.

Unless the unknown thing is also unknown to the character whose point of view we are following, you ought not show the character boggling over this unknown thing any more than you would have a modern-day character boggling over a microwave oven.

So how would we introduce the microwave to a reader from, say, the 1940's? The 1940 reader might know that microwaves are electromagnetic waves with a wavelength shorter than that of a normal radio wave but longer than those of infrared radiation. She would have no clue as to what nuke means in that context. To let her know what microwave and nuke means in this story, you could have the character pull his cup of coffee out of the microwave, sip it, and be annoyed that after forty-five seconds of nuking it, the coffee was still lukewarm. It must be time to replace the oven. Or you could have the character yell at the alien, "No! You can't put metal in the microwave. It will spark and blow up. Here." She takes the spoon out of the bowl and reinserts the bowl into the oven. "Press sixty seconds if you want your soup boiling hot." (And then maybe later blowing something up in the microwave could be an important plot point.)

There are all sorts of ways to demonstrate new concepts or inventions without stopping the story to insert a definition. There are times though, when a single sentence definition is useful. In Hunger Games, Suzanne Collins sometimes inserts a short definition of a horrific animal or device in the middle of action so that the action can be understood. Short. Not long. Few are the readers who want a device and how it works explained in great detail. Most readers only want to know what the character is going to do with the thing, or what the thing is going to do to the character. By all means, do understand for yourself how a device works, but don't bore the reader with that information.

Apparently contradicting what I just said, remember at all times that the reader cannot read your mind. She can only read the words on the page, and you won't be there in the bookstore to tell her what you meant. Yes, we readers of science fiction want new ideas and the skillful use of science fiction tropes, but we also need clear illustrations to understand what we are reading. Unless you are writing clichéd stories where every sentence is a cliché, clarity can be hard to achieve. The balance between action and information is tricky. That balance is still worth the effort.

Activities:

A. *Read*:

'Don't you leave this room, Blaine Colton!'

'Whatever!' Blaine snatched his jacket from the back of his chair. As an abrupt excuse for a wave, he swiped his hand towards the woman opposite him. 'Catch you at the next "science freak-boy" appointment.'

'Clearly you do *not* understand!' Dr. Melissa Hartfield's eyes probed him with the sharpness of a biopsy needle. 'According to current law, *all* experimental such as this must be contained within the facility, *particularly* GMOs. And those not approved—'

'Genetically modified organisms?' Blain held up the jacket and backed towards the door. 'Not my problem, Doc. Besides, you don't own me.'

She held up a form and tapped one of the points. 'Actually, as I was just explaining, technically you belong to this research institute. Not that you heard a word I said while you were browsing social media sites on your phone.'

Heat crept up Blaine's neck and over his face. He'd kept the iPhone near his knee and hadn't thought she'd seen it from the other side of her desk. 'Well, *I* didn't sign that form, my parents did!'

'Until you're of legal age, you can't reverse that authority without contesting it in a court of law.'

'And that's next month. Hard luck, lady. I'm out of here!'

The sound of the slamming door echoed through the corridor. Blaine's heart lurched in his chest with each stride. His new joggers squeaked their own rhythm against the impervious, laboratory-grade linoleum.

Taking his iPhone from his pocket, he started texting his mum. Hearing other footsteps much heavier than his own, he glanced over his shoulder. Two large men in security uniforms were jogging towards him.

'Mr. Colton, why don't you make this easy?'

Blaine's gait stalled and he gripped his jacket tighter. They were comparative giants. Yet in his new life he had discovered himself to be wiry and fast. 'Bite me, Baldy!'

Having spent most of his years incapable of feeling the power of his muscles, adrenaline hit him like a shot of speed. He bolted towards the exit. The corridors were strangely deserted. That worked to his advantage.

With freedom in sight, Blain skidded to a stop as Dr. Hartfield pushed through a side door and blocked his path. She held one hand behind her back. 'Blaine, I tried to explain your recent test results.'

Blaine slipped his phone into his pocket and pretended to listen, all the while inching to a better position to side-step her.

'They show the unprecedented success of your gene therapy was not complementation of the mutated regions in your nuclear and mitochondrial genomes, as predicted, but the result of integration.'

He glanced over his shoulder. The security guards were walking now, but closing in.

'In my opinion, as this institute's Biosafety Committee Chair, the procedure wasn't approved by the appropriate regulating body. And *I'm* responsible for managing such indiscretions, including illegal GMOs.'

Again Blaine looked from her to the guards. 'I don't care about your "indiscretions". The therapy was thirty-five months ago. History! I just want to get out of here and go home.'

She produced what looked like an auto-injector. Instinct kicked in. Darting nearer the wall, Blaine dropped his shoulder to barge her aside.

The collision nearly toppled him over. *But at least she's down*. He righted himself and regained his momentum.

Footsteps thudded behind him as he tore down the corridor. The guards were charging, grunting like slow, clumsy bulls. He was at the door when he felt a fistful of his shirt grabbed from behind. A huge arm reached over his shoulder, spun him around and pushed him back into the corridor. He struggled as Dr. Hartfield strode towards him. She gripped his wrist and plunged the auto-injector towards his arm. The sting whacked him sideways. A wave of nausea coursed through his body.

He looked to his upper arm and caught a hazy glimpse of the auto-injector, now delivering its venom. His jacket slid from his arm to the floor with a plop. It was like he'd been submerged in a giant tub of honey.

Still he struggled. 'Stop! You can't do this!'

The thugs had him pinned. Dr. Hartfield shook her head. 'We can, Blaine. If you'd been listening, you'd know that.' Her words wafted like jarring noises through his mind. 'Blaine, you're the illegal GMO!'

Illegal … GMO … me…?

'Take him to the observation room.'

Adele Jones *Integrate*

1) What have you heard about the controversies about genetically modified organisms?
2) What do you think the conflict here will be?
3) Why weren't the thugs named?

B. *Read*:

 Izrael Irizarry stepped through a bright-scarred airlock onto Kadath Station, lurching a little as he adjusted to station gravity. On his shoulder, Mongoose extended her neck, her barbels flaring, flicked her tongue out to taste the air, and colored a question. Another few steps, and he smelled what Mongoose smelled, the sharp stink of toves, ammonia, and bitter.

 He touched the tentacle coiled around his throat with the quick double tap that meant *soon*. Mongoose colored displeasure, and Irizarry stroked the slick velvet wedge of her head in consolation and restraint. Her four compound and twelve simple eyes glittered and her color softened, but did not change, as she leaned into the caress. She was eager to hunt and he didn't blame her. The boojum *Manfred von Richthofen* took care of its own vermin. Mongoose had had to make do with a share of Irizarry's rations, and she hated eating dead things.

Sarah Monette and Elizabeth Bear *Mongoose*

1) What do you think a tove is?
2) What do you think a boojum is? What are the clues?
3) This is certainly not a Rikki-Tikki-Tavi mongoose. What is it?

C. *Read*:

 Carter Cho was trying to camouflage the lifepod when the hunter-killer found him.

 Carter had matched spin with the fragment of shattered comet nucleus, excavated a neat hole with a judicious burn of the lifepod's motor and eased the sturdy little ship inside; then he had sealed up his p-suit and clambered out of the airlock, intending to hide the pod's infrared and radar signatures by covering the hole with fullerene superconducting cloth. He was trying to work methodically, clamping clips to the edge of the cloth and spiking the clips deep into the slumped rim of dirty water ice, but the cloth, forty meters square and just sixty carbon atoms thick, massed a little less than a butterfly's wing, and it fluttered and billowed like a live thing as gas and dust vented from fractured ice. Carter had fastened down less than half of it when the scientist shouted, "Heads up! Incoming!"

That's when Carter discovered she'd locked him out of the pod's control systems.

He said, "What have you done?"

"Heads up! It's coming right at us!"

The woman was hysterical.

Carter looked up.

The sky was apocalyptic. Pieces of comet nucleus were tumbling away in every direction, casting long cones of shadow through veils and streamers of gas lit by the red dwarf's half-eclipsed disc. The nucleus had been a single body ten kilometers long before the Fanatic singleship had cut across its orbit and carved it open and destroyed the science platform hidden inside it with X-ray lasers and kinetic bomblets.

Paul McAuley *Rats of the System*

1) There are at least two hooks in the very first sentence. What are they?

2) What do you think the p-suit is? Why? Does the writer stop the story to explain every function of the p-suit?

3) There is some striking description in this excerpt. What keeps it from being static and/or boring?

Day 4 is the trope a cliché?

Every story is going to use tropes the reader is familiar with. The word trope has a number of meanings. One of them is a building block for a story. Another one is a stale cliché. A space ship does not need to be a stale cliché, any more than a car in a horror story needs to be. Characters need to get around somehow. However, if every single device and function of a space ship replicates exactly that of a famous television or movie space ship, the writer might want to do some changeouts to keep the ship from becoming a stale cliché.

Activities:

1) What are the tropes you are using in your story so far?

2) What emotion are you trying to evoke in your reader?

3) Are all your characters reacting the same way in your story? How might you vary their reactions to events?

Day 5 the end is nigh

You should be close to finishing or have finished your story. Now is the time you get to examine your story and take some things out and put some things in.

Activities:

1) Look over your rough draft. Are there clichés you need to remove? Remove them.

2) Look over your bleeding draft. Are there any tropes you can add that will evoke the emotion you want from your reader? Mark where you will add them. Then add them.

CHAPTER SEVENTEEN:

FANTASY

Fantasy is the literature of maps and books that weigh five pounds. Sometimes it seems that the writers think that you spent so much effort to get into their world, you might as well stick around for a while.

No, there is a little bit more to fantasy than that. Fantasy is the parent of science fiction and horror. The earliest literature of mankind includes fantasy.

On the website A Pilgrim in Narnia, Tim Willard posted an essay in which he wrote:

> In 1942 J.R.R. Tolkien penned the essay, "On Faerie-stories." The essay became the touchstone work of fantasy fiction, illuminating the genre. Tolkien ends the essay by discussing the "consolations of the happy ending," what he calls the *eucatastrophe*.
>
> A eucatastrophe is the opposite of a catastrophe. Whereas the catastrophe might be employed in tragedy, and is regarded as the down-turn of a story, Tolkien's eucatastrophe is the shift in the faerie story for the good. It's "the sudden joyous turn." The eucatastrophe says that just when all hope appears to be lost, just when circumstances cannot get much bleaker, hope emerges.
>
> Tolkien said eucatastrophe does not deny a sudden failure by the protagonist (*dyscatastrophe*). Rather, "it denies universal final defeat and in so far is *evangelium*, giving a fleeting glimpse of Joy, Joy beyond the walls of the world, poignant as grief." Tolkien uses the Latin *evangelium*, meaning "good news" or in Old English "godspel," fully aware of the Christian undertone.
>
> Universal final defeat was exactly what Norse mythology offered. What's more, it was compounded by endless repetition. Ragnarök, the Norse apocalypse was cyclical: the giants destroy the gods and all humankind in a final battle only for the earth to rise again out of primordial waters, the gods to be reborn along with humans, and the cycle to begin afresh. Medievalist scholar and Tolkien expert Tom Shippey suggests Tolkien wanted to offer something more than this cycle of doom and was attempting to "retain the feel or 'flavour' of Norse myth, while hinting at the happier ending of Christian myth behind it."

    Tim Willard *Eucatastrophe: J. R. R. Tolkein & C. S. Lewis's Magic Formula*
                           for Hope

Today, the word myth carries the connotation of that which is not true. That is not what either Tolkein or Lewis meant by the word. To them, myth meant any way in which the world is explained, including the true Christian Myth.

G. K. Chesterton said this about fairytales:

> "Fairy tales do not tell children the dragons exist. Children already know that dragons exist. Fairy tales tell children the dragons can be killed."

Day 1 why fantasy?

C. S. Lewis, in his book Four Loves, wrote, "Friendship is unnecessary, like philosophy, like art, like the universe itself (for God did not need to create). It has no survival value, rather it is one of those things which give value to survival." In other words, art, which includes literature, is one of the things that gives value to our lives.

Around AD 865, Johannes Scotus Erigena, an Irish philosopher proposed a doctrine that had the idea that the natural world was a manifestation of God in four separate divisions that were contained in the singularity of God. Scotus said that God was the sole Creator, Sustainer, and True Source of all that exists, the first division. The second division was supernature, a separate, invisible, other nature that was composed of all primordial ideas, forces, and archetypes, (a Neoplatonist idea) which he called the Form of forms. This Otherworld is where the idea of beauty comes from.

In *The Song of Albion* by Stephen R. Lawhead, a character named Professor Nettleton tells the main character about the ideas of Scotus,

> … "The Otherworld does not supply the meaning of life. Rather, the Otherworld describes *being alive*. Life in all its glory—warts and all, so to speak. The Otherworld provides meaning by example, by exhibition, by illustration if you will. Do you see the difference?
>
> "Through the Otherworld we learn what it is to be alive, to be human: good and evil, heart-break and ecstasy, victory and defeat, everything. It is all contained in the treasury, you see. The Otherworld is the storehouse of archetypal life imagery—it is the wellspring of all our dreams, you might say."

Stephen R. Lawhead   *The Song of Albion*

C. S. Lewis thought that the longing that fantasy can arouse in a person was one of the signs that this world is not all there is for humans.

Other people claim that fantasy contains moral training. Well, maybe. Some fantasy contains a morality I approve of, and some, like everything else on earth, contains nasty evil. Discernment is needed.

Others feel about fantasy the way Emily Dickinson explains in her poem:

> Tell all the truth but tell it slant —
>
> Success in Circuit lies
>
> Too bright for our infirm Delight
>
> The Truth's superb surprise
>
> As Lightning to the Children eased
>
> With explanation kind
>
> The Truth must dazzle gradually
>
> Or every man be blind —

Why did Jesus the Christ couch so much of His truth within parables? Perhaps the usefulness of fantasy is to tell the truth slant so that we can bear to hear it.

Activities:

A. *Read*:

Drawing in a breath full of story, Alia began.

"Once upon a time, there was a powerful wizard who lived hidden among a brave and noble people and who married and had three daughters and used magic to protect them from the evil rampant in the lands around them—"

"Sha'kath!" Aron hissed.

Alia frowned, "Are you going to let me tell this story, or do you want to tell it?"

Aron pinched his lips shut and shook his head. She waited for the wiggling to stop.

"However, the threat of evil grew so great, the wizard had no other choice but to use magic to hide the people of the great ancient kingdom of Moreb, and so, when Sha'kath was not looking, a great rent ripped the ground open, and all the frightened people of Moreb fled underground—"

"Far, far underground!" Aron chimed in.

Alia chuckled at his excitement over hearing the same story over and over. He never seemed to tire of it, reminding her of God's delight in repetition. For every day, in constant and perfect patterns, galaxies and planets and moons repeated their orbits, and on many planets, day and night, summer and winter, never ceased. As if God alone had pure childlike delight in his creation and said to the sun, "Do it again. And again!" Never tiring, never losing the wonder.

She understood now, looking at Aron, why God wanted all his creatures to be like small children. It was the path to joy.

"And the wizard with great magic, formed a beautiful kingdom far below the earth's surface in which all could live—man and beast alike. And in time, the people forgot they were underground. They forgot the real world above, and the centuries drifted by, and wizard watched and waited, ever alert. For although the people lived in safety and peace, the wizard knew it was only a matter of time . . ."

Alia let her soft words trail off as the quiet, rhythmic breaths puffed out of Aron's mouth, as his head slumped against Big Pig's plush cheek. Carefully, she extricated herself from the arms and animals and got to her feet.

She stood by the window, the three moons now cresting the dome of night in tandem, and let out a sigh.

She remembered back to those years, those centuries of smuggled peace and prosperity. Remembered how her power had gradually waned, the artificial light dimming more and more until she'd nearly lost hope of sustaining them any longer. She recalled the hard choice before her—to let her people wither and die in darkness or do the unthinkable—abandon their land and return to the surface to face whatever they would find there. But then, unexpectedly, the door to the secret room, long sealed, opened. And the choice was made for her.

No, she would never forget. It was her task to remember. Her duty.

Her promise.

If humans had learned only one lesson from the thousands of years of evil and suffering, it was this.

Never forget the stories.

C. S. Lakin *The Hidden Kingdom*

1) What might the author think the purpose of stories is?

2) What have we learned about this world from this excerpt?

3) Which kind of fantasy is this?

B. *Read*:

Looking back, I shiver to think how little I understood, not only the peril I was in, but the true extent of the power I fled. I did know better than to make for Sumildene, where a stranger stands out like a sailor in a convent; but if I had had the brains of a bedbug, I'd never have tried to cut through the marshes toward the Queen's Road. In the first place, that grand highway is laced with toll bridges, manned by toll collectors, every four or five miles; in the second, the Queen's Road is so well-banked and pruned and well-maintained that should you be caught out there by daylight, there's no cover, nowhere to run—no rutted smuggler's alley to duck into, not so much as a proper tree to climb. But I didn't know that then, among other things.

What I did understand, beyond doubt, was that they could not afford to let me leave. I do not say *escape*, because they would never have thought of it in such a way. To their minds, they had offered me their greatest honor, never before granted one so young, and I had not only rejected it, but lied in their clever, clever faces, accepting so humbly, falteringly telling them again and again of my bewildered gratitude, unworthy peasant that I was. And even then I did know that they were not deceived for a single moment, and they knew I knew, and blessed me, one after the other, to let me know. I dream of that twilight chamber still—the tall chairs, the cold stone table, the tiny green *tintan* birds murmuring themselves to sleep in the vines outside the window, those smiling, wise, gentle eyes on me—and each time I wake between sweated sheets, my mouth wrenched with pleas for my life. Old as I am, and still.

If I were to leave, and it became known that I had done so, and without any retribution, others would go too, in time. Not very many—there were as yet only a few who shared my disquiet and my growing suspicions—but even one unpunished deserter was more than they could afford to tolerate.

I had no doubt at all that they would grieve my death. They were not unkind people, for monsters.

Peter S Beagle *Quarry*

1) If the author had started with, "I lived with monsters," would the effect have the same impact it does where he did place that information?

2) What might these monsters be?

3) What geography is important in this story? Why?

C. *Read*:

"Are you afraid to answer?" the Chronicler asked.

Leta drew a deep breath. Then she nodded.

"Why?"

Even that was a dangerous question. Clutching the book in both hands, scarcely daring to raise her gaze from it, she said, "Because I don't think you'll like it."

He snorted. "What does that matter? Think something; think something on your own. Not what *they* tell you to think or what *I* tell you to think. You are Leta of Aiven. I want to hear *your* thoughts, for they are neither mine nor anyone else's. Only yours. This makes them interesting."

His words pierced the numbness she had felt since meeting Lady Mintha, since coming to Gaheris, since the moment her father had told her she would wed and did not consult her wishes on the matter.

Tell him what you think! her rebellious side cried. Tell him!

He'll believe you such a fool, her practical side rejoined.

Tell him anyway! Tell him!

So she said, "I think you're wrong."

Then she blushed and pressed a hand to her mouth. Never in her life had she dared to cross the will or opinions of anyone! The glory of freedom surged in her heart. Before she could stifle the words, she repeated, "I think you're wrong!"

The Chronicler laughed a genuine laugh, and the great stones of the Wall crumbled away in that sound. "Do you, now?" he said, his eyes sparkling with mirth and, wonderfully, interest. "Why is that?"

Anne Elizabeth Stengl   *Dragonwitch*

1) What can we deduce from this short excerpt about the storyworld?
2) What might the character of Leta be like?
3) How do you react to people who say you are wrong?

Day 2 drawing lines

Everybody draws a line in their writing somewhere. Some don't draw the line at language, imagery, and violence until they reach child pornography. Some draw the line at one swear word and will not read past the point of that word, because the people who have practiced the discipline of not swearing don't appreciate being made even to think the swear word.

Some people won't read a book that contains positive references to delusional religion. Others won't read a book that doesn't exalt their God whom they love. Some people detest having sovereign God as a character in a book speaking words the writer makes up. Some writers get around that by still using God as a character in their books but only what is written in Scripture is used for His dialogue. Some readers frown on using angels as anything but a messenger of God, and they really hate it when an angel falls in love with a human.

There are readers who despise the use of dragons in literature unless the dragon is a metaphor for malevolent chaos as it is used in the Bible. Writing dragons as characters of good will is, to those readers, akin to putting a friendly face on an Ebola virus. Some writers refute that attitude by noting that dragons are considered beneficent creatures in China and Japan (and bats are symbols of good luck, and toads symbolize prosperity.) Other writers will note that God can redeem anything with His extravagant grace. Friendly dragons can be a metaphor for redemption.

Friendly demons can be considered even more egregious than the use of dragons in a story. Having sweet girls fall in love with bad-boy demons can be offensive to potential readers.

That might seem like a lot of fussing over fictional creatures. After all, most readers (except some history buffs) don't mind fictional fiction even when real people are included. But when it comes to fictionalizing that which is holy, fictionalizing that which has eternal consequences, many people think it's evil to desacralize such ideas. Other people will think it's okay to fictionalize even sacred concepts because that is a way to express important ideas. Where will you draw the line for your fiction?

As for other lines, some people don't want to read realistic violence, while others scoff at non-realistic violence. Ditto sex. Ditto magic spells. Ditto drug use.

Some of us can't stand reading a book with many grammatical errors outside of dialogue, while others really don't care.

If you want to have commercial success (i.e. sell lots of books) you need to know where your target audience draws the lines and stay within those lines. Books that cross those lines will not be read unless an instructor commands them to be read.

The reader owes you nothing. They are not required to buy your book or like your writing. They are not required to read past the things to which they object in order to read the rest of your brilliant prose. They are not required to write a good review. They are not required to say nice things about your book or you.

Instead, you owe the reader. You owe the reader the emotional experience you promised with your choice of genre, subgenre, blurb, and tone of the first page.

If the reader ignored every clue about what was in the book and still read what he didn't like, okay, that's on him. If she says negative things about the book or you in public places, here is the protocol for dealing with such readers: Ignore them. If people who are not your target audience don't like the book, you don't care. You weren't writing the story for them.

Even the target audience owes you nothing.

You owe the target audience.

Today, your instructor is your target. (If you want a good grade)

Tomorrow?

Activities:

A. *Read*:

In previous pages we found out Liz can see the demons and angels no one else can see. Sometimes she fights a demon to its death.

> The moon appeared and lit the night. By its glow, she could make out his hands clasped in front of him and a smile on his face. Not a drop of tension stiffened his body. He moved forward slowly as if trying not to scare her. Liz drew in a sharp breath and staggered as he walked out of the shadows.
>
> The mystery blond.
>
> He loomed over her. His electric-blue eyes glowing in the dark, sapphire orbs ablaze. Expansive shoulders topped impressive arms. He had the rugged look of a

warrior, yet features so pristine they were elegant. A peculiar aura encircled him, majestic and out of place in the rural setting.

Fear tickled Liz's senses, and the fleeting thought she had no control over the situation gave it solid purpose. Yet she was captivated.

"Who are you?" Liz couldn't keep the wonder out of her words.

"I am Arie-Chayal." His voice was oddly familiar.

The back of her neck prickled. What do you want?"

"I am here for you."

Those five words snapped her chin lower and her shoulders back. Liz's grip tightened on her paltry weapon. "What's that supposed to mean?" She edged toward the door.

"You need not fear me." He followed her retreat. "I have been sent by the Master. It is time." He followed her retreat. He spread his arms and gave a small bow. "I am your guardian and teacher."

The branch fell from her hand to the pine needles below. Liz's head roared, and her stomach churned. It was him. The angel. That softening spot in her heart grew. Teacher? There was something she was supposed to learn to do? The thought simultaneously terrified and thrilled her. Yet her shield of cynicism refused to be laid down.

Liz put her hands on her hips. "Wait. All these years. Now all of a sudden, it's time. Time for what?" She glared at him. "Have I suffered enough and now I'm worthy?"

Heat boiled in her belly. God and His merry band of angels had hung her out to dry for years. Now out of nowhere an angel stood in front of her, saying he was her guardian. Where was he when she'd needed him? Where was God?

Amy Brock McNew   *Rebirth: Book One of the Reluctant Warrior Chronicles*

1) What is the target audience for this book? (Hint: The target audience for this book is people who like fantasy that has ____ and is ____.)

2) Is that the same target audience as your story? Pretend you are out of school and writing on your own. Who is your target audience?

3) What do you think is the story question for this book? Compare answers with others. Perhaps one of you will obtain the book and find out who was correct about where the book was going.

B. *Read*:

I met Mal the day he tried to kill my boyfriend.

It happened in February, because that's when they delivered the bees for our almond orchard. The semi woke me up at four in the morning—a descending roar of diesel engine, a yelp of air brakes, then the constant beeping as it backed up.

A little thrill raced through me. I sat up in bed and peered out my window, but the fog created a solid wall of nothing outside.

My breath rattled in my lungs, and I inhaled slowly. I had to struggle to slide off my bed and stand up. Stupid Valley Fever. It'd been six months, for crying out loud. It was like having tuberculosis.

Dishes clattered downstairs, and Mom and Dad talked in low voices. A whiff of coffee floated up the stairs. My stomach did this uneasy slithering thing that meant I was hungry.

I dressed in a fresh pair of sweats, and brushed my hair a few times. It fell to my waist, and since I spent so much time in bed, it kept trying to convert to dreadlocks. Someday I'm going to cut it all off. I pulled it back in a loose ponytail to keep it out of my face. Then I scooped my lockblade and smartphone off my dresser and into my pocket, and dragged myself down stairs. Maybe my body would cooperate and let me eat food for once. Between the meds and the sickness, I didn't eat much these days. Most girls would love to lose the amount of weight I'd lost. Me—well, I wasn't exactly fat to begin with.

Dad disappeared out the back door with a breakfast burrito as I entered the kitchen. Mom swirled around the kitchen, emptying the dishwasher, then froze with a handful of plates. "Libby! What're you doing up?"

I flopped into my chair at the kitchen table. "Can I have some toast?" My legs trembled from the trek downstairs. Mom dropped a slice of homemade bread in the toaster. The overhead light caught the silver in her hair. My parents are older—they had already sent my four brothers through college when I came along. Mom's nice looking—light hair, dark eyes, and a comfortable round face without being fat. I take after my dad—chocolate-colored hair and skinny as a rake handle.

"I'm glad to see you up, baby. Are you feeling any better?"

"I shook my head. "Nope. The bee truck woke me up."

Mom smiled. "Yes, we're lucky to have them. Honeybees are dying out and the orchards fight over them."

"I'm going to go see them." I watched the beekeepers set up every year, and a crummy sickness wouldn't change my tradition.

                    K. M. Carroll   *Malevolent (The Puzzle Box Trilogy Book 1)*

1) What keeps you reading through the establishment of this character's normal?

2) What is the first question, the first hook, in this story?

3) How old do you think the main character is? What are the clues?

C. *Read*:
Somewhere over Zaethien.

The bloody image of King Zireli fell away as Chima lifted into the ash-riddled air. Smoke and flames streaked into the skies, not only of their own violent will, but wielded at the hand of a master accelerant. Searching. Hunting for Haegan as he fled the hopeless battle that had cost his parents their lives. He squeezed his eyes shut against the devastation, his hands gripping the raqine's dense fur. But no distance or expanse could separate him from the visage of his father in death.

Zireli's son, heir of the Fire King, Haegan glanced back to the smoldering keep. In that heartbeat, he saw the Deliverers standing amid the ruin. Remembered as acid on his tongue the terror they had struck in him. And the furor as they forbade him from killing Poired.

Why? Why would Abiassa stay his hand? Deliverers were her justice embodied. All-powerful. All knowing.

And they had forbidden him from slaying the beast who had ravaged the kingdoms. Terrorized the people. Murdered his father.

Everything in him wanted to turn back. What justice was there when Abiassa allowed evil to go unchecked? Had not the Council of Nine said Haegan was the Fierian, Her chosen warrior? Was is not his role to mete out her retribution?

He dug his knees into Chima's side, forcing her to angle to the left. To bring her around and head back to the keep.

White-hot fire shot through his wrist. Haegan screamed as the pain blazed across his arm. Glowing. Red. As if an ember itself had embedded itself in his forearm.

You are forbidden, Fierian. This is not yours to do. The Deliverer's reminder scorched his mind as its touch had his wrist.

A throttling-staccato angry purr rippled through Chima. Even with the wind tearing at his ears, Haegan heard her refusal. He turned his face to the sky and let loose a cry of anguish and frustration.

Chastised. Defeated. Humiliated. Haegan, prince of Zaethien and all the Nine, hunched forward over the sleek red neck of the raqine and stared down at the limp body of his sister slung in front of him.

Ronie Kendig   *Accelerant (Abiassa's Fire Book Two)*

1) What is the conflict here?

2) Haegan has a lot of anguish. What are the things causing it?

3) If you have not read the first book, you don't know a lot about Haegan. Is there anything in these first few paragraphs of book two that engage you, that cause you to have sympathy for him? Do you want to keep reading?

Day 3 inner conflict externalized

In an essay on writing for children, C. S. Lewis said:

… Since it is so likely that [children] will meet cruel enemies, let them at least have heard of brave knights and heroic courage. Otherwise you are making their destiny not brighter but darker. Nor do most of us find that violence and bloodshed, in a story, produce any haunting dread in the minds of children. As far as that goes, I side impenitently with the human race against the modern reformer. Let there be wicked kings and beheadings, battles and dungeons, giants and dragons, and let villains be soundly killed at the end the book. ... It would be nice if no little boy in bed, hearing, or thinking he hears, a sound, were ever at all frightened. But if he is going to be frightened, I think it better that he should think of giants and dragons than merely of burglars. And I think St. George, or any bright champion in armour, is a better comfort than the idea of the police.

Gracy Olmstead in an open letter to Professor Dawkins that was first published in The American Conservative and then republished on the website theimaginativeconservative.org said:

> Lewis saw a potent metaphorical force in the fairy tale: it helped children battle the pains and frustrations of reality through its images of valor and heroism. None of us ought to read children news stories about serial killers and tragic accidents. These things are too graphic and frightening for their young minds. But by reading them stories of evil monsters, and by telling them of knights and heroes who bravely stood up to such monsters, they receive greater mental and moral strength. When they grow older, they'll have to fight their own real-life villains and calamities. The fairy tale's metaphorical power gives real strength to them as they grow.
>
> Of course it's statistically improbable that any child will ever be required to carry a magic ring across a perilous land ravaged by monsters, toward an evil, all-seeing eye and its dark kingdom, in order to save all of humanity. But how many of the children who read *The Lord of the Rings* will grow up to fight injustice and oppression in its real forms? Might some of them become doctors on the frontlines of fighting cancer, teachers willing to work in the most troubled school districts, social workers eager to combat corruption and manipulation in the foster care system?
>
> ...
>
> You could also note the observations of J.R.R. Tolkien, the author of the aforementioned fantasy trilogy, one of the greatest masters of fantasy fiction. In a fascinating essay on fairy tales, he wrote the following:
>
> Fantasy is a natural human activity. It certainly does not destroy or even insult Reason; and it does not either blunt the appetite for, nor obscure the perception of, scientific verity. On the contrary. The keener and the clearer is the reason, the better fantasy will it make. If men were ever in a state in which they did not want to know or could not perceive truth (facts or evidence), then Fantasy would languish until they were cured. If they ever get into that state (it would not seem at all impossible), Fantasy will perish, and become Morbid Delusion.
>
> For creative Fantasy is founded upon the hard recognition that things are so in the world as it appears under the sun; on a recognition of fact, but not a slavery to it. So upon logic was founded the nonsense that displays itself in the tales and rhymes of Lewis Carroll. If men really could not distinguish between frogs and men, fairy-stories about frog-kings would not have arisen.
>
> Fantasy can, of course, be carried to excess. It can be ill done. It can be put to evil uses. It may even delude the minds out of which it came. But of what human thing in this fallen world is that not true? Men have conceived not only of elves, but they have imagined gods, and worshipped them, even worshipped those most deformed by their authors' own evil. But they have made false gods out of other materials: their notions, their banners, their monies; even their sciences and their social and economic theories have demanded human sacrifice.
>
> Interestingly, Tolkien's argument suggests that even you, Mr. Dawkins, could fall prey to fantasy of a sort: could it be that you worship statistical probability to some

excess, to a degree that necessitates the disposal (or at least shackling) of creative imagination?

Gracy Olmstead   *Why Fairy Tales are Dangerous*

What do you think of her argument?

Some people who analyze fantasy and its impact upon readers say the fantasy is inner conflict externalized. What they mean by that is a story about anxiety, an inner emotion, can be expressed with outer forms, such fighting dragons.

Activities:

A. *Read*:

My son, the shapeshifter starts the school day as a honey badger--thirty pounds of coiled muscle and a quarter-inch of thick skin. The predators will stay away today, and even the serpents with their venom will do him no harm.

"Let them stare. You're small but fierce," I say. "And I love you just the same."

When I tuck my son into bed that night, he reverts to a boy, swallowed beneath the blankets, a tuft of thin hair all that I can see in the gloom. I touch his frail legs through the material and hear the wheeze in his breathing.

I pray that tomorrow he wakes as a fire-breathing dragon.

* * *

My son morphs into a stork on the way to the doctor, one bent wing tucked up against his body. He tries to flap it in the backseat and squawks more and more frantically with each failed attempt.

"You'll make it worse," I say. "Don't worry. You'll fly again soon."

I watch him in the rear-view mirror, and I fear that this time even braces of aluminum and plastic won't make my promise true.

When we arrive, I gather my broken bird in my arms and carry him through the revolving doors. The nurses stroke his beak as I hurry him through the corridors, and his clawed feet flap at the ends of limp legs.

The doctor pokes and prods the broken wing with a grimace. When I ask him if my little bird will ever kiss the sky again, he shakes his head. *Not this time,* he tells me. *Not ever again.*

Shane D. Rhinewald   *My Son, the Shapeshifter*

1. What story is being told here in disguise?

2. How could a little boy be compared to a honey badger?

3. What is the tone of this story?

B. *Read*:

Sir Charles Hallwyn was riding at the head of his retinue when he spotted it, an arrow-flight away across the wasteland: an angel sitting on a rock.

Heart pounding, he halted the others. What could it want? Half-forgotten stories swirled through his head. Why did angels usually appear? Was he being assigned a great task?

Knowing knights weren't supposed to run away, he rode toward it instead, sword sheathed. The brush crackled as the horse pushed through, and a cloud of dust followed their passage. Perhaps that was why his mouth had gone dry.

The angel wore a linen robe and a gold cape that covered most of the stone on which he sat, and he carried his wings tucked up so they touched neither the ground nor the rock. Standing he would have towered a head taller than Sir Charles (whose broad shoulders and short stature had earned him the school nickname "whiskey bottle"). At full extent the angel's wings would have spread to twice his height, and the feathers glistened silvery blue in the straight noontime sunlight.

The angel smiled. "Thanks for stopping. Not many pass this way."

Shaking inside, the knight dismounted and removed his helmet, then brushed his sweat-drenched brown curls from his eyes. He bowed as well as he could manage wearing leather mail, and his sword clanked against its scabbard as he genuflected.

"Please don't." The angel wore a no-nonsense expression in his brown eyes. "The only one to worship is God, and anyhow, I simply wanted to talk."

Sir Charles took in the angel's slender features, his relaxed poise, the way the breeze lifted the straight ends of the angel's black hair. The air around the angel carried the scent of tea leaves, leaving him dizzy. "Do you bear a message for me?"

The angel shrugged. "Nothing specific. Where are you going?"

Sir Charles gestured toward the foothills twenty miles away.

The angel sat taller. "Dragons live there. You're planning to fight one?"

Sir Charles chuckled. "I'm not that skilled a knight. I raise dragons."

The angel cocked his head. "Now that's a reversal. I'm glad some of your kind can see them as intelligent and beautiful creatures. It saddens me how often knights venture out to slaughter one, and how many of them either fail to return or else parade home dragging their victim's severed heads as if homicide were a mark of glory."

Sir Charles shivered. "I'd be among those who didn't return." He paused. "If it isn't untoward—"

"Why is an angel sitting on a stone in the middle of the wilderness?" The angel regarded himself ruefully. "Almost three years ago, a friend of mine asked me to accompany her before the Throne of God to pray for the soul in her care. The man's soul was an absolute abyss as far as grace was concerned."

Without understanding why, Sir Charles perceived a series of images: an angel with red-barred black wings and purple eyes, sadness etching her heart-shaped face as she knelt before God. A blond-haired man with calculating eyes. Fire. Deep dread.

"We were praying for the soul's conversion, and when my friend begged for some hope, God said no one is without hope. And I," the angel said, his gaze lowering, "said Sure there's a Japanese proverb '*Ishi no ue ni mo sannen.*'" The angel shook his head. "Even a stone will warm up if you sit on it for three years."

Sir Charles flinched.

The angel knit his hands. "I succeeded in making my friend burst into tears, and God sent me here, showed me this stone, and ordered me to find out if the proverb was true."

Jane Lebak *Even a Stone*

1) Analyze the voice of this excerpt.

2) What is the hook? What do you think the story question might be?

3) What do you think the climax might involve?

C. *Read*:

It wouldn't be long now. Sitting atop the gray skyscraper with my feet dangling carelessly over the ledge, I was concealed by the dark of the early evening. They existed down there, sure, but up here, it was just me and my marks. People were fools, generally speaking. They believed in only what they could see in front of them, or what they were certain existed above or below. Who was I to complain? If they were a little more observant, maybe less arrogant, my life wouldn't be nearly as successful. Fools were great for business.

I exhaled, watching the thin white cloud of my breath appear and then dissipate. I wondered somewhat morbidly I supposed, what it would feel like if I shifted too suddenly, lost my balance, and didn't stop myself. What would it feel like to simply—fall? Would I try to catch myself, would I cry out—or would it be like this moment—so completely, perfectly peaceful? I held my breath. If I could have stopped time, I would have then. Just frozen the whole thing. Nights like this had held a strange comfort for me lately. At eighteen, the darkness was the closest thing I'd ever had to a romance. Its cover was almost a caress. Letting my lungs deflate in a rush, I blinked the thought away. The evening was passing and it would soon be time to make my move.

I raised the binoculars to my eyes and peered through. I'd done it so often they almost felt like an extension of my fingertips. The man in the high-rise condo across from me was putting on his black suit coat, with that easy, familiar motion exhibited by every wealthy, faceless mark I'd chosen this month. His wife was generic. She'd be glued to him all evening.

…

Their limousine pulled up—I recognized it from two nights prior when they had attended an art gala for a client—and they would soon make their way down. Stretching my long legs straight in front of me and my arms over my head, I looked up into the clouded, starless sky and counted the hours until the sun came up and stole my freedom. For now, the height of my perch and color of night made me invisible to the people below and around me. I didn't need the light to see. It was one of the few perks of being me.

When I was going through a stage last year, I spent an inordinate number of nights in darkened libraries. I read everything I could find about flying people. Books about beings with white, feathered, angel-like annexes—eagle men. I read one story about a girl with reptilian wings that were scaled and sharp and fire red. Some writers imagined the ability to fly came with extraordinary speed or unparalleled strength. Maybe if you were Superman, it did. If you were Joshua Miller, it only came with a set of four translucent wings, a love of the cold, night vision, and the inability to sleep comfortably on your back.

Alyssa Thiessen   *Dragonfly*

1) What fantasy power does the protagonist have?

2) The protagonist is a thief. Does that make him an anti-hero?

3) Why do you think he is thinking about falling?

Day 4 keeping the reader

The fantasy reader opens a book willing to suspend disbelief, wanting to suspend disbelief and be carried away to another world. You, the writer, need to make it easy on the reader and not toss anvils at them so they crash and burn and toss aside your book. To give a silly example, if you have knights jousting and all through the book and said knights have been using courtly language, and then one breaks a lance and shouts, "Hey, Dude!" your reader will be thrown right out of the story.

There are a number of ways you can help the reader suspend their disbelief.

Consistency in language and behavior and rules of magic.

Get the facts right on all the things that aren't fantasy.

Sensory details that help the reader ground herself in the protagonist's head. Sight, touch, smell, taste, hearing.

Make the characters have realistic reactions.

Follow a general logical progression of events and actions.

Foreshadowing so things don't pop up suddenly.

Activity:

1) Go through your manuscript and make sure there is at least one sensory detail per page. Use more senses than sight.

Day 5 keep calm

You should be in the serious editing and revising stage of your story by now. Keep calm and continue.

CHAPTER EIGHTEEN:

HORROR

Horror is the genre that is most likely to elicit strong feelings of like or dislike. Perhaps the reason for this is that horror is specifically written to evoke the emotions that most of us do not want to feel: fear, dread, and revulsion.

I suggest that since the reading of horror can cause distress, any student who feels they cannot or must not read horror should be allowed to opt out of this section of the course. They could engage in some of the extra credit activities listed elsewhere in the textbook instead.

We urge those who love horror to not mock those who choose to not read or watch horror. One cannot help the body and physiology one is born with. Some people metabolize the adrenaline that fear produces well and other people do not. I would have rather clawed my way out of a metal box than read or watch horror the first four decades of my life. A rush of adrenaline leaves me shaking and nauseated, sometimes for days after the initial stimulus. Nights of nightmares leave me groggy. Even now I will sometimes vent my ire upon my fellow writers whose stories have left me feeling sick and filled with dread for days. They have become used to receiving messages from me that open with, "I hate you!"

I also urge those who hate horror to not condemn those who love the genre. Those who love horror are having a different experience while reading it than you are. The last few years I have gotten to know a number of horror writers and have found most of them to be among the sweetest people on earth. I have spent decades trying to understand why anybody, especially all those sweet people, would read, let alone write horror. If you have the same question, keep reading this chapter.

Horror will usually use the elements of things that make us uneasy: darkness, death, disease, decay, deformity, distortion, evil, filth, things usually hidden, foreboding, separation, vulnerability, threat to a loved one, inability to control where one is going, pain, chaos, brokenness, the feeling of being lost, the unknown, rain and thunder, the underground, the breaking of social taboos, malice, and insanity. It is possible to write a horror story set in a sunny day with crowds of people around, but it is difficult.

As in science fiction and fantasy, while you need to sow the seeds of what bad stuff is coming, you first need to establish the protagonist as someone we will care about.

Day 1 why?

Why, oh, why does anyone want to feel the fear and dread that accompanies the reading of horror? One writer has said he likes confronting his fears in a safe arena, one he can step away from if he needs to. Another writer has said she enjoys the thrill of fear, but she does not ever want to watch a real monster eat a real person.

Dean Koontz described the feeling of dread in *The Taking* this way:

> The chill that spread through Molly was different from any that she had experienced previously. It was not a quivery thing localized along the spine or the nape of the neck, did not shiver through her like a vagrant breath of eternity, but lingered. A coldness seemed to be spawned in the very cavities of her bones, in the red-and-yellow mush of marrow, from which it spread outward to every cell in every extremity.

Dean Koontz   *The Taking*

Again we ask, *Why* would anyone want to feel like that? Dean Koontz says elsewhere in The Taking:

Derek shook his head. "Better to seize what pleasure you can. Make love. Raid Norman Ling's market for your favorite foods before the place is underwater. Settle into a comforting haze of gin. If others want to go out with a bang . . . well, let them. But pursue what pleasures are still available to you before we're all washed into that long, perfect, ginless darkness."

He turned away from them once more and went to the back of the tavern.

Watching him, hesitating to follow, Molly saw Derek Sawtelle as she had never seen him before. He was still a friend but also other than a friend; he was now the embodiment of a mortal temptation—the temptation to despair.

She did not want to see what he wished to show them. Yet the refusal to look would be a tacit acknowledgement that she feared his evidence would be convincing: therefore, refusal would be the first step on a different road to despair.

Only by seeing his evidence could she test the fabric of her faith and have a chance to hold fast to her hope.

Dean Koontz *The Taking*

Maybe the author here is saying that looking at horror tests us to prove what we really believe.

Here's something Mike Duran wrote in his intriguing book *Christian Horror   On the Compatibility of a Biblical Worldview and the Horror Genre*

Because the real world is full of horrors, so our stories "must contain monsters and demons." *It is simply unbiblical for a Christian artist to avoid portraying the realities of evil.*

Of course, there is a fine line between portraying evil and celebrating it. Indeed, artists who choose to portray evil will, at some point, run the risk of being accused of celebrating it. The only way to avoid such accusations is to forgo portraying evil out of fear of offending someone. But the fear of offending someone with a portrayal of evil can be just as misguided as celebrating evil. By being fearful of making others afraid, we are succumbing to fear.

This is a very important point. *Christian horror should not shy away from portraying evil, even at the expense of being misinterpreted.* The believing artist must be free to "depict the full range of the grotesque."

…

Art, like life, is always open to interpretation. Sometimes it is difficult to clearly categorize anyone or anything as purely "good" or "evil." The "good guys" don't always wear white hats; the "bad guys" don't always wear black hats. Even some of the most beloved Bible heroes had dark sides. King David was "a man after God's own heart" (Acts 13:22). Nevertheless he was also an adulterer and a murderer. Scripture does not glorify David's sin. In fact, his household and his kingdom eventually suffered because of it. This true of the Bible's portrayal of evil across the board. Making evil appear cool, sin as inconsequential, sadism as tolerable, hell as "fun," Satan as liberator, or occultism as simply an alternative religion is misguided, if not intentionally deceptive. Evil must appear evil, unnatural. It is not without consequence. It never ultimately fulfills. And we mustn't portray it as such. As the prophet intoned, "Woe to those who call evil good and good evil."

Mike Duran   Christian Horror

Here I would like to make what is likely an obvious point. All writing—all literature, non-fiction and fiction, all genres, not just horror, not just fantasy or science fiction, but definitely including them—can glorify evil. Discernment is needed for reading everything. Discernment is needed for writing everything.

Activities:

A. *Read*:

-1-

It rained the day the world ended.

That's how she remembered it.

The rain fell cold and hard. That day and every time the world ended. For Lilah there wasn't just one apocalypse. They kept happening to her.

And each time it was raining.

-2-

The first time was when she was little. Too little to really understand what was happening. She was just learning to speak, barely able to walk, hardly able to form the kind of memories that could be taken out later and looked at. She remembered a woman's face. Her mother's, but Lilah didn't really understand what that meant. George had to explain it to her later.

Lilah remembered her mother holding her, and running. And other people holding her. And running.

And the monsters chasing.

Grabbing. Tearing. Taking. Biting. Eating.

Always.

One of them had bitten Mom. Lilah had seen it happen but did not know what the bright colors and loud shrieks meant. Not then. Not until later.

She remembered the house where her mother and the other grownups had hidden. She remembered her mother screaming. Mommy, with her big, swollen belly. Screaming.

That's when Annie was born.

Lilah did not understand birth, either.

Or the death that followed.

Or what happened when Mom woke up.

Jonathan Maberry   *Sisters (A Story of The Rot and Ruin)*

1) List the elements of horror in this excerpt.

2) Which POV is this written in?

3) What makes this voice sound like a young child's?

B. *Read*:

It had been a long day, and all I really wanted was to come home, get something to eat, and fall asleep on the couch watching Family Feud. But even as I turned the handle to my apartment door, I knew that wasn't going to happen.

"Nick," a voice floated through the air from my living room. "Niiick . . ."

I closed my eyes and, for just a second, considered turning around and finding a hotel. But I'd have to come back here sooner or later anyway, seeing as I lived here. And so did Larry. Well, not really. See, Larry was my roommate, but not the normal kind.

Before I could sum up the will power to open the door, Larry's head stuck out from the middle. "Nick!" He shouted. "You're late. Come on, get in here, I'm starving."

I shook my head and pushed the door open through him. "You shouldn't be able to eat, you're a ghost. It should just fall through you." I pushed past him, or tried to—with ghosts, you end up just walking through them—into my apartment.

"Nu-uh," Larry whined, following me down the hall. "I can eat."

"Then why is it that whenever it's your turn to clean the apartment your hands always go right through the vacuum cleaner?"

I didn't bother to look over my shoulder, but I knew he was making the same hurt expression he always did. "I don't know, I guess metal interferes with it. Lay off, I feel bad enough about it already."

"The vacuum's plastic, Larry." Not that it really mattered. He was always going to find some way to weasel out of doing his share of the chores, and I'd learned to deal with that long ago.

I went into the kitchen, ignoring his protests, and opened up the fridge. The only thing in there was a pizza box.

I spun around to glare at Larry, but I couldn't see him. "Don't turn invisible," I snapped, "I know you're still there."

A haze appeared just to my left, and it resolved into Larry, wearing a sheepish grin. "Told you I could eat."

Matthew Sketchley   *Ghost Roommate*   *Mythic Orbits 2016*

1) List the elements of horror in this excerpt.

2) Take one of the paragraphs and analyze the voice in quantifiable terms.

3) Which POV is this written in?

C. *Read*:

May of 1885—Northern California

Hunger drove Raven Worth to the big tent revival that night, but it wasn't what made him stay. Usually in such a public gathering he'd have lurked just beyond the edge of the crowd to scan the fringes for stragglers. In other setting he'd often harvest the ones who looked the most destitute or lonely.

He could relate to them. He knew their pain.

But not that night. The crowd seemed devoid of the transients and homeless nobodies Raven preferred. Everyone beamed with happiness—they enjoyed the service, the evangelist's booming voice, and each other in a form of unity Raven hadn't seen since before he'd turned.

Then again, that was almost a hundred years ago. Sometimes it felt more like a thousand.

A few children wandered along the crowd's outer ring, not engaged by the service in the least. One of them, a small girl with hair so blonde that it seemed to glow under the moonlight, sat alone on the ground and played with a rag doll.

Raven couldn't help but stare at her.

Who would leave such a beautiful child unattended? Raven clenched his fists. Didn't her parents know what kinds of horrors roamed the night in search of weak, vulnerable prey exactly like her?

A rumble in Raven's stomach reminded him why he'd come tonight. He shook off the weakness and resigned himself to his task.

She was a small girl, small and alone, but she would do. Perhaps if he could restrain himself enough, she wouldn't die after he finished.

Either way, if he didn't feed, he wouldn't survive.

She's just an orphan. She has no one. No one will miss her.

Ben Wolf   *Blood for Blood*

1) Whose point of view is this from?
2) What is the hook?
3) What are the conflicting emotions in Raven? In your story, are there any characters with conflicting emotions?

Day 2 ratcheting

Horror is known for the buildup of tension or the ratcheting of fear. How do writers achieve that? Let's look at what J. S. Bailey did in the short story *The Ghosts of Memories*.

"I'd love to hear this place's story," Paige said as she nudged a dog's rope toy with her shoe. "If only walls could talk."

"I'm almost afraid to hear what they'd say," I murmured. This place was giving me the creeps more than I liked to admit. What could cause a family of four to leave all their things behind like this? Had they all died in an accident? Had they really all been murdered?

I vowed then that I would research this house and learn its secrets once I was safely nestled in my spider-free apartment.

In the meantime, I moved on to the spacious kitchen, which presented even more of an enigma than the living room. A table set for four sat in the center of the open space. My flashlight revealed mouse droppings scattered across the tabletop and plates which I'm sure at one point held the remains of this family's dinner before it was consumed by rodent and insect life.

Cynthia went to the counter and prodded an uncertain finger at a stack of envelopes, then picked one up and turned it over. "This looks like a medical bill. It's still sealed."

"What's the name on it?" I asked, craning for a better look.

"William Arnold. Postmarked October 2, 1986."

William Arnold must have been the bug-eyed man in the photograph out in the living room. I shivered. Part of me was tempted to tear open the envelope and see what exactly he'd been billed for. Had he been in poor health? Had he passed away?

That still wouldn't explain why the entire family vanished.

"Come on, let's keep going," I said. Standing in one place for too long was making me uncomfortable. I swept the room with the thermal imaging camera, spotting nothing abnormally cold nor warm.

We proceeded up the stairs and investigated the bathroom and bedrooms, finding exactly what you'd expect in a place like this: dusty toothbrushes sitting in a holder on the sink, limp towels draped over a rod, beds covered in rumpled blankets. A smattering of building blocks spread across the carpet in the girls' bedroom, and a single pink bunny slipper stared at me with beady plastic eyes.

The air smelled of mildew and decay, like a tomb.

Thunder rumbled as we regrouped on the landing.

"I don't know about you, but I've seen all I need to see," Darren said.

"As if you aren't as intrigued as the rest of us," Paige said while a second roll of thunder rattled the windows.

I caught sight of another spindly spider scuttling across the floor and decided it would be in my best interests to vacate the premises as soon as possible. "Darren's right. We should get going."

"Best idea I've heard all night," Darren muttered. Then, "Wait a minute. Look at this." He held up the K-II meter, which suddenly registered EMFs too high to be normal. "This is crazy."

J. S. Bailey *The Ghosts of Memory*

The story begins with the introduction of the ghost-hunter foursome, the discussion of some local legends, the sight of the spooky, abandoned house, and the decision to enter despite misgivings. This excerpt starts after they have entered the house and looked over the living room. Bit by bit the spooky details pile up and begin to overwhelm the mundane details. There are normal building blocks strewn across the floor, and then there's the single bunny slipper. Single indicates that something is lost. Single breaks the wholeness of a pair. And not only that, but the slipper is staring at them. And a thunderstorm is coming. And then something crazy registers on the meter......

The timing of a character at a resting state, ie. normal and calm, and then growing more tense ratchets up the tension in the story and the reader.

This ratcheting allows the reader to anticipate and then feel the impact of the event more fully than if the event happens so quickly that the reader needs to stop and ask, "What just happened?"

Activities:

A. *Read*:

Zeph glanced from one man to the other, and then he edged toward the corpse.

Its flesh appeared dull, and the closer he got, the less it actually looked like skin. Perhaps the body had been drained of blood or bleached by the desert sun. He inched closer. Sunken pockets appeared along the torso, and he found himself wondering what could have possibly happened to this person.

The head lay tilted back, its bony jaw upturned, cords of muscle taut across a gangly neck. A white sheet draped the body at the chest, and just above it a single bloodless hole about the size of a nickel notched the sternum. He crept forward, trying to distinguish the person's face. First he glimpsed nostrils, then teeth, and then . . . something else.

That *something else* brought Zeph to a standstill.

How could it be? Build. *Facial features. Hair color.* This person looked exactly like him. There was even a Star of David tattooed on the right arm, above the bicep—the same as Zeph's.

What were the chances, the mathematical probabilities, that one human being could look so identical to another? Especially in a town the size of Endurance?

"Is this . . ." Zeph's tone was detached, his eyes fixed on the body. "Is this some kinda joke?"

The detectives hunkered back into the shadows without responding.

Goose bumps rose on Zeph's forearms as the overhead vent rattled to life, sluicing cool air into the room. He took another step closer to the cadaver until his thigh nudged the table, jolting the stiff and bringing Zeph to a sudden stop. He peered at the bizarre figure.

Their similarities were unmistakable. The lanky torso and appendages. The tousled sandy hair. Thick brows over deep-set eyes. *This guy looks exactly like me!*

However, it was one feature—the most defining feature of Zeph Walker's existence—that left him teetering in disbelief: the four-inch scar that sheared the corpse's mouth.

Zeph stumbled back, lungs frozen, hand clasped over the ugly scar on his own face.

Mike Duran   *The Telling*

1) In a prior paragraph the desert setting and heat had been established. The mention of the desert sun at the beginning of this section reminds us that that protagonist has been in the heat. How does the protagonist go from the heat to the stage of frozen lungs?

2) How else is the tension slowly ratcheted up in this scene?

3) Why doesn't the writer have the protagonist immediately recognize the body on the table?

B. *Read*:

The moon was rising when Sankofa came up the dirt road. Her leather sandals softly slapped her heels as she walked. Small swift steps made with small swift feet. When she passed, the crickets did not stop singing, the owls did not stop hooting, and the aardvark in the bushes beside the road did not stop foraging for termites.

Sankofa was thirteen years old, but her petite frame and chubby cheeks made her look closer to ten. Her outfit was a miniature version of what the older more affluent women of northern Ghana wore—a hand-dyed long yellow skirt, a matching top embroidered with expensive lace and a purple and yellow headband made of twisted cloth. She'd done the headband exactly as her mother used to when she visited friends. Sankofa covered her bald head with a short-haired black wig. She'd slathered her scalp with two extra coats of thick shea butter, so the wig wasn't itchy at all. Despite the night's cloying heat, the shea butter and her elaborate heavy outfit, she felt quite cool—at the moment.

A young man leaned against a mud hut smoking a cigarette in the dark. As he was blowing out smoke, he spotted her. Choking on the last puff, he cupped his hand over his mouth. "Sankofa is coming," he hollered in Ewe, grabbing the doorknob and shoving the door open. "Sankofa is coming!"

People peeked out windows, doorways, from around corners and over their shoulders. Noses flared, eyes were wide, mouths opened and healthy hearts pounded like crazy.

"Sankofa. *Na* come!" someone shouted in Pidgin English.

"Sankofa is here!"

"Sankofa strolling!"

"Sankofa, *Sankofa*, o!"

"Here she comes!"

"Beware of remote control, o!"

"Sankofa bird landing!"

Women scooped up toddlers playing in the dirt and ushered them inside. Doors slammed. Steps quickened. Car doors slammed and cars sped off.

The girl called Sankofa walked up the quiet deserted road of the town that was pretending to be full of ghosts. Her face was dark and sweet and her jaw was set. The only item she carried as the amulet bag the juju man had given her five years ago not long after she left home. The size of a grown man's fist, it softly bounced against her hip. Its contents were simple: a roll of money that she rarely needed, a wind-up watch, a large jar of shea butter, a hand drawn map of Accra and a tightly rolled up book. For the last week, her book had been a copy of *No Orchids for Miss Blandish*, a paper novel she barely understood yet enjoyed reading. Before that, a crumbling copy of *Gulliver's Travels*.

The town was obviously not poor. There were huts but they were well built and this night, though dark as caves, Sankofa could see hints of bright light coming from within. People feared her but they still wanted to watch television. These mud huts had electricity. Beside the huts were modern homes, which equally feigned vacancy. Sankofa felt the town staring at her as she walked. Hoping, wishing, praying that she would pass through, a wraith in the darkness.

Nnedi Okorafor   *Sankofa*

1) When do you figure out the girl is more than she seems?
2) Why do you think the people fear her?
3) What do you think will happen next? Are you hooked by the beginning of this short story?

C. *Read*:

The monster had him boxed in and it wasn't even close to sunup.

"Rabbit! Give it up! You don't have a chance!"

Schaffer cringed at the sentiment and tiptoed faster along the corrugated tin wall. Up ahead he could see the exit; a huge door that emptied out into the dark night beyond. The warehouse sat on the river's edge—how far from the pier was he? Maybe fifty feet once he cleared the threshold. There was a good chance he could jump into the water and swim away. Didn't these aberrations of nature abhor running water? Schaffer didn't have time to think too hard about it. Taking one deep breath to gather his nerve, he burst forward suddenly, commanding his legs to propel him faster than they ever had before. But it wasn't fast enough.

Not by a mile.

Schaffer slammed into the outstretched arm of his enemy after only four strides.

"Oops. Down you go, Rabbit."

Schaffer struggled to get to his feet, but the monster grabbed him by the collar and dragged him back the way they had come. His boot heels plowed the red clay in the dirt parking lot, making furrows no one would notice.

"Come on, silly Wabbit . . . we have a big night ahead of us."

Schaffer wrestled against his attacker's grip to no avail. The creature that held him fast was not his master, but he was still one of *them*. One of the Brethren. A Rakum. A devilish miscreant with ancient roots no one remembered; whose strength was only outdone by his cruelty. And they would be sure to punish Schaffer for the stunt he pulled against their Elder, Rufus.

Schaffer fought futilely until they reached the monster's aged and dented Dodge pickup parked in the unlit abandoned lot. He got a glimpse of the Rakum's face—it was not one he recognized. But that mattered little—once he was marked as a Rabbit, they would come from all over.

"In ya go, Rabbit."

The Rakum grabbed Schaffer's belt along with his collar and tossed him into the passenger seat in one fluid motion. Schaffer grunted with discomfort as his attacker quickly zip-tied his hands together. He then zip-tied his wrists to the headrest behind, yanking his arms up above his head. Schaffer cried out but only a few syllables escaped his lips before the monster shoved a greasy rag into his mouth.

"Where're your matches now, Rabbit?"

Schaffer had set Rufus on fire.

Yeah, it had been a glorious sight. But he didn't get away fast enough. He blinked back tears, gagged and watched with round eyes as his attacker settled into the driver's seat and switched on the truck.

"Might be fun to burn you up, Rabbit. See what that smells like."

Schaffer moaned. An hour after he set Rufus aflame, he had been captured and marked by one of the Elders. The creature told him to start running.

Schaffer looked out the passenger side window as they sped through a thick forest. If only he'd planned an escape route. Now this monster was taking him to his private killing field. As the morbid thought crossed his mind an Airstream trailer emerged from the woods on the side of the grassed-over road.

"Oh my. All for me."

The Rakum hit the brakes hard and didn't bother to come around to extricate his catch. Instead, he jumped down and reached in to yank Schaffer out the driver's side. The stiff plastic ties raked across his flesh and he yelped through the filthy towel as his skin gave way. His wrist bones fractured as his hands popped free of the bonds. The Rakum chuckled and tossed Schaffer bleeding and crying over his shoulder and headed for the trailer.

Ellen C. Maze   *Rabbit: Chasing Beth Rider*

1) Are you horrified that Schaffer set Rufus on fire? Why or why not?
2) What might another name for Rakum be? Why do you say that?
3) List the elements of horror in this excerpt.

Day 3 fear

What are you afraid of?

Many people are afraid of the dark. You can't see what's out there in the dark. It could be anything. It could be a huge spider slowly lowering itself from ceiling or tree to land on you.

It could be spiders. Some of us have screamed and flailed when walking face first into a spider web and the spider less than an inch from our eye so it looks as large as a boulder. When a spider drops unexpectedly on us, even those of us who aren't afraid of spiders can wake the neighbors.

Perhaps you're afraid of pain: from knives or stingers or bites or poison or acid.

Perhaps you're afraid of being closed in a tight spot and unable to protect yourself as your car drifts under the river, as dirt is shoveled onto your coffin, as someone hides you behind a wall of bricks so you can die of thirst and hunger, unable to reach anybody you love. Many of us have prayed that we would never end up paralyzed, or worse, paralyzed and mute.

Perhaps you're afraid of loss, of losing somebody you love, of losing your sanity to schizophrenia or psychosis, of losing your intelligence to Alzheimer's or brain injury, of losing a body part. Those of us who are already blind might be snickering at the terror of darkness or of losing one's eyes, but for those of us who still have sight, the thought of losing it is horrifying.

Some of us are afraid of anything sticky. Hey, if you have any sensory hypersensitivities, the fear is real.

Most of us fear humiliation. Most of us shudder at thinking about being watched and judged when we thought we were in private. Think of how much of every day is spent with you trying to avoid embarrassment and humiliation.

Even those of us who felt at peace when we thought we were dying suddenly can still feel dread at seeing death close but not here yet, maybe days or weeks or months to come, but definitely coming.

Some of us fear how evil we would be if we let ourselves go. What if our evil thoughts could take physical manifestation?

How about abandonment?

A few of us fear doing something without knowing what the consequences will be, and then those consequences turning around and killing us.

All of us fear being helpless among our enemies, depending on mercy from someone who has no mercy.

You can take your personal fears and turn them into horror stories. Suppose you're afraid of getting cancer. Let's look at that a moment. Cancer eats you up from inside. It's like your body has betrayed you. Sometimes cancer hurts. How could you turn those elements into a horror story? You could think about the mass growing inside and turn it into supernatural maggots, an alien egg that hatches and literally eats you, a spot of evil that grows until you are that evil infecting other people, a spore you accidentally eat and in a few hours you've turned into a fungal mass bursting with spores.

Ewww. Anything that makes you gag is likely to make other people gag. Take your fear, tweak it, think about it some more, tweak it again, come up with a likeable potential victim, (remembering to show its state of normal before the creepy stuff starts) and you can write a story that will terrify other people. And they will be happy you did so.

Activities:

A. *Read*:

When the palace women had brought the child to the kappa, all these questions had been asked, but the kappa had received no satisfactory answers.

"Does she have a name?" the kappa had asked the women. One had merely stared, face flat and blank, suggesting concentration upon some inner programming rather than the scene before her. The other woman, the kappa thought, had a touch of the tiger: a yellow sunlit gaze, unnatural height, a faint stripe to the skin. A typical bodyguard. The kappa took care to keep her manner appropriately subservient.

"She has no name," the tiger woman said. "She is *ikiryoh*." The word was a growl.

"I am afraid I am very stupid," the kappa said humbly. "I do not know what that means."

"It does not matter," the tiger woman said. "Look after her, as best you can. You will be paid. You used to be a guardian of children, did you not?"

"Yes, for the one who was—" the kappa hesitated.

"The goddess before I-Nami," the tiger woman said. "It is all right. You may speak her name. She died in honor."

"I was the court nurse," the kappa said, eyes downward. She did not want the tiger-woman to glimpse the thought like a carp in a pool: *yes, if honor requires that someone should have you poisoned.* "I took care of the growing bags for the goddess Than Geng."

"And one of the goddess Than Geng's children was, of course, I-Nami. Now, the goddess remembers you, and is grateful."

She had me sent here, in the purge after Than Geng's death. I was lucky she did not have me killed. Why then is she asking me to guard her own child? the kappa wondered, but did not say.

"And this child *is* the goddess I-Nami's?" she queried, just to make sure.

"She is *ikiryyoh*," the tiger woman said. Faced with such truculent conversational circularity, the kappa asked no more questions.

In the days that followed it was impossible not to see that the child was disturbed. Silent for much of the time, the *ikiryoh* was prone to fits, unlike anything the kappa had seen: back-arching episodes in which the child would shout fragmented streams of invective, curses relating to disease and disfigurement, the worst words of all. At other times, she would crouch shuddering in a corner of the temple, eyes wide with horror, staring at nothing. The kappa had learned that attempts at reassurance only made matters worse, resulting in bites and scratches that left little impression upon the kappa's thick skin, but a substantial impression upon her mind. Now she left the child alone when the fits came and only watched from a dismayed distance, to make sure no lasting harm befell her.

The sun had sunk down behind the creeper trees, but the air was still warm, heavy and humid following the afternoon downpour. Mosquitoes hummed across the water and the kappa's long tongue flickered out to spear them before they could alight on the child's delicate skin. The kappa rose and her reflection shimmered in the green water, a squat toad-being. Obediently, the child rose, too, and reached out to clasp the kappa's webbed hand awkwardly in her own. Together, they climbed the steps to the water-temple.

Liz Williams   Ikiryoh

1) List three questions raised in this excerpt.

2) Notice how the careful details grounded you in the character. List some of the concrete details.

3) If this was the beginning of your story, what would happen next?

B. *Read*:

Present Day

The stairs wandered to the right—old wooden stairs. With the first step they groaned, and she hesitated. Small candles sat on the steps, spread out—only one every four or five steps. They oozed lifeless blood that pooled at their base and coagulated into white scabs. She broke a candle free and continued her ascent, tilting it so it bled on the planks.

Darkness pressed in from beyond the candlelight. The shadows behind her taunted her by name, while the shadows above beckoned with false hope. More than once, she thought she recognized a shape—a person or animal—in the shadows, only to have the light flicker and send the phantom away. Slotted windows perforated the outer wall every few feet, staring at her with cold, lidless eyes.

She passed a rough wooden door with an iron handle. It was not her destination, so she continued. On her journey she passed many doors the same as the first. The stairs dissolved into black eternity. Her feet hurt, her knees hurt, and her heart pounded with cold dread. Each footstep echoed in the empty stairwell, answered by moans from the wooden steps. She wanted to flee—to turn and go back. But she couldn't. She must continue. Sweat leaked from her body, matting her clothes to her skin. A bitter breeze drifted through a window and she shuddered.

Finally, the endless line of candles stopped before a door just like all the others she had passed. She reached out and brushed the handle with the tips of her fingers. It felt cold. Cold radiated from the floor like heat from a furnace. Evil waited beyond this door . . . expecting her. She could feel it, and the instinct to flee seized her stronger than ever. Every hair on her body stood rigid, and she trembled with anticipation. Her arms and legs numbed, but she knew she must enter. Here lay her destiny—her calling. She grabbed the handle, took a deep, desperate breath, and pushed.

Inside was a round room. She hesitated before entering, heart pounding. Fear grabbed her and wouldn't let go, and her knees threatened to buckle. Never had she seen such a sight.

Blood flowed down the walls like cascading waterfalls. Blood rained down from the ceiling like a summer shower. Blood pooled over every inch of the floor like glassy oil. It was as if she had stepped into the very bowels of Hell itself.

In the center stood a man. No . . . not a man. A demon. The grotesque black creature reached out a scaly, bony hand to her. It smiled, revealing long, pointed teeth.

"Winterrrr," it hissed, calling her by name with a roll of the final R. "Winterrrr."

* * *

"Winter."

Winter sat up and stared out the rain-streaked window of her dad's Dodge Dakota. The windshield wipers squeaked in paused intervals as Randy Travis wailed in the background. The pine tree air freshener's smell mingled with that of motor oil. Winter closed her eyes and sighed, trying to shake away the hellish nightmare.

"Winter?"

This time she turned to face her dad, making her expression blank. Her jet-black hair brushed against her face.

"I think we're here." He hoisted his travel coffee mug to his lips.

They turned off the interstate and passed beneath the boughs covering Hoole Boulevard. Extra-large drops of water fell from the branches, striking the windshield with small splashes.

Winter leaned her elbow on the door and watched collegiate suburbia pass by. After a few miles, the arched gateway of Tishbe University loomed before them. Winter's dad stopped at the guardhouse.

"Moving in," he told the guard.

The guard smiled and greeted them, then passed them a map of the campus before turning his attention to the next vehicle.

Winter didn't even try to follow the twists and turns of the school roads. At one point she saw a large lawn between two buildings. A few people walked along pathways crisscrossing the well-manicured grass. Some held umbrellas or wore ponchos, some just slumped beneath the weight of their backpacks. Winter took it all in during the second before they passed behind the next building.

Eventually, they found their destination—a large dorm in the shape of a U. A parking lot lay between the arms, and small grassy knolls padded the ends of each. The grassy area to the right displayed a blue plaque reading "Carmichael Hall."

"Looks nice," her dad said. Winter grunted and shifted in her seat. He pulled into the parking lot across two spaces to allow for the trailer. "All right," he said, "are you ready?"

Winter looked back to the covered entrance for a moment, then opened the door, being sure to take her time. She wore black carpenter pants and a baggy black Jack the Pumpkin King T-shirt. The chain dangling from her belt loops jingled as she walked. She kept her arms crossed and watched the pavement between her feet.

Pounding steps on wet pavement announced someone rushing to them. Winter cut her eyes up and saw a grinning girl with hair so rain-soaked it was impossible to tell whether she was blond or brunette.

"Hello!" the girl said. "I'm Amber. Welcome to Carmichael Hall!"

"Hi, Amber. I'm Steve Maessen. This is my daughter, Winter."

Amber grinned. Winter scowled and Amber's grin melted away.

Keven Newsome *Winter*

1) You will be told over and over again not to start your story with a dream. Generally, that's a good rule and you should try to adhere to it. Why do you think the author broke that rule for this story?

2) List the elements of horror used in this excerpt.

3) What are the questions raised in these first paragraphs of the novel?

C. *Read*:

I fully recognize that I have an amazing gift, even if it feels more like a curse. I'm still trying to figure out why me. I suppose I'm expected to do something good with it, to help people. Sometimes I succeed.

Yet other that this odd talent, there are many people with backgrounds similar to mine. Kids abused by their parents, taken away by authorities, placed in children's homes, abused, bounced around foster homes, abused. I've known a few of these kids while they were still alive. Sadly, I've known some who are now dead. My brother and sister among them.

Not all foster homes are bad. Some are wonderful and save children. I've just been unlucky at a few places.

So the math is a family of five, four gone, one left. Both parents and two siblings. How is that possible? Here's a spoiler. It has to do with my demon father.

The very idea that a man possessed by such pure, concentrated evil could be the same man that brought me into this world makes me want to revolt against the slightest recognition, not to mention the acceptance, that there is a God. To believe a person could be so completely devoid of moral character, be a black hole that destroyed all goodness around it, is further proof against the existence of God.

Yet, despite the damning evidence that was my father, evidence that has played a major role in my life, I believe the contrary.

Faith is a funny thing.

This is the last time I will refer to him with a term as intimate as *father*. I only do so now as the word is an immediate definition of my genealogy. Going forward, he will be referenced by his first name, Allister.

As for what happened to my mother, she died after Allister gave her some bad drugs.

And Allister? I killed him.

Frank Redman *Elijah*

1) I sincerely hope that this character's normal is not your normal. What is his normal?

2) What are the elements of horror in this excerpt?

3) How does the calmness of this writing contribute to the shock at the end of this excerpt?

D. *Read:*

Laughter barks around me as I finish my breakfast. It's been a long time since anyone has called me by my given name—but I hear it whispered soon enough. Two men with sallow skin and long braided hair sneer as they pass me on their way to the field. One of them breathes, "Anna," in my ear as his left hand lingers on my thigh. I shove him away. Behind me, the morning skies fill with a multitude of dark clouds, casting more shadow than light down on our camp. A hundred gray tents line the riverbank—the same river where the Chasers caught me, just last week—and all of the tent flaps are tied down in case the wind picks up again.

I pause, plate in hand as I glance up at the sky, wondering what it's going to give us today. Ever since the Last War, everyone west of the Mississippi's been tormented by lightning storms, demon winds and earthquakes. Sunshine comes like a fiery flash, straight out of nowhere and it always passes before you can enjoy it.

Never can count on a sunny day anymore.

Thanks to those Chasers and that blasted sun, today I'm heading into a war field, where I'm almost instantly surrounded by dead bodies, knee-deep in blood and gore, shovel in one hand, bucket in the other. A thick canvas apron covered me from neck to ankle and a plastic visor shields my face. Flies buzz from one carcass to the next while the other Cleaners are already grumbling that I'm taking too long, hunting for valuables.

"Get a move on there, dearie!"

"Just look for somethin' shiny and hurry up—"

"Never shoulda taken that Runner, she doesn't have a stomach for blood—"

I ignore them as I flip a body on its back, then run a gaze over it, looking for anything worth a coin or two.

Right about then, the sun creeps out like the sneaky devil it is, scaring away all the clouds, charming steam to rise up from the heath and turning the field to haze. I've learned that sometimes a sudden change in temperature can cause the dead bodies to shift and moan, and more than one Cleaner has let out a startled cry when that happens.

Not me.

I refuse to cry out. No matter how terrified I am.

Merrie Destefano *The Plague Carrier*

1) What the horror elements in this excerpt?
2) What are the science fiction elements in this excerpt?
3) Are there supernatural elements such as magic or spirits in this excerpt?

Day 4 facing fear

In a 1933 sermon on Matthew 8: 23-27, entitled "Overcoming Fear." Dietrich Bonhoeffer said,

Fear is, somehow or other, the archenemy itself. It crouches in people's hearts. It hollows out their insides, until their resistance and strength are spent and they suddenly break down. Fear secretly gnaws and eats away at all the ties that bind a person to God and to others, and when in a time of need that person reaches for those ties and clings to them, they break and the individual sinks back into himself or herself, helpless and despairing, while hell rejoices.

Josh Larsen in a September 2, 2015 post on the website Think Christian said about Dietrich's sermon:

This grim homily sounds about right, whether we're talking about the world-shaking fears Bonhoeffer faced in relation to Nazi Germany, the universal fear of illness which he later references or simply the primal fears we're seemingly born with. (Say, of the dark.) Strikingly, Bonhoeffer doesn't deny those fears, but acknowledges them, just as Matthew 8 acknowledges the storm. And this is not an isolated incident in Scripture.

The expression of fear is a more Christian response than the repression of it.

The Bible doesn't balk at fear. Scripture is wide awake to horror, from the bloodlust of Cain to the zombies of Ezekiel to the more existential despair of the psalms of lament. And so it seems to me that the expression of fear is a more Christian response than the repression of it. Horror in the Bible exists partly to evoke a darkness that will provide context for God's shining light, but also to acknowledge the deep-seated terror (of violence, of mortality, of despair) we experience in this broken world. To sweep away this fear runs against the grain of the Bible. If we deny fear, we can't defeat it. So horror helps us take that crucial first step of confrontation.

All of this fearfulness is rooted in one fact: a deep uneasiness over our separation from God, and the broken world that is the result. To that, the Gospel has an answer, described quite eloquently by Bonhoeffer: *"We name the one who overcame fear and led it captive in the victory procession, who nailed it to the cross and committed it to oblivion; we name the One who is the shout of victory of humankind redeemed from the fear of death – Jesus Christ, the Crucified and Living One."*

Josh Larsen   *Wes Craven, Dietrich Bonhoeffer and a Christian defense of horror* (note: format has been changed)

I take umbrage at the assertion that the risen bodies in the valley of dry bones in Ezekiel are zombies. The rest of his assertions are interesting. What do you think?

Here's another excerpt from Mike Duran's book, *Christian Horror*

> But perhaps the most terrible of all biblical visions is that of sinful man's encounter with a holy God. The apostle Paul, after declaring that all believers must stand before the judgment seat of Christ to give account for their deeds, concluded,'
>
> "Knowing therefore the terror of the Lord, we persuade men" (2Cor. 5:11 KJV)
>
> Some versions translate terror as "fear." But the idea is clear: an encounter with God is a potentially fearful, terrifying reality. The writer of Hebrews echoes this sentiment.
>
> "It is a dreadful thing to fall into the hands of the living God" (Heb. 10:31)
>
> Yes, God loves us immensely. But giving account of our deeds on earth, especially apart from a relationship with Christ, is a dreadful, terrifying reality we all must face.
>
> While the Bible is often referred to as The Good Book, within its pages are some truly bad, disturbing, awful things—depravity, judgment, the crucifixion, angels, demons, and an impending apocalypse. One argument for the compatibility of a biblical worldview with the horror genre is the amount of horrific images and potentially disturbing concepts found in the Bible. Which is why the recurrent intersections of religion and horror are not coincidental. Scripture frames "a compelling moral vision" of the world. A world where the ugly and the beautiful coexist; where a fantastical world of angels and demons interact with ordinary humans; where real evil exists and those created in God's image can potentially become monstrous and face the torments of hell.
>
> *Religious themes occur so often in horror because horror themes occur so often in religion.*

Mike Duran *Christian Horror* On the Compatibility of a Biblical Worldview and the Horror Genre

Activity:

1) Proofread your short story. Check for grammar issues, homonym errors, redundant words, spacing errors, spelling errors, verb tense errors etc. I know you won't find everything, but that is no excuse for sloppiness. Find all you can and fix them.

Day 5 open minds

If you are not a Christian, I can understand why pulling in all these references to the genre of horror and the Bible can be offensive. Even some Christians will find some of the excerpts offensive. This is where you get to practice saying, "That's interesting. Why do you think that?"

One reason I quote a lot from Mike Duran's book is that he is the one that opened my mind to the possibilities of horror. In the following five years I read more horror than I had in the previous *cough* years. I discovered some marvelous books that I had liked before that were horror, but I had defined them as not-horror because I hated horror. If this exploration into the horror genre were a story, it would be called The Hero Learns Better. I wish I could quote the entire book in this textbook, but we will need to settle for one last excerpt from *Christian Horror*.

> If we simply limit our scope of what's "Christian" to art that satisfies the evangelical censors or makes positive references to God or the Gospel, we may miss many, many glimpses of the sacred all around us. The same is true for the artistic representations of horror. Just because a work contains dark, disturbing, or "secular" elements, does not automatically mean that the "kingdom of heaven" is not in it.
>
> Of course, this is not to suggest that all expressions of horror and the grotesque contain something sacred or redemptive. I once spoke to an indie film director who had recently discovered a vibrant Asian market for low-budget splatter flicks. It was clear from our discussion that he had no desire to craft a film with redemptive value or deeper meaning. To him, it was about making cheap, short, gross-out flicks as quickly as possible. Likewise, some representations of horror should be seen for what they are—exploitive garbage. Despite the protestation of their makers, tales simply designed to disturb or repulse audiences, much less ones that celebrate gore, often have little redeeming value.
>
> *In this sense, Christian horror should aspire to do much more than just scare, unnerve, or gross people out.*
>
> Once again, the Bible is a great example of such an approach. Though Scripture often describes horrific or disturbing events, (…), it does so in the context of a larger narrative. For example, the telling of the destruction of Sodom and Gomorrah (Gen. 18-19) with its raining down of fire and brimstone on the city and inhabitants, is not recorded simply to scare people. Though the account *is* deeply disturbing and scary, the story is told as part of a larger narrative. In part, it serves as an example of the pervasive nature of sin and the testimony of God's judgement. It also reveals God's desire to rescue His people out from such evil, as he did with Abraham and Lot's family. Furthermore, Jesus referred to Lot's wife who, when fleeing the city, looked back, defying God's explicit command, and was turned into a pillar of salt. In one of the shortest verses in Scripture, He said,
>
> Remember Lot's wife! (Luke 17:32)
>
> Scripture is full of such stories. Though they contain dark, horrific elements, they are not recorded simply for shock value.

Mike Duran   *Christian Horror*

Activity:

1) Ready or not, now you face the horror of turning in your short story. One last walk-through, and turn in your story.

If you procrastinated on writing your story, aren't you sorry now? Vow to not do that anymore. If you worked steadily and finished your short story in time, aren't you glad?
Or maybe you're not. Maybe you think your story is utter drek and is too embarrassing to turn in. Turn it in anyway.

AFTERWORD

Here's a thing you need to know. Professional writers work with deadlines. They often whoosh past them, but the deadlines exist. Professional writers do not keep polishing the first page for a year, for ten years, for twenty years. They realize the story they produced is not perfect, again. They promise themselves they will do better next time, and start the next story. There comes a time when you are changing words but no longer improving the story. There comes a time you must let go of a story that still does not satisfy you and Move On To The Next Story.

Here's another thing: If you are like most writers, one day you will think your story is brilliant and another day you will think it is wretched. This is normal. Persevere. It is also normal to start a story with great enthusiasm and before you reach the end, grow to hate the work. You meant to build a Taj Mahal, and you're holding a birdhouse. If you are going to be a professional, you will keep on keeping on.

And the final thing you must learn for you to have any pleasure in writing: Your story is not you. Yeah, you bled on the paper, you bared your soul, you gave birth to a baby book, and all those other things writers say about writing. The words on the page are still not you. Your story is a product, a product that can be altered any number of ways and still be your story. If you want your target audience to enjoy your work, you will tailor your work to their expectations and to professional standards. Some people call that selling out. I call that being practical.

Once you take to heart the knowledge that your story is not you—it is a product you produced—you will be able to step back from the work and accept advice that will improve your work. You will understand why you should not bother people outside of your target audience about your book. You will understand that people can dislike your story and still like you. You can stay calm if you join a critique group, a self-help group of writers who are trying to improve their writing by reading each other's work and offering helpful advice and encouragement. (If there is only discouragement and no helpful advice, find a different critique group.) You need to be teachable if you want to improve your product.

Now that you have finished the course, you should look at the recommended reading list. Then you should take *at least* two of the books about writing, read them, and reread them. Then reread them again. Where advice conflicts, take the advice that best fits the likes of your intended audience. If you follow the instructions in any of those books for at least a year, your writing will improve.

Go forth and conquer.

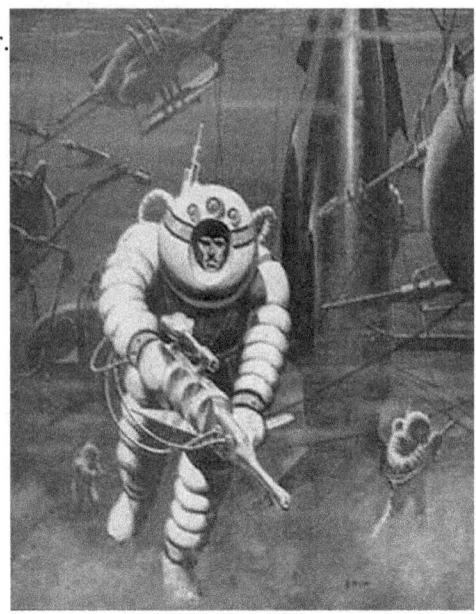

EXTRA CREDIT ACTIVITIES

A. Read a short story of one's choice and answer the following questions:

    1) What is the genre, subgenre, and point of view?

    2) Is the point of view the writer chose an effective one for telling the story? Why?

    3) What is this writer's voice?

B. Read a work longer than 30,000 words and answer the following questions:

    1) What was the inciting incident?

    2) What was the climax?

    3) What skill or characteristic of the protagonist displayed in the beginning of the book was used in the climax?

C. Submit your short story to a magazine, anthology, or website designed to showcase teen writing

GLOSSARY

. . . : Indicates the voice trailing off without finishing the sentence.
…: Indicates missing words, paragraphs, or chapters from the original writing
—: m dash. Used to indicate a voice cutting off suddenly without finishing the sentence. Also sometimes replaces a pair of commas or a pair of parentheses. In USA English fiction, there is no space between the words and the m dash.
-: n dash. Used as a hyphen in many word processors. Used to connect two words being used as an adjective.
* * *: indicates a change of scene
Action Beat: The action a character does before, during, or after a line of dialogue. The action beat is an alternative way to tag the speaker instead of (whoever) said.
Agency: The freedom and capacity to live or act within a defined world.
AKA: Also Known As
Antagonist: The force, villain, or system that denies the protagonist what she wants, and thus, she must fight.
Antihero: A protagonist who lacks conventional heroic qualities such as idealism, courage, or morality.
Arc: The change from one state to another.
Aspiring Writer: What Kristen Lamb says you must not call yourself. She wears a Viking helmet with horns, so you should listen to her.
Bad: What some people call a book they don't like whether or not it is written skillfully.
Bafflegab: Science and technology words that are used to explain a phenomenon that's impossible, so the reader can suspend her disbelief.
Big Boss Battle: The climax.
Character: A thing or person with particular qualities in a story, usually referring to someone who has some agency.
Climax: Where the conflict rises to the largest and final battle and the protagonist either finally wins or finally loses.
Coherent: United as, or forming a whole. Not fragmented or containing parts that have no relation to each other. Understandable.
Concrete Noun: An object that can be seen or touched, i.e. table, chair vs. an abstract noun that is an idea, i.e. liberty, justice.
Conflict: The struggle between the protagonist who wants something and the antagonist who is blocking the protagonist from achieving or getting the something.
Contagonist: A character that helps the protagonist. One form of contagonist is the sidekick.
Denouement: The final part of the story where everything is resolved.
Driver: In this context, the thing that pushes a plot along.
Enemy: Someone who wants to hurt or destroy another person.
Engaged: When the reader is reluctant to stop reading because the book is too interesting, the reader is engaged.
Flash Fiction: Wikipedia defines it as an umbrella term used to describe any fictional work of extreme brevity, including the Six-Word Story, 140-character stories, also known as twitterature, the dribble (50 words), the drabble (100 words), and sudden *fiction* (750 words). Other people say that all fiction under a thousand words is flash fiction and don't bother to name all the other sizes.
Frame: A frame story is an overall unifying story within which one or more tales are related. In a single story, the opening and closing constitutes a frame. In the Canterbury Tales by Chaucer, the frame is the pilgrims sitting around a campfire telling each other stories.
Flying Snowman: A term invented by Adam Bryant that means implausible elements or events in science fiction or fantasy that throw you out of the story, even if you've accepted other, previous implausible elements or events. That moment when the reader or movie-watcher can no longer suspend disbelief.
Foreshadow: An advanced sign or warning of what is to come.
Genre: A subdivision of literature characterized by tropes particular to that genre.
Good: What some people call a book they like whether or not it is written skillfully.
Hero: In literature, the main character, or protagonist, who has agency and whose actions drive the plot.
Hyperbole: Exaggeration.
I.e.: That is. For example.

Inciting Incident: The event or decision that begins the story problem. Everything before the inciting incident is backstory. Everything after is the story.
Irritation Quotient: The thing that makes the reader quit reading in disgust after too many encounters with it.
Kishotenketsu: A type of plot that has a four act story structure and that does not have conflict built into the structure.
Literal: The taking of words in their basic or real sense instead of as metaphor or allegory.
Laconic: Terse
Loose End: A metaphor based on the craft of cloth weaving that means a question in the story that is not answered.
Manuscript: A writer's text that has not yet been published.
Melodrama: Oversensational and overemotional writing. Many readers laugh at melodrama while others find that is the literature they love best.
Metaphor: A figure of speech which makes an implicit, implied or hidden comparison between two things that are unrelated but share some common characteristics. In other words, a resemblance of two contradictory or different objects is made based on a single or some common characteristics.
Moment of Truth: The point in the story where the hero finally realizes what the cost of being a hero is going to be, and decides to be one anyway. Or, the point in the story where the protagonist realizes that what he is doing isn't working, and decides to be a different person. A dictionary says it is a time when a person or thing is tested, a decision has to be made, or a crisis has to be faced.
Motif: A repeating image, idea, or symbol that develops or explains a theme.
MRU: Motivation reaction unit
ms: Manuscript
Narrator: The one telling the story.
Noir: Type of detective story with a grim worldview and extravagant metaphors.
Opponent: someone who opposes something. Seldom the same as enemy.
Pet the Kitty: The moment a hero shows tenderness to something vulnerable. It does not need to be a literal cat or dog. It is a literary device that will manipulate the reader into loving the hero. Readers want to be manipulated into having emotional experiences while reading and suspending their disbelief, so manipulation in this context is not evil.
Pinch point: Larry Brooks in *Story Engineering*, says it is "an example, or a reminder, of the nature and implications of the antagonistic force." A pinch point is meant to show the reader the powerful forces pushing against a hero.
Protagonist: The hero, the one the reader wants to "win." Usually the point of view from which the story is told, but not always.
Quantifiable: Measurable, able to be measured.
Resonate: A story resonates when the emotion within the hero evokes the same emotion within the reader.
Save The Kitty: The moment a hero saves a vulnerable victim.
Rubric: In this context, rubric means an authoritative rule by which to judge (whatever.)
Sibilance: Hissing
Sidekick: The contagonist who helps the hero achieve her quest and is a close friend.
Simile: a figure of speech involving the comparison of one thing with another thing of a different kind, used to make a description more emphatic or vivid. Uses the words like or as.
Spear-carrier: An unnamed character who is there for purposes of scenery.
Story Question: The main question of a story and the question for which the story was written to answer.
Storyworld: The world, real or imaginary or any combination thereof that the story is set in. Sometimes referred to as Universe.
Subgenre: A subcategory of a particular genre.
Subvert, Subversion: The act of undermining respect for a certain idea.
Suspension of disbelief: A willingness to suspend one's critical faculties and believe the unbelievable; sacrifice of realism and logic for the sake of enjoyment.
Technobabble: What Star Trek is full of. Science and technological words that are thrown together to make the characters sound like they're talking about future tech.
Tension: While conflict is the confrontation of protagonist and antagonist, tension is the threat of conflict. One thing that raises tension well is the Ticking Clock.
Terraforming: Transforming an uninhabitable planet into one that humans can live on in the open.
Terse: Short.

Ticking Clock: The bad thing that will happen if the hero doesn't save the day in time. Soldiers searching for a stowaway hero is a ticking clock. The closer to the hidden hero the soldiers get, the higher the tension.

Theme: An idea or philosophy that a story presents whether or not the writer is aware of it, i.e. Love conquers all. Belief will make things happen. People are vile. You are more important than you think. The Dodgers are better than the Yankees. A theme can be grand or trivial.

Trope: Used to mean a figure of speech. Now it means an overused plot device or sometimes a concept that is common in any particular genre. The broke, cynical PI is a trope of noir. A generation space ship is a trope of science fiction. A magic wand is a trope of fantasy. A decayed corpse is one in horror.

Umbrage: Offense

Universe: The storyworld the story is set in. Can be one town, one country, one planet, one galaxy, or even the universe.

Writer: Someone who puts words on a page, hopefully in coherent sentences.

LISTS OF RECOMMENDED WORKS

WRITING

Aliens and Alien Societies by Stanley Schmidt

The Art & Craft of Writing Christian Fiction by Jeff Gerke

Eats, Shoots & Leaves by Lynne Truss

Fiction Writing 101: A Home Study Course by Mike Dellosso

The First 50 Pages by Jeff Gerke

How to Write Science Fiction and Fantasy by Orson Scott Card

How to Write a Novel Using the Snowflake Method by Randy Ingermanson

The Irresistible Novel by Jeff Gerke

Rivet Your Readers with Deep Point Of View by Jill Elizabeth Nelson

"Shut up!" He Explained by William Noble

Space Travel: A writer's guide to the science of interplanetary and interstellar travel by Ben Bova and Anthony R. Lewis

Story World First: Creating a Unique Fantasy World for Your Novel by Jill Williamson

World-Building: A writer's guide to constructing star systems and life-supporting planets by Stephen L. Gillett

World-Building From the Inside Out by Janeen Ippolito

World-Building From the Inside Out Workbook by Janeen Ippolito

Writing Active Hooks by Mary Buckham

Writing Fiction for Dummies by Randy Ingermanson and Peter Economy

Writer's Guide to Creating a Science Fiction Universe by George Ochoa and Jeffrey Osier

Write Your Novel From the Middle by James Scott Bell

A Writer's Guide to Active Setting: How to Enhance Your Fiction with More Descriptive, Dynamic Settings by Mary Buckham and Dianna Love

Writing to the Point: A Complete Guide to Selling Fiction by Algis Budrys

SCIENCE FICTION

Alpha Redemption by P. A. Baines

Arena by Karen Hancock

Ashes by A. C. Williams

Ashlyn's Dreams by Julie Gilbert

Avenir Eclectia by Grace Bridges, Jeff C. Carter, Jeff Chapman, Frank Creed, Pauline Creeden, Karina Fabian, Joseph H. Ficor, Kat Heckenbach, Holly Heisey, Kaye Jeffreys, Greg Mitchell, Keven Newsome, Travis Perry, Mary Ruth Pursselley, J. L. Rowan, Walt Staples, H. A. Titus, and Fred Warren.

Binti by Nnedi Okorafor

Black Tiger by Sara Baysinger

The Bricks of Eta Cassiopeiae by Brad R Torgersen

Captives (The Safe Lands) by Jill Williamson

The Chaplain's War by Brad R Torgersen

Chasing Lady Midnight by C. L. Ragsdale

Cinder by Marissa Meyer

Circular Horizon by Bokerah Brumley

The Chronetic Perspective by Kim K. O'Hara

Curio by Evangeline Denmark

Dark Side of the Moon by Terri Main

Deadman Switch by Timothy Zahn

Discovery by Karina Fabian

Divergent by Veronica Roth

Dragon's Rook by Keanan Brand

Edge of Oblivion by Joshua A. Johnston

Enduring Endurance by Amy Spahn

Eternity Falls by Kirk Outerbridge

Failstate by John W. Otte

Flashpoint by Frank Creed

For Us Humans by Steve Rzasa

The Gypsy Pearl by Lia London

Heavy Planet by Hal Clement

Hero by Jim Miles

The Hidden Level by A. J. Bakke

The Hive by John W. Otte

The Hitchhiker's Guide to the Galaxy by Douglas Adams

Hunger Games by Suzanne Collins

Infected: The Shiners by Tara Ellis

In Plain Sight by Marlayne Jan Giron

Integrate by Adele Jones

Jupiter Winds by C. J. Darlington

Knox's Irregulars by J Wesley Bush

The League of Freaks by Alberto Hazan, MD

The Leviathan Trilogy by Scott Westerfield
Like Herding the Wind by Cindy Koepp
Lingua Franca by Carole McDonnell
Little One by Nate Philbrick
Logic's End by Robinson Keith
Medieval Mars edited by Travis Perry
Minister Without Portfolio by Mildred Clingerman
A New Threat by Aaron DeMott
The New Recruit by Jill Williamson
Night Hawk by Jolene Loraine
Nyssa Glass and the House of Mirrors by H. L. Burke
Orlo: The Created by Lauren H. Brandenburg
Oxygen by John B. Olson and Randy Ingermanson
Quartz by Rabia Gale
The Paradise Protocol by Anna Zogg
Rainbird by Rabia Gale
Red Rain by Aubrey Hensen
Respite by Autumn Rachel Dryden
The Restorer by Sharon Hinck
The Riddle of Prague by Laura DeBruce
The Scarred King by Josh Foreman
Search for Eden by Mark Venturini
Sentinel by Jamie Foley
Shivering World by Kathy Tyers
Slave by Laura Frances
Slumbering by C. S. Johnson
Somewither: A Tale of the Unwithering Realm by John C. Wright
Space Drifters: The Emerald Enigma by Paul Regnier
A Star Curiously Singing by Kerry Nietz
A Curriculum Guide to A Star Curiously Singing by Kerry Nietz
Starfire by Stuart Vaughn Stockton
Supervillain of the Day by Katie Lynn Daniels
There Goes the Galaxy by Jenn Thorson
Thorn by Intisar Khanani
A Time to Die by Nadine Brandes
Today I Am Paul by Martin L. Shoemaker
Thunder by Bonnie S. Calhoun
The Truce by Michelle Levigne
Tycho by William Woodall
Waiting for Appa by Mirtika Schultz
Waking Beauty by Sarah E. Morin
Whispers of a Faded Dreamer by Celesta Thiessen

The Word Reclaimed by Steve Rzasa
The Worker Prince by Bryan Thomas Schmidt

FANTASY
The Adventures of Zero by Vincent Trigili
Albion Academy by Elijah David
Accelerant by Ronie Kendig
Animal Farm by George Orwell
The Beast from Talesend by Kyle Robert Shultz
Beast Hunter by Michele Israel Harper
Bellanok: The Reluctant Savior by Ralene Burke
Blood Moon by S. D. Grimm
The Book of Feasts and Seasons by John C. Wright
Captive of Raven Castle by Jessica Greyson
Celebration by Arthur Daigle
The Collar and the Cavverach by Annie Douglas Lima
Daughter of Anasca by RC Tolbert
Daughter of Light by Morgan L. Busse
The Destiny of One by Sarah Holman
Domino by Kia Heavey
The Door Within by Wayne Thomas Batson
Dragon Airways by Brian Rathbone
Dragonfly by Alyssa Thiessen
Dragonlight by Donita K. Paul
Dragon's Rook by Keanan Brand
Dragonwitch by Anne Elisabeth Stengl
Dreams of Caladria by Joseph Bentz
Even a Stone by Jane Lebak
Father of Dragons by L. B. Graham
Finding Angel by Kat Heckenbach
The Firebird Trilogy by Kathy Tyers
The Firethorn Crown by Lea Doue`
Flatland by Edwin Abbott
Forged Steel: The Crucible by H. A. Titus
The Ghost of Briardale by Grace Mullins
Healer's Curse by Kathrese McKee
The Healer's Rune by Lauricia Matuska
The Hidden Kingdom by C. S. Lakin
Hero Second Class by Mitchell Bonds
Into the Fire (Under Fire) by Kim Vandel
Jack Staples and the Ring of Time by Mark Batterson and Joel N. Clark

Kingdom's Call by Chuck Black
Knife by R. J. Anderson
The Last Unicorn by Peter S. Beagle
Life After by Julie Hall
Lost Mission by Athol Dickson
Malevolent by K. M. Carroll
Merlin's Blade by Robert Treskillard
The Mermaid's Sister by Carrie Ann Noble
My Son, the Shapeshifter by Shane D. Rhinewald
Orphan's Song by Gillian Bronte Adams
Paper Crowns by Mirriam Neal
Pelmen the Powershaper series by Robert Don Hughes.
Pilgrim's Progress by John Bunyan
Quintessence by David Walton
Rebirth: Book One of the Reluctant Warrior Chronicles by Amy Brock McNew
Redeemer Chronicles: Awakening by Julie Gilbert
Resistance by Jaye L. Knight
Scarlet Moon by S. D. Grimm
Secrets Kept by J. L. Mbewe
The Shock of Night by Patrick Carr
A Shadow on the Land by Krystine Kercher
Shadow over Kiriath by Karen Hancock
Song Keeper by Gillian Bronte Adams
Song of Albion by Stephen R. Lawhead
Song of the Mountain by Michelle Isenhoff
Song of the Stoneshell by Brian Tashima
Song of the Storm Dragon by Marc Secchia
Spindle Cursed by Michelle Pennington
Star of Wonder by Tracy Higley
The Strange Man by Greg Mitchell
Swan Knight's Son, The Green Knight's Squire, Book One by John C. Wright
The Tethered World by Heather L. L. FitzGerald
To Save Two Worlds (is twice as fun) A. J. Bakke
Thorn by Intisar Khanani
Three Steaks and a Box of Chocolates by A. R. Silverberry
The Trojan Horse Traitor by Amy C. Blake
Truce at Bakura by Kathy Tyers
The Tree Remembers by Thea van Diepen
A Twist of Fae by Rebekah Shafer
Waking Beauty by Sarah E. Morin
Where the Woods Grow Wild by Nate Philbrick
The Windrider Saga by Rebecca P. Minor

HORROR
Bait by Laura VanArendonk Baugh

Blood for Blood by Ben Wolf

Dragon's Tooth by N. D. Wilson

Edgar Allan Poe Complete Tales and Poems, Castle Books

Elijah by Frank Redman

Explaining Cthulhu to Grandma by Alex Shvartsman

Fearless by Mike Dellosso

Forlorn by Bret Carter in anthology *Mysterion*.

Ghost Roommate by Matthew Sketchley

House of Dark Shadows by Robert Liparulo

Ikiryoh by Liz Williams

In the Lamplight by L. Jagi Lamplighter

Never to Live by Just B. Jordan

Perfect Blood Innocent Blood by Cindy Emmet Smith

The Plague Carrier by Merrie Destefano

Rabbit: Chasing Beth Rider by Ellen C. Maze

The Salvation of Jeffrey Lapin by Summer Kinard

Servant by J. S. Bailey

The Taking by Dean Koontz

The Telling by Mike Duran

Winter by Keven Newsome

Wrath and Ruin by C. W. Briar

Zombie Takeover by Michele Israel Harper

WORDS AND WORLDVIEW

Christian Horror: On the Compatibility of a Biblical Worldview and the Horror Genre by Mike Duran

Culture Making by Andy Crouch

Notes from the Tilt-A-Whirl by N. D. Wilson

The Righteous Mind: Why Good People Are Divided By Politics and Religion by Jonathan Haidt

The Universe Next Door by James W. Sire

You Are What You Love by James K. A. Smith

HELPFUL WEBSITES ACTIVE AT TIME OF PUBLICATION

http://www.advancdfictionwriting.com/ezine/

https://birdfacewendy.wordpress.com/

www.theblazingcenter.com

http://brandonsanderson.com/sandersons-second-law/

https://thecatholicgeeks.com/

https://christandpopculture.com/

http://dive-into-worldbuilding.blogspot.com/

http://www.donitakpaul.com

http://goteenwriters.blogspot.com/

www.theimaginativeconservative.org

http://www.mikeduran.com

http://novelteen.wordpress.com

https://owl.english.purdue.edu/

http://wordmastercommunications.blogspot.com/

http://www.reformedfellowship.net/fictions-delight-and-truth

http://www.speculativefaith.com

http://teenageauthor.wordpress.com

https://thinkchristian.reframemedia.com/

http://www.wherethemapends.com/main.htm

https://warriorwriters.wordpress.com/

https://storybird.com

INDEX
(Note: Does not include front material or quizzes.)

A

Abbott, Edwin	10, 323
Accelerant	288-289, 323
Adams, Douglas	9, 321
Adams, Gillian Bronte	134, 324
The Adventures of Zero	53, 323
Albion Academy by Elijah David	323
Aliens	10, 37, 38, 59, 66, 69, 95, 141, 143, 162, 240, 250, 259, 264-268, 271, 320
Anderson, R. J.	324
Angels	11, 184, 240, 252, 265, 273, 274, 285, 286, 287, 292, 313
Angles of Incidence	270
Animal Farm	85, 323
Aliens and Alien Societies	320
Arena	87, 104, 296
Arena by Karen Hancock	320
The Art & Craft of Writing Christian Fiction	320
Ashes	122, 321
Ashlyn's Dreams	179, 321
Asteroid 745: Mauritia	244
Avenir Eclectia	61, 112, 321

B

Bailey, J. S	301, 302, 325
Bait	324
Bakke, A. J.	10, 96, 139, 321, 324
Batson, Wayne Thomas	212, 323
Batterson Mark, and Clark, Joel N.	323
Baugh, Laura VanArendonk	324
Baysinger, Sara	9, 208, 321
Beagle, Peter S.	284, 324
Bear, Elizabeth	278
The Beast from Talesend	323
Beast Hunter	97, 323
Scott Bell, James	320
Bellanok: The Reluctant Savior	218, 323
Bentz, Joseph	323
Binti	8, 321
Bird Face Wendy	114, 127
Black, Chuck	324
Black Tiger	9, 208, 321
Blake, Amy C.	143, 324
Blood for Blood	300, 325

Blood Moon	323
The Blue Afternoon That Lasted Forever	232
Bodard, Aliette de	273
Bova, Ben and. Lewis, Anthony R	320
Brumley, Bokerah	321
Bonds, Mitchell	323
Brand, Keanan	321, 323
Brandenburg, Lauren H.	26, 217, 322
Brandes, Nadine	9, 233, 247, 322
Briar, C. W.	256, 325
The Bricks of Eta Cassiopeiae	63, 321
Bridges, Grace	61, 321
Brin, David	29
Brozak, Jennifer	184
Buckham, Mary	99, 320
Budrys, Algis	72, 320
Bunyan, John	10, 12, 324
Burke, H. L.	10, 214, 322
Burke, Ralene	218, 323
Burnett, E. Stephen	257
Bush, J Wesley	9, 32, 178, 321
Busse, Morgan L.	91, 323

C

The Call of Cthulhu	246
Called Warrior	149
Calhoun, Bonnie S.	9, 322
Captive of Raven Castle	323
Card, Orson Scott	8, 75, 275, 320
Carr, Patrick W.	31, 61, 166, 172, 176, 324
Carroll, K. M.	288, 324
Carter, Bret	253, 325
Causes and Effects	18
Celebration	48, 323
Christian Horror	297-298, 313-314, 325
Clement, Hal	9, 321
The Collar and the Cravverach	180, 321
Collins, Suzanne	9, 276, 321
Creed, Frank	9, 245, 3
Culture Making by Andy Crouch	325
A Curriculum Guide to A Star Curiously Singing	322
Captives (The Safe Lands)	9, 321
The Chaplain's War	9, 142, 321
Chasing Lady Midnight	35, 321
Cinder by Marissa Meyer	9, 321
Circular Horizon	321
The Chronetic Perspective	321
Curio	10, 321
Czerneda, Julie E.	63, 67, 68

D

Daigle, Arthur	48, 323	Fantasy	8,9,10,11-12, 15, 16, 24, 40, 48, 53, 58, 59, 74, 82, 89, 150, 162, 176, 182, 193, 207, 216, 226, 258-260, 275, 280-294, 298, 298, 317, 319, 320, 323-324
Daniels, Katie Lynn	322		
Darlington, C. J.	189, 322		
Dark Side of the Moon	10, 83, 135, 140, 321		
Daughter of Anasca	47, 323		
Daughter of Light	91, 323		
Deadman Switch	321		
Death's Doors	183		
DeBruce, Laura	322		
Dellosso, Mike	320, 325	*Father of Dragons*	323
Demon	11, 15, 18, 37, 99, 149, 218, 240, 266, 267, 286, 297, 309, 310, 311, 313	*Fearless*	325
		Fiction Writing 101: A Home Study Course	320
		Finding Angel	11, 93, 261, 323
		The Firebird Trilogy	126-128, 323
DeMott, Aaron	9, 269, 322		
Denmark, Evangeline	10, 321	*The Firethorn Crown*	323
Destefano, Merrie	311, 325	*The First 50 Pages*	320
The Destiny of One	323	FitzGerald, Heather L. L.	11, 51, 182, 324
Dickson, Athol	11, 324	*Flashpoint*	9, 245, 321
Dickinson, Emily	282	*Flatland*	10, 323
Diepen, Thea van	324	Foley, Jamie	103, 322
Dinner at Deviant's Palace	168	Foreman, Josh	189, 322
Discovery	109-111, 321	Foreman, Lelia Rose	156-159, 159, 332
Divergent	9, 321		
Domino	323	*Forged Steel: The Crucible*	126, 323
The Door Within	323	*Forlorn*	253, 325
Doue`, Lea	323	*Foreshadowing vs Telegraphing*	180
Dragon Airways	20, 323	*For Us Humans*	321
Dragonfly	294, 323	Frances, Laura	322
Dragonlight	323	Fulda, Nancy	270, 272
Dragon's Rook	321, 323		
Dragonwitch	285, 323	**G**	
Dreams of Caladria	323		
Dragon's Tooth	325	Gale, Rabia	101, 236, 322
Dragon's Rook	321, 323	Gardner, Rachelle	180
Dryden, Autumn Rachel	69, 322	Gerke, Jeff	89, 186, 187, 207, 320
Duran, Mike	168, 170, 210, 250-252, 257, 297, 298, 303, 313-314, 325, 326, 332	*The Ghost of Briardale*	12, 134, 135, 323
		Ghost Roommate	299, 325
		Gilbert, Julie	153-154, 179, 321, 324
Dust Angels	184	Gillett, Stephen L.	320
		Giron, Marlayne Jan	83, 321
E		Graham, L. B.	260, 323
		Greyson, Jessica	323
Edge of Oblivion	9, 229, 321	Grimm, S. D.	323, 324
Eats, Shoots & Leaves	320	*The Gypsy Pearl*	98, 321
Editing	17, 18, 180, 192-205, 294		
		H	
Elijah	311, 325		
Ellis, Tara	141, 321	*Halo*	94
Enduring Endurance	321	Haidt, Jonathon	325
Eternity Falls	35, 322	Hall, Julie	324
Eucatastrophe	281	Hancock, Karen	320, 324
Even a Stone	293, 324	Harper, Michele Israel	97, 153, 323, 325
Explaining Cthulhu to Grandma	325	Hazan, MD, Alberto	321
		Healer's Curse	14, 323
F		*The Healer's Rune*	80, 323
		Heavey, Kia	323
Fabian, Karina	11, 111, 321	Heckenbach, Kat	11, 93, 261, 321, 323
Failstate	10, 321		

Hensen, Aubrey	322	Knox's Irregulars	9, 32, 178, 321
Hero	321	Koepp, Cindy	166, 322
Hero's Journey	75	Koontz, Dean	13, 17, 230, 296-297, 325
Hero Second Class	323		
Heavy Planet	321	Kress, Nancy	66
The Hidden Kingdom	284, 323		
The Hidden Level	10, 139, 321	**L**	
Higley, Tracy	52, 324	Lakin, C. S.	284, 323
Hinck, Sharon	322	Lamplighter, L. Jagi	325
The Hitchhiker's Guide to the Galaxy	9, 321	Larson, Josh	312
The Hive	321	*The Last Unicorn*	324
Holman, Sarah	323	Lawhead, Stephen R.	282
Horror	8, 10, 12-13, 15, 17, 19, 21, 40, 58, 84, 134, 152, 162, 171, 207, 225, 239, 250-251, 256, 258, 275, 279, 281, 295-314, 319, 324-325	*The League of Freaks*	321
		Lebak, Jane	293, 323
		The Leviathan Trilogy	9, 321
		Levigne, Michelle	322
		Lewis, C. S.	11, 259, 260, 266, 281, 282, 289, 290
		Life After	324
House of Dark Shadows	325	*Like Herding the Wind*	166, 322
How to Write Science Fiction and Fantasy	8, 320	Lima, Annie Douglas	180, 321
How to Write a Novel Using the Snowflake Method	107, 320	*Lingua Franca*	36, 42, 322
		Liparulo, Robert	325
Hoyt, Sarah A.	164	*Little One*	45, 322
Hughes, Robert Don	16, 27, 41, 324	*Logic's End*	322
Hunger Games	9, 276, 321	London, Lia	98, 321
		Loraine, Jolene	215, 322
I		*Lost Mission*	11, 324
		Lovecraft, H. P.	246
Ikiryoh	307-308, 325		
Ingermanson, Randy	25, 107, 136, 146, 320, 322	**M**	
		Maberry, Jonathon	299
Infected: The Shiners	141, 321	Main, Terri	10, 83. 135, 140, 321
Infinities	255		
In Plain Sight	83, 321	*Malevolent*	288, 324
Integrate	278, 321	Matuska, Lauricia	80, 323
In the Lamplight	325	Maze, Ellen C.	306, 325
Ippolito, Janeen	24, 25, 40, 43, 44, 48, 49, 55, 56, 320	Mbewe, J. L.	221, 324
		McAuley, Paul	59, 224, 279
		McCay, EJ	149
The Irresistible Novel	89, 320	McKee, Kathrese	14, 323
Irritation quotient	123, 318	McDonnell, Carole	36, 42, 322, 333
Isenhoff, Michelle	324	McNew, Amy Brock	287, 324
		Medieval Mars	322
J		*Merlin's Blade*	324
		The Mermaid's Sister	11, 209, 324
Jack Staples and the Ring of Time	323	*Minister Without Portfolio*	322
Johnson, C. S.	248, 322	Miles, Jim	10, 321
Johnston, Joshua A.	9, 229, 321	Minor, Rebecca P.	234, 325
Jones, Adele	277, 321	*Migration*	66
Jordan, Just B.	325	Mitchell, Greg	113, 324
Jupiter Winds	189, 322	Monette, Sarah	278
		Mongoose	278
K		Morin, Sarah E.	171, 322, 324
		Morris, William	228
Kendig, Ronie	173, 289, 323	Mullins, Grace	12, 135, 323
Khanani, Intisar	43, 322	*My Son, the Shapeshifter*	291, 324
Kinard, Summer	325		
Kingdom's Call	324	**N**	
Knife	324		
Knight, Jaye L.	324	Neal, Mirriam	82, 230, 324

Nelson, Jill Elizabeth	199, 320	*Rabbit: Chasing Beth Rider*	306, 325
A New Threat	9, 269, 322	Ragsdale, C. L.	35, 321
The New Recruit	322	*Rainbird*	100-101, 322
Newsome, Keven	310, 325	Rathbone, Brian	20, 321
Never to Live	325	*Rats of the System*	279
Nietz, Kerry	9, 77, 79, 185, 225, 322	*Reap the Wild Wind*	63, 67, 68
		Rebirth: Book One of the Reluctant Warrior Chronicles	287, 324
Night Hawk	215, 322		
Noble, Carrie Ann	11, 209, 324	*Recollection*	272
Noble, William	320	*Red Rain*	322
Nyssa Glass and the House of Mirrors	10, 212-214, 322	*Redeemer Chronicles: Awakening*	154
		Redman, Frank	311, 325
O		*Reef*	224
		Regnier, Paul	322
Ochoa, George	320	*Resistance*	324
O'Hara, Kim K.	321	*Respite*	69, 322
Okorafor, Nnedi	8, 304, 321	*The Restorer*	322
Olmstead, Grace	290	Rhinewald, Shane D.	291, 324
Olson, John B.	322	*The Riddle of Prague*	322
Orlo: The Created	26, 322	*The Righteous Mind*	325
Orphan's Song	134, 324	*Rivet Your Readers with Deep Point Of View*	320
Orwell, George	10, 85, 323		
Osier, Jeffrey	320	Robinson, Keith	60, 322
The Other Edge	256	Roth, Veronica	9, 321
Otte, John W.	10, 321	Rzasa, Steve	169, 321, 323
Outerbridge, Kirk	35, 322		
Oxygen	322	**S**	
		The Salvation of Jeffrey Lapin	325
P		*Sankofa*	304
		To Save Two Worlds (is twice as fun)	96, 324
Paper Crowns	82, 230, 324	*Scarlet Moon*	324
The Paradise Protocol	14, 322	*The Scarred King*	190, 322
Paul, Donita K.	323, 326	Schmidt, Bryan Thomas	9, 323
Pelmen the Powershaper series	16, 32, 33, 324	Schmidt, Stanley	320
Pennington, Michelle	138, 324	Science Fiction	8-10, 14, 16, 18, 21, 24, 29, 32, 40, 58, 66, 82, 162, 188, 207, 216, 224, 225, 250, 251, 252, 258, 259, 263-279, 298, 312, 317, 319, 320-323
Perfect Blood Innocent Blood	325		
Perry, Travis	242, 258-262, 264-268, 321, 333		
Philbrick, Nate	45, 322, 324		
Pilgrim's Progress	10, 324		
The Plague Carrier	315, 329		
Planet of Fear	59		
Poe, Edgar Allan	13, 15, 19, 325		
Powers, Tim	168	*Search for Eden*	274, 322
		Secchia, Marc	162, 324
Q		*Secret of the Songshell*	121, 324
		Secrets Kept	221, 324
Quartz	236, 322	*Sentinel*	103, 322
Question, hook	72, 99-101, 104-105, 108, 182, 184, 217, 279, 288, 293, 300, 304, 320	*Servant*	325
		Shadow over Kiriath	324
		Shafer, Rebekah	11, 324
		Shivering World	322
		The Shock of Night	31, 61, 170, 172, 322
Question, story	89, 99-100, 104, 176, 208, 287, 293, 318		
		Shoemaker, Martin L.	16, 322
		Shroeder, Karl	94
Quintessence	227, 248-250, 323	Shultz, Kyle Robert	151-152, 323
		Shultz, Mirtika	188, 327
		"Shut up!" He Explained	320
R		Shvartsman, Alex	325

Silverberry, A. R.	226, 324
Singh, Vandana	255
Sire, James W.	239-240, 325
Sisters	299
Sketchley, Matthew	299, 325
Slave	322
Slumbering	248, 322
Smith, Cindy Emmet	325
Smith, James K. A.	325
Somewither: A Tale of the Unwithering Realm	119, 268, 322
Song Keeper	324
The Song of Albion	282
Song of the Mountain	324
Song of the Storm Dragon	162, 324
Space Drifters: The Emerald Enigma	322
Space Travel: A writer's guide to the science of interplanetary and interstellar travel	320
Spahn, Amy	321
Sparhawk, Bud	18
Spindle Cursed	138, 324
Staples, Walter	112, 322
A Star Curiously Singing	9, 77-79, 322
Starfire	235, 322
Star of Wonder	52, 324
Stengl Anne Elisabeth	285, 323
Stockton, Stuart Vaughn	235, 322
Story World First: Creating a Unique Fantasy World for Your Novel	320
The Strange Man	113, 324
Supervillain of the Day	322
Swan Knight's Son	100, 124, 324

T

The Taking	17, 230, 296--297, 325
Tashima, Brian	121, 324
The Telling	168, 170, 209-210, 325
The Tethered World	11, 51, 181, 182, 324
There Goes the Galaxy	9, 231, 322
Thiessen, Alyssa	294, 323
Thiessen, Celesta	322
Thorn	43, 322
Thorson, Jenn	9, 231, 322
Three Cups of Grief, By Starlight	273
Three Steaks and a Box of Chocolates	226, 324
Thunder	9, 322
A Time to Die	9, 233, 247, 322
Titus, H. A.	126, 323
Today I Am Paul	16, 322
Tolbert, RC	47, 165, 323
Toney, Cynthia T.	114
Torgersen, Brad R	9, 65, 142, 321
The Tree Remembers	324
Treskillard, Robert	324
Trigili, Vincent	53, 323
The Trojan Horse Traitor	143, 324
The Truce	322
Truce at Bakura	9, 324
Truss, Lynne	320
A Twist of Fae	11, 324
Tycho	322
Tyers, Kathy	9, 128, 322, 323, 324

U

The Universe Next Door	239, 325

V

Venturini, Mark	274, 322
Vogler, Christopher	75

W

Waiting for Appa	188, 324
Waking Beauty	171, 322, 324
Walker, Lars	183
Walton, David	227, 248-250, 324
Website	5, 6, 59, 114, 203, 257, 281, 290, 312, 316, 326
The Well at the World's End	228
Westerfield, Scott	9, 322
Where the Woods Grow Wild	324
Whispers of a Faded Dreamer	322
Why Fairytales Are Dangerous	290
Willard, Tim	281
Williams, A.C.	122
Williams, Liz	308, 325
Williamson, Jill	9, 147, 150, 320, 321, 322
Wilson, Daniel H.	232
Wilson, N. D.	325
The Windrider Saga	234, 325
Winter	314, 329
Wollheim, Donald A.	244
Woodall, William	322
The Worker Prince	9, 323
World-Building: A writer's guide to constructing star systems and life-supporting planets	320
The Word Reclaimed	169, 323
Wolf, Ben	300, 325
World-Building From the Inside Out	24, 25, 40, 43, 44, 48, 55, 56, 320
Worldview	9, 11, 24, 25, 107, 123, 136, 145, 238-262, 268, 297, 313, 318, 325
Wrath and Ruin	256, 325
Wright, John C.	100, 119, 124, 268, 322, 323, 324
Writing Active Hooks	99, 320
A Writer's Guide to Active Setting	320

Writer's Guide to Creating a Science
  Fiction Universe 320
Writing Fiction for Dummies 25, 136, 320
Writing to the Point 72, 320
Write Your Novel From the Middle 320

X

Y

You Are What You Love 325

Z

Zahn, Timothy 321
Zogg, Anna 14, 322
Zombie Takeover 153, 32

AUTHOR

Lelia Rose Foreman: When she was in the fifth grade and working her way through the long row of Reader's Digest Condensed Books on her mother's shelf, she ran across *A Fall of Moondust* by Arthur C. Clarke. It was though a fuse had been lit and fireworks went off. Next she read every speculative fiction book in her small town library. (There were a lot fewer then.) In high school she discovered J. R. R. Tolkien and fell in love with fantasy as well. As for horror, she's still working on appreciating the genre.

She obtained a B.S. in Medical Technology, raised and released five children, all of whom survived, and followed her husband in the U.S.A.F to bases in Japan, Texas, and Alaska. She is the author of *A Shattered World* and a number of short stories in anthologies.

CONTRIBUTORS:

The following people are contributors in the sense that while my advice is derived from hundreds of writing books and writer's conferences, these people contributed direct conversations, advice, and information during the making of the textbook.

MIKE DURAN is a novelist, blogger, and speaker, whose short stories, essays, and commentary have appeared in Relief Journal, Relevant Online, Bewildering Stories, Rue Morgue, Zombies magazine, Breakpoint, and other print and digital outlets. He is the author of *THE GHOST BOX* (Blue Crescent Press, 2014), which was selected by Publishers Weekly as one of the best indie novels of 2015 and first in a paranoir series that continues with *SAINT DEATH* (2016), a Southern Gothic Horror short *WICKERS BOG* (2016), a short story anthology *SUBTERRANEA* (Blue Crescent Press, 2013), the supernatural thrillers THE TELLING (Realms May 2012) and THE RESURRECTION (Realms, 2011), an e-book fantasy novella entitled *WINTERLAND* (Amazon digital, Oct. 2011), and a non-fiction exploration on the intersection between the horror genre and evangelical fiction entitled *CHRISTIAN HORROR* (Blue Crescent Press May 2015). You can learn more about Mike Duran, his writing projects, cultural commentary, philosophical musings, and arcane interests, at www.mikeduran.com.

Janeen Ippolito is two authors for the price of one! She's an experienced teacher who writes quirky nonfiction world-building and writing resources, plus she's an author of speculative fiction with a side of romance. She's also the Fearless Leader (president) of Uncommon Universes Press. In her spare time, she enjoys sword-fighting, reading, learning random facts, and making brownie batter. Two of her goals are eating fried tarantulas and traveling to Antarctica.

Carole McDonnell is a writer of Christian, supernatural, and ethnic stories. Her writings appear in various anthologies, including So Long Been Dreaming: *Postcolonialism in Science Fiction*, edited by Nalo Hopkinson and published by Arsenal Pulp Press; *Jigsaw Nation*, published by Spyre Books; and *Life Spices from Seasoned Sistahs: Writings by Mature Women of Color* among others. Her reviews appear at various online sites. Her story collections are *Spirit Fruit: Collected Speculative Fiction* by Carole McDonnell and Flight and other stories of the fae. Her novels are the Christian speculative fiction and include, *Wind Follower, My Life as an Onion, The Constant Tower, A Town for Timothy, The Daughters of Men, Turn Back O Time, The Charcoal Bride, Black Girls Have Always Loved Cowboys, and Who Gave Sleep and Who Has Taken It Away*. Her Bible studies include: *Seeds of Bible Study, Blogging the Psalms, A Fool's Journey Through Proverbs, Great Sufferers of the Bible*. She lives in New York with her husband, two sons, and their pets.

Travis Perry was born in Montana in 1968 and raised in that state. *The Crystal Portal*, published in 2011, was his first novel. He also contributed to the short story collections *Stories From a Soldiers Heart, Aquasynthesis, Aquasynthesis Again, Avenir Eclectia Volume 1, Colony Zero, No Revolution Too Big, Medieval Mars,* and *Avatars of Web Surfer*. An Army Reserve officer who deployed for the Gulf War and later to Iraq, Afghanistan, and Africa, his writing reflects his lifelong interest in science fiction and fantasy, his strong Christian beliefs, and his knowledge of warfare.

VOCABULARY QUIZ ONE

DEFINE THE FOLLOWING WORDS:

Action Beat:

Agency:

Antagonist:

Antihero:

Arc:

Character:

Climax:

Coherent:

Concrete Noun:

Conflict:

VOCABULARY QUIZ TWO
DEFINE THE FOLLOWING WORDS:

Contagonist:

Denouement:

Driver:

Enemy:

Engaged:

Foreshadow:

Genre:

Hero:

Hyperbole:

I.e.:

VOCABULARY QUIZ THREE

DEFINE THE FOLLOWING WORDS:

Inciting Incident:

Literal:

Loose End:

Manuscript:

Metaphor:

Motif:

Narrator:

Resonate:

Story Question:

Suspension of Disbelief:

Bear Publications is a Christian publisher of speculative fiction. We are expanding and developing the titles we support, including publishing this textbook. Learn more about us at:

www.bearpublications.com

www.ingramcontent.com/pod-product-compliance
Lightning Source LLC
Chambersburg PA
CBHW080036100526
44584CB00023BA/3226